Getting Away With Genocide?

Getting Away With Genocide?

Elusive Justice and the Khmer Rouge Tribunal

Tom Fawthrop and Helen Jarvis

Pluto Press

LONDON • ANN ARBOR, MI

First published 2004 by Pluto Press
345 Archway Road, London N6 5AA
and 839 Greene Street, Ann Arbor, MI 48106

www.plutobooks.com

British Library Cataloguing in Publication Data
A catalogue record for this book is available from the British Library

ISBN   0 7453 2028 7 hardback
ISBN   0 7453 2027 9 paperback

Library of Congress Cataloging in Publication Data applied for

10   9   8   7   6   5   4   3   2   1

Designed and produced for Pluto Press by
Chase Publishing Services, Fortescue, Sidmouth, EX10 9QG, England
Typeset from disk by Stanford DTP Services, Northampton, England
Printed and bound in Canada by Transcontinental Printing

Contents

List of Photographs

Foreword

Roland Joffe

Soon after the Vietnamese left Cambodia in 1989 I found myself
standing on the sweating tarmac of Cambodia's Pochentong
airport, expectantly clutching my passport, trying not to stare at
the bedraggled line of Vietnam War-era helicopters, rusting away
under the sugar palms. This felt familiar: I'd been here before. I hadn't
though – not physically at least.

Forty minutes later, visa stamped, luggage loaded into a Toyota
van, I was heading out of the airport and onto the main road that
led to Phnom Penh. As we pulled onto it, heading into a stream of
cycles, ox carts, motor scooters and overloaded old buses I felt it
again, this overwhelming sense of coming home, home to a place
I'd never been to.

Five years before, I'd have struggled, if asked, to place Cambodia
accurately on a map. I'd heard of it, certainly, I knew it boasted fabulous
temples lying overgrown in its jungles, I knew it was in Southeast
Asia, I knew the French had colonised it, but that was the sum total
of my knowledge. Oh, and that it had in some way been embroiled
in the ghastly mess that we knew as the war in Vietnam!

Then one day, in 1982, the film producer David Putnam gave me a
script to read. It was based on an article that had appeared a year or
so before in the *New York Times Magazine*. The article was by Sidney
Schanberg. It was about Cambodia. It was about his time there as a
journalist. Most importantly of all it was about Sidney's extraordinary
assistant, the courageous, resourceful and loyal Dith Pran.[1] Even
more, it was a searing portrait of a country's hidden agony, a heartfelt
indictment of the brutal international realpolitik that then held the
world in its crudely Darwinist grip – that, in modified form, as recent
events in Iraq show, still does. I couldn't put the screenplay down. I
read it with growing horror and fascination. Horror at the cruelty that
infected the very sinews of the little nation of Cambodia. Fascination
at the strength of ordinary Cambodians, who with heroic guts refused
to yield up their humanity to the atrocious fantasy that the deluded
and paranoid neo-Stalinist Khmer Rouge called 'Kampuchea'. That
script eventually became the film called *The Killing Fields*.

On the evening of my first day in Phnom Penh, I walked with Heng, my Cambodian interpreter, to the Central Market. The old yellow stucco colonial buildings were half deserted, cooking fires smouldered on the pavements, rubbish and wrecked cars were still scattered about, but the air was filled with the sounds of life, babies crying, mothers calling out, children giggling, the unmistakable rumble and slap of a skateboard. Life had returned to this sleepy, stylish capital – a capital that a few years before had been drained of its population, left as an empty shell, inhabited by mindless torturers and their deranged masters, the Khmer Rouge leadership.

As I stood in the moist air, the lowering sun gradually washing the scene with a luminous pink, I caught Mr Heng's eye. He dropped his gaze. I asked him what he was thinking. It took him a long time to answer. We stood in silence while he struggled with himself. When he looked up, I could see the tears coursing slowly down his face. 'Why?' he asked simply. A battalion of answers flooded into my mind. After a slight pause Mr Heng continued, 'Why? Why didn't we count? Why did no one do anything?'

Again, answers flitted through my mind – Cambodia was a sideshow to the bigger war, to the ideological struggle that underpinned the cold war. But that wasn't the question Mr Heng had in mind. 'Why?' he asked quietly, 'when your British government knew what the Khmer Rouge was doing, about the mass killings and suffering, did it send men from your special forces to train Khmer Rouge soldiers?'[2] The skateboard clattered to a stop, a stifling sense of shame welled up inside me.

Later, after an evening at the Foreign Correspondents Club (a rather sweet little restaurant much frequented by young NGO workers), where the discussion about how a country could apparently commit genocide on itself ebbed and flowed, I went for a walk along the banks of the Mekong river. It wasn't that the discussion at the press club didn't interest me: it did. Whatever had happened in the inner depths of those damaged psyches that became the Khmer Rouge needed to be urgently understood. But I was occupied by the question that Mr Heng had put to me, and by another thought – or rather a memory. The river flowed by peacefully. On the opposite side, from where the Khmer Rouge had shelled the city, lights twinkled, signalling the presence of the innumerable little brothels that had sprung up to service UN soldiers, amongst others. The moist air clung to my skin and lovers whispered in the shifting patterns of moonlight. In my mind, though, I was somewhere else, somewhere that Mr Heng's question had dredged up in my mind.

I'd been working on the setting up of *The Killing Fields* for a month or so when I got a visit from an overly-dogmatic left-wing friend. After some time he got around to what was the real purpose of his visit. He suggested that I should think twice before continuing work on the film. His reason, deftly and confidently explained, was that Cambodia was an 'aberration'. By that he meant that it was a bad example of a Marxist state, because it had gone off the rails, and to publicise it would damage the cause. I was stunned at the mental gymnastics that got him to that point, so stunned that I not only ignored his request, but put it out of my mind. Now walking along the Mekong, my mind racing with the effect of Mr Heng's question, I saw a grisly link between it and that request of a few years before that I abandon the film.

The link is this. Both sides in the cold war were linked by a view of reality that existed outside their commitment to their respective 'isms'. That link was the geo-political philosophy of *realpolitik*, or, as the American State Department puts it, 'reality politics'. This philosophy has underpinned the foreign policy of nations since the 1870s. It was the brainchild of Bismarck, the war-hungry and expansionist German chancellor.

In essence it goes like this. It is every government's job to protect the interests of its own nation state at all costs. It follows from this that no nation state can treat the rest of the world as composed of anything other than a set of shifting self-interested alliances. This view enshrouds its profound cynicism in the banner of intellectual rigour and historical precedent. The fact that it is an excuse for the most profound immorality is defended with the argument that since there is no court of appeal in international affairs to guarantee fairness, each nation must fend for itself, in ceaseless attempts to undermine the influence and effectiveness of competing nation states.

This self serving, pseudo-Darwinist view of international relations has corrupted not only the foreign policies of the nations that subscribe to it, but arguably the very ethical foundations of those states themselves. It forms the central tenet of the foreign policies of the world's major – and not so major – powers.

So, both my friend and the conservative Margaret Thatcher – one wanting the truth ignored, if not concealed, the other sending soldiers to train the murderous troops of a demented Stalinist Khmer Rouge – were united in feeling that the noble sword of national or ideological self interest should be used to cut a justifiable swathe through the prickly thickets of ethical behaviour.

One evening, while I was researching *The Killing Fields*, I found myself in heated conversation, in a Bangkok bar, with an ex-CIA operative. Let's call him Billy Boy. Billy Boy had a grisly but acerbic intelligence. I was supposedly probing him about his devious and covert experiences in Cambodia, but he was more professional at ducking and weaving than I was at probing. Billy Boy, however was a man in a rage. The focus of his rage was the way the world had ignored the suffering of Cambodia under the Khmer Rouge. He had particular scorn for Noam Chomsky, who at one time had been accused of discrediting refugee accounts and denying that any genocide had taken place.

The rest of his vituperation was aimed at the State Department, or 'state', as he called it. The word came shooting out of his mouth, like a rocket-propelled grenade. He had spent months huddled over his radio listening as his operatives were picked off one by one by the Khmer Rouge. 'No one back home cared,' Billy Boy said bitterly. 'Because the buzzword was *détente* with China. Democratic Kampuchea, the Khmer Rouge state, was a client of China's. The Chinese have a beef with the Vietnamese, so do the Thai. Get the picture? And that's without factoring in local circumstances such as logging, gems and corruption!' That's the ugly reality behind the intellectual justifications of *realpolitik*. As Billy Boy put it: 'You wanna know why things happen in Cambodia, Limey? Go look in the White House. Wanna know why they get ignored? Go look under the carpet in Drowning Street [*sic*], or whatever you call your prime minister's residence!'

William Shawcross's compelling study of Cambodia's fate during the Vietnam War, *Sideshow*, draws a bitter picture of precisely how this small nation was sacrificed to the wider interests of the global games of the Cold War, and in particular the ferocious US bombing campaign.

Once the war in southeast Asia was over in 1975, interest in the fate of Cambodia and its people faded utterly. Not that governments around the world didn't know about what was going on in Cambodia. They did. But they barely seemed to care. A few brave and honest voices across the political spectrum spoke up, struggling to be heard through a fog of disinterest. Disinterest, as I've noted, compounded by denial from some quarters including some doctrinaire sections of the left.[3] Denial that helped stifle any concerted effort to focus the world's attention on the agony that was the daily life of ordinary Cambodian men and women under the Khmer Rouge. 'Grow up, man. Truth is always a f****ing inconvenience,' sneered Billy Boy, chillingly. 'You know I'm right!'

It's nearly 30 years since the Khmer Rouge atrocities began. It's been 25 or so since they were swept out of power. As yet there have been no war-crimes trials, no trials for crimes against humanity. It's not in many people's self interest, at least those that count, to dig up the truth.[4]

In whose interest would these trials be? Funnily enough the answer is incised in stone in the bas-reliefs that line the lower walls of the vast and ancient Khmer Temple of Angkor Wat. A line of carvings depict various wars, real and mythological, fought during the time of the Khmer Empire that dominated the landscape of southeast Asia from the ninth to thirteenth centuries. Huge warriors are locked in timeless stone battle. Amidst their giant feet, crushed, one might believe, there are plants and houses. And, yes, look closer – tiny figures: farmers, merchants, peasants and their wives and children, ordinary Cambodians, the 'little people' of the day.

Just before I left the bar in Bangkok, Billy Boy had raised a weary hand in the air. 'But go ahead Limey – speak up for the little people!' he'd said, before sinking another beer. But something in his tone let me know that he meant it, that it was important that cynicism and self- interest be confronted. That it may even be a duty.

What can the Khmer Rouge Tribunal achieve? Well, in Billy Boy's tipsy phrase, it could honour the 'little people'. It would demonstrate accountability. It would show that it isn't – and will never be – possible for the powerful to escape responsibility for the suffering they cause. The trial would show that self-interest, even for nations, can never, ever, excuse inhumane acts or crimes against humanity.

Further it might encourage public discussion and learning about what forces, social and psychological, led a group of Cambodians, intellectuals and peasants, to murder and torture their fellow citizens. There's much to be learned there, learning that might absolve Cambodians in general from suffering the anguish of feeling that there is something specific to their culture or make up that produced this violence. A vital absolution if the country is to move on.

Then there is the closure of punishment, perhaps the least regenerative aspect of the trials. I wonder whether the Cambodians might want to take a leaf out of that great humanitarian Nelson Mandela's book, and use the tribunal as a forum of understanding and admission that can lead to reconciliation and healing, perhaps even to forgiveness. That's not for me to say. It is though for all of us to think about, if indeed we are to help the 'little people' of Cambodia to find a voice. After all, the voice they find, dear reader, may turn out, in the final analysis, to be our own.

> Roland Joffe
> London
> 2004

Roland Joffe is director of: *The Killing Fields* (1984), *The Mission* (1986) and *City of Joy* (1992). His strong interest in Cambodia has continued through his work with the British NGO The Cambodia Trust, which is providing prosthetics for the countless victims of landmines.

NOTES ADDED BY THE AUTHORS

1. Dith Pran's role in *The Killing Fields* was played by Dr Haing Ngor, another survivor of that holocaust. See Chapter 6 for references to Dr Ngor.
2. The UK government eventually owned-up to sending SAS military advisors in 1985–89, to train anti-Phnom Penh guerrilla forces, but denied any involvement with the Khmer Rouge. However all three forces were military allies as part of a Khmer Rouge-dominated CDGK coalition (see Chapter 4).
3. While a few on the left indeed continued to defend the Khmer Rouge, it should be noted that others, like journalist John Pilger, were among the strongest voices documenting the horrors of the Pol Pot regime inside Cambodia in 1979 and calling for an end to the continuing political and military support for the perpetrators of these crimes (see Chapters 5 and 7).
4. In August 1979 Pol Pot and Ieng Sary were tried and convicted *in absentia* for the crime of genocide by the People's Revolutionary Tribunal in Phnom Penh (see Chapter 3).

Acknowledgements

We embarked upon writing this book in December 1999. The idea emerged over a convivial dinner in a house on the bank of the Mekong. Tom sketched an outline the very next morning and emailed it to Helen, who received it via mobile phone in a taxi en route to Phnom Penh airport.

In those first enthusiastic beginnings, neither author imagined that, like the Khmer Rouge trials themselves, the project would take years to complete. Progress was frequently disrupted by other commitments: Tom covered East Timor from 1999–2000 and has been frequently out of Cambodia ever since. Helen's work as advisor to the Cambodian Task Force setting up the tribunal also put constraints on the time she had to finish the book.

This text is the result of a joint writing enterprise between the two authors. We bring to our account two differing yet complementary backgrounds – one academic and the other journalistic. We trust that the merging of these differing lenses will help elucidate the complexities of Cambodia's recent history.

Although we have collaborated on the overall text and exchanged comments and suggestions, it may be useful to indicate that principal authorship for Chapters 1, 2, 4, 6, 8 and 12 rests with Tom Fawthrop, while Helen Jarvis penned the Introduction and Chapters 3, 5, 7, 9, 10 and 11. Because each chapter was composed to deal with a particular issue or perspective, inevitably some material may be relevant to more than one chapter and may appear more than once.

We gratefully acknowledge the assistance of many people who helped and encouraged us to write this book. Above all, we thank those Cambodians who shared their memories with us, despite their grief at rekindling the trauma and the pain that they suffered. Support was given from people across the political spectrum, in government, in opposition ranks, in non-governmental organisations, the media, academe and ordinary citizens of Cambodia. It is our hope that this book will make a useful contribution to one of the most important debates in Cambodia today.

Special mention should be made of cooperation from Chum Mey and Vann Nath (both survivors of Tuol Sleng), Chey Sopheara (the director of Tuol Sleng Genocide Museum), Youk Chhang and his team at the Documentation Center of Cambodia. Two other survivors that helped to inspire this book were Pin Yathay and the late Haing Ngor.

We would like to thank Khieu Kanharith, the former editor of *Kampuchea Weekly*, and Sum Mean, the former news editor of SPK, the Cambodian News agency for help and information. Thanks also to all others we have interviewed, who are mentioned individually in our bibliography.

We owe a deep debt of gratitude Bill Herod who took the trouble and time to read the entire manuscript and provided invaluable advice and suggestions. We also wish to thank David Hawk, who kindly arranged access for us to his CDC files from the 1980s and who, as acting head of the UN Human Rights Centre in Cambodia from 1997–1999, continued his spirited advocacy of the tribunal. Similarly David Roberts and Gregory Stanton both made important contributions to the book.

Nayan Chanda, Allen Kesee and Adrian Edwards contributed to our efforts. Roland Neveu and John Vink kindly shared their photographs. Among dozens of diplomats and UN officials that the authors have dealt with, Verghese Mathews, Stephen Bridges, Kent Wiedemann and Benny Widyono were particularly helpful.

Tom Fawthrop conducted many interviews with and gained many insights from: Bou Saroen, Chantou Boua, Chea Sophara, Chea Vannath, Dr Craig Etcheson, Im Sethy, Dr Kao Kim Hourn, Long Visalo, Lor Chandara (of the Tuol Sleng genocide museum, rather than his namesake at *The Cambodia Daily*), Dr Lao Mong Hay, Ok Serei Sopheak, Prum Sokha, Seng Theary, Dr Thong Khon, Thun Saray, They Sambo and Thai Senator Kraisak Choonhavan.

He also wishes to express special thanks to Novib (the Dutch NGO) for partial funding of his research and to Guy Stringer of Oxfam UK. Thanks also for support from: Dominic Cardy, Cindy Coffill, David Cowell, Khieu Kola, Meng Phalla, Sar Sambath, Theerada Suphaphong and Dr Shane Tarr, who all played a part in making this book happen.

Helen Jarvis gives special thanks to Peter Annear, Michel Bonnieu, Helen Brady, Tara Gutman, Sally Low and Tara Urs, as well as to Allen Myers, Mina Bui Jones and the rest of the Left Bank for comments on various portions of the text and for constant encouragement and light relief. She acknowledges Ben Kiernan's invaluable contributions to an understanding of the Khmer Rouge in power and for his directorship of the Cambodian Genocide Program.

She wishes to express her gratitude to Senior Minister Sok An for pressing her to translate her support for the Khmer Rouge trials into an on-the-ground commitment to work with the Cambodian government into bringing the idea into reality, and thanks also to fellow members of the Cambodian delegation through all the long negotiations with the United Nations, especially Sean Visoth and Tony Kranh.

We pay tribute to Onesta Carpene, the feisty Italian who first came to Cambodia in 1979, along with post-Pol Pot pioneer in development and rebuilding the country, Eva Mysliwiec, who edited the famous Oxfam booklet *Punishment of the Poor*.

Finally, the authors wish to thank our editors at Pluto Books, Roger van Zwanenberg and Julie Stoll, who committed themselves to the project and showed such understanding and patience as deadlines slipped. Thanks and appreciation also to our copy-editor Rebecca Wise and managing editor Robert Webb.

The cover of the paperback edition shows 'The Evil Smile of Pol Pot' from an original painting by Cambodian artist Hen Sophal. Pol Pot cheated justice and got away with genocide by his death. Sophal yearns for justice and a tribunal to be held for the survivors.

List of Abbreviations and Acronyms

Adhoc – Cambodian Human Rights and Development Association
Asean – Association of Southeast Asian Nations
ANS – Sihanoukist National Army
CDC – Cambodian Documentation Committee
CGDK – Coalition Government of Democratic Kampuchea
CDP – Cambodian Defenders' Programme
CGP – Cambodian Genocide Program
CICP – Cambodian Institute for Cooperation and Peace
CIVPOL – Civilian police
CORKR – Campaign to Oppose the Return of the Khmer Rouge
CPP – Cambodian People's Party
DC-Cam – Documentation Center of Cambodia
DK – Democratic Kampuchea
DNUM – Democratic National Unity Movement
FAO – Food and Agriculture Organisation
Funcinpec – National United Front for an Independent Neutral, Peaceful and Cooperative Cambodia
GRUNK – Royal Government of the National Union of Kampuchea
HRW – Human Rights Watch
ICC – International Criminal Court
ICJ – International Court of Justice (World Court)
ICRC – International Committee of the Red Cross
ICTR – International Criminal Tribunal for Rwanda
ICTY – International Criminal Tribunal for the Former Yugolsavia
JIM – Jakarta Informal Meeting
KEG – Kampuchea Emergency Group
KID – Khmer Institute for Democracy
KPNLF – Khmer People's National Liberation Front
MAG – Mines Advisory Group
OLA – Office of Legal Affairs
PRK – People's Republic of Kampuchea (official name of the Cambodian state 1979–1989)
PRT – People's Revolutionary Tribunal
SOC – State of Cambodia (1989–1993)

UNAKRT – United Nations Assistance to the Khmer Rouge Tribunal
UNCHR – United Nations Commission on Human Rights
UNDP – United Nations Development Programme
UNGA – United Nations General Assembly
UNSC – United Nations Security Council
UNTAC – United Nations Transitional Authority in Cambodia
WHO – World Health Organization

Introduction

Bringing the leaders of the Khmer Rouge to justice is the focus of this book. These are some of the worst mass murderers of the twentieth century who plunged their country into an unspeakable horror, often termed the darkest period in Cambodia's history. Over 25 per cent of the population died under their rule between 1975 and 1979. Why, a quarter of a century after the Pol Pot regime was ousted, has no one stood in court to answer for these terrible crimes?

We trace in the first half of the book how the very governments that so often speak the language of human rights shielded Pol Pot and his lieutenants from prosecution during the 1980s, massively contributing to impunity for crimes against the people of Cambodia.

Most governments ignored efforts inside Cambodia to document and prosecute the crimes of Democratic Kampuchea, the official name of the Pol Pot regime. For over a decade appeals from Cambodians inside and outside the country for a Khmer Rouge tribunal fell on deaf ears. The Khmer Rouge were aided and abetted, rebuilt as a military force and accorded the right to sit in the United Nations as the 'legitimate representatives of the Cambodian people'.

Only after the Khmer Rouge no longer posed a political or military threat did the United Nations, in 1997, come round to condemning their crimes, following a request from the Cambodian government for international assistance to bring the perpetrators to justice.

The final quarter of the twentieth century witnessed enormous changes in the international political landscape. Moves towards setting up a Khmer Rouge tribunal were but one strand among many in the weaving of the new cloth of international humanitarian law and justice.

Following the Second World War there had been a flurry of activity in the name of 'never again'. The Nuremberg and Tokyo tribunals were intended to lay the groundwork for setting international safeguards to prevent such horrendous crimes from ever being repeated. However, they were also subject to the label of victor's justice – no one on the winning side was ever charged for war crimes, even for the utilisation of weapons of mass destruction such as the atomic bomb, or for the fire-bombing of civilian populations.

Post-war enthusiasm for a new world order led not only to the founding of the United Nations, but also to an advance in the codification of customary international humanitarian law. One result of these deliberations was the adoption in 1948 of the Genocide Convention. In the following year the Geneva Convention defined and proscribed all manner of war crimes.

But that was where things stayed – on paper for almost half a century – as both sides in the cold war played out their mutual hostilities through proxy wars in the Third World. Although the International Court of Justice (World Court) had the authority to try disputes between states, it had no powers to enforce its rulings, and no international court had jurisdiction over individual perpetrators. The new conventions were simply ignored, each side holding a veto power preventing the Security Council from bringing any country on its side to account for crimes committed.

The collapse of the Soviet Union in 1989 ushered in a new era of international intervention. With Russia anxious to establish its new credentials in the halls of its former opponents, the western powers were able to take action in the name of the United Nations as long as they could secure the acquiescence of China. In 1993 the Security Council decided to establish the International Criminal Tribunal for the Former Yugoslavia and in 1994 the International Criminal Tribunal for Rwanda. Cambodia was still not on the map of international justice. Any prospect of the UN Security Council approving the same kind of international tribunal for Cambodia always appeared doomed by the implacable opposition and veto power of China.

Establishing *ad hoc* tribunals for every new violation of international humanitarian law was clearly untenable as a long-term approach to the problem and a new campaign was launched to establish a permanent International Criminal Court. The International Criminal Court had been envisaged even before the Second World War, but had fallen by the wayside – a victim of cold-war suspicions. In the 1980s the concept was resurrected and years of detailed negotiations resulted in the adoption of the Statute of Rome in 1998 outlining the ICC's structure and powers. In 2002 Cambodia, to its credit, became one of the founding states and the International Criminal Court was formally established in March 2003.

It was against this background of emerging possibilities for international justice, and domestically amid the final stages of the disintegration of the Khmer Rouge, that in June 1997 the Cambodian government requested the United Nations to provide assistance in finally holding accountable the senior Khmer Rouge leaders who had masterminded massive human rights violations some 20 years before.

It took a further six years for Cambodia and the United Nations to agree on what should be done. The second half of this book recounts the twists and turns along the road to passing a Cambodian law to establish a tribunal in 2001 and reaching agreement with the United Nations in 2003 on its role. These chapters cover many aspects of the tussles between the UN Secretariat and Cambodia, which in reality were more about politics than justice.

The Cambodian formula for a mixed tribunal was unprecedented when first outlined in 1999. Both national and international judges and prosecutors would try crimes under both national and international law. This hybrid approach, sometimes termed 'the Cambodian model', has since been used as the basis for the Special Court for Sierra Leone, established in 2002, and in East Timor and Kosovo, where international judges have been invited to sit on the bench in the national courts.

THREE MAJOR CONTROVERSIES

At the outset the authors feel three controversial questions have to be addressed:

1) How many people died as a result of the policies and practices of the Khmer Rouge regime?
2) Was it genocide?
3) Why will the prosecution be limited to the period of the Pol Pot regime (17 April 1975 – 6 January 1979)?[1]

The death toll 1975–79

During the three years, eight months and twenty days that the Khmer Rouge held power it is estimated that around 2 million people perished – over one quarter of the total population – from torture and execution or from starvation and untreated illness.

The issue of the numbers who perished remains a matter of heated debate. Serious estimates range from 740,000 to 3.314 million. Recent studies seem to be converging, with historian Ben Kiernan estimating 1,671,000 and demographer Marek Sliwinski 1.8 million on the basis of extrapolations from very different samples. New calculations based on demographic reconstruction by Patrick Heuveline lead to a similar picture. Working forward from the 1960 census and backwards from the 1992 UNTAC electoral lists, Heuveline suggests a range of from 1.17 million to 3.42 million deaths in excess of what could have been expected in the period. While the data gives a medium estimate of 2.52 million, Heuveline comes very close to Kiernan and Sliwinski in his subjective estimation of 'between 1.5 to 2 million'.[2]

While it may be argued that those holding power in a country are responsible for all 'excess deaths' in the population under their control, it is clear that the subjective intentions and actions of the government are not always to blame, as objective and external factors can play an even stronger part. What is far clearer, however, is the direct responsibility of the authorities for executions, torture and deliberate starvation.

Sliwinski estimates that of the overall deaths from 1975–79, 39.3 per cent resulted from execution and 36.3 per cent from famine, with only 9.9 per cent from natural causes. Heuveline refers to 'violent mortality', which he estimates at between 600,000 and 2.2 million, with a central value of 1.1 million.[3]

Any trial of the Khmer Rouge would need to address the questions of what crimes were committed and by whom. Overwhelming evidence of horrendous crimes has been amassed over the past two decades. The challenge for the prosecution will be to marshal sufficient evidence to establish individual culpability for genocide, crimes against humanity, war crimes, homicide, torture and religious persecution. This challenge is explored in the penultimate chapter.

Was it genocide?

We have chosen in this book to use the term 'genocide' as a shorthand for the large number of horrendous crimes committed by the Khmer Rouge in Cambodia.

We are mindful of the fact that many scholars and legal experts maintain that successful prosecution of the Khmer Rouge for the crime of genocide might be difficult to achieve. Many of the atrocities fall more readily under the rubric of other crimes, and the narrow definition of genocide under the 1948 Genocide Convention will present difficulties for the prosecution even on those acts that are closest to the legal definition.

An extensive body of literature has been penned on the interpretation of the definition of genocide in general, and on the Cambodian case in particular,[4] and we canvass the issues in more detail in Chapter 11.

We decided to use the term genocide principally because in Cambodia the crimes of the Khmer Rouge have been referred to consistently since mid-1978 as genocide – by those who overthrew the Khmer Rouge, by all subsequent governments and in common parlance. Genocide was the only charge prosecuted by the 1979 People's Revolutionary Tribunal (discussed in Chapter 3). Many Cambodians have expressed their insistence that the Khmer Rouge be tried for this 'crime of crimes', asserting that any other charge would somehow diminish the offence.

Outside Cambodia, too, the term genocide has been used in many journalistic and scholarly reports, and in political and legal campaigns to seek judicial accountability by the Khmer Rouge for the crimes they committed. In this sense, we speak of genocide in a generic or sociological sense, fully aware of its legal constraints.

All or nothing? The contradictions of selective justice

Cambodia is a case study in double standards and the selectivity of international humanitarian law. While the call for 'an end to impunity' is shouted from the rooftops, political interests and global power still determine who shall be prosecuted and when.

It was not politically convenient to prosecute the Khmer Rouge during the 1980s. When finally in the late 1990s it became opportune for previously opposing governments to move towards a trial, their support was contingent upon limiting prosecution to the period of Pol Pot control.

The *New York Times* fully understood the dilemmas of many governments who feared that some part of their own dirty deeds might be revealed by an open-ended tribunal. 'All Security Council members ... might spare themselves embarrassment by restricting the scope of prosecution to those crimes committed inside Cambodia during the four horrific years of Khmer Rouge rule.'[5]

In 1969 the US had unleashed a ferocious bombing of Cambodia directed against Vietcong supply lines along the Ho Chi Minh trail, passing through parts of Laos and Cambodia. Between 18 March 1969 and May 1970 a staggering 3,630 B-52 bombing raids were flown over Cambodia. This intensive bombing campaign was directed against neutral Cambodia in a clear violation of international law.

In a second assault in the final throes of the US war, B-52s pounded Cambodia for 160 consecutive days in 1973, dropping more than 240,000 tons of bombs on rice fields, water buffalo and villages – 50 per cent more than the Allies dropped on Japan during the Second

World War. Hundreds of thousands of people were killed in the holocaust of these two bombing campaigns.[6]

Setting up selective tribunals for some war criminals and genocidists while letting off the hook others such as former US Secretary of State Henry Kissinger, who masterminded the bombing of Cambodia, clearly presents a legal and moral contradiction. Where is the universality of international justice if it targets only Third World leaders, and only those despots and generals who are not too closely linked to western governments? Why are powerful western statesmen and women who stand accused by many as culpable of war crimes apparently immune from prosecution?

The International Criminal Court is intended to universalise responsibility for crimes under international humanitarian law. But the United States has refused to become a party to the ICC, and in 2003 undertook a campaign to pressurise other countries that are members of the ICC to sign specific agreements under Article 98 to exempt US personnel from possible prosecution under its powers.

Cambodia was one such small and weak state that was unable to resist this pressure despite its expressed pride at being the only southeast Asian country to be among the ICC's founding states. In June 2003, during a brief visit to Cambodia, US Secretary of State Colin Powell convinced Prime Minister Hun Sen to support an Article 98 agreement. The agreement was later signed and then endorsed by the Cambodian government on 3 October 2003 and sent to the National Assembly for ratification.

While many reject the hypocrisy of such selective justice, a few analysts go further and maintain that no tribunal is credible if it does not address all the crimes committed in Cambodia – including the bombing and other crimes against humanity. But any attempt to extend the period available for prosecution beyond the Khmer Rouge regime was a sure formula for preventing any tribunal taking place at all. As a result of strong pressures exerted on the Cambodian government, jurisdiction of the Khmer Rouge tribunal will be strictly limited to the period between 17 April 1975 and 6 January 1979.

Only the Khmer Rouge will stand in the dock. Those whose actions helped bring them to power pre-1975, succoured them while in power and revived them post-1979 will be exempt from prosecution. The tribunal has no mandate to judge whether or not the US 'secret' bombing of Cambodia in the 1970s constituted war crimes. The reasons for the temporal exclusions of US bombing, and likewise the Chinese and others support for the Pol Pot regime, have little to do with any principle of justice and everything to do with international politics.

Outside the main framework of the established international legal system, however, in recent years a number of individual initiatives have been taken to launch prosecution cases for violations of international law, such as against Henry Kissinger and the former Chilean dictator Augusto Pinochet. While these legal actions have so far been stymied by various means, they have served notice to the perpetrators of monumental crimes that they can no longer assume themselves to be safe from prosecution by virtue of their power. These legal cases have also been accompanied by public campaigns to expose and shame them and those who continue to give them comfort.

Back in Cambodia there is a growing sense of confidence that the trial will at last be held. The long road since the overthrow of the Khmer Rouge is tantalisingly close to its destination. Pol Pot cheated justice with his death in 1998. The authors hope that in spite of all the pressures and obstacles, the Cambodian people will not be cheated again and that all Pol Pot's chief co-conspirators will soon face their day in court.

We write this book in memory of all those who died at the hands of the murderous regime of the Khmer Rouge and for those who rebuilt the country afterwards. For all the survivors we hope that this long-delayed tribunal may bring answers to their angst, the justice they have long been seeking and, above all, peace of mind.

1
Rebirth of a Nation – and the Beginning of the Long Struggle for Justice

Chaktomuk Theatre at the confluence of the Mekong and the Tonle Sap – the symbolic heart of Cambodia: the packed auditorium fell still as the speaker's voice came over the microphone. 'Did we not know? Could we not have prevented what happened? What did we do to stop the atrocities?'

It was 6 June 2003 and the questioner was Hans Corell, Under Secretary General and Legal Counsel of the United Nations on the occasion of the signing of the Agreement between the United Nations and the Royal Government of Cambodia Concerning the Prosecution under Cambodian Law of Crimes Committed during the Period of Democratic Kampuchea.

The Cambodian signatory – Sok An, Senior Minister in Charge of the Office of the Council of Ministers – responded:

This is indeed a historic day for Cambodia and for all humanity. I stand here today humbled by the task ahead of us as we move forward in partnership with the United Nations to bring to account the perpetrators of one of the greatest crimes of the 20th century, in which more than one third of the population of Cambodia lost their lives.

I recall clearly the hushed atmosphere in August 1979, as witness after witness gave moving testimony, speaking graphically of their own personal experiences or presenting reports of field investigations on the common graves found throughout the country and on the social problems faced by all sectors of the surviving population.

In this very room we held the world's first genocide trial.[1] At the time President Heng Samrin expressed the confidence that 'the tribunal of history, the tribunal of mankind's conscience…will join with the Kampuchean people in pronouncing its verdict.'

We have waited a long time for this prediction to come true. Almost a quarter of a century – a whole generation – has passed, during which geopolitical complexities stood in the way of a proper international recognition of the crimes committed.

On 7 January 1979 the Khmer Rouge were driven from Phnom Penh. The Pol Pot regime had been overthrown by 150,000 Vietnamese troops assisted by 15,000 anti-Khmer Rouge Cambodian soldiers who had previously fled to Vietnam. On the following day the most grisly evidence of the crimes of the Khmer Rouge was found. Two Vietnamese photojournalists 'were drawn to a particular compound by the smell of decomposing bodies. The silent malodorous site was surrounded by a corrugated tin fence topped with coils of barbed wire.'[2] The former Tuol Sleng high school had been transformed by Pol Pot's regime into its central prison and interrogation centre, known as S-21. The bodies of recently killed prisoners were found, some shackled to iron bed frames, with blood on the floor below. They had been killed as their captors made their escape, leaving behind documentary and photographic evidence of the detention of more than 15,000 people.[3] If they survived the interrogation and systematic torture, they were routinely executed on the outskirts of the city at Cheung Ek, one of many 'Killing Fields' throughout the country. Only a handful escaped this fate – in 1979 the number was put at seven, but several more have since been identified.

Even amid the chaos, the destitution and all the shortages faced by the new government in 1979, the importance of dealing with the crimes of the Pol Pot regime both for domestic and international reasons was clearly understood. The new authorities hastened to bring evidence of these crimes to international attention. A group of journalists, mostly from the former Soviet bloc countries and Cuba, were brought to S-21. In February the Vietnamese museum curator Mai Lam, who had worked on the Museum of American War Crimes in Ho Chi Minh City, was brought to oversee the conversion of S-21 into the Tuol Sleng Museum of Genocidal Crimes, which was officially opened on 17 April 1979, the anniversary of the Khmer Rouge coming to power four years earlier.[4]

Among the first actions of the newly established Ministry of Information and Culture was to send directives to all provinces to 'preserve mass graves, the skeletons and all other evidence of genocidal crimes'.

Tuol Sleng and Cheung Ek were designated historic sites. But they are only two out of hundreds of mass graves and prisons uncovered in every province, proof that the same gruesome horror had been a nationwide phenomenon.[5]

The door was also open to the world's media. Harish Chandola writing for *Asiaweek* and Nayan Chanda of the *Far Eastern Economic Review* were among the first to provide eye-witness accounts. Journalists from the non-communist world had to overcome the west's diplomatic boycott in order to secure visas.

'Every night we dreamed about having food, another world ... we could do anything we want in our dreams, we were free, it was our only escape,' Im Sethy recalled. Sethy, one of the intellectuals who survived the 'Killing Fields' regime, is today a secretary of state in the Ministry of Education. He vividly remembers that after nights of dreaming 'we returned to a daytime hell. Above all we dreamed that some force, some country would liberate us.'[6]

Tey Sambo had been deported by the Khmer Rouge in 1975 to Battambang province. Four years later, when she heard the boom of heavy guns and artillery, she was more worried than hopeful. Then aged 25, Sambo recalled 'My husband was seriously ill with dysentery, and my mother had just died that same day. I dared not think that anything better was about to happen.' But amidst her deep grief and the constant sound of shelling getting closer, a sympathetic villager suggested 'the soul of your mother is calling somebody to liberate us; do not be afraid.'[7]

Chea Vannath, consigned to a labour camp in Kandal Province, had a different reaction when she first heard the sounds of unidentified attackers. 'We were all so happy to hear the sound of shelling because we knew something was up. We didn't care who was coming, so long as Cambodia was liberated from the Khmer Rouge. We felt so excited, and the Khmer Rouge were panicking.'[8]

The Khmer Rouge forces in Kandal urged people to follow them to the west, to escape from the advancing Vietnamese troops. Then, for the first time, people grasped the identity of their liberators.

In many different villages and districts in the first week of January 1979 Khmer Rouge officials attempted to force civilians to accompany them as a hostage population, with dire warnings of horrible atrocities to come at the hands of the Vietnamese for those who refused to go.

Chea Vannath and most people from her village stayed behind. The next morning was a revelation. The Khmer Rouge had fled. Vannath, who is today the president of the Center for Social Development, a Cambodian NGO, vividly remembers 7 January 1979, 'We felt like birds being released from a cage. We had a feeling of joy and looked at countryside with new eyes. We people from the city saw its beauty for the first time.' For the first time since the day when the Khmer Rouge had seized power in 1975, there was no 4.00 am gong, no wake-up call to send them to slave-labour in the fields.

Many Cambodians like Im Sethy had assumed and expected that any liberation would come from a western country, a liberation from the west rather than from the east. He was surprised to see the round pith helmets of Vietnamese soldiers.

The Vietnamese military offensive, launched on 25 December 1978, captured the Cambodian capital in just 14 days. So speedy was their advance that Hanoi's tanks ran out of fuel and were unable to finish off the enemy. The Khmer Rouge fled towards the Thai frontier to the west, and the Vietnamese troops reached a section of the Thai border on 17 January. But the long nightmare was not yet over for inhabitants of large parts of the western districts, including the towns of Battambang, Sisophon and Poipet, which were not liberated until April.

Like so many others, Tey Sambo had no idea about events in the rest of the country but, in the areas they still controlled, the Khmer Rouge continued and in many cases even intensified their killings as the Vietnamese troops drew closer.[9]

In village after village Cambodians welcomed the arrival of Vietnamese soldiers, according to dozens of eyewitness reports. Chea Vannath observed 'the Vietnamese were our friends. Villagers lined the street to applaud them, and provided them with sugar cane and water. We did not see them as invaders.'[10]

Rice granaries were broken open and food stocks distributed among the hungry and emaciated population. Hundreds of thousands enjoyed their first square meal for years.

In some districts festivities were held to celebrate the overthrow of the Pol Pot regime. Traditional dances and songs were performed for the first time in nearly four years. But the sudden change of regime brought not only joy and relief, but also a strong sense of confusion, shock and disorientation. Their Khmer Rouge jailors had fled. Now they were free ... free to go anywhere. But where?

FRANTIC SEARCH FOR RELATIVES, SECURITY AND A FUTURE

During the first half of 1979 a new phenomenon gripped the nation, dominating all other activity. Long columns of emaciated human beings slowly trudged in all directions across the country, searching for news of their loved ones, hoping to find some relatives still alive in their home villages. Some people hitched rides on Vietnamese trucks, others procured bicycles, but mostly they had to walk every kilometre.

In April 1975 the new regime had ordered the mass evacuation of Phnom Penh and other towns, resulting in a mass deportation from urban to rural areas, and hundreds of thousands of people in rural areas were uprooted from their native districts in Pol Pot's grand Orwellian experiment in social engineering. In 1979 the survivors embarked on a reverse path, hundreds of thousands heading on a long march back to their roots, the very roots that the Democratic Kampuchea regime had tried so hard to eradicate.

Bui Tin, a Vietnamese advisor to Cambodia's newly established SPK news agency, reported, 'hundreds of thousands of gaunt and diseased people, dazed as if they were returning from hell, wandered shoeless along dusty roads ... reduced to a state where they did not speak or smile any more.'[11]

Dressed in the egalitarian black of the Khmer Rouge regime, their frail bodies were driven onwards. Some travelled to Phnom Penh seeking employment with the new authorities. All were trying to pick up the pieces of their shattered lives, and pondering the uncertain future. For more than six months a great demographic flow coursed the main highways of Cambodia from west to east, north and south, with long lines passing in opposite directions.

The first edicts of the Salvation Front[12] both encouraged and endorsed this population movement, proclaiming that 'citizens are authorised to return to their villages and places of origin, and to choose their residence as they wish.'

PHNOM PENH – A CITY OF GHOSTS

Cambodian dissidents and Vietnamese divisions entered the deserted Cambodian capital on 7 January 1979, the official date of liberation from the Khmer Rouge reign of terror. Dr Thong Khon, a former medical student, recalled the eerie silence of the city, broken only by the occasional buzzing of flies and mosquitos – a Phnom Penh without people, without cars, without traffic.[13] Only a few military trucks and jeeps with Cambodian and Vietnamese soldiers rumbled by, otherwise it was a city of ghosts[14] – a movie set without extras.

It resembled the aftermath of a massive typhoon, with street after street of derelict houses along which were to be found piles of books, TVs and old Peugeot and Citroen *deux chevaux* cars. The tree-lined boulevards of the once beautiful capital were abandoned and deserted. Pieces of paper and old money were blowing along the gutters. Thousands of shoes littered the entrance to Psar Thmei, the city's main market. It was a scene straight out of Dante's *Inferno*.

Within hours of capturing Phnom Penh on 17 April 1975, Pol Pot's forces had directed one of history's greatest urban evacuations, clearing some 2 million people out of the city over a matter of days.[15] During the following four years of Khmer Rouge rule, the city was inhabited mainly by the top political leaders, their families and the administrative apparatus, military personnel and a small number of workers in repair shops and small-scale factories that were reopened or established anew with a total population estimated at under 20,000.[16]

The National Bank of Cambodia had been blown up in line with the Khmer Rouge scheme to abolish money. The Catholic cathedral and the main Cao Dai church had been dismantled stone by stone to become building material for new construction – reportedly mainly to extend the port of Phnom Penh. The spacious National Library grounds had been used to hold pigs, ducks and chickens, and books were pushed off the shelves to make way for kitchen utensils. It served the next-door Hotel Le Royal, which was the main residence of the many Chinese advisers and technicians during the Pol Pot regime. Most of the city's buildings were intact, but suffering from total neglect and decay. Grass and banana trees were growing among the deserted tenements. The water supply didn't function because most of the waterpumps had been removed by the Khmer Rouge and diverted for use in the countryside. A foul stench wafted up from the city's drains.

By January 1979 Cambodia had been reduced to a primitive state with no markets, no power supply, no safe drinking water, no sanitation and no money. After liberation the first fragile steps were taken in setting up a new Cambodian government named the People's Republic of Kampuchea, formed out of the Salvation Front, in whose name the invasion was undertaken. It was a government that lacked everything. Amidst the debris of the still deserted city, the 14-member Revolutionary Council, aided by Vietnamese advisors, planned the setting up of ministries and the creation of a new social order.

Tens of thousands of people started to gather on the outskirts of Phnom Penh, pleading with Vietnamese soldiers guarding the checkpoints at all major points of entry to the capital to be allowed to pass into the derelict city.

Hun Sen later estimated that when Phnom Penh was liberated on 7 January 1979 only 70 residents remained.[17] The city's most recent residents had boarded the special westward bound trains as the Vietnamese troops came into the city.

All who saw the place in 1979 expressed shock at the degree of devastation. A few years later a Vietnamese journalist reflected,

> At the birth of the People's Republic of Kampuchea even the most optimistic observers had no idea how the new regime was going to restore life back to normal on the immense ruins of a whole society, which included the ruins of all communities and all families.... The homeland of Angkor was like an anthill crushed under cruel boots, people were dazed and confused and wondered what the future held in store for them.[18]

During the three years, eight months and twenty days that the Khmer Rouge held power, it is estimated that around 2 million people perished, over one quarter of the total population. Some died from brutal torture or execution, while others coughed their last in miserable circumstances of starvation and untreated illness.[19]

The toll was spread unevenly. The figures given by Cambodian historian Ben Kiernan indicate that 29 per cent of 'new people' from the cities and areas recently taken over by the Khmer Rouge, and 16 per cent of 'base people' were victims. Some ethnic minorities clearly suffered well above the average, with nearly 100 per cent of those Vietnamese who had not been driven out of the country being killed, while other minorities suffered heavy losses: Chinese (50 per cent), Thai and Lao (both 40 per cent) and Cham (36 per cent). Rural Khmer people and upland minorities suffered relatively less, but still lost 15% of their total populations.[20]

Among the urban people, the death-toll for professionals and those with any form of tertiary education (often termed intellectuals) was particularly high, although it should be noted that the extremely low figures often given for 'survivors', reflect the absence not only of those who perished but also the high proportion of surviving professionals who fled the country. Out of the estimated 450 qualified doctors in

Cambodia in the early 1970s, only 43 remained after the Pol Pot era. Only seven lawyers were reported to have survived.

A report from September 1983 gave the following figures for those who died: 594 doctors, pharmacists and dentists; 675 lawyers and professors; 18,000 teachers; 10,550 students; 191 journalists; and 1,120 artists.[21] The ranks of this Buddhist nation's monks were also decimated. The same document reported that 25,168 had been killed, while many others died of starvation and disease. Before Pol Pot there were around 50,000 monks, of whom only 800–1000 returned to their temples inside Cambodia, although others were among those who fled to the Thai refugee camps.[22]

This legacy of the 'Killing Fields' today still cripples Cambodia. In 1979 it had left the country utterly dependent and in desperate need of all kinds of foreign aid and assistance. The fledgling People's Republic of Kampuchea and its Vietnamese backers were grappling with a million problems in trying to restore normal life just in the capital Phnom Penh. They faced monumental shortages of everything from food and shelter, to trained staff, to a simple lack of typewriters and paper. Vietnamese, and later Russian, engineers and plumbers arrived to wrestle with the long-neglected water supply and the power station in an attempt to restore basic services, but it would take time to repair the extensive damage. Former residents of Phnom Penh were given day-passes permitting them to return to their houses and retrieve their property and valuables, but the authorities decided on a policy to restore basic services before allowing people to move back into the city.

Outside the city people ate whatever they could lay their hands on – wild roots, crabs, snails, snakes, rodents and grasshoppers. For the first year farmers were either too busy finding their relatives or too traumatised to concentrate on the rice-planting and cultivation of the next harvest, and the liberation war of 1978–79 had completely disrupted the previous harvest.

Among the swelling multitudes gathering on the outskirts of Phnom Penh was Sum Mean, who had been a student in Phnom Penh before 1975. At first he remembers that 'it was exciting, we were singing and dancing, I was eager to help rebuild my country'.[23] But, not permitted to enter the city, he became frustrated. He hit on the idea of trying to band together with other students and knocked up a simple sign on a piece of wood using charcoal to scrawl 'Student Survivors of the Genocide', placing it in a highly visible position in a tree. About 15 other students gravitated to Sum Mean's banner and they set up one of the first activist groups of the new Cambodia.

The problem for Sum Mean's group was to gain the attention of those in control – to let them know that they were waiting on the outskirts of Phnom Penh, waiting to be called upon to help rebuild their country. Frustrated by the difficulty of making their desires known, Sum Mean jumped in front of a car driven by a Vietnamese officer. The car stopped and the Cambodian student leader made a desperate plea in French imploring the officer to take him into the city, 'I want you to tell the Cambodian leaders the students are gathered here.'

The same Vietnamese official later returned with a good supply of food and a message that the Cambodian leaders were interested in meeting them. Only six of the students dared to go into Phnom Penh, the others said they were afraid that 'the Vietnamese will kill us'.

By the end of January the regulated re-population of the capital had started. First priority was given to government employees and their families, who comprised some 70 per cent of the residents during the next few months. The Ministry of Information issued an urgent appeal for all former intellectuals and technicians to offer their services in the cause of rebuilding the country.

Other Cambodians who did get into the city became an army of scavengers, ransacking houses and apartments. After the euphoria of being freed from the Khmer Rouge regime, people were now frantically searching for plates, cutlery, bicycles, hidden caches of gold, jewellery – anything to ensure their families' survival in a country where no one really knew where the next meal was coming from.

REBUILDING A NATION

The People's Revolutionary Council of Kampuchea announced on 8 January 1979 consisted of eight men: Heng Samrin was President; Pen Sovann was Vice-President and in charge of National Defence; the others were responsible for the Interior (Chea Sim); Foreign Affairs (Hun Sen); Information, Press and Culture (Keo Chenda); Education (Chan Ven); Health and Social Affairs (Dr Nou Beng); and Economy and Living Conditions (Mok Sakun).

These men reflected the three currents that had come together to form the Salvation Front: old members of the Communist Party of Kampuchea who had stayed in Hanoi after the Geneva Accords in 1954; Khmer Rouge dissidents who had fled to Vietnam in 1978 and 1979; and individuals with no communist or revolutionary experience.

The first job of each minister was to find a suitable building to house his ministry, and the second task was to search for former employees and any survivors with some basic education. After hunting on the outskirts of Phnom Penh for former officials, civil servants or students and teachers, the next item on the agenda was to scavenge basic furniture and office equipment: paper, chairs, desks and the ultimate luxury – any rusting old typewriter rescued from the scrap heaps!

The hope that had been generated by the overthrow of the Pol Pot regime was not easy to sustain with a gutted capital and no working telephones. This was year zero and everything, including a new Cambodian state and society, had to be created out of the ashes and ruins.

Dr Thong Khon, a deputy mayor and later mayor of Phnom Penh from 1983–85, recalled those early days. The Khmer Rouge regime had brought an abrupt end to Khon's medical studies. He lost 18 members of his family and in early 1979 he was one of the former students seeking to help rebuild their country.

'We were able to find only 105 surviving students and intellectuals', of whom 32 were designated to work on the restoration of Phnom Penh city.[24] Thong Khon became chief of personnel and was given the responsibility to find more staff. A new police force was launched with just twelve recruits who were put through a short training programme.

The Khmer Rouge regime had closed down all the schools. Chan Ven, a former maths teacher, was now given the daunting task of re-establishing a basic educational system.[25] Teachers along with other professionals had been prime targets of Pol Pot's policy of purification and the elimination of foreign influences. Mobilising the pitifully few remaining qualified teachers, Chan Ven launched a nationwide literacy and educational campaign with the maxim: 'those who are well-educated must teach those people who only know a little, and those who know only a little must educate those who know nothing.'

On 24 September 1979 the Ministry of Education was able to take pride in having completed the reopening of all the pre-1975 schools in Phnom Penh, without any aid at all from the United Nations or western countries. The only supplies of paper, pens and notebooks had come from Vietnam, the USSR and Eastern Europe. On 14 October the following additional six ministries were established: Commerce, Industry, Agriculture, Finance, Social Affairs and Special Affairs (in charge of the rudimentary judicial system and tasked with drafting the new Constitution). Western media routinely reported the threat of famine, refugees and Vietnamese occupation, but only the few correspondents who made the effort to visit Phnom Penh paid any attention to these critical first steps at nation-building.

OUTSIDE ASSISTANCE

Pol Pot 's brand of ultra-collectivist agrarian revolution based on the peasantry had no scope for any intellectuals apart from their own tightly knit group, the Khmer Rouge leadership core, who had all studied together in Paris during the 1960s. Cambodia's professional and intellectual classes were identified as a potential threat and as natural opponents of the Khmer Rouge new order based on an agrarian utopia. In 1975 the new regime called upon students and workers abroad to return and help build the new Cambodia, but it was a cruel trick. Many of them were leftists who had gone into exile during the late Sihanouk or Lon Nol periods, but they were not trusted by the Khmer Rouge. They were held in camps and many were executed. Those who were released from the camps were generally put to work at heavy manual tasks rather than utilising their skills.

The resultant intellectual and professional vacuum in 1979 was partially filled in the short term by an influx of several thousand Vietnamese experts including doctors, journalists, teachers and at least one librarian, soon supplemented by others from the Soviet Union, Eastern Europe and Cuba.

The 1980s embodied a far more complicated Vietnamese-Cambodian relationship than the cold war propaganda label of a 'Vietnamese puppet regime', imposed on the population by an invasion force of 150,000 troops.[26]

Vietnamese advisors were attached to both party and State. Many advisors provided valuable technical and professional skills. Others were political cadres and security personnel dispatched to Cambodia to further Hanoi's political suzerainty over the infant republic. So many and complex were these ties that in 1984 the Council of Ministers reported that it had no way of figuring out how many advisors had come – and gone, or stayed on. In 1985 they reported that there were currently 310 Soviet advisors, 52 from other friendly countries and 22 international NGOs based in Phnom Penh.[27]

Strident calls from Asean countries, China and the West for 'unconditional and immediate Vietnamese withdrawal' and for self-determination seemed to take no account of the reality of a shattered nation that was in no shape to determine fully its own future until foreign aid from whatever source had delivered some degree of resuscitation.

The new government included intellectuals who were neither former Khmer Rouge nor communist veterans who had settled in Hanoi after the 1954 Geneva Peace Accords. Im Sethy, Dr My Samedy, Kong Sam-Ol and other professionals who chose to stay and rebuild their country cannot fairly be labelled as Hanoi puppets. Rather it was a case of being trapped in circumstances not of their own choosing.

All Cambodians – both inside and outside the country – could agree with the goal of self-determination. But there was a massive ideological chasm emerging between Cambodians inside and outside the country on how to achieve it and how to save their nation. Prum Sokha, at the time a trade-union official, said, 'What counted is we survived. Vietnam — we respect their contribution to save Cambodian people but we never accepted Vietnamese domination.'[28]

No western government rushed to send humanitarian aid to the new Cambodia, not even diplomatic observers or a fact-finding mission. The US and British governments even sought to block later NGO attempts to get emergency aid into Phnom Penh. Not all the fault was on one side. Vietnam and the People's Republic of Kampuchea tried to stop any aid being sent to the refugee settlements linked to the Khmer Rouge along the border and in Thailand. The politics of food aid in Cambodia was hotly debated at the time and the complexity that lay behind this tragedy forms the focus of Chapter 4 below.[29]

In July and August 1979 joint exploratory missions were sent into Phnom Penh by Unicef and the International Committee of the Red Cross, and in September they launched an international emergency relief campaign, but most of the aid was channelled to the refugee camps inside Thailand, rather than to the population inside Cambodia itself.

Oxfam UK was the first international NGO to break through the cold war boycott of post-Pol Pot Cambodia by delivering food aid, fertiliser and other basic necessities. It sent three relief flights into Phnom Penh in August and September, defying the negative advice from the UK's Foreign Office, which clearly did not want any western NGO to break the isolation of Phnom Penh. After negotiating numerous obstacles Oxfam's Jim Howard managed to charter a boat laden with humanitarian supplies from Singapore to Kampong Som (Sihanoukville), arriving on 14 October 1979 and followed by 43 barges. More than 25 years later Cambodians still fondly remember Oxfam's commitment and determination.[30]

THE HARD CHOICE FOR THE SURVIVING INTELLECTUALS : TO REBUILD THE COUNTRY OR FLEE ABROAD?

The intellectuals and other well-qualified professionals who had by some miracle survived the holocaust were now confronted by a very difficult choice. Liberation from Pol Pot brought the opportunity either to flee and seek exile abroad or to help build a new Cambodia. The option to get out became more appealing as it became increasingly evident that the People's Republic of Kampuchea was not going to be recognised by the west and that privation would remain the order of the day. Clearly it would be a long time before Cambodia would return to the 'golden age' of the 1960s that many harboured in their dreams.[31]

Should they rally round the new administration or head into exile? Given the wholesale destruction, the chronic food shortages and the obvious weakness and fragility of any new regime, the temptation to flee to the border was hard to resist.

France would have been only too happy to welcome French-trained radiologist Dr My Samedy, with many relatives already living in Paris. In the old days before the Khmer Rouge regime, Dr Samedy was a wealthy doctor who could afford to send his five children to France for their education and to buy an apartment in Paris in 1974. Im Sethy, a French-speaking teacher and later education official, also had relatives in France.

No doubt the British government would similarly have welcomed an asylum application from Dr Kry Beng Hong, the first Cambodian postgraduate from University College, London, who survived the Pol Pot regime.

From a Thai refugee camp to resettlement in a western country would have been little more than a formality for these non-communist intellectuals. Indeed hundreds of professionals, including a number of doctors, did choose this course.

In spite of the confusion, and temptations of seeking a sanctuary in the west, a body of professionals and intellectuals did respond to the plaintive appeals for qualified people to come forward and serve the nation. Prum Sokha later summed it up: 'If in 1979 everyone had gone to a refugee camp, there would have been no more Cambodia.'[32]

The new regime recruited civil servants and administrators from both the Prince Sihanouk era of the 1960s and the Lon Nol regime (1970–75). Behind the Marxist-Leninist rhetoric and the security provided by the Vietnamese army was another reality. The new government was a coalition of the survivors – Khmer Rouge rebels, Khmer veterans from the early 1950s struggle against French colonialism returned from Hanoi and a motley collection of intellectuals and professionals who held the key to nation building.

Dr My Samedy was appointed Secretary General of the Cambodian Red Cross on 16 May 1979 (a position he still holds today) but soon afterwards his wife begged him to leave for Paris via the Thai border. 'Every day my wife urged me to go to France,' Dr My Samedy recalled. Like most new government employees in Phnom Penh he knew that many people were still leaving the country. 'My friends and relatives ran away to Battambang and then to refugee camps in Thailand, but I did not want to leave my country. I consider my life was saved by the Vietnamese. They gave me a second life. And now I made a commitment to save the life of my people. I could not leave.'[33]

The new education minister, Chan Ven, had been a mathematics teacher in Svay Rieng province before the Pol Pot regime, and fled to Vietnam in 1978. He was recruited to the original 14-member Revolutionary Council – the only member without any communist or revolutionary background. Appointed as Minister of Education on 8 January 1979 he became the highest ranking non-communist in the new government.

In 1979 Chan Ven searched among those gathered on the outskirts of Phnom Penh for qualified survivors. He found his former colleague from the old days, Im Sethy, and persuaded him to resume his old job at the education ministry.

Im Sethy had every personal incentive to leave Cambodia. His brothers and sisters in Paris sent money to Phnom Penh and urged him to flee to Thailand. An easier life with his relatives in France beckoned. Why did he resist the temptations that others succumbed to? Sethy explained, 'I am too linked to the country, I had survived the killing and now we hoped to rebuild our country. We must share the hardship and survive, it is in the soul of the Khmer to survive and to prevent the return of the Khmer Rouge.'

Kong Sam-Ol had more reasons than most to flee abroad. Almost his entire family had been killed, including his wife, parents, brothers and sisters. Fluent in English, he had friends and excellent contacts in the US. He was an agronomist who had graduated from the University of Georgia in the US with a diploma in rice production, had all the right credentials to join the Khmer exile community in Long Beach, California or Lowell, Massachusetts.

A pre-1975 anti-communist magazine, *Free Asia*, had prominently featured him, then director of rice planning in the Lon Nol regime, as one of the bright prospects among US-educated Asians. As a result, Hanoi could well have been suspicious of his having CIA connections, surely another reason why he might have had serious doubts about his future in a pro-Vietnamese government.

But Kong Sam-Ol was appointed deputy minister of agriculture and later deputy prime minister. Dr My Samedy took charge of Cambodian Red Cross, and by 1980 he had managed to re-open the Faculty of Medicine. Dr Kry Beng Hong worked with the Phnom Penh municipality, and became deputy mayor in the late 1980s.

The 1979 Minister of Education, Chan Ven, is now deputy secretary general of the National Assembly, Im Sethy is today secretary of state for education and Prum Sokha is a secretary of state at the Ministry of Interior. Dr Thong Khon became deputy mayor of Phnom Penh in 1983 and launched a mass literacy campaign. He went on to become successively Phnom Penh mayor, a deputy in the National Assembly and currently holds the position of secretary of state in the Ministry of Tourism. In 1993 Kong Sam-Ol was appointed to be minister for the palace, in charge of relations between re-instated King Sihanouk and the government.

All of them could so easily have gone abroad, and gained good professional jobs in exile. But it was a matter of conscience, the spirit of public service and a strong patriotic desire to help rebuild their shattered nation that inspired them to stay, whatever the ideological complexion and rhetoric of the new regime. Working with Vietnam for the rebirth of Cambodia, fleeing the country or joining with the Khmer Rouge to fight Vietnamese troops were the stark choices imposed by the cold war alignments.

Dr Thong Khon commented, 'In 1993 I welcomed Funcinpec coming back (they returned from the Thai border and refugee camps). I asked only two things: "Don't call me a communist and don't call me a Vietnamese puppet."'

These were the epithets thrown at Cambodia's new government in 1979, used to justify a policy of delivering support rather than justice to the Khmer Rouge criminals. And over the next ten years the US government and their allies in the cold war sought to belittle and deny Phnom Penh any credit or legitimacy solely on the basis that they had been liberated by the wrong country.

2
Keeping Pol Pot in the UN Cambodia Seat

In 1979 Cambodia had stepped back from the abyss. The rebirth of a nation had begun and, in the face of colossal deprivations, life gradually returned to some semblance of normality. But the release from Pol Pot's genocidal rule, that had brought such relief inside the country, was met by consternation and denunciations of Vietnamese aggression from Washington and other western capitals, as well as from Beijing.

A sharp dichotomy developed between the view from inside Cambodia and the cold war-tinted perspective generated from Bangkok and beyond. Inside the country people were consumed with anger against the Khmer Rouge, overflowing with grief for their missing relatives and broken families. The first steps towards documenting the genocide and preparing for a Khmer Rouge tribunal were under way.

But neighbouring countries and western governments had no contact at all with Phnom Penh and no first-hand information about what was happening inside the country. Beyond the bare facts – that the Vietnamese army had ousted the Pol Pot regime and were chasing the fleeing Khmer Rouge towards the Thai frontier – the world knew precious little about the real situation. What made matters worse was the evident lack of interest in finding out more, as observations from the few journalists and aid workers who did visit Cambodia received scant attention in the western press or in government circles.

In spite of the fact that the end of the Khmer Rouge regime ushered in a new era, western governments shunned the opportunity to send observers or any fact-finding missions to Phnom Penh. If the British Foreign Office or the French Ministry of Foreign Affairs had sent a fact-finding mission to Phnom Penh in early 1979 it would not have necessarily implied diplomatic recognition, only diplomatic interest and concern. Hanoi at the time would certainly have welcomed it. However a former British ambassador to Cambodia has confirmed to the authors that this kind of initiative was never even considered.[1]

If Vietnam had imagined that it could garner support or perhaps even be applauded for getting rid of such a widely detested regime, it must have been taken aback by the speed with which western governments shifted from human rights concerns about the Pol Pot regime to cold war preoccupations with the geopolitical chessboard.

But, aside from the altruism of rescuing the Cambodian people from their current fate, Vietnam had other motives that gave them the right under international law to intervene. From the very first days of the Khmer Rouge regime, attacks were mounted across the border into islands regarded as Vietnamese by previous Cambodian governments and a major cross-border assault was mounted on 30 April 1977, the second anniversary of the end of the war in Vietnam. In December 1977, Democratic Kampuchea broke off diplomatic relations with Vietnam, which then launched its first serious retaliation to a series of assaults. By June 1978 over three-quarters of a million Vietnamese had been displaced from their homes in border provinces, which were also unable to be farmed, and Vietnam had received over 300,000 Cambodians who fled across the border seeking refuge.[2]

China and the US, which had just normalised relations in 1978, had their first taste of working together in the effort to prevent Vietnam from obtaining international acceptance of its crushing defeat of the Pol Pot regime.

An emergency session of the United Nations Security Council was hastily arranged for 11 January 1979, one day prior to the formal declaration of the People's Republic of Kampuchea – the new government in Phnom Penh.

At the UN, Prince Norodom Sihanouk, often termed 'the last of the Cambodian God-kings',[3] played a critical role during this new phase of the cold war tussle over this small southeast Asian nation sandwiched between its more powerful neighbours Thailand and Vietnam. He had been installed on the throne by the French colonial authorities in 1941. Soon after Cambodia achieved independence in 1954, he abdicated and ruled Cambodia as an autocratic prime minister until he was ousted by a military coup in 1970. He then went into exile in Beijing, assuming the position as the nominal leader of the resistance to the Lon Nol regime, and the head of a government-in-exile.

Sihanouk returned to Cambodia after the Khmer Rouge victory in 1975 and accepted the position as figurehead president of Pol Pot's 'Democratic' Kampuchea, over which he had not the slightest influence, and was held a virtual prisoner in his own palace. He resigned from this post in 1976.

During Pol Pot's final days in power he ordered the royal prisoner to be brought to his office. With Cambodian dissidents and Vietnamese forces almost at the gates of Phnom Penh, Pol Pot adopted an apologetic tone and appealed to Sihanouk – the VIP hostage – to accept a special assignment on behalf of a doomed regime.

It was a supremely ironic encounter only days before the fall of Phnom Penh. Pol Pot, who had shown no qualms about permitting the killing of 19 members of Sihanouk's family, implored the prince to become the Khmer Rouge special emissary to the UN. His mission: to persuade the UN to support the regime of 'Democratic Kampuchea against Vietnamese aggression'.

The hostage prince was persuaded to fly to Beijing and on to the UN in New York to plead the cause of the Democratic Kampuchea regime as a victim of foreign aggression. Sihanouk, the hostage, readily agreed. Had anybody ever said no to Pol Pot and lived to tell the tale?

On 6 January a Chinese Boeing 707 arrived at Pochentong airport, Phnom Penh, to whisk Sihanouk off to safety. Other passengers on board the plane included Khmer Rouge escorts – Pol Pot-appointed 'minders' – Chinese advisors and diplomats.

On arrival in New York the prince and his entourage were installed in the luxury suite of New York's Waldorf-Astoria Hotel, all expenses underwritten by China. Taking no chances with the Cambodian prince, his Khmer Rouge minders – Thiounn Prasith and Keat Chhon – were under orders to share the suite and keep a permanent watch.[4]

The members of the UN Security Council listened to Prince Sihanouk, in his new role as Pol Pot's special emissary, passionately denouncing the Vietnamese invasion and violation of Cambodian sovereignty. Sihanouk enjoyed considerable prestige in the Third World as one of the founders of the Non-Aligned Movement. He had attended the 1955 Bandung Conference alongside Egypt's Nasser, India's Nehru, Indonesia's Sukarno and Yugoslavia's Tito.

China called for the immediate withdrawal of all foreign troops and 13 out of 15 Security Council members voted to support the resolution. The ambassador of Guinea spoke for many when he told the long-respected Cambodian statesman: 'This is a victory for you, Prince Sihanouk ... That is why the member countries kept quiet, so as not to hinder you in the Security Council and the international scene. If you were not here as the representative of Democratic Kampuchea, we would come out and say that the government [of Pol Pot] only got what was coming to it.'[5]

Realising that he was still a Khmer Rouge prisoner even while staying in a New York luxury hotel, the prince made a short-lived midnight dash for freedom, applied for political asylum in the US and checked into a hospital for a medical check-up and rest. But not for long, as the US government succumbed to Chinese pressure to reject his bid for asylum. This was a time of strenuous efforts by the US to turn the clinks of the champagne glasses heralding a new era in US-China relations into more substantial bonds. Cambodia was an opportunity handed to them on a plate. From this point on, not upsetting China over Cambodia became a major plank in western governments' approach to resolving the conflict, right up to the drafting and signing of the Paris Peace Agreement twelve years later.

Although China's motion at the UN Security Council calling for the withdrawal of all foreign troops from Cambodia was vetoed by the Soviet Union, the debate clearly strengthened prospects for the diplomatic survival of the Khmer Rouge. The real test came later at the 34th session of the UN General Assembly meeting in New York September 1979.

In August Prince Sihanouk started to lobby member states to leave the Cambodia seat vacant, reversing his earlier plea in the UN Security Council. In the intervening months since his role as Pol Pot's emissary back in January, Sihanouk had manoeuvred to escape from the clutches of the Khmer Rouge. While accepting financial underwriting from China, including accommodation for his family and retinue in Beijing, he headed off to Pyongyang, North Korea, and proceeded to unleash scathing attacks on the barbaric rule of the Khmer Rouge, calling on China to cease its support. From his sanctuary in Pyongyang Sihanouk now appealed to the world to stop diplomatic support for the Pol Pot regime.

However, the US, China and the Asean countries, confident of their ability to muster the numbers, ignored Sihanouk's open letter and went all out to retain the seat for the Khmer Rouge delegation.

How could the UN recognise an ex-regime that no longer fulfilled the basic requirements for diplomatic recognition? Democratic Kampuchea no longer controlled any significant amount of territory. It did not exercise effective authority and no longer commanded any administration inside Cambodia. A plausible case could be made that these criteria were more or less fulfilled by the newly-installed Heng

OPEN LETTER TO MEMBER STATES OF THE UN
FROM PRINCE NORODOM SIHANOUK
(excerpts)

At the approach of the opening of the next session of the General Assembly of the United Nations ... I should like to underline the following:

1) I fully approve, in advance, of your refusal, which maybe anticipated, to admit to your organization the pretended 'government of the People's Republic of Kampuchea' which is only too obviously the creature of a foreign power whose armed forces occupy my country.

2) I implore you with the utmost urgency to revise your attitude, which has too long been benevolent, towards Mr Pol Pot's 'government of Democratic Kampuchea' which you unduly consider to be the sole and authentic representative of the Khmer nation and people ...

As far as I know, you have never protested, let alone asked those responsible who were sitting among you, for an account of this genocide worse than the one committed by the detestable 'Nazis'.

This miserable silence in the face of this enormous crime against humanity does not – to say the least of it – enhance the image of your organization. Immediately after the Second World War, before the Tribunal of Nuremburg [sic], the high-ranking personages responsible for Hitler's excesses paid [for] their evil crimes with their own lives. For the past four years those whom you know perfectly well to be the hangmen of a whole people have taken part in your deliberations, talking from your platform and throwing in their ballots. International morals have decidedly declined rather deeply today when honest people and whom all know to be murderers, work together in perfect serenity ...

The solution which I have the honour of proposing to you, is as follows:

1) to declare that, at the present time, Cambodia has no longer a national government and therefore allow her seat at the UNO to remain *vacant*.

2) solemnly invite the Khmer Rouge and the Vietnamese to put an end to their fighting;

– demand the Khmer Rouge put down their arms under the control of a peace force of the United Nations (Blue Helmets) and that the armed forces of Vietnam leave the Cambodian territory...

3) appoint an International Control Commission of the 'Geneva 1954' type to watch over the return of peace and independence to Cambodia ...

Norodom Sihanouk of Cambodia
Pyongyang, September 1979[6]

Samrin government, but how could it possibly apply to a defunct and deposed *ancien régime*?

At the September session of the nine-member UN credentials committee, Bulgaria formally challenged the status of the Pol Pot regime and its right to represent Cambodia in the UN General Assembly. The Congo came up with a compromise proposal that would have left Cambodia's UN seat open but this was ignored and the Committee voted six to three to award the UN credentials to the Khmer Rouge. The vote was taken without even reviewing the credentials of the People's Republic of Kampuchea duly submitted by the head of state, Heng Samrin, in accordance with the Rules of Procedure of the General Assembly.[7]

'I was told to engineer the result on the Credentials Committee,' said Robert Rosenstock, the US delegate, 'so I engineered the result.'[8] He argued that the Credentials Committee was not concerned with the conduct of a regime towards (or against) its own people but was purely technical in nature. Since the KR credentials had been accepted at the 1978 session of the General Assembly, they should be accepted again.

No one was more delighted with the results of US diplomacy than Ieng Sary, the leader of the Pol Pot delegation. After the tally he approached Rosenstock the US delegate and proffered his hand. 'Thank you so much for everything you have done for us,' he said. Rosenstock shook his hand and told a colleague, 'I think I now know how Pontius Pilate must have felt.'[9] The motion was then submitted to the General Assembly.

A major battle over the credentials of the Pol Pot regime was gearing up for a showdown on the floor of the UN General Assembly which had to consider whether to accept or reject the six to three resolution referred from the UN's Credentials Committee.[10]

Bulgarian Ambassador Yankov submitted a resolution to recognise the newly-installed Heng Samrin government. During the course of a heated debate several communist states cited the Genocide Convention which they said required them to withhold recognition from a genocidal regime. Far from deserving the UN seat, they argued, Pol Pot and Ieng Sary should be tried for genocide.

India, one of the non-aligned leaders, argued for a political compromise between the two rival claims to the Cambodian seat. Instead of seating the newly proclaimed Peoples Republic of Kampuchea, or continuing to recognise the *status quo ante* – the deposed regime that had ceased to exist as a government – New Delhi's delegation appealed for sober reflection and taking the middle course of leaving the seat vacant.

Indian Ambassador Mishra introduced an amendment to the report of the Credentials Committee – a decision that would have brought the UN position in line with the position adopted by the non-aligned countries in Havana just prior to the General Assembly session. However, Ambassador Tommy Koh from Singapore argued that the Indian proposal was not an amendment but a new proposal, which should therefore be put to the vote after the resolution of the Credentials Committee. This argument was accepted by the General Assembly. As the report of the Credentials Committee was adopted, the Bulgarian and Indian proposals were never put to the vote.

The legal precedents concerning both credentials and Cambodian representation demonstrated clear contradictions and inconsistency in UN member states' policies, not only with other cases in 1979 but with the specific case of Cambodia almost a decade earlier. The 1970 military coup that had toppled Prince Sihanouk's government had led to a similar conflict of claims to the UN Cambodia seat, but with a vastly different outcome. Prince Sihanouk claimed that the UN should not recognise a new regime illegally installed by a process of military force. However, the UNGA chose to accept the credentials of General Lon Nol's regime. Sihanouk's protests that his government-in-exile should be recognised were rejected by the UN.

In the 1979 vote in the General Assembly, 71 countries backed the credentials of the ousted Pol Pot regime including the US, UK, Canada and Australia, with 35 votes against, led by Vietnam, the Soviet bloc and some non-aligned countries. There were 34 abstentions including France and Sweden.[11] Some argued that neither of the claimants had the necessary control of territory or population. Other governments saw it as more of a human rights issue. They could not stomach voting for an evil regime, but at the same time considered the new PRK regime as too much the creature of Hanoi and foreign invasion. For many of these governments the empty seat formula was the only acceptable outcome.

Robert Rosenstock from the US delegation at the UN provided an explanation for its pro-Pol Pot stance, 'The choice for us was between moral principles and international law. The scale weighed in favour of law, because that also served our security interests.'[12]

Another North American took a totally different view. Father Theodore Hesburgh, then president of Notre Dame University in Indiana, was disgusted by the result. During a visit to Phnom Penh in 1979 with Unicef information officer Jacques Danois, Hesburgh declared: 'Pol Pot shouldn't be accepted anywhere except perhaps in prison. Giving Pol Pot a seat at the United Nations is the same as seating Hitler.' Fr Hesburgh elaborated, 'I think recognising and accepting the Pol Pot Government at the UN is an insult to humanity. Personally, I would like derecognition of Pol Pot's Government because it's a government of murderers, and brigands. Not one civilised country should recognise it.'[13]

International law and the UN seating issue came to be tested several times that year. In 1979 several brutal regimes were overthrown. Idi Amin, the Ugandan dictator, was ousted by foreign intervention from Tanzania. In the same year French troops moved against Emperor Bokassa to topple his Central African Empire regime. During the 1980s the US government clearly violated national sovereignty in Grenada (1983) and Panama (1989) to install pro-US regimes.

Although foreign troops in all four cases committed similar invasions of the territory of another country, the hue and cry raised with such vehemence against Vietnam was curiously absent. In all these cases the UN credentials committee approved the standing of the new claimants to their nation's seating in the General Assembly with few objections and little fuss.

One might also point instructively to the contrary reaction to Indonesia's invasion and occupation of East Timor in December 1975 which, although never endorsed by the United Nations and only *de jure* by a single country – Australia – was accepted *de facto* by many countries. Indonesia was never seriously challenged or punished for its invasion and annexation despite several UN resolutions that upheld East Timor's right of self-determination. Despite their protestations to that effect, clearly most countries that voted for Pol Pot's credentials as the ' legitimate representative of the Kampuchean people' at the UN were not principally concerned with the sanctity of international law.

The prime movers in denying the Cambodian seat to the new regime installed by Vietnam were determined to block by any means what they perceived to be a strategic advance of the USSR and its allies in southeast Asia. It was primarily a cold war manoeuvre with little concern for international law.

Intense lobbying by the US, China and the Asean group led by Singapore was effective in winning over the minnows in the UN General Assembly. Some small countries remote from the process were wined and dined at the best restaurants in New York with offers of aid linked to their UN voting behaviour.[14] The 71 votes mustered in favour of the Pol Pot regime's credentials stand out in UN history as a major embarrassment and a poignant reflection of cold war alignments and power politics.

The USSR and Vietnam were outmanoeuvred by a new coalition between China, the US and the Asean nations, now shamelessly aligned with Democratic Kampuchea. It was the most important seating controversy since the exclusion of mainland China and the endorsement of the island of Taiwan as the UN's choice to represent nearly 1 billion people. The world's largest nation was deprived of representation as a result of US machinations in support of the defeated Kuomintang who fled from the mainland and seized control over the island of Taiwan. Instead of China sitting on the UN Security Council, Taiwan preposterously claimed to represent all of China and refused to give up its seat in favour of the People's Republic of China until the landmark United Nations General Assembly vote in 1971. In 1979, with the farce over the representation of China still fresh in the minds of many, the UN's reputation took another nosedive with the UNGA's affirmation of the legitimacy of the 'Killing Fields' regime and its right to represent its victims.

Most diplomats paid lip service to the moral issue and heaped condemnation on the Pol Pot regime, largely to satisfy public opinion at home. But from 1979 until 1990 this apparent disgust failed to stir the conscience of any western government sufficiently to vote against the Khmer Rouge.

Australia and the UK did eventually de-recognise the Democratic Kampuchea regime under intense domestic public pressure. But these gestures made no practical difference to the seating of the Khmer Rouge in the UN. Western governments made no attempt to deprive the Khmer Rouge of their diplomatic status at the UN, declining even to support India in its lobby for an empty seat arrangement.

If the abstainers had voted with the 35 nations that had emphatically rejected the Khmer Rouge credentials, their numbers, 35 plus the 34 abstentions, would have come close to defeating the 71 votes in favour. Then if only a single country could have been convinced to switch its vote, Pol Pot's credentials would have been rejected. Moral decency and rationality could have prevailed if abstainers and pro-PRK nations had come to an understanding that could then have paved the way for a second vote on India's resolution to leave the Cambodia seat vacant. At the same time western nations could have been assured that any motion to seat the new claimants, the People's Republic of Kampuchea, would still be comfortably defeated.

Derek Tonkin, the British ambassador in Hanoi at the time, recommended this course of action to the Foreign Office but they rebuffed him. In the less crucial forum of the Non-Aligned Movement, however, the Indian formula prevailed and the Cambodia seat was left vacant in 1979.

The failure of the United States and other western governments to pursue the empty seat option allowed the Khmer Rouge extraordinary diplomatic advantages which they exploited to the hilt, obstructing any UN development aid for rebuilding the nation that they had done so much to destroy. Oxfam and other NGOs striving to help rebuild Cambodia bitterly condemned this 'poverty of diplomacy', which condemned Cambodia to an aid boycott and ten more years of war.

As Ramses Amer pointed out in 1990, 'None of the Western democracies have ever voted against the acceptance of DK's credentials.' Most supported Democratic Kampuchea on each of the four occasions its credentials were put to the vote (Belgium, Canada, Denmark, Federal Republic of Germany, Greece, Italy, Japan, Luxembourg, New Zealand, Portugal, United Kingdom and the United States). Five countries abstained in all four votes (Austria, Finland, France, Ireland and Sweden). Others had mixed positions: Netherlands abstaining from 1979–1981 and voting in favour of the DK in 1982; Spain abstaining in 1979–80 and voting in favour in 1981–82; while Australia moved in the other direction, voting in favour of the DK in 1979–80 and then abstaining in 1981–82; as did Iceland and Norway, voting for the DK in 1979 but then abstaining in 1980–82.[15]

India had warned the UN General Assembly that ignoring the reality of a government that did exist in Cambodia, and choosing instead to recognise a phantom regime that existed only as a terrorist administration in some refugee camps, was to fall into the same trap that had undermined the UN's credibility in the past, when for 21 years China had been kept out of the UN.

In spite of India's warning to the UN, the majority of member states once again embraced the diplomatic absurdity of recognising a regime that did not control or administer the territory that they claimed to represent. Taiwan was not China and the Khmer Rouge no longer controlled Cambodia.

Although the credentials of Democratic Kampuchea, or the Coalition Government of Democratic Kampuchea (CGDK), were no longer challenged by Vietnam after 1982, international governmental opinion continued to be monitored by an annual vote on an Asean-sponsored resolution calling for 'the withdrawal of all foreign forces' (i.e., Vietnam) from Cambodia. As will be chronicled in Chapter 7 below, only in 1988 was an oblique reference to the Khmer Rouge's crimes made by the General Assembly in speaking of 'the non-return of the universally condemned policies and practices of a recent past'.

The UK Foreign Secretary, Douglas Hurd, proclaimed that Britain's vote to accept the credentials of the CGDK 'in no way implies readiness to deal with the coalition government of Democratic Kampuchea as a government, much less support for the Khmer Rouge'. But the result of the vote was indeed to keep the Khmer Rouge alive for more than a decade after its overthrow.

Thanks to the extraordinary UN vote in 1979, the Khmer Rouge's diplomatic status in the world was renewed, and their political survival bolstered, even though some 2 million people – over a quarter of the population – had been either murdered or 'manslaughtered', having died as a direct result of their policies.

People inside Cambodia were dumbfounded by this international recognition of Pol Pot. During Tom Fawthrop's first visit to Phnom Penh representing the *Irish Times* newspaper in January 1981, he was bombarded with questions from ordinary people : 'Why does the UN recognise Pol Pot? The UN should help us capture Pol Pot – why are they protecting him?' Many correspondents found themselves facing the same despairing questions: 'How can it be?' 'Don't they know Pol Pot killed my husband and my two brothers?' 'They killed my whole family and yet why does the UN support them?'

It is no easy task to provide simple answers to explain the perversity of international diplomacy. What answer could be given other than that the world had gone mad? Many western governments, for all their prattling about human rights, proved to be opportunistic and cynical when it came to taking sides on the Cambodia issue.

Sir Robert Jackson, placed in charge of UN Emergency Aid for Cambodia in November 1979, had previously dealt with survivors of the Nazi concentration camps. After his first visit to Phnom Penh he reported that, 'a quarter of the entire population perished, representing genocide on a scale never before witnessed in terms of a single country.' In similar vein, Jackson concluded, 'Without doubt, it is the greatest human tragedy of the twentieth century.'[16] And yet the perpetrators had just been given a renewed diplomatic licence to represent their victims. After the liberation in 1945, it would have been unthinkable for Hitler and his supporters to represent West Germany or East Germany in the newly formed UN. Cambodians asked why after their liberation the same standards of morality, integrity and justice did not apply.

No less outrageous for some UN officials was the unseemly sight of Khmer Rouge commanders having fled Cambodia now exercising their reign of terror over the refugee population at Sa Kaeo in Thailand under the noses of international organisations. International Red Cross officials, Oxfam and other western aid agencies operating inside Cambodia were shocked and embarrassed by the UN allowing active combatants on behalf of a genocidal regime to recuperate in 'refugee' camps in Thailand administered, supplied and protected by the UN High Commissioner for Refugees.

THE FAILURE OF THE UN COMMISSION ON HUMAN RIGHTS

Instead of nations complying with their obligations under the Convention on the Prevention and Punishment of the Crime of Genocide of 1948 and calling in Interpol to track down the leaders as after 1945 to hunt down the Nazis, they ignored the crimes of the Pol Pot regime and its UN representatives led by Ieng Sary were once again granted all the privileges of diplomatic immunity and VIP status.

When the Khmer Rouge were still in power, the UN Commission on Human Rights based in Geneva had launched an investigation into the Khmer Rouge regime in 1978. Hearings were held in Geneva, with testimony taken from a number of refugees and human rights bodies. Mr Abdelwahab Boudhiba from Algeria was appointed UN Special Rapporteur and mandated to assess the documentation of the Khmer Rouge regime's human rights violations. His conclusion did not mince words and referred to violations of genocidal proportions and represented the 'the worst to have occurred anywhere in the world since Nazism.'[17] But the Khmer Rouge and their allies were effective in stopping the report from ever reaching the floor of the commission.

In a tragic twist, in February 1979 the USSR, the entire Soviet bloc and the non-aligned movement voted not to consider the Boudhiba report at the Human Rights Commission just a month after the Vietnamese, with Soviet support, had ousted Pol Pot.

It was appallingly sloppy diplomacy or a feeble lack of diplomatic coordination that, at the same time as Vietnamese experts were already using the documentation submitted to the UN in 1978 to justify their invasion on the grounds of humanitarian intervention, no new instructions were issued from Moscow to Soviet bloc diplomats at the commission, who held to the line of opposition to any investigation.

The ousted Pol Pot regime continued to sit as Cambodia's representatives in the Human Rights Commission in Geneva, and they were able to exploit all opportunities to hijack the agenda and bury the genocide issue. The Khmer Rouge delegates in Geneva and their allies manoeuvred to drop any further investigation into the genocide, diverting attention from their bloody record by introducing resolutions attacking Vietnam's invasion and occupation as violations of human rights and the right to self-determination. The countries that in 1978 had so stridently called for the investigation of human rights abuses by the Khmer Rouge, now suddenly lost all interest in pursuing resolutions that would put the Khmer Rouge in a bad light. David Hawk, a founder of the Cambodian Documentation Commission, summed up the situation in *The New Republic*: 'The problem of Cambodian self-determination has almost entirely superseded the problem of the Cambodian genocide. Now the Human Rights Commission is treated to the ironic spectacle of human rights complaints filed by the Khmer Rouge who when in power promised to make 'mince-meat' of the imperialist manoeuvres at the Commission.'[18]

The 1978 Boudhiba report on the Khmer Rouge genocide was never even considered, let alone voted on. Now it was the turn of western countries to match the opportunism of the USSR and its allies. Britain, Canada and Norway, which had led the 1978 efforts to document the human rights record in Cambodia, abruptly dropped the issue of the Pol Pot regime's accountability in line with the new policy dictated by Washington. A second Special Rapporteur's Report on Kampuchea issued in late 1979 for consideration at the 1980 Commission held that Cambodia faced two human rights problems: a 'terrible genocide'; and the denial of the right to self-determination. For a second year in a row the UN member states at the Commission decided to ignore a report of genocide by an officially appointed UN human rights special reporter.

The decade of the 1980s was marked by the singular absence of any western initiative at the UN to return to the fundamental human rights issue that had been had been canvassed so strongly before Vietnam had entered the picture. Cambodia in 1979 presented a historic opportunity for the UN to apply and enforce for the first time its own treaty – the Convention on the Prevention and Punishment of the Crime of Genocide of 1948.

Was it a case of monumental amnesia on the part of the whole UN apparatus that nobody raised the issue from 1979 until 1997 – a full 18 years of forgetting? Or is it the case as Sir Robert Jackson remarked:

> I know of no parallel to the conditions which have been experienced in Cambodia over the past decade to any other experience I have had. In the case of post-war Europe, there is the vast tragedy of the concentration camps . . . but thank God, the world had an immediate reaction and to this moment, there has been a sensitivity to events which happened forty years ago. But, in the case of Cambodia, for some extraordinary reason, I am left with the strong impression that the world wants to forget the tragedy in Cambodia – they *want* to forget it![19]

After the conclusion of the August 1979 People's Revolutionary Tribunal in Phnom Penh, which sentenced Pol Pot and Ieng Sary to death in absentia, copies of the court records and a report on the legal proceedings were officially transmitted to the UN in New York. If Britain, Canada and Norway still had any desire to document the human rights situation under Khmer Rouge rule, then they had only to study the detailed testimony of Pol Pot's victims. However, none of these countries made any attempt either to send observers to the Tribunal or to follow up and scrutinise the wealth of evidence that the tribunal had recorded and published, which went far beyond the scope of their own deliberations in 1978.

UN'S TARNISHED REPUTATION AND ITS CAMBODIAN LEGACY

The determination of at least two members of the Security Council, the US and China, to enforce rigorously the UN's recognition of the Khmer Rouge regime in exile ensured that UN agencies were not permitted to sign any agreements with the real but 'illegal' government in Phnom Penh.

The UN's recognition of the Pol Pot regime meant that the only functioning Cambodian administration, the Heng Samrin government, had no legal existence in the eyes of the UN. Nearly all the UN agencies that would normally undertake major programmes to rehabilitate the country were banned from dealings with Phnom Penh as long as the Pol Pot group occupied the Cambodia seat in New York.

UN agencies could have helped Cambodia so much: WHO to assist with the chronic health problems of a country without a health system, UNESCO to help rebuild the school system, FAO for the rehabilitation of agriculture, and UNDP to support development programmes. But only Unicef was given an operational mandate inside Cambodia.

A handful of powerful states had conspired to abuse the United Nations, standing both reality and morality on their head. They enforced the fiction that the Pol Pot regime – the government of Democratic Kampuchea that did not exist outside its terrorist control of some refugee camps – was the legitimate government of Cambodia.

Some UN staff dealing with Cambodia during the emergency period chafed at these farcical constraints imposed on them by the fact that the Khmer Rouge government-in-exile was deemed to be the *de jure* entity for UN agencies to deal with in carrying out humanitarian and development programmes.

To add insult to injury, Pol Pot's representatives would periodically turn up at major conferences of UN agencies solely for the purpose of reminding a WHO meeting that the regime that had destroyed hospitals and clinics was still entitled to represent the health interests of Cambodian people. When the WHO debated an epidemic of cerebral malaria sweeping Cambodia in 1979, the representative of Democratic Kampuchea had nothing to say, whereas people from the country's Ministry of Health were barred from attending.

During the period when the Pol Pot regime did control Cambodia they seldom attended any UN forums. Now they were out of power, their functionaries were dispatched to even the least known UN agencies. The newly-discovered enthusiasm of the Khmer Rouge to attend all UN conferences included those of the International Civil Aviation Organization, the Inter-governmental Maritime Consultative Organisation and the Universal Postal Union. Given the fact that Khmer Rouge had no planes, no ships and no postal service, their contributions to these UN affairs were at best irrelevant. Their ritual denunciations of Vietnamese occupation interrupting the otherwise technical and scientific deliberations could have provided fertile material for a Monty Python comedy script.[20]

Contrary to normal UN practice, most refugees in the border camps were subject to daily control and intimidation by either the Khmer Rouge or their battlefield allies – the Royalist guerrillas and the rightist soldiers loyal to former prime minister Son Sann.

Humanitarian assistance was channelled to those political organisations through the UNBRO (United Nations Border Relief Operation) instead of through the UNHCR (United Nations High Commissioner for Refugees), which normally administers refugee camps. As Ramses Amer commented: 'This situation of UN assistance being given without UNBRO being in a position to fully control distribution is a result of political considerations stemming from the decision to grant de facto international recognition to the Khmer Rouge alone as the legal and lawful representative of the Kampuchean nation from 1979 to 1981 and the CGDK from 1982.'[21]

The bottom line in diplomatic thinking was brutal: without development aid Hanoi could not consolidate its stranglehold over Cambodia, the fledgling 'puppet regime' would soon collapse and then pro-western forces would take over the rebuilding of Cambodia according to their preferred model and in conjunction with forces that could perhaps be described as beholden to them.

'No humanitarian operation in this century has been so totally and continuously influenced by political factors,' Sir Robert Jackson told a meeting of foreign correspondents at the Dusit Thani hotel in Bangkok in 1980.

Considerations of humanity, human rights and justice were swept aside during the 1980s, not only by dictatorships in China, Thailand, Indonesia and by other Asean members but also by western countries, led by the United States, that continued to proclaim loudly their concern for these matters.

During the 1990s UN human rights investigators coined the phrase the 'culture of impunity' to characterise the failure of the authorities and the justice system to investigate, arrest and prosecute political murderers and any case in which high ranking military or police were the main suspects. But nothing contributed more to this prevailing culture of getting away with murder than the support given to Khmer Rouge leaders by western nations that sheltered them from prosecution from 1979–1997. Getting away with genocide can be considered as the foundation of Cambodia's culture of impunity.

3
The World's First Genocide Trial

It was a tall order to expect that an internationally credible trial of
the Khmer Rouge regime could be mounted in Cambodia in 1979.
The legal system had to be rebuilt from scratch and resources – even
paper and typewriters, let alone skilled translators and court officials
– were sadly lacking. As one international participant, John Quigley,
later remarked, 'My initial reaction on arriving in Phnom Penh was
to wonder why anyone was bothering to hold a criminal trial, when
so much needed to be done to restore normal life.'[1] But the level of
organisation shown in the conduct of the trial – preparing a vast
quantity of testimony in three languages and coping with a large
delegation of foreigners needing to be housed, fed and taken to
various genocide sites in and around Phnom Penh as well as in Siem
Reap – indicated the high priority given by the government to this
effort. Its legal shortcomings will be discussed below.

From the beginning, the Cambodian political forces and their
Vietnamese backers who overthrew the Khmer Rouge enumerated a
dual policy with regard to punishment of those who had committed
crimes. The founding document of the Salvation Front, using the
language of the day, pronounced, 'All reactionary ringleaders, who
stubbornly oppose the people and owe a heavy blood-debt to them,
should be sternly punished,' while going on to assure clemency for
those who confessed and joined the effort to reconstruct the country.[2]
During January 1979, as the very first steps were being taken to re-
establish governmental structures, the issue of legal accountability
for Khmer Rouge crimes was pursued.

The eight-member People's Revolutionary Council of Kampuchea
functioned as the cabinet until after the 1981 election. Initially
there was little distinction between different branches of the state
(legislative, executive and judiciary). By August ten ministries were
functioning.

Keo Chenda was responsible for Information, Press and Culture
and it was within this part of the government that the rudimentary
judicial system was formed. A small legal unit was set up on the third
floor of the Information building, headed by Dith Munty, a former

deputy prosecutor in the Phnom Penh court. Dith Munty scoured the camps on the outskirts of Phnom Penh seeking other people with legal experience to join him and he found Chhuor Leang Huot, a former judge, and Min Khin, a former clerk in the Phnom Penh municipal court.

These were among the few surviving Cambodian lawyers: out of those legally trained personnel from the pre-1975 period only seven remained. Not only did this chronic lack of qualified lawyers hamper efforts to collect evidence back in 1979, but its legacy continues to cast a long shadow over the country's very weak legal system today, an important factor in the 2002 breakdown in negotiations between the UN legal panel and the Cambodian task force for setting up a tribunal.

In 1979 the three-member legal section's most pressing assignment was to document the crimes committed by the Khmer Rouge. In and around Phnom Penh, Min Khin carried out his task of seeking witnesses and evidence in preparation for a trial held only seven months later. People who had been imprisoned or tortured by the Khmer Rouge were interviewed about their ordeal.

Some key testimony was provided by a number of Khmer Rouge cadre who had been arrested in January as they tried to flee Phnom Penh, and were being held in T3, the old colonial prison in the centre of the city. One of these men confessed to having personally killed 300 people. When Min Khin started work in February 1979, S-21 (Tuol Sleng) had already been discovered and it was part of his responsibility, under conservator Mai Lam's guidance, to preserve the evidence and document the horrors that had happened there. Min Khin recalls sending instructions out through the governmental apparatus to village level, asking the people not to touch the remaining physical or documentary evidence of the crimes committed. While this was indeed done in some places, in others the local population tore down prisons both to vent their anger and also to salvage building materials.

A three-person Vietnamese legal team came to Phnom Penh to advise on the tribunal. It was headed by Tran Huu Duc, a member of the Central Committee of the Vietnamese Communist Party.[3] Min Khin recalls that the Vietnamese and Cambodian teams spoke French as they worked together.

On 15 July 1979 the government passed Decree Law No. 1 establishing the People's Revolutionary Tribunal (PRT) 'to try the Pol Pot – Ieng Sary Clique for the Crime of Genocide'. Two further charges of 'betraying the revolution and fatherland' and 'creating war by invading Vietnam' initially planned for inclusion in the indictment were dropped and the final text was limited to the charge of genocide.[4]

The scope of the crime of genocide outlined in Decree Law No. 1 was not taken directly from the 1948 Genocide Convention, although the acts described in the Convention's Article 1 certainly resonated in the Decree Law's list of crimes: 'planned massacres of groups of innocent people; expulsion of inhabitants of cities and villages in order to concentrate them and force them to do hard labour in conditions leading to their physical and mental destruction; wiping out religion; destroying political, cultural and social structures and family and social relations'.[5]

The Decree Law maintained the Salvation Front approach in stipulating 'leniency towards those people who participated in the armed forces or the administration of the Pol Pot – Ieng Sary Clique but are sincerely repentant'. The decision to limit the prosecution, and indeed the name of the tribunal itself, to Pol Pot and Ieng Sary, was, according to Min Khin, because the new government in 1979 was still hoping for a split in the Khmer Rouge, including defections by Khieu Samphan and Nuon Chea.[6]

As the time for the tribunal grew closer, the legal groups moved their office and the ever-growing number of files to a riverside building near the palace, close to the trial venue. This building had been Ieng Sary's office as Minister for Foreign Affairs in Democratic Kampuchea. Some 22 years later, when the authors interviewed him in March 2001, Min Khin was still occupying the same office, in which he had served successively as the administrative officer for the PRT, then a senior official in the Salvation Front, and most recently, after the restitution of the monarchy in 1993, as the head of the Permanent Organising Committee for National and International Ceremonies, responsible for organising both royal and governmental ceremonies. And in early 2004 the same building was under consideration as one of the offices for the new Khmer Rouge tribunal.

On 20 July 1979 the members of the PRT were announced: Presiding Judge Keo Chenda, Alternate Presiding Judge Chim Chendara and ten 'people's assessors', including former judge Chhuor Leang Huot, a teacher, a classical dancer, a doctor, a soldier, two electrical workers and representatives of women, youth and the party.[7]

Five days later the investigation was officially opened by the Chief Prosecutor, Mat Ly, who had himself been a Khmer Rouge cadre and vice-president of the (non-functioning) Democratic Kampuchea People's Assembly before fleeing to Vietnam in May 1978. On 26 July arrest warrants were issued for Pol Pot and Ieng Sary, together with a call for them to surrender to the authorities. The warrants were posted in Phnom Penh city hall, and then broadcast on National Radio of Kampuchea news frequencies for seven consecutive days from 8 August.

On 4 August Keo Chenda issued a declaration outlining 22 points of trial procedure to be followed. These included details of the rights of the defence (including the right to advance exonerating evidence, and to present a defence, to question victims and witnesses in court); participation of representatives of mass organisations to 'express the people's will regarding the punishment'; details of the kinds of evidence that might be tendered; prosecuting procedure (public trial, order of procedure, inclusion of complaints by victims); recording of all the proceedings; and execution of the judgment. Defendants were to have the right to self-representation, to ask a lawyer or Cambodian citizen to represent them or, if absent, to be represented by someone appointed by the Tribunal. Decree Law No. 1 had stated, 'The choice of a lawyer of foreign nationality, or of a defender who is not a lawyer, must be approved by the Presiding Judge.'

The trial date was set for 15 August and a list was issued of 54 witnesses and experts to be called to testify and an inventory of evidence to be submitted. In the absence of the defendants, Dith Munty and Yuos Por were appointed by the Tribunal as the Cambodian defence lawyers. Twenty four foreign observers, including representatives of international organisations, and 29 foreign journalists were invited, but not all of them turned up for the trial. Lawyers from the following countries were invited to participate: Algeria, Cuba, India, Japan, Laos, Syria, USSR, USA and Vietnam.[8]

The following international organisations were represented: World Council of Peace (Bhagat Vats, India); Afro-Asian People's Solidarity Organisation (Pacine Bangouna, Guinea, and Eva Ramawara, Sri Lanka); Solidarity Organisation of the People of Asia, Africa and Latin America (Gabriel Clarapora, Cuba); Asian Christian Council (Yap Kim Hao, Malaysia, Frans Tumiwa, Indonesia, Robert Congid, Philippines, and Peter Paul Van Lelyveld, Netherlands). This was happening in the late 1970s, before the more recent mushrooming of organisations concerned with human rights and international humanitarian law, but there is no indication that existing organisations like Amnesty International or the International Commission of Jurists, for instance, received invitations. Their absence was regrettable. The list shows mainly individuals and organisations that could be considered firmly in the pro-Soviet camp, and the foreign jurists and legal observers were limited to people prepared to buck the boycott and be seen to be working in cooperation with Vietnam.[9]

The 'People's Revolutionary Tribunal held in Phnom Penh for the trial of the genocide crime of the Pol Pot–Ieng Sary clique' took place over the brief period of 15–19 August 1979, in Chaktomuk Theatre. Pol Pot and Ieng Sary had taken sanctuary in Thailand, thereby avoiding any chance of being arrested. The trial had to take place without the defendants. It was still a highly charged week. Witnesses and observers alike frequently broke into tears as the horrors they had survived were recounted in graphic detail. 'Around the auditorium with seats for 500, where the trial was held, an overflow audience milled, anxious to talk with anyone who would listen about what they and their families had suffered under the Khmer Rouge.'

Among those who attended was Sok An, appointed 20 years later to head the government Task Force to negotiate with the UN on the Khmer Rouge Law. In 2003 he recalled the extreme emotion of the hearings.[10] The proceedings were broadcast by loudspeakers set up around the building and throughout the country via the Voice of Kampuchea Radio, while the weekly *Kampuchea* newspaper devoted a full issue to extended transcripts and photographs.

On the eve of the trial Presiding Judge Keo Chenda made a highly political statement on the objectives of the trial, which indicated how predetermined the verdict was: 'Trying the Pol Pot-Ieng Sary clique for the crime of genocide will on the one hand expose all the criminal acts that they have committed and mobilise the Kampuchean people more actively to defend and build up the people's power, and on the other hand show the peoples of the whole world the true face of the criminals who are posing as the representatives of the people of Kampuchea'.[11]

Although the indictments cited only domestic law (Decree Law No.1 and Point 8 of the Salvation Front founding Declaration), the conclusion and judgment made explicit reference 'to international law punishing the crime of genocide, in particular the Convention on the Prevention and Punishment of the Crime of Genocide of December 9, 1948'.[12]

In accordance with the civil law tradition, the prosecutor read the lengthy indictment that had been presented by the Clerk of the

Court at the commencement of the trial. The charge read to the court comprised three parts: the description of the crimes and the methods used; establishing the premeditated nature of the criminal acts, their motives and foreign support; and juridical arguments that these acts constituted the crime of genocide.

After five days of hearing reports from eight commissions, testimony from 39 witnesses, films of exhumations and sites of destruction and visits to Tuol Sleng and to Siem Reap, closing statements were made.

Closing arguments were presented by the three defence lawyers (Hope Stevens, Yuos Por and Dith Munty), Mohammed Hikmet Turkmanee argued for compensation for the victims, John Quigley gave an opinion as to the extent to which genocide had been proven, making reference to the Genocide Convention and its obligation on states to prevent and punish genocide, and the Japanese and Cuban lawyers made statements.

Following a brief adjournment the Presiding Judge read the verdict reached by himself and the People's Assessors. Keo Chenda enumerated the crimes on which both defendants had been found guilty:

- systematic implementation of a plan to kill many strata of the population on an increasingly ferocious scale; indiscriminate extermination of nearly all the officers and soldiers of the former regime; liquidation of the intelligentsia, and all persons and organizations deemed to be opposed to the regime;
- killing of clergy and believers, and eradication of religion; systematic killing of members of ethnic minorities to force them to assimilate; extermination of foreign residents;
- forcible evacuation of the population from Phnom Penh and other liberated towns and villages; the breaking and upsetting of family and social structures; mass killings and mass executions;
- the herding of the population into 'people's communes', which were disguised concentration camps, where they were forced to work and live in physically and morally destructive conditions that caused deaths in large numbers;
- massacre of small children, persecution and moral poisoning of the youth, transforming them into cruel thugs devoid of human feelings;
- destruction of the structure of the national economy, and destruction of the national culture, the educational system and the health care system;

- after their overthrow by the genuine revolutionary forces, Pol Pot and Ieng Sary are still committing new crimes and are still killing those people who refuse to follow them;
- during their four years in power, Pol Pot and Ieng Sary and their associates used extremely savage methods of torture and killing, as well as many techniques designed to terrorise the people.

The crimes enumerated actually went far beyond genocide, and included many crimes considered under customary international law to be crimes against humanity, as well as a number of other acts that were not crimes at all under either international or Cambodian domestic law.

The court found 'an intention of genocide' on the basis of the systematic and nationwide nature of the criminal acts, as documented in resolutions and directives of the party and state. 'After examining the investigation reports presented at the hearing, the findings of a sample census conducted in a number of villages and sub-districts, and other information in the case file, the tribunal finds well-founded the estimate that more than three million people were killed or otherwise succumbed because of the torture or the poor conditions of life'. The judgment asserted that 'the Peking reactionaries were the invidious instigators of this plan'.

Specific judgments outlined the personal responsibility of the two defendants as follows:

Pol Pot, as Secretary of Angkar[13] and Prime Minister of the government, bearing ultimate responsibility for directing the entire state bureaucracy, mapped out the general lines and orientation of domestic and foreign policy and directed their implementation. Pol Pot himself on many occasions toured different localities to direct and inspect personally the purges of forces accused of opposition. Pol Pot is an extremely dangerous criminal deserving no degree of leniency.

Ieng Sary, as a standing member of the political bureau of *Angkar* and deputy prime minister of the government in charge of foreign affairs, holding high offices and wielding real power, worked with Pol Pot in the leadership. He built up and conducted collusion with the Peking reactionary forces and other international reactionaries and defended the criminal acts of genocide committed by his clique in international fora. Ieng Sary ordered the issuance of the invitation to return to intellectuals and students working or studying abroad. The accused Ieng Sary is an extremely dangerous criminal deserving no degree of leniency.[14]

The tribunal found the two accused guilty of the crime of genocide and sentenced them to death *in absentia* and ordered confiscation of all their property. The judgment was rendered as a matter of last instance, although appeal for reduction in sentence was permitted within seven days.

Western media paid scant attention to the trial and the genocide verdicts and most governments peremptorily dismissed the tribunal as a mere 'show trial' without making the slightest effort to study the evidence or monitor the proceedings.

Some of the criticisms of the PRT focus on aspects of the trial that, while unfamiliar to those used to the common law or adversary procedure practised in the Anglo-American legal tradition, are quite normal in the civil law, or Romano-Germanic tradition, as pointed out by John Quigley, one of the US lawyers at the People's Revolutionary Tribunal.[15] This legal system was established in Cambodia (and Vietnam) under French colonialism. But the PRT also revealed many elements that are characteristic of the Soviet legal system, also inherited by Vietnam.

On *in absentia* trials, for instance, the French system permits the trial and sentence to take place, but if the convicted person is ever apprehended or surrenders to the court, then they have the opportunity to argue mitigating circumstances before the sentence is imposed. In 1977 the Human Rights Committee of the United Nations ruled that the right to be tried in one's presence in the International Covenant on Civil and Political Rights is not violated if the defendants have been properly informed of the proceedings and choose not to appear.[16]

Other features from the civil law tradition include the brevity of the court procedure itself, compared to the scale and weight of evidence prepared during the investigative pre-trial phase; the inclusion of a civil claim by victims for compensation in the criminal proceeding; and the mixed panel of people's assessors, made up of both legal and lay people, making decisions regarding both judgment and penalty.

More serious criticisms of the People's Revolutionary Tribunal are those that pertain not to the procedures followed, but to the trial's character and foregone conclusions and its scripted nature. The detailed timetable for the proceedings that had been issued five days in advance of the tribunal indicated that the length, course and the outcome of the process had been predetermined. The witness statements (many of which used derogatory jargon) were composed in similar if not identical wording.

Above all, the pathetic main line of the defence has to be condemned. The defence lawyers tamely accepted all the crimes of which the accused were charged and made virtually no cross-examination of witnesses, even though this right was specifically enumerated beforehand. The defence should have been as good as possible and still resulted in a conviction.

In his closing arguments for the defence, US lawyer Hope Stevens proclaimed Pol Pot and Ieng Sary to be 'criminally insane monsters carrying out a program the script of which was written elsewhere'. The Cambodian defence lawyer, Yuos Por, added that, 'Behind the defendants are unacknowledged forces that incited, encouraged, pressured and protected them. These unacknowledged forces, despite all their efforts to conceal themselves, have shown their ugly face on the immense crime scene that is our country. This criminal, this highly dangerous abettor, is a mystery for no one. It is the hegemonist expansionists of Peking.'[17]

China's unique stance of steadfast support to the DK regime supplying more than 15,000 military and civilian advisors, artillery and tanks should surely have been examined by the court, but no serious effort was even made to support their case that Beijing had incited or directed the Pol Pot regime to slaughter their own people. The politically opportune attempt by both prosecution and defence to place the principal blame on China, and not to attempt to establish specific and criminal responsibility by the defendants, certainly did not serve the cause of truth, justice and historical accountability.

Neither did the defence take the opportunity to advance various lines of argument on behalf of their absentee clients, such as denying personal responsibility, refuting the systematic nature of the crimes, or claiming necessity due to the after-effects of the war and particularly the US bombing. Nor did they raise any legal challenges such as the use of the term 'genocide' for the enumerated crimes, the court's decision to use a definition different from that given in the Genocide Convention, or the jurisdiction of the court over their clients. The sole plea for mitigation on the grounds that China had instigated Pol Pot and Ieng Sary to commit these terrible crimes further undermined the tribunal's credibility and clearly transposed Hanoi's ideological line into the courtroom.

The decision taken by the authorities to limit the indictment to only two leaders – Pol Pot and Ieng Sary – and not the whole leadership of the Khmer Rouge also damaged the credibility of the proceedings, engendering doubts as to how complete was the break with the Khmer Rouge past.

These shortcomings, especially the abysmal defence, did a huge disservice to Cambodian intellectuals and survivors who gathered, organised and set forth a large body of documentation that would in the main stand the test of time and legal scrutiny. As in political trials described so evocatively by Albert Camus in *The Outsider*, the defendants were guilty until proven innocent, and no real attempt was made to do that. The PRT's image as a show trial continues to haunt efforts towards the establishment of a new mixed tribunal.

But was it justified to write off the whole affair as a propaganda show, and for other countries to make no effort to apprehend or even ostracise those convicted of genocide? The answer has to be No. The Cambodians who retold their sufferings did so as witnesses would have done in any credible court of justice. Their moving testimony should have been noted by international jurists of all political persuasions and from all parts of the world.

An alternative to peremptory dismissal and denunciation of the PRT would have been an offer of expert legal assistance to enable the trial to be conducted according to the very best standards, and for those who were so keen in 1978 to bring the Khmer Rouge crimes before the United Nations Commission on Human Rights to pursue other prosecution options.

Min Khin recalled his impressions: 'I felt that fair justice had been done for the great crimes committed by the powerful *Angkar*. While the trial had no defendants present, the people felt that it was appropriate that these "engines" *[kbal mesin]* of the crimes were charged. We did a good job, and we had foreign participation. Those who criticise the trial look down on the victims of the Khmer Rouge.'

When the People's Revolutionary Tribunal was wound up, Min Khin continued his work of collecting data on Khmer Rouge crimes in his capacity as an official of the Salvation Front.

Vietnam sought to disseminate some of the PRT's findings as part of its ongoing effort to discredit Democratic Kampuchea and to bring about a reversal of the decision of the UN General Assembly's Credentials Committee to allow it to occupy the Cambodian seat. On 17 September 1979, the judgment was sent to the Secretary General from Ha Van Lau, Permanent Representative of Vietnam to the UN, with a request that it be circulated as an official UN document, which was done.[18] In the following months various other items from the People's Revolutionary Tribunal, including the indictment, the report on crimes against religions and believers, on the population of Phnom Penh, and statements by lawyers and jurists were introduced as documents of the 1979 General Assembly under the agenda items on 'International Covenants on Human Rights' and 'Elimination of all forms of religious intolerance'.

The major documents from the People's Revolutionary Tribunal were published inside Cambodia in Khmer in 1981 and in English and French in the late 1980s.[19]

The Russian judge at the trial, Valentine Choubine, who held the position of Deputy Presiding Judge of the Supreme Court of RSFSR, published his report of the trial *Kampuchea : the people's verdict* in Russian in 1980, and later wrote a booklet translated into French and published by Novosti in 1986 as *Le Genocide de Pol Pot devant le tribunal de l'histoire*. Choubine maintains: 'The polpotist executioners, responsible for the death of millions of their compatriots, were chased from the country. They had to answer for their crimes. It was to this end, above all, that the People's Revolutionary Tribunal was constituted.'

But the People's Revolutionary Tribunal received no serious exposure in the west until John Quigley decided to compile the trial documents and several introductory essays as the volume *Genocide in Cambodia*, published in 2000 by the University of Pennsylvania Press.

As John Quigley concluded:

> Beyond its significance for events in Cambodia, the trial of Pol Pot and Ieng Sary was important in several other respects. It was the first trial of a government or of anyone else, under the Genocide Convention. The trial, moreover, was held at a time when the perpetrators of genocide still controlled territory. Thus, the trial might serve to deter future atrocities by the defendants. The Nuremberg and Tokyo trials were held only after the forces represented by the defendants were no longer active.
>
> In this respect, the trial of Pol Pot and Ieng Sary was the precursor of the judicial proceedings that would be instituted in 1993 regarding atrocities in Bosnia. ...[The adoption of the Rome Statute in 1998] bespeaks the importance attached by the international community to promoting judicial remedies as one

avenue for preventing atrocities. The trial of Pol Pot and Ieng Sary was a step in that direction.[20]

Others consider that the unfair nature of the PRT, in the mould of 'victor's justice' echoing Nuremberg and Tokyo, actually set back international humanitarian law.[21]

But regardless of the legal shortcomings of the PRT, it was the cold logic of the cold war that determined that its verdict would be ignored. Contrary to the hope that those who organised and participated in the trial placed in 'the tribunal of history, the tribunal of mankind's conscience', as expressed by President Heng Samrin in the closing reception, those convicted of genocide in 1979 continued to be accorded wide international recognition and assistance throughout the following decade and beyond. The following chapters address the 'geopolitical complexities' referred to by Sok An on 6 June 2003 that left the Khmer Rouge crimes unaccounted for and remaining as a matter of unfinished business into the next century.

4
Sympathy for the Devil

The news of the capture of Phnom Penh and the overthrow of the Pol Pot regime was not received with the same enthusiasm in Bangkok, Beijing and western capitals as it was by the survivors in Cambodia. In addition to the UN General Assembly vote on who should occupy the Cambodia seat (see Chapter 2), year after year the Asean group (Association of South East Asian Nations) sponsored a resolution on the Cambodia conflict that called for the 'unconditional and immediate withdrawal of all Vietnamese forces in Cambodia'.

It was not the kind of resolution that was likely to encourage Vietnam to relax its grip on Cambodia, or inspire any confidence that western countries, China, Asean and the UN were concerned about rebuilding the shattered nation. Asean's resolution called for self-determination while ignoring the realities of a total political and social vacuum in the wake of Pol Pot's destruction. One of the key issues that the UN resolution failed to address was who would fill that power vacuum the day after Vietnamese troops departed?

One clear answer came from the pen of Prince Norodom Sihanouk: 'they knowingly neglected to mention that once such unconditional withdrawal had taken place, Pol Pot, Ieng Sary and their 'SS' would resume their horror show and once again transform all of Kampuchea into a vast gulag, an immense slaughterhouse worthy of Auschwitz.'[1]

Sir Robert Jackson, UN Under-Secretary, who was appointed as a special coordinator for the Kampuchea Emergency 1979–83, insisted that 'every single western leader should ask himself – if the Vietnamese withdraw, how can the Khmer Rouge be stopped?' Jackson, one of the few westerners who were eyewitnesses inside Cambodia during these critical times after 1979, concluded: 'Khmers above all fear the return of the Khmer Rouge ... that is absolutely basic.'[2] But during the 1980s there was scant evidence that western leaders lost any sleep over the answer to such a key question. The fear of a Khmer Rouge return to power and a recurrence of the 'Killing Fields' would continue to haunt Cambodians well into the 1990s.

David Hawk, from the US Cambodian Documentation Commission, pointed out 'it was a resolution premised on total cynicism based on the assumption that Vietnam would not withdraw, and therefore there was no need to worry about the implications of implementing the resolution.'[3] But the resolution was sweet music to Khmer Rouge ears.

Whereas recent US invasions of Kosovo (1999), Afghanistan (2001) and even Iraq (2003) have been at least partially justified on the basis of humanitarian intervention, positive aspects of Vietnam's intervention in 1979, which actually did remove a genocidal regime and set about a process of nation-building, engendered a very different reception.

In the early 1980s fear of Soviet-backed communism gripped Asian regional capitals: fear that could readily be exploited by China and the US in such a way that the complexity of China-Vietnam and Cambodia relations could be ignored or glossed over.

While the patient, having just survived the Pol Pot regime, was still in intensive care, suffering post-traumatic stress and dependent on life-support systems provided by Vietnam and the Soviet Union, it appeared that the cold warriors in the west preferred the infant regime to die, rather than a new society to be born under Hanoi's sphere of influence.

REVIVING THE KHMER ROUGE: THE THAI-CHINESE PIPELINE REBUILDS POL POT'S ARMY

China and the US decided they needed to rescue and revive the dying beast. This revival was the first step in the process of unleashing a new war staged from rear bases in Thailand against Vietnamese forces and the fragile new government in Phnom Penh. Rebuilding and recycling the Khmer Rouge army became their shared agenda. While Beijing concentrated on the military side of this enterprise, Washington worked publicly on the diplomatic front, while ensuring adequate material supplies were delivered.

By 17 January 1979 the Vietnamese army had seized control all the way to the Thai-Cambodian border. On 21 January the Thai military regime, led by Prime Minister General Kriangsak Chomanand and backed by the US, announced its continued recognition of Democratic Kampuchea.[4]

During the months after Vietnam launched its offensive in support of the Cambodian Salvation Front, the battered (but still armed) remnants of the Khmer Rouge army fled to Thailand. Tens of thousands of hungry and malaria-ridden black-clad refugees crossed the border into Thailand and gained instant access to refugee camps and humanitarian aid. Rosalynn Carter's visit to Khmer Rouge-controlled refugee camps in November 1979 put pictures of starving Khmer Rouge on the covers of *Time* and *Newsweek* as the image of Cambodia.

By May 1979 all of Cambodia was liberated from the Khmer Rouge and its army was battered, debilitated and demoralised. Prince Norodom Sihanouk considers that the Khmer Rouge nightmare could have been terminated at that moment.

1   Prince Norodom Sihanouk, over the years king, statesman, head of state, and film-maker, pictured here at a ceremony inside the Royal Palace celebrating his return home after twelve years of self-imposed exile, Phnom Penh, October 1991. (Tom Fawthrop)

'In 1979 and 1980,' Sihanouk claimed, 'I begged your government not to support the Khmer Rouge.' But he reported the US wouldn't listen to him. 'The US still uses the Khmer Rouge, and the CIA is involved in supporting the Khmer Rouge even now.' He challenged the US, saying: 'So now [in 1989] when the USA pretends that the Khmer Rouge are unacceptable, it is hypocrisy.' Continuing with his *tour de force* the prince, who was at that moment the president of a coalition with Pol Pot forces, accused the Americans of bringing the Khmer Rouge back to life. 'To save Cambodia, all you had to do was let Pol Pot die ... Pol Pot was dying and you brought him back to life.' The prince concluded, 'It is true ... from the ashes the phoenix rises! Was reborn and sent to the battle front! To kill! To kill! To kill!'[5]

Even before Cambodia had been completely liberated from the clutches of Pol Pot forces, a new round of Indochina warfare was unleashed. Ieng Sary, Pol Pot's foreign minister, rushed to Beijing on 11 January, meeting Hua Guofeng (the Chinese premier) and Deng Xiaoping (the Vice Premier in 1999) two days later.

IENG SARY Aliase Van DK Deputy Prime Minister Foreign Affairs.
KHIEU THIRITH Alias Ieng Thirith, DK Minister of Social Action Education.
(Mme.Ieng Sary) Alias Phea,Hong (Phnom Malay –1993).

2   Ieng Sary, Pol Pot's foreign minister was the chief conduit for Chinese aid flowing through Thailand to the Khmer Rouge bases on the border. Next to him is Ieng Thirith, his wife, who ran education and social affairs for the DK regime. Photographed in Phnom Malai, 1988. (Tom Fawthrop archives)

According to a transcript of their conversation, China scolded the Khmer Rouge for their 'sectarian mistakes' while in power and urged Pol Pot forces to form a united anti-Vietnamese front with Prince Norodom Sihanouk and other non-communist forces. The Chinese agreed to support a Khmer Rouge-led guerilla war with both massive arms shipments and generous funding in hard cash. Documents captured from the Khmer Rouge base at Ta Sanh and published by Phnom Penh's foreign ministry in 1982 included this excerpt:

BEIJING MEETING BETWEEN DENG XIAOPING
AND IENG SARY IN JANUARY 1979

DENG XIAOPING (to Ieng Sary): How do we supply you with money? Send it to Bangkok? Or to Kriangsak [the Thai prime minister]? Or deposit in Thai banks? You can withdraw it at any time. We can deposit five million dollars subject to withdrawal at any moment. We can deposit it in Thai banks, or leave it with the Chinese embassy, or the Kampuchean embassy in Thailand.
IENG SARY: We will take it from the Chinese embassy in Bangkok.[6]

Indeed Ieng Sary continued to do exactly that – collecting the cash from the Chinese embassy for the next ten years.

From 1979 until 1989 China maintained a direct aid programme worth between $80–100 million a year. Lee Kuan Yew's memoirs put it at 1 billion dollars over the decade.[7] In 1990 20 Chinese T59 tanks were delivered, most deployed in Pailin, according to *Jane's Intelligence Review*.[8]

China had promised arms, ammunition and massive financial support. But delivery depended on Thailand's full cooperation. To work out the sensitive details of Chinese arms shipments destined for the Khmer Rouge bases in Thailand, two top Chinese officials were dispatched for urgent meetings in Bangkok.

Ieng Sary, the foreign minister of the regime that abolished money, was sent to Beijing to sort out the cash flow. On the same day, 13 January 1979, Han Nianlong, China's Deputy Minister for Foreign Affairs, and Geng Biao, chief of the Chinese Military Commission, met in secret with the Thai prime minister in Bangkok. A further meeting with Thai officials took place at the U-tapao military airbase.

In the secret session with Prime Minister General Kriangsak Chomanand, the Chinese urged Thailand to provide sanctuary and shelter to Khmer Rouge units and their political leaders. An

3   Pol Pot with Chinese ambassador Sun Hao at Phnom Penh airport. When Khmer Rouge were in power from 1975–79, the only link to the outside world was a weekly flight to Beijing. (AKP press agency archives)

4   Nuon Chea, following close behind his leader Pol Pot, in keeping with their ranking in the Khmer Rouge hierarchy as Brothers Number One and Two, Thailand in the 1980s. (Khmer Rouge photos)

understanding was reached on the use of Thai territory as the pipeline for arms and other equipment destined for Pol Pot's army.[9]

5   Left to right: Chinese military, third, Son Sen, next, Khieu Samphan, Chinese diplomat, and Ieng Sary, near Surin Thailand 1980s. The Chinese military officers and Khmer Rouge leaders after signing deal to supply Pol Pot forces with military aid through Thailand. (Nhem Eng, KR photographer)

By April Thailand's National Security Council had taken steps to seal many parts of the border. Although Pol Pot forces were in poor shape and still fleeing to Thailand, the Sino-Thai plan to rebuild the Khmer Rouge was already being implemented with the establishment of Khmer Rouge camps and the stockpiling of weapons.

Arms and other supplies could be shipped to the ports of Bangkok, Sattahip and Klong Yai and the airport at Takli could be utilised under the terms of the Thai-Chinese agreement concluded with Geng Biao. One month later Chinese cargo ships laden with arms made their first deliveries across the South China Sea to Thai ports and islands. The Malaysian *Star* newspaper reported that 'Chinese cargo ships are secretly carrying arms for Pol Pot troops to Thailand's Kut Island.' From Kut Island Thai trawlers ferried the arms to the port of Klong Yai where they were unloaded and transported by Thai army 6x6 trucks to camps and warehouses set up for the Khmer Rouge near the border.[10] Khmer Rouge warehouses stretched from Borai in Trat province in the south to Ban Leam, a depot close to Aranyaprathet, with at least four arms depots in Sisaket province including O Trao, Khun Han, Kantharalak and Nam Yum.

The Thai government adopted a policy of total denial about the flood of Chinese arms passing through Thailand to the Cambodian border. In an attempt to sustain this fiction, the whole length of the 800 kilometre border was placed under martial law and all sensitive areas, including Khmer Rouge sanctuaries and military warehouses, were sealed off as 'No-Go' areas by Thai military checkpoints and placed beyond the prying eyes of journalists and international aid workers.

The nerve-centre for this vast supply operation – tens of thousands of tons of arms and ammunition (including AK-47 rifles, hand-grenades, cannons, mortars and B-40 rockets) – was the People's Republic of China embassy in Bangkok. The former Chinese ambassador in Phnom Penh, Sun Hao, who had cooperated so closely with the Pol Pot regime, was re-assigned to the Bangkok embassy as the pivotal figure for coordinating Beijing's support for the new war. A second Chinese diplomat, the fluent Khmer speaker Fu Zue Zhang, spent some months working directly in the Khmer Rouge camps both inside Thailand and in the Phnom Malai area as far south as Ban Laem, one of their many bases strung along the border and protected by the Thai military.[11] Fu Zue Zhang, who had also served in the Chinese embassy during the Pol Pot regime, was nominated as their ambassador to Cambodia's Supreme National Council in 1991.

A new Thai military unit, Unit 838, was established in 1979 primarily to provide sanctuary, liaison and protection to the Khmer Rouge leadership on Thai soil. Unit 838 soldiers were drawn from the Special Warfare Division of the Thai army based in Lopburi. They organised the setting up of secret training camps and safe sanctuaries along the border, logistics and transportation.

Taskforce 80 was set up under the Supreme Command of the Thai army to police and control all Cambodian refugee camps, but its prime purpose was to promote and coordinate cooperation between all the factions engaged in launching anti-Vietnamese guerrilla operations from Thai soil.

Another shadowy military group, Unit 315 based in Bangkok, planned Cambodian strategy and cooperation with Khmer Rouge leaders.

US DUPLICITY AND SECRET SUPPORT FOR THE KHMER ROUGE

In 1978 US President Jimmy Carter had condemned the Khmer Rouge regime with the declaration, 'America cannot avoid the responsibility to speak out in condemnation of the Cambodian Government, the worst violator of human rights in the world today.'[12]

At the time China was the one country that supplied aid to the Pol Pot regime. Yet only one year later the two nations were both giving it succour. Beijing did it openly, while Washington professed abhorrence, engaging in 'hold your nose' diplomacy to block out the Pol Pot odour, but proceeding to supply their lifelines just the same.

The locations of Khmer Rouge zones in Thailand were well known to military attaches and intelligence agencies including the CIA. But arresting Pol Pot and Ieng Sary was clearly not part of the Carter script.

Washington and its allies showed no interest in rounding up the perpetrators of the Cambodian genocide and convening an international tribunal. It was also not on Interpol's agenda. And it was President Carter, the human rights advocate, who in 1979 gave the green light to support the genocidal credentials of the Pol Pot regime at the UN General Assembly.

Today the former president is a roving campaigner for peace, human rights and a more just world. In 2002 he was awarded the Nobel Peace prize. The authors contacted the Carter Foundation and the Carter Center in Atlanta to find out why a man with such strong convictions about human rights could have cast the US vote in favour of one of the worst regimes of the 20th century.

One of Carter's aides, Steve Hochmann, responded to the authors of this book. He sent a memo quoting Cyrus Vance, Carter's Secretary of State, on the Cambodia vote: 'There are times when your obligations as a senior government official force you to take a position which, although essential for our national interests, is at the same time extremely distasteful.'

Hochmann went on to claim,

The United States declared that it was voting in this manner for technical reasons and did not favour the return to power of the Khmer Rouge. Nevertheless, as Cyrus Vance points out in his account, several high-ranking Carter administration officials argued strongly against this vote. They thought it could be interpreted as supporting the Khmer Rouge.[13]

Carter failed to side with those who argued that it would be unconscionable to back the Khmer Rouge, and instead sided with the *realpolitik* lobby led by national security advisor, Zbigniew Brzezinski. Brzezinski later spilled the beans: 'I encouraged the Chinese to support Pol Pot. I encouraged the Thai to help the DK [Democratic Kampuchea]. The question was how to help the Cambodian people. Pol Pot was an abomination. We could never support him but China could.'[14]

The reasons for supporting the Khmer Rouge claim to the Cambodia seat at the UN were clearly not technical at all. It was a highly political decision to play the China card against Vietnam, so that the Khmer Rouge, as the enemy of my enemy, was now Washington's friend. This meant holding the Cambodian people hostage, sweeping aside all considerations of human rights, the interests of Cambodian survivors and international humanitarian law. Even Steve Hochmann pointed to the work of US writer Christopher Brady, who put it that the Carter administration chose *realpolitik* rather than human rights as the basis for policy in southeast Asia.[15] An alternative choice would not have been so difficult, if the White House had taken a closer look at the Indian initiative to leave the Cambodia seat vacant.

Carter's avowed human rights policy, already looking sadly moth-eaten and frayed well before 1979, was buried by Zbigniew Brzezinski, his extremely anti-Soviet national security advisor. Brzezinski steered the Carter administration, first to normalise relations with China and then to play the China card against Vietnam and the Soviet Union. Support for the Khmer Rouge in 1979 was a predictable consequence of this strategy. Brzezinski encouraged China to rebuild the Khmer Rouge army in order to launch a new Indochina war, this time directed against Vietnam's forces in Cambodia. Brzezinski worked closely with the Chinese foreign ministry and the chairman of the Thai National Security Council, Squadron Leader Prasong Soonsiri, another inveterate cold warrior.

REFUGEES AS PAWNS

In 1979 the US embassy in Bangkok spawned a greatly expanded refugee section. It was eventually to be headed not by any expert on humanitarian affairs, but by Colonel Michael Eiland from the Defence

Intelligence Agency, who had a track record in covert operations, codenamed Daniel Boone, launched from South Vietnam in late 1960s against Cambodia.[16]

Eiland's prime mission was not to coordinate US aid for the refugees, but rather to gather intelligence from the hundreds of thousands who had fled to the border with Thailand seeking food, shelter and news of their relatives. The US refugee section included a number of intelligence operatives who had long been involved in the Indochina war. Since the US client regimes in Vietnam, Cambodia and Laos had all collapsed it was not surprising that from 1975 onwards Bangkok hosted the bulk of the US intelligence community in southeast Asia.

In order specifically to coordinate US intelligence operations along the border, the Kampuchea Emergency Group, known as KEG, was established in 1980, with its major operations centre based along the Thai-Cambodian border close to the town of Aranyaprathet. As well as Eiland, it included Lionel Rosenblatt, a former advisor in South Vietnam during the war, as well as the embassy's Cambodia expert, Tim Carney.[17]

Coordination meant close contact with all parties opposed to the government in Phnom Penh. That included Thailand's military Taskforce 80, Special Forces unit 838, various Cambodian warlords and guerrillas camped along the border and most importantly the Khmer Rouge. Direct relations between US agents and the Khmer Rouge officially didn't happen. But in reality Colonel Dennison Lane, Defence Intelligence operative from the US embassy in Bangkok, who at one stage was assigned as the American representative with the United Nations Border Relief Operation (UNBRO), enjoyed regular contact with the Khmer Rouge during the 1980s. It has also been established that in November 1980, Ray Cline, former Deputy Director of the CIA and senior foreign-policy adviser to President-elect Ronald Reagan, made a trip to the Thai-Cambodian border. After he had visited a Pol Pot zone a Khmer Rouge press release noted that Cline 'was warmly greeted by thousands of villagers'.[18]

The much-touted policy of no dealings with the Khmer Rouge was largely a diplomatic shadow play. US diplomats staged walkouts from some international conferences when a Khmer Rouge diplomat started to speak. And during the Reagan administration the State Department issued an internal memo about politically correct behaviour, which included not shaking hands with the likes of Ieng Sary and Khieu Samphan.

These gestures were certainly designed to indicate a modicum of disgust. But Khmer Rouge diplomats around the world were certainly not perturbed by the theatrics, as long as they could count on US support on such issues as delivering food to Khmer Rouge zones along the Thai-Cambodian border.

At the UN-sponsored International Conference on Kampuchea held in New York in July 1981 President Reagan's administration rubbed shoulders with Pol Pot's foreign minister, Ieng Sary. General Alexander Haig, US Secretary of State, found himself standing with China and the Khmer Rouge. Ten years earlier this was the man who had directed the 'secret' bombing of Cambodia and the Khmer Rouge under the orders of Henry Kissinger, Nixon's foreign affairs chief. History had come full circle: in the vortex of the cold war yesterday's enemies, Ieng Sary and Al Haig, were now allied against Phnom Penh and Hanoi.

Ieng Sary was under sentence of death in Cambodia following his conviction for genocide by the 1979 Phnom Penh Tribunal. But ironically, in the glittering UN reception in New York hosted by Austria (the conference chair), Ieng Sary, a deputy prime minister in a regime that routinely starved its own people, was one of the VIPs elegantly sipping champagne and gorging himself on the best caviar.

At the reception, the Khmer Rouge delegates chased General Haig's coterie around the room with the intention of publicly expressing their thanks to the US government for invaluable diplomatic support. But the US diplomats bobbed and weaved beyond the grasp of would-be Khmer Rouge handshakes. Afterwards John Holdridge, the new assistant secretary of East Asia and Pacific proudly related their success in avoiding Ieng Sary.[19]

However, this little charade was a mere diversion from the real US policy. If Washington had been anti-Khmer Rouge then it would have readily supported Asean's call to disarm the Pol Pot forces as part of a political settlement. But China was strongly opposed. Washington sided with China and the Khmer Rouge, and Asean caved in to Washington's pressure.

Aid from western governments and NGOs flowed freely to the Thai-Cambodian border. However, complementary attempts to ensure humanitarian aid was also distributed to the more than 80 per cent of the population still inside Cambodia, and not yet drawn to the border, were hampered and often blocked by the US and Thai governments as a weapon in their struggle with the new authorities in Phnom

Penh. The US policy of denying development aid to Phnom Penh led to constant arguments. Bill Herod, then Church World Service liaison officer in Washington DC, had to fight for exemptions with the Treasury Department on an almost daily basis. 'An ice-making machine, primary school kits – even a pencil – were deemed to be development aid' and were therefore, Herod remembers, among the many items of contention.[20]

Two American aid workers, Linda Mason and Roger Brown, wrote:

> Thailand, the country that hosted the relief operation, and the US government, which funded the bulk of the relief operation, insisted that the Khmer Rouge be fed. In the 1979–81 period, the World Food Program, which was strongly under US influence, gave almost $12 million in food to the Thai Army to distribute to predominantly Khmer Rouge camps along the border.[21]

Total aid from the United Nations in 1986 was $142 per head for the 300,000 on the border, but only $1.50 per head for the 7 million inside Cambodia itself (supplemented by a further $1.50 per head from international NGOs).[22]

Sir Robert Jackson, a veteran of many UN aid missions, was appointed in November 1979 as the Personal Representative of the UN Secretary General to take charge of coordinating the different UN agencies' emergency aid to Cambodia. In his introduction to the Oxfam publication on Cambodia entitled *Punishing the Poor,* Jackson wrote,

> in my experience no humanitarian operation in this century has been so totally and continuously influenced by political factors, with the result that hundreds of thousands of men, women and children who had already undergone untold pain, agony and despair are still, today, deprived of elementary needs of life because of international political confrontations of which they are innocent victims.[23]

From July 1979 regular convoys of trucks carrying hundreds of tons of rice and other basic foods left Bangkok for the Thai-Cambodian border refugee camps and aid poured into this western-government supported relief zone; it was quite a different story when aid agencies tried to carry out a similar humanitarian mission on behalf of the

80 per cent of the Cambodian population who still lived inside the country. Many obstacles were deliberately placed in the way of those who sought to balance aid to the border area with equal concern to push aid into a Cambodia ruled by a government that the western world and its allies in Asia had chosen not to recognise.

In October 1979 the UK development agency Oxfam pioneered the complicated process of delivering aid inside Cambodia. Jim Howard, Oxfam's senior specialist in disaster missions, chartered a DC8 cargo plane to fly to Phnom Penh. Both the British and the Thai governments tried to block this urgently needed humanitarian aid. The UK Foreign Office warned that if they flew into the Cambodian capital they might be fired upon and proffered disinformation that the Vietnamese were obstructing aid.

No western government had any observer mission inside the country and the UK Foreign Office confirmed to us that they made no request to open one. Hence the British government had no reliable source of information and no credible basis for their warnings to Oxfam.

In Bangkok the Thai regime refused to allow Oxfam to fly direct to Phnom Penh, forcing them to waste money on extra fuel and flight

6   With friends like these who needs enemies? Prince Norodom Sihanouk in the company of leading candidates for the Khmer Rouge tribunal. Right, the smiling Prince, to his left Khieu Samphan and Ieng Sary (second left) in the days of the CGDK the Khmer Rouge-dominated coalition. (Roland Neveu, all rights reserved/www.asiahorizons.com)

costs by flying via Ho Chi Minh city and then changing course back to Phnom Penh. The Thai government also blocked Oxfam's request to send a barge of relief aid by sea from the port of Bangkok. This necessitated Oxfam re-locating to Singapore and organising all the logistics from that more distant location.

After overcoming all the odds the first major shipment of aid from the west (including 1,500 tons of relief aid and rice seed) arrived in Cambodia's main sea-port of Kampong Som on 14 October 1979. It was a breakthrough and soon led to ICRC and UNICEF jointly running the Kampuchea Emergency Programme with offices in Phnom Penh.

Whilst most of the obstructions to international aid came from the west, the new Cambodian government and their Vietnamese advisors attempted to impose conditions that delayed the delivery of aid. Permits for delivery of aid to Phnom Penh were made conditional upon the donor organisation agreeing to cease assisting refugees along the border, on the grounds that most of that aid was going to the Khmer Rouge.[24]

CONTRAS ON THE BORDER AND COBBLING TOGETHER A COALITION

How much longer could the Khmer Rouge hang onto the Cambodia seat in the UN? It was a question that increasingly preoccupied the minds of US diplomats and their Asean counterparts during 1980 and 1981. As the story of what had happened under the Khmer Rouge and the existence of mass graves throughout the country circulated abroad, it became all the harder for many governments to justify supporting Pol Pot in the UN.

Activist campaigns in several countries pressured their governments to abandon their vote in support of the Khmer Rouge regime. Iceland, Norway and Australia changed their votes on DK's credentials from 'yes' to abstention and other European countries indicated their reluctance to deliver any further direct support for the Khmer Rouge. In July 1980 India formally recognised the People's Republic of Kampuchea. The anti-Vietnamese camp was getting nervous that the UN General Assembly support for the Khmer Rouge would slip away as the tide started to turn against them. These diplomats needed a new rabbit to be pulled out of the hat.

China, Thailand, Singapore and the US soon reached a consensus on the size and shape of the new rabbit to conjure before the international community. More acceptable faces of Cambodian resistance, especially Prince Norodom Sihanouk and ex-prime minister Son Sann, were needed to lead the anti-Vietnamese coalition, camouflaging its Khmer Rouge core.

But press ganging Prince Sihanouk to form another alliance with the Khmer Rouge was not easy. His experience of first allying with the Khmer Rouge against the Lon Nol regime from 1970–75, then becoming their prisoner from 1975–79, must have cautioned him against making the same mistake again.

Sihanouk's earlier deal with the Pol Pot forces led to the enslavement of the Cambodian people and the death of 19 members of the royal family, including five of his children. He was appalled at the proposal put forward by Singapore and Thailand that he should get back into bed with the Pol Potists. Son Sann, although rabidly anti-Vietnamese, also detested the Khmer Rouge and all that they stood for. They both expressed serious reluctance to join the coalition being foisted on them by China, Asean and the United States.

But the moral qualms and political judgement of these two leaders were gradually swept aside. Ok Serei Sopheak, during the 1980s an intelligence officer with Son Sann's KPNLF forces, recalls, 'the Thai army called all the shots at the border and if we did not want to cooperate with the Khmer Rouge they could make life very difficult for us'.[25] China, Thailand, the US and Singapore piled on the pressure at every level – military, diplomatic and economic – to ensure that their 'coalition of the unwilling' came into existence.

The Coalition Government of Democratic Kampuchea (CGDK) was launched on 22 June 1982 in Kuala Lumpur. It was a total misnomer, neither a true coalition, nor a government; even less was it democratic, and it barely had any presence within the borders of Cambodia. But the CIA and the Kampuchea Emergency Group operatives were delighted with their grand illusion. Like the Nicaraguan Contras set up by the CIA after the overthrow of the Samoza regime, the coalition project in Cambodia was the creature of external forces.

Each member of the CGDK controlled its own segments of the refugee diaspora camped just inside Thailand. Each faction treated the camps as recruitment bases and cover for a guerrilla war against Phnom Penh. Neither the UN nor the International Committee of the Red Cross were able to protect the refugees from becoming hostages in a new war not of their choosing.

The formation of the coalition enabled the US to provide public support for Sihanouk and Son Sann with overt 'humanitarian' and 'non lethal' military aid, helping them to organise their own guerrilla armies from the refugee population in the camps. These camps were a critical factor in the ability of the Khmer Rouge's National Army of Democratic Kampuchea, the Sihanoukist National Army (ANS) and Son Sann's Khmer People's National Liberation Front (KPNLF) to wage war against the Hun Sen government.

The CGDK also proved to be an excellent vehicle for diverting attention from support for the Khmer Rouge allowing the repeated declarations that the US, UK and Asean nations backed only the 'democratic', or 'non-communist' forces within the coalition, the Sihanoukists and the KPNLF. These efforts to boost the non-communist components of the coalition did not lessen the danger of an eventual Khmer Rouge victory, courtesy of Washington and Beijing.

When the US Congress approved the $5 million aid package for the ANS and KPNLF in 1985, it prohibited use of the aid '... for the purpose or with the effect of promoting, sustaining or augmenting, directly or indirectly, the capacity of the Khmer Rouge ... to conduct military or paramilitary operations in Cambodia or elsewhere ... '.

The British SAS provided training to CGDK forces in military camps in Thailand and Malaysia. The UK government has always denied that they ever trained Khmer Rouge members of the CGDK. Prior to 1989 UK defence and foreign affairs had denied with equal vehemence any suggestion of SAS deployment at all. The then prime minister, Margaret Thatcher, wrote to Neil Kinnock: 'I confirm that there is no British government involvement of any kind in training, equipping or co-operating with Khmer Rouge forces or those allied to them.' On 25 June 1991, after two years of denial, the government finally admitted that the SAS had been secretly training the 'resistance' since 1985. Rae McGrath, an expert in defusing landmines for MAG (Mines Advisory Group), wrote a report for Asia Watch that detailed how the SAS had taught 'the use of improvised explosive devices, booby traps and the manufacture and use of time-delay devices'. He also wrote in the *Guardian* newspaper that 'the SAS training was a criminally irresponsible and cynical policy'.[26]

Given the first Foreign Office lie, the fallback position of the UK government and of the US (that only the 'good guys' in the coalition were aided and not the 'bad guys') has a hollow ring to it. The pretence that no support was being given to help the Khmer Rouge was one more fable in a coalition riddled with myths. All the guerrilla factions including the Khmer Rouge belonged to the same coalition and as such were therefore in a state of military alliance.

An honest assessment of the relationship of forces was revealed by a US government official: 'Of course, if the coalition wins, the Khmer Rouge will eat the others alive.'[27]

Aside from military gains, the coalition provided important propaganda value for the Khmer Rouge and their supporters. By dragging the two non-communist factions into the coalition they were able to guarantee their silence on any moves to hold the Khmer Rouge accountable for their crimes. Further, the coalition successfully steered the discourse of reporting on the Cambodian conflict to focus on Vietnamese occupation and alleged colonisation, diverting attention and obscuring the need to put Pol Pot and the Khmer Rouge on trial. The campaign to paint the Vietnamese role as one of brutal annexation, as bad if not worse than the Pol Pot regime, became a useful propaganda tool for keeping a tribunal off the international agenda.[28]

The CIA's master illusion, the CGDK coalition, fulfilled one key function for those nations that were desperate to prevent the UN from recognising a pro-Vietnamese government in Cambodia. Prince Norodom Sihanouk, a respected international statesman of the 1960s and a founding member of the non-aligned movement, was the perfect figurehead for the new coalition. Lobbying for Prince Sihanouk's coalition at the UN was a far easier task than trying to justify votes for Pol Pot's gang. UN delegations failed to notice how little had changed – the Khmer Rouge still retained its diplomats in their postings and Pol Pot's flag still fluttered outside the UN headquarters.

The formation of the CGDK was a huge success for the Khmer Rouge; indeed it could almost be classified as a diplomatic coup. They kept the UN Cambodia seat firmly in their grasp just by tolerating the expansion of their delegation to include a few Sihanoukist and KPNLF representatives.

It was a primarily cosmetic arrangement. Selling the CDGK to the world amounted to marketing a product to deodorise the genocidal smell. In order fully to develop the fiction, the Khmer Rouge announced the early retirement of Pol Pot as party chief to keep the most notorious face of the Khmer Rouge out of public view. Inside the coalition Pol Pot's mouthpiece and chief diplomat was the smiling Khieu Samphan. He was the more acceptable face of the Khmer Rouge that former UK prime minister Margaret Thatcher was to refer to as one of the 'moderates' with whom Britain could do business.[29]

5
Challenging the History of Forgetting

Above the deafening din of the cold war led by President Reagan and the hawks in the Pentagon, voices from inside and outside Cambodia demanded a hearing. Both in Phnom Penh and in New York Cambodians and friends of Cambodia urgently pleaded that the world must not forget the genocide.

It is assumed by many commentators that serious attempts to put the Khmer Rouge on trial started only in the late 1990s. This is not the case. Human rights specialists, legal scholars, academics, students and Cambodians in exile grappled with ways to document and seek accountability for the extreme violations of human rights under Khmer Rouge rule. As well as mounting its own trial in 1979 (discussed in Chapter 3) the Cambodian government took important measures to protect the physical evidence of mass graves and to construct memorials. Small numbers of Cambodia specialists visited Phnom Penh in 1979 and 1980 and were granted access to the S-21 archives.[1] The ugly secrets of the Tuol Sleng torture and extermination centre started to become known.

Gregory Stanton, who in 1980 interrupted his studies in international law at Yale University to direct the Church World Service/CARE field office in Phnom Penh recalls:

> I realized that because Cambodia was a state-party to the Genocide Convention, and because the Khmer Rouge still held Cambodia's seat in the United Nations, a compelling case could be taken against Cambodia to the World Court for breach of the Genocide Convention, and the very people who committed the crimes would still be legally required to answer the charges. It was a unique opportunity ... In June, 1980 on my way into Cambodia, I met David Hawk, the former executive director of Amnesty International USA, who was then working for the World Conference on Religion and Peace in Bangkok, and proposed my plan to him. In Cambodia, I discussed my idea with government officials. Ben Kiernan, currently professor of history at Yale University and

director of the Yale Genocide Studies Program, was in Cambodia doing research for his Ph.D. dissertation on the Khmer Rouge, and we also discussed the plan. We have worked together ever since to document the crimes of the Khmer Rouge and to bring their leaders to justice.

Ben and I were among the first Westerners to see the newly opened mass grave at Choeung Ek, where the Khmer Rouge buried over 7000 victims of the Tuol Sleng extermination prison in Phnom Penh. There were so many bodies in the mass graves that the decomposition was not yet complete. Flesh still clung to human bones. The stench of death seared my nostrils. The stories of survivors still haunt me. Every Cambodian had lost family members, and their stories crushed my soul. In our interviews in Cham Muslim villages, Ben Kiernan and I learned that the Chams and other minorities were singled out for extermination.[2]

On returning to the US in 1981, Stanton searched for allies in taking the Khmer Rouge case to the World Court, turning first to the International Commission of Jurists. To his shock and consternation the Chairman of the American Association of the ICJ, lawyer William Butler, responded negatively after discussing the idea with the US State Department, which opposed the plan. Butler and others in the ICJ both in the United States and elsewhere questioned whether the killings in Cambodia constituted genocide.

Stanton was now face to face with the politico-legal obstacles that are central to this book. He commented, 'such "definitionalism" has plagued the anti-genocide movement since Stalin got political mass murder removed from the Genocide Convention in 1948. It has paralysed the will of thousands of lawyers. Stalin's ghost must snicker that he again used the appearance of law to deny justice.'

Hawk and Stanton travelled back to Cambodia in early 1982 seeking evidence and, importantly, Cambodian government support for this campaign. In mid-1982 Stanton incorporated the Cambodian Genocide Project as a non-profit, tax-exempt organisation under US law and began soliciting funds for what would be a long and arduous fight. For various reasons, both political and personal, Hawk and Stanton were unable to keep working together, though each continued in their own way the commitment to seek justice for the Cambodian people.

Stanton continued to work on ways to hold the Khmer Rouge leadership accountable through the Cambodian Genocide Project and later also through the Campaign to Oppose the Return of the Khmer Rouge and Genocide Watch, while Hawk operated initially under sponsorship of the Columbia University Center for the Study of Human Rights, and later through an organisation he established, the Cambodia Documentation Commission.

Both the Cambodian Genocide Project and the Cambodian Documentation Commission worked through the 1980s to collect crucial evidence, archival documents and photographs from Tuol Sleng and of the disinterment of mass graves in Cambodia, as well as oral histories from select categories of Cambodian survivors, including representatives of different ethnic and religious communities and those who had emerged alive from Khmer Rouge prisons and execution centres.

In 1986 David Hawk and Hurst Hannum drew up a 200-page model legal brief for presentation to the International Court of Justice. Entitled 'The Case Against the Standing Committee of the Central Committee of the Communist Party of Kampuchea', it established a *prima facie* case for the Khmer Rouge violation of the Genocide Convention and other instruments of international law. Hawk and Hannum argued that there were no legal or jurisdictional impediments to launching an Interstate Complaint to the International Court of Justice (commonly known as the World Court) under Article 9 of the Genocide Convention.

Inside Cambodia the government continued to assemble documentation. On 5 October 1982 the Salvation Front established a Research Committee into the Crimes of the Pol Pot Regime, headed by Min Khin, who had in 1979 led the work of collecting evidence for the People's Revolutionary Tribunal. His new brief was to prepare an overview of the crimes committed and to compile documents to be disseminated both within the country and internationally.

Why, almost three years after the trial, was this initiative launched? By October 1982, it was clear that the verdict of the People's Revolutionary Tribunal had made no impact at all on pro-western governments regarding the status of the Cambodia seating at the UN. Vietnam and the PRK were isolated and condemned rather than assisted in the work of reconstructing Cambodia.

The fourth and final attempt in the General Assembly to canvass in favour of the PRK credentials as Cambodia's representative had failed yet again, with the vote swinging even more against the PRK, as the Khmer Rouge put on its new garb as the Coalition Government of Democratic Kampuchea, headed by Prince Sihanouk.

The Research Committee began the Herculean task of travelling throughout the country to gather petitions from the people. The Report from the Research Committee, dated 25 July 1983, reported a figure of 3,314,768 deaths on the basis of petitions signed or thumb printed by 1,166,307 people in villages, cooperatives and government offices in 19 provinces. From the wording of the petitions it is clear that they were directed at the United Nations in an appeal to deny recognition to the Khmer Rouge. But for some reason the petitions were never presented to the UN, nor made known to those campaigning for an international trial; rather they lay in boxes in the Salvation Front office until handed over to the Cambodian Genocide Program in 1995.

The figure of 3.3 million deaths was ridiculed at the time as Vietnamese propaganda massively exaggerating the death toll. The precision of the figure is itself problematic. While it was arrived at from a straightforward addition of each province's figure of reported deaths, those interim figures were composed of estimates as well as precise numbers, and also did not take into account the certainty of double reporting – one person's death can be reported by many different family members. Subsequent research by various scholars now indicates that the most likely estimate is close to 1.7 million people who died as a result of the regime's policies, although the Cambodian government has never issued a revised figure.[3]

The government and Salvation Front made efforts to disseminate the findings of the Research Committee and to utilise them in its struggle for recognition. On 18 August 1983 the National Assembly passed a resolution receiving and endorsing the findings of the Research Committee and establishing 20 May as a day to commemorate the sufferings inflicted by the crimes of the regime led by Pol Pot, Ieng Sary and Khieu Samphan. It also called for the construction of inscriptions and memorials in Phnom Penh, provinces and communes, asking each locality to forward reports to the National Assembly, to preserve any local documents and to prepare follow-up reports to send to the National Assembly. We have found no records of such follow-up reports at the central level, but several provincial reports were given to research teams from the Documentation Center of Cambodia and the Cambodian Genocide Program as they travelled through the country in the late 1990s.

On 12 September 1983 a conference of 300 'intellectuals and religious people ' was held in the Salvation Front headquarters in Phnom Penh to discuss the findings of the Research Committee. They issued a moving Open Letter addressed to their counterparts around the world and to international organisations, appealing to them to 'denounce any international power that is aiding and abetting the Pol Pot, Ieng Sary and Khieu Samphan clique and other Khmer reactionaries to revive the genocidal regime, and to expel these fakers from the United Nations'.[4]

The decision to nominate a day of commemoration was widely welcomed. In the end 20 May was selected, according to the 1983 conference report, on the grounds that it was the date in 1976 'when the gang began to carry out their policy of continuous genocide openly and cruelly throughout the entire country'. This was evidently also the date in 1973 when the Khmer Rouge proclaimed the collectivisation movement in southern Takeo. When instituted in 1983 this day was given the name *T'veer Chong Kamhaeng* – literally the 'Day for Tying Anger'. While often translated into English as 'Day of Hatred', the spirit of the Khmer words is more accurately rendered as 'Day of Maintaining Rage'. Throughout the 1980s 20 May was commemorated and then again since the late 1990s, after a brief hiatus around the time of UNTAC, when the Khmer Rouge was being accorded political legitimacy. In 2001 it took on a new demeanour, being referred to officially as a 'Day of Remembrance'.[5]

Every year the survivors flock to Choeung Ek, the best-known 'Killing Fields' site about eight kilometres outside Phnom Penh, to attend solemn ceremonies with Buddhist payers and chanting monks, supplemented by pageants and songs from the next generation. Chea Sophara, the governor of Phnom Penh (from November 1999 to February 2003), whose own family was decimated, usually presided over this annual event officially organised by the Phnom Penh municipality and this tradition was continued in 2003 by Sophara's successor as governor, Kep Chuktema. In spite of the commitment of political parties to national reconciliation, the other parties have shown little interest in attending what they have seen as an event organised under the auspices of Hun Sen's Cambodian People's Party, rather than as a national day of mourning.

CAMPAIGNS AROUND THE WORLD

These efforts by the Cambodian government were paralleled by campaigns in a number of countries. The NGOs that brought aid to Cambodia in 1979 – most notably Oxfam, Cooperation Internationale pour le Développement et la Solidarité (CIDSE) and the American Friends Services Committee (AFSC) – also spoke out, adopting an unusually high-profile role in publishing such tracts as Oxfam's *The Poverty of Diplomacy*, which argued that British diplomacy was serving 'to perpetuate fear and prevent development'. Oxfam called for Britain to vote in support of a temporary one-year vacant Cambodia seat at the UN 'while urgent efforts are made to find a more permanent solution' and for an immediate resumption of development aid.[6]

Of the western NGOs operating inside Cambodia, 15 felt the need to document and publicise real developments inside Cambodia as a counter to the one-sided reporting of the Cambodian conflict by the chiefly Bangkok-based media. In 1986 they financed the publication of Eva Mysliwiec's aptly titled view from inside Cambodia, *Punishing the poor*. In June 1987 they decided to establish the NGO Forum on Cambodia as a permanent organisation to exert more influence as an independent lobby on governments to reverse the boycott and end the isolation of Cambodia. The former British diplomat John Pedlar was appointed in 1989 as the NGO Forum's 'diplomatic counsellor', a position held from 1990 to 1994 by the Belgian political analyst Raoul Jennar.[7]

Some NGOs limited their campaigning to the humanitarian issue of aid. Others took a wider view of the need for advocacy against cold war politics. A third strand focused on the legal side, calling for the Khmer Rouge to be brought to justice for their crimes and seeing the need to gather and preserve evidence for any such future trial.

In addition to the consciousness-raising work of the NGOs, pressure was also placed on governments by solidarity campaigns, much of whose energy came from veterans of the antiwar movement in the US, Europe and Australia, combined with new and younger people urged into action on seeing the injustice of a world that aided and armed the genocidists instead of bringing them to trial. The US-Indochina Reconciliation Project, the Vietnam, Cambodia, Laos Committee in Sweden and other peace committees around the world gave some focus to these issues, and later in the 1980s committees began to be formed focusing specifically on Cambodia (or Kampuchea as it was still widely known). The Australia-Kampuchea Solidarity Committee and some others broadened their call beyond provision of aid to include recognition of the People's Republic of Kampuchea.

As early as 1979 visits began, not only by solidarity groups from the socialist bloc countries which were supporting the People's Republic of Kampuchea, but also by academics, unionists, women and peace activists from the countries that were supporting the boycott. A group of Australian women visited Cambodia in December 1979. One member of the group, Helen Ester, wrote a vivid account of the devastation caused by Khmer Rouge attacks into the border areas of Vietnam, of the new Tuol Sleng museum and the confessions of two Australians who had been executed by the Khmer Rouge, and her interviews with women workers and Cambodia's young foreign minister, Hun Sen.[8]

Cambodian scholars who had worked in Cambodia in pre-Khmer Rouge times, such as David Chandler, Michael Vickery, Ben Kiernan and Serge Thion, followed their mid-1979 visit with their own quite different analyses that documented and condemned the crimes that had been committed both by Cambodians and by others on Cambodians.[9]

Journalist John Pilger and film director David Munro visited Cambodia in 1979 and were shocked by what they saw. Their reaction was to produce the documentary *Year Zero*, shown on British ITV. So powerful were the images and cries of this film that its initial screening led to an unprecedented outpouring of public donation and galvanised public opinion in the UK against British foreign policy on Cambodia. John Pilger continued his efforts in documenting the plight of Cambodia throughout the decade of its isolation, with five documentaries that included *Cambodia – the Betrayal*, complemented by his books and articles, mainly in the *New Statesman*.

Delegates from the PRK government travelled abroad to speak at peace conferences and seminars, and invited foreigners to visit Cambodia and see for themselves the evidence of Khmer Rouge crimes and the country's rehabilitation.

India, a leader of the non-aligned world, was one of the few countries outside the Soviet bloc that extended diplomatic recognition to the People's Republic of Kampuchea. Strong pressure from the Asean countries led the embassy to keep a low profile with only a *chargé d'affaires* to run the mission, but India was nevertheless able to play an important part in helping to develop Cambodia's contacts with the wider world.

At the same time those supporting the Khmer Rouge government-in-exile also mounted a vigorous international campaign. Pro-Democratic Kampuchea solidarity groups were formed in a number of countries and they held a number of international conferences. The influence of these groups was, however, insignificant when compared to the diplomatic recognition accorded to the Khmer Rouge by the United States, China and Asean.

HAYDEN'S BID TO GET GENOCIDE
ON THE INTERNATIONAL AGENDA

A few western governments continued to feel queasy about UN endorsement of the Khmer Rouge during the 1980s. To various degrees France, the Netherlands, Ireland, and Sweden expressed their distaste with this state of affairs. These governments were approached by the Cambodian Documentation Commission (CDC) in New York to take legal action. David Hawk, CDC chairman, lamented that they all invoked various legal and political arguments or excuses for declining to be associated with any kind of legal proceedings against the Pol Pot regime.

The only exception to this dismal record was the 1986 initiative of Australian foreign minister Bill Hayden. It was the one candle that sputtered briefly in the dark, while not a single government showed enough political will to launch a prosecution of Khmer Rouge leaders in the World Court.

In 1983 the Australian Labor Party won the country's general election. There was strong support among the rank and file of the Australian Labor Party to adopt a foreign policy that sought to end the cold war isolation of Cambodia and Vietnam. Gregory Stanton's Australia visit in mid-1986 was well timed. During this time he was a consultant to the Australian Department of Foreign Affairs, briefing them on the possibilities for action.

The Australian government saw an opportunity to start a dialogue with Hanoi and act as a mediator between the Asean countries and Vietnam, in a worthy attempt to break the diplomatic impasse. This was part of a new era in Canberra's foreign policy, with Australia striving for the first time to establish itself as an Asia-Pacific country, not just a colonial or neo-colonial outpost. The Asian lobby was riding high in the Department of Foreign Affairs and Hayden quickly responded to Stanton's proposal, announcing his support for a tribunal to try the Khmer Rouge the day after Stanton's first appearances on Australian television and radio.

Hayden had already blazed a trail by meeting Vietnamese foreign minister Nguyen Co Thach in Hanoi in 1983, and to the further dismay of all the anti-Hanoi hawks, he also met with Hun Sen, the young Cambodian foreign minister in Ho Chi Minh city in 1985.[10]

The essential elements of a settlement of the Cambodian conflict had started to coalesce in Hayden's thinking in mid-1986.

The foreign minister could see that if countries in the region really wanted to negotiate Vietnam's complete troop withdrawal from Cambodia, then they also had to address the legitimate fears of Phnom Penh and Hanoi of a resurgent Khmer Rouge, backed by China and the Thai army. One way of neutralising the Khmer Rouge threat, advancing the peace process and delivering justice all at the same time would be to prosecute the KR leadership for genocide and war crimes.

Stanton convinced the Department of Foreign Affairs in Canberra that Australia was one of the best-placed countries to invoke the UN Genocide Convention for the first time other than Cambodia's little recognised 1979 People's Revolutionary Tribunal. Australia was one of the group of countries in dispute with the DK regime, having in 1978 raised the issue in the UN together with Canada, Norway and the United Kingdom (see Chapter 2). This satisfied the requirement of Article 9 of the Genocide Convention that states bringing the case needed to be a party to the dispute with the accused state and that both countries were signatories of the convention.

Canberra's credible legal standing in such a case was also based on the impact of the genocide causing a massive refugee influx and subsequent relief programmes, as well as the fact that two Australian citizens were among the 79 foreigners incarcerated in the S-21 extermination centre and subsequently murdered along with more than 15,000 Cambodian prisoners.

At the Asean foreign ministers' summit in June 1986 Hayden publicly floated the idea of putting the KR leadership on trial as part of an overall Cambodian settlement, breaking the diplomatic log-jam that had already lasted seven years since the overthrow of the Pol Pot regime. This caused a furore, with Singapore and Thailand immediately viewing it as a move that could undermine the united front against Vietnam.

The Australian ambassador to the UN took up the theme in his address to the UNGA in October that year, arguing that if 'a mechanism could be established to determine once and for all the culpability of the Pol Pot leadership' it would clear the way for the Khmer Rouge rank and file to participate in moves towards a settlement.

The Australian initiative gave the UN Secretary General the opportunity to express concern about the flouting of international law. Although the seating of Khmer Rouge in the UNGA was ultimately the decision of member states, clearly every UN Secretary General has an opportunity to raise issues and lobby member states. The record shows that throughout the 1980s, successive UN Secretaries General paid scant attention to this gross abuse in which the world's most important international assembly continued to respect the credentials of Pol Pot's delegation in New York.

Back in Canberra the government's legal affairs department was asked to explore the feasibility of bringing a case at the International Court of Justice (World Court) in The Hague. But by 1987 Canberra was under pressure to drop the initiative. Stanton commented 'the Australian government finally declined to take the case on the erroneous ground that to do so would be to "recognize" the Khmer Rouge, even though cases in the World Court are brought by states against other states, not by governments as governments.'

But behind the legal rationalisations lurked the closeness of US-Australia relations. Later Stanton found out that 'the Australians had consulted the US State Department, which remained opposed to the prosecution because it might legitimise the Vietnamese-backed regime in Phnom Penh, and undermine the opposition coalition backed by Washington, a coalition that included the Khmer Rouge.'

The US State Department decided to go behind Hayden's back with discreet warnings to prime minister Bob Hawke that the US-Australia alliance would come under serious strain if Canberra pursued the tribunal concept. Two former Australian ambassadors confirmed that Hawke responded by promptly ordering his foreign minister to abandon the plan to hold the Khmer Rouge accountable, for the sake of preserving US-Australia relations and Asean unity.

Stanton reported with some gloom:

Neither David Hawk, who took the case to Sweden, nor I could convince any other government to take the case to the World Court … I had learned lesson number one about the struggle against genocide: Genocide continues and its perpetrators escape with impunity because of failure of political will to enforce the law. The Genocide Convention is international law. But law is not effective until there is [an] authoritative decision to enforce it.

By April 1987 the Cambodian Documentation Commission redirected its energies into a more public campaign. Some 200 survivors of the Cambodian genocide, including Dith Pran and Haing Ngor (famous from *The Killing Fields* movie), wrote to all the heads of government of countries that had signed up to both the Genocide Convention and the World Court, requesting them to file a complaint against Democratic Kampuchea. They were joined in the press conference launching the campaign by Elie Wiesel, a survivor from Auschwitz and Buchenwald, and recipient of the 1986 Nobel Peace Prize.

The way various governments responded to their personal appeal showed in a nutshell the farrago of alibis that have prevented action against the Khmer Rouge for so many years.[11]

President Ronald Reagan did not reply – this task was delegated right down the line to the Deputy Assistant Secretary of State for East Asian and Pacific Affairs, David Lamberton. He proclaimed the Administration's abhorrence of the Khmer Rouge brutality and heinous disregard for human rights and assured the petitioners that the US administration shared their deep and lasting concern that the Khmer Rouge leaders responsible should be punished. But, Lamberton demurred, the proposal to seek redress under the Genocide Convention 'raises serious, complex legal and practical difficulties'.

One of these difficulties was the United States' ambivalent attitude to the Genocide Convention, drawn up 40 years previously. Not until February 1986 did the Senate ratify it, but it was not until later, in October 1988, that the Genocide Convention Implementation Act was passed, making genocide punishable in the US. However, even then, the Senate added a 'sovereignty package' of reservations denying the automatic jurisdiction of the World Court, and in so doing 'rendered the US ratification a symbolic act'.[12]

At the Thai foreign ministry Arsa Sarasin likewise expressed appreciation and sympathy with the petitioners, but added: 'a sense of realism must guide our common efforts. Nothing should sidetrack us from mustering all our resources at this present time toward what must be the immediate priority, namely, to free the Cambodian people from the yoke of Vietnamese aggression.'

Indonesian Foreign Minister Mochtar Kusuma-Atmadja cautioned that

> more serious consideration must be given to the political implications which will arise from such an effort ... [which] will lead to events which will turn out to be counter-productive. The effort and the world-wide publicity it will create will tarnish the image of the Coalition Government of Democratic Kampuchea and Prince Sihanouk ... The objective ... can best be pursued through

[quiet] diplomacy as part of a comprehensive political solution to the Kampuchean problem.

It was not too surprising that these strong proponents of the embargo on the People's Republic of Kampuchea, and sponsors of the Coalition Government of Democratic Kampuchea government, which included the Khmer Rouge, would not be swayed. More hope might have been placed in the governments of the European Union and of Australia, which had indicated interest in a more flexible political accommodation, but such hope was misplaced.

Australian Prime Minister Bob Hawke said he was deeply moved by the letter and referred to Foreign Minister Bill Hayden's initiative with Asean a year earlier. But Hawke went on to echo the Indonesian viewpoint: 'we are conscious ... of the potential difficulties, both political and legal, in carrying forward any initiative in this area ... Care would need to be taken to ensure that such an action does not in any way risk unintended and possibly counter-productive results.'

And Swedish Prime Minister Ingvar Carlsson recycled Australia's rationalisation that to 'take legal action against the Khmer Rouge ... would constitute a *de facto* recognition' of the CGDK of which the Khmer Rouge forms a part 'and we are not prepared to make such recognition'.

Advocates of taking the Khmer Rouge to the World Court felt they were caught in a classic Catch 22 situation – those governments that supported the Khmer Rouge politically and militarily would scarcely confront them legally, while those that withheld political support used this as a reason for staying aloof from any legal action.

In addition to action resulting from interstate complaint, which was clearly not succeeding, another approach was allowed under the Genocide Convention's Article 8, which enabled the UN itself to take action to prevent or suppress genocide. So the case was mounted in the early 1980s that the Khmer Rouge was still a clear and present threat. Individual letters signed by over 1,000 Cambodian survivors were sent to the head of government and UN Permanent Representative of every Member State. Hannum and Hawk tried to get the United Nations Commission on Human Rights (UNCHR) to act and contributed their findings to assist the UN Special Rapporteur to prepare his 1986 'Revised and Updated Report on the Question of the Prevention and Punishment of the Crime of Genocide'. But the commission never voted to accept the report and it was shelved as its predecessor had been in 1979.

Despite compelling and thoroughly researched legal arguments, strong support from the émigré survivors and imaginative means of presentation, all these initiatives foundered on the rocks of geopolitics. But the documentation, especially the legal briefs so painstakingly prepared, convinced many jurists and academics that the case was worth pursuing and it may yet see its day in court.

THE PATH TO PEACE, PARIS AND ERASING THE GENOCIDE ISSUE

From 1979–1986 the cold war strategy of bleeding Vietnam white and keeping it bogged down in the Cambodian jungle was largely successful. The war dragged on and the few and feeble attempts at breaking the stalemate did not manage to disturb this strategy, nor the consciences of any politician advancing it.

Far from seeking peace, Washington and Beijing adroitly blocked tentative peace initiatives along with any moves towards targeting the KR leadership for a tribunal. Every year the Cambodian government continued to call for the trial of the leaders of the Pol Pot regime rather than their continued recognition, terming this offensive to the memory of those who died under its rule. For example, on 17 September 1986 Hun Sen wrote to the Secretary General calling for the unseating of the CGDK delegation and for an international trial of the 'Polpotists'.[13] Likewise in December 1988 the Salvation Front organised a conference to mark the 40th anniversary of the Genocide Convention, calling on the international community to cease recognition of and to take legal action against Cambodia's genocidists as it had with the Nazis.[14] Sadly these appeals went unheeded.

Several attempts by Hun Sen to hold talks with Prince Norodom Sihanouk, the president of the CGDK coalition, were thwarted by China with US approval. President Reagan's Secretary of State George Schultz actually went so far as to warn Asean nations not to enter into any kind of peace dialogue. The *Bangkok Post* reported that 'a senior US official said Schultz cautioned Asean to be extremely careful in formulating peace proposals for Kampuchea because Vietnam might one day accept them.'[15] Indeed this approach was precisely the nature of all the UN General Assembly resolutions up to 1988.

Sihanouk understood that China and the US were quite happy to let the Khmer Rouge and their allies make Cambodia into 'Vietnam's Vietnam' and he expressed disgust and despair for the way Cambodia's need for peace was sidelined by cynical global designs on the world chessboard. 'The Kampuchean people have been dismembered, crushed by the unbearable weight of an endless war a few foreign powers are keeping alive ... until the last Kampuchean is dead.'[16]

But the prince was also heavily indebted to China. An old friend of Beijing, especially of former Chinese foreign minister Chou En Lai, Sihanouk had been given sanctuary and support by China for five years after being ousted in the 1970 Lon Nol coup. In 1979 the former statesman and founder of the nation's independence was once again in exile, and once more Beijing's rulers placed a sumptuous palace at his disposal and supplied him with a stipend of $300,000 a year, as he confided to journalist T.D. Allman during a lengthy interview in Beijing.[17] Not surprisingly Beijing exercised enormous leverage in keeping their royal guest married to the Khmer Rouge-dominated coalition. If Sihanouk had been a free agent he could perhaps have charted a course for peace much earlier than the breakthrough that was finally achieved.

In December 1987, after years of sterile diplomacy and regional impasse between Asean and Indochina, the two leaders – Prince Norodom Sihanouk, the President of CGDK, and Prime Minister Hun Sen – met for the very first time.

The untold story behind this landmark meeting starts neither in Asia nor in Europe, but in Africa. In 1984 Hun Sen as foreign minister visited Angola where he met a French diplomat, Jean-Jacques Galabru, and his Cambodian wife, Kek Galabru. Hun Sen conveyed his strong desire to forge peace talks with Prince Sihanouk and the Galabru couple agreed to help make it happen.[18]

France did not have diplomatic relations with Phnom Penh, in deference to the United States, but Mitterand made some tentative overtures during the 1980s, including sending foreign minister Claude Cheysson to visit Phnom Penh. Phnom Penh's communications to the UN and western countries were dependent on Vietnam, the USSR and occasionally India as go-betweens. After the Angola visit Hun Sen astutely cultivated France as a new conduit of foreign policy.

Madame Galabru's father, Pung Peng Cheng, provided the vital connection. From 1960–70 he had been one of Sihanouk's top advisors as Secretary General to the Throne Council, later holding the position of Prince Sihanouk's *chef du cabinet* during his exile in Beijing from 1970–75. But Pung Peng Cheng never trusted the Khmer Rouge. He refused to accompany Sihanouk on his return to Phnom Penh under Khmer Rouge rule and in 1982 when Sihanouk joined the Pol Pot dominated CGDK coalition, he again parted company with Prince Sihanouk.

Over a six-hour dinner Cheng persuaded Sihanouk to accept Hun Sen's invitation, prevailing over strong Chinese blandishments and objections, which had blocked several attempted meetings between the two, including one scheduled in July 1987 in Pyongyang. Again there were last minute attempts to stop it happening. Objections from the French foreign ministry to granting visas to the Phnom Penh delegation were overcome only by personal intervention by Prince Sihanouk at the request of the Galabrus, who acted as go-betweens to facilitate one of the most delicate diplomatic operations in the 1980s.

The descendant of the great god-kings of the Angkor empire finally agreed to a dialogue with the self-educated son of a humble rice-farming family from Kampong Cham. The social chasm between the two leaders was far greater than the ideological divide. Hun Sen could not afford to rent a hotel room in the expensive resort of Fère-en-Tardenois where Sihanouk had rented a chateau. The delegation was forced to seek more humble lodgings at a motel about 20 kilometres away.

The meeting heralded the beginning of a peace process. Sihanouk, the veteran statesman and father of independence aged 65, warmed to the 36-year-old confident young upstart from Phnom Penh. The chemistry was surprisingly good and broad principles for a peace settlement were agreed.

Several months prior to this summit Hun Sen had launched an initiative for peace and national reconciliation. Overseas Cambodians were invited to return to the homeland and amnesty was offered to rank and file Khmer Rouge soldiers and the other factions who laid down their arms and defected to the government. Only 'the criminal Pol Pot and his close acolytes' were excluded from this amnesty offer.

1988 AND THE WIND OF CHANGE

The Hun Sen–Sihanouk meeting in France had broken the ice. The peace process then received a major shot in the arm from the 1988 elections in Thailand. Chatichai Choonhavan became the first elected civilian prime minister after more than a decade of military rule. He immediately embarked on a diplomatic offensive encapsulated in the slogan 'Let us transform the battlefields into marketplaces'. Spurning the cold war posturing against Phnom Penh, the Thai prime minister invited Hun Sen to Bangkok in spite of the absence of diplomatic relations, opposition from his foreign ministry and friction with his military.

A wind of change was blowing through Indochina, the region and beyond. A generation of hardliners and cold war apostles was being pressured to stand aside while those advocating peace, flexibility and international cooperation had briefly taken centre stage. Mikhail Gorbachev had opened the era of *Glasnost* (openness) that would eventually result in the dismantlement of the Soviet Union and the ending of the economic sustenance it had been able to provide to Cambodia.

Hardliners in both Thailand and Vietnam were either on their way out, or had already been replaced. The Vietnamese old guard of Le Duc Tho and Truong Chinh were no more. In 1986 new party chief in Hanoi, Nguyen Van Linh, brought *Doi Moi* (renovation) and a greater eagerness for a peaceful settlement of the Cambodian conflict. In Thailand cold warriors like Foreign Minister Siddhi Savetsila, close to US intelligence, were sidelined by the new Prime Minister Chatichai Choonhavan.

By June 1988 another partial withdrawal of Vietnamese troops gave a boost to those seeking an opportunity to advance the peace process. In demonstrating that Hanoi was serious in implementing its long-term timetable for complete unilateral withdrawal, it put pressure on all parties to come up with a settlement.

The lobby by overseas Cambodians and other activists started to have some discernible impact. Dr Haing Ngor and Dith Pran had constantly criticised Asean-sponsored UN resolutions on Kampuchea for being one-sided. In their view withdrawal of Vietnamese troops had to be linked to guarantees of a non-return of the Khmer Rouge regime. It was the same link that former Australian foreign minister Bill Hayden had pursued with little success in 1986. European nations and New Zealand were persuaded that now it was time to insist that Asean countries should modify their stand.

House Joint Resolution 602 in the US Congress took up the same theme. The moving force behind it was Stephen Solarz, a prominent Democratic Member of Congress who then held the position of Chair of the East Asia and Pacific Subcommittee of the House of Representatives Foreign Affairs Committee. The resolution calling for the 'non-return to power by the genocidal Khmer Rouge' was launched on 28 June 1988 at a press conference in Washington, DC, organised by the Cambodian Documentation Commission with Dith Pran, Haing Ngor, Kassie Neou and Senators Kennedy and Hatfield and Congressmen Atkins, Leach, Ridge and Dornan. It was passed by Congress and signed by Reagan on 18 October, marking a major shift by incorporating an explicit anti-KR provision into US policy.

In July 1988 Indonesia launched its 'cocktail diplomacy', bringing together all four Cambodian parties including the Khmer Rouge delegation in the first JIM (Jakarta Informal Meeting). Khieu Samphan, by some diplomats termed 'the smiling face of the Khmer Rouge', travelled first class on Thai International from Bangkok to Jakarta.

The talks were deliberately informal, with six representatives from Phnom Penh squared off against two representatives from each of the three coalition factions. The six Asean nations plus Laos and Vietnam also participated, with Indonesia chairing the proceedings.

A few months later in 1988 the Asean resolution in the UN General Assembly included for the first time a reference to the mass killings – the euphemistic formulation of 'non-return to universally condemned policies and practices of the past' – but it avoided mentioning either the Khmer Rouge by name, or using the highly charged term 'genocide'.[19] US Ambassador Vernon Walters criticised China and Thailand on the floor of the General Assembly for continuing to support the Khmer Rouge and cited House Joint Resolution 602, signed just days before.

A peace process had been launched. But there was still a fundamental divide between the CGDK backed by China, Asean and the US on the one side, and the Phnom Penh government and anti-Khmer Rouge lobbyists on the other. While the first bloc insisted that the Khmer Rouge must be part of the Cambodian solution and included in a four-party coalition government, Cambodian campaigners in exile argued that, on the contrary, the Pol Pot faction was at the heart of the problem and should therefore not form part of any solution.

In February 1989 Dr Haing Ngor travelled to Jakarta to urge the second JIM meeting of all Cambodian factions to keep the Khmer Rouge leaders outside any power-sharing agreement. Whereas Khieu Samphan, the man with so much blood on his hands, received the VIP treatment inside the conference chamber, Dr Haing Ngor was denied entry. Seeing him parade outside the conference centre with a sandwich board reading: 'Keep the Khmer Rouge out of the Peace Settlement' was sadly pathetic.

Back in Phnom Penh Hun Sen and his party had declared a similar position at a press conference held on 16 December 1988. He named the senior Khmer Rouge leaders as Pol Pot, still number one, followed by Ieng Sary, Son Sen, Ta Mok, Nuon Chea, Ke Pauk and Khieu Samphan, all of whom he insisted should be excluded from a peace settlement.

Excluding a cabal of mass murderers from a peace settlement containing explicit adherence to human rights should not be so very controversial and one might have expected western governments to have readily accepted it. After all, such a principle had been advanced in excluding former Nazi leaders from participating in post-1945 German governments – whether East or West – and one of Interpol's first mandates had been to hunt down former Nazi leaders. Hun Sen and overseas Cambodians like Haing Ngor called for the same respect for survivors of the Cambodian holocaust. The message from Phnom Penh was that the likes of Pol Pot, Nuon Chea and Ieng Sary should be standing trial for their crimes against humanity, not considered as part of a diplomatic equation. It was a message that fell on deaf ears among the very countries that most often speak about human rights.

One of the few governments that did display some sensitivity to the need for a solution without the Khmer Rouge was Thailand, or at least that part of the government led by Prime Minister Chatichai Choonhavan. In a meeting with Deputy Assistant Secretary of State for Asia and Pacific, Richard Solomon, it was suggested by an advisor to the Thai Prime Minister that 'the CIA might consider carrying out executive action to terminate Pol Pot with extreme prejudice'. Solomon looked slightly horrified, as if such things were never discussed in polite company.[20]

Senator Kraisak Choonhavan recalls that Washington reacted with alarm to his father's foreign policy initiatives to move outside of the US-China-Asean formula for a 'comprehensive settlement' and resorted to several economic threats in an attempt to bring Thailand back into line. At the same time the US ambassador in Bangkok insisted that the Khmer Rouge could not be excluded from any future Cambodian government.[21]

The Chatichai government had a different view. 'We were trying to end the military's backing for the Khmer Rouge and [advocate] a peace agreement between Funcinpec and the Cambodian People's Party that excluded the Pol Pot faction,' Senator Kraisak said.[22]

Among the factors that led to the 1991 Thai military coup that toppled prime minister Chatichai Choonhavan, according to his son Senator Kraisak, was precisely their efforts to stop the military alliance with Pol Pot forces.

Among Thai politicians Senator Kraisak is almost unique in his frank admission that 'Thailand shamelessly supported the Khmer Rouge' and he apologised to Cambodia in a 2001 interview with the *Phnom Penh Post*. Thai support for the Khmer Rouge, pushed by both the Thai military and the foreign ministry, did enormous damage to Thai–Cambodian relations. Kraisak argued 'now is the time for Thailand to admit it was a wrong policy.'[23]

During the course of 1989 France and Indonesia became convinced that such was the momentum of the peace process, with so many countries eager to contribute to a settlement, that the time was ripe for a grand peace conference. They served as the co-hosts for the Paris Peace Conference of July 1989, attended by 19 foreign ministers, including the region's main countries (the six Asean nations plus Vietnam and Laos), the P5 (the five permanent members of the UN Security Council), two members of the International Control Commission (Canada and India) and the then chair of the non-aligned movement (Zimbabwe) as well as all four Cambodian parties – the Hun Sen government and the three members of the CGDK coalition.

In preparation for the Paris conference, Cambodia hosted the International Seminar on the 'Genocide Phenomena and Prevention of their Return' to remind the world of the crimes of the Khmer Rouge and of their continued recognition. The seminar, held in Phnom Penh and organised by the Salvation Front and the Ministry of Information, appealed for:

> international lawyers and democratic governments to assist in bringing the Khmer Rouge leadership and organisation to the International Court of Justice in conformity with the UN Convention on the Prevention and Punishment of the Crime of Genocide;
>
> the Cambodia UN seat to be vacated until a fairly and democratically elected government can claim it;
>
> to stop all military aid to the Khmer Rouge, and to pressure them to demobilise, to surrender their arms to an International Control Mechanism and to go home;
>
> to oppose any power-sharing arrangement with the Khmer Rouge prior to any elections;
>
> to force the Khmer Rouge and other warlords to liberate all their hostages held in pseudo refugee camps, and to allow them freedom to return home under international assistance.[24]

At the Paris Peace Conference a week later the Hun Sen delegation officially submitted a summary report on genocide committed by the Khmer Rouge regime, to support their position that the issue should be addressed clearly by the conference.[25] While listed as an official conference document, it received little public airing or comment at the time.

From the opening session, though, it was clear that the genocide issue would block any chances of a peace settlement. While Prince Sihanouk had indicated he would consider dumping the Khmer Rouge in talks with Hun Sen in May 1989, he had in the meantime returned to Beijing and was once more back on board with the Khmer Rouge. China insisted there could be no peace without the Khmer Rouge as a full partner in any coalition government.

Prince Sihanouk proposed he would be prime minister and there would be one deputy prime minister for each faction: Hun Sen from the State of Cambodia government (the new name for the People's Republic of Kampuchea, adopted in April 1989); Sihanouk's son Prince Ranariddh for the Royalist faction; Son Sann for the KPNLF and Khieu Samphan for the Pol Potist faction.

This formula for a quadripartite interim coalition had been dismissed by Phnom Penh back in 1988. The security implications of Sihanouk's proposal for such a coalition government to bring four warring factions under one umbrella in the capital were addressed by Hun Sen in an interview with Tom Fawthrop. The Cambodian premier drew a parallel with warring military factions and militias in Beirut at the time insisting: 'If there are four armies fighting each other here in the city [Phnom Penh], this is not a solution. If the country will be turned into a second Lebanon, it is better not to have any agreement.'[26]

Sihanouk and his Coalition Government of Democratic Kampuchea knew in advance of Paris, then, that Phnom Penh was totally opposed to any interim arrangement that included power sharing with the Khmer Rouge.

In spite of all the professions of concern from the US government that there should be no return to power of the Khmer Rouge, no support at all was given by Washington and its allies for any of the safeguards advocated by Phnom Penh, including the exclusion of the top genocidal leaders.

The P5 majority, US, UK and France, were far more concerned with placating China than in providing any guarantees to the Cambodian people against a Khmer Rouge return to power. This even extended to the seating arrangements of the four Cambodian delegations. The conference organisers asked Hun Sen to be seated with the CGDK tripartite delegation. But he adamantly refused: 'I rejected that idea, saying that I could not sit in the chair of Democratic Kampuchea which is stained with the Cambodian people's blood.'[27]

The USSR was the only member of the P5 to show any understanding of Phnom Penh's concerns and the dangerous implications of a four-party coalition that would legitimise some 20,000 Khmer Rouge insurgents, leaving them free to roam the streets of Phnom Penh.

The Paris Peace Conference stalled and in August the talks were adjourned indefinitely. The acute contradictions of US policy were manifested when James Baker, US Secretary of State, blamed Vietnam and Hun Sen for the Paris failure, characterising him as 'stubborn'. In fact, Hun Sen's stand against inclusion of the Khmer Rouge was implementing the spirit of the congressional resolution 'to prevent the return of the KR regime', whereas the US government and the majority of participants were pushing for a dangerous collaboration. Most of the US press including the *Washington Post* and the *New York Times* ignored the perversity of Baker's remarks.

Speaking to Senator Muskie, a former US Secretary of State, in Phnom Penh on 9 October 1989, Hun Sen summed up a central issue that triggered the collapse of the 1989 Peace talks. 'The problem is whether to reward or condemn the Pol Potists. I don't understand why the crimes and the killings should be rewarded by giving them a share of power.' The Cambodian prime minister cited those who say 'we should give some power to the Khmer Rouge to satisfy China. This is using Cambodia to satisfy China, it is not in the best interests of the Cambodian people.' In the meeting with Muskie Hun Sen also spoke of Sihanouk's alignment with China.

> He is more or less a hostage to the Khmer Rouge. He has lost 19 children and grand children (during the Pol Pot regime) but at Paris he demanded the omission of the word genocide. The Cambodian people cannot allow that. Should we respect the UN genocide Convention, or should we reward those criminals?[28]

Before the Cambodian premier had left Paris for Phnom Penh he gave a press conference. Referring to Baker's accusations he conceded,

> in stopping any comeback by the Khmer Rouge I am happy to be called 'stubborn'. If we agreed to hand power to the Khmer Rouge

we would betray the memories of those who died. If the Khmer Rouge want to get power again they will have to kill Hun Sen to enter Phnom Penh.[29]

It is ironic that among all the Cambodian leaders in Paris, the only leader who steadfastly refused bestowing legitimacy on the Pol Pot faction and vowed to prevent their return to power was himself a former young soldier in the Khmer Rouge army, who had metamorphosed into their most bitter enemy.

After the Paris collapse the situation looked bleak. The final unilateral Vietnamese troop withdrawal took place in October 1989 but without any international verification. China and CGDK denounced it as a fraud. The US insisted on the retention of the economic and political boycott of Cambodia and Vietnam. Sihanouk called for a 'general uprising' and the KR launched a military offensive culminating in the capture of Pailin in late October. Australia, Indonesia and the Chatichai government in Thailand renewed their efforts to bring all parties back to the negotiating table.

On 24 November 1989 Australian Foreign Minister Gareth Evans announced the Australian peace proposal with an 'enhanced role for the United Nations in the transitional period leading to free and fair elections', building on proposals floated by US Congressman Stephen Solarz and by Norodom Sihanouk, as a means to side-step the power sharing issue that had failed to be resolved in Paris.

The State of Cambodia (SOC) agreed to a UN role providing that the Cambodian seat at the UN was no longer held by the CGDK; the government stated that it was not willing to dismantle itself before elections, but suggested the establishment of a Supreme National Council with equal representation of both SOC and CGDK, including the Khmer Rouge. The SOC even agreed to cut off Soviet military supplies if China would also cut its aid to the Khmer Rouge.

Meanwhile, SOC forces retook much ground from the coalition forces in western Cambodia, although the town of Pailin remained in the hands of the CGDK.

At a second round of the JIM peace talks held in Jakarta February 1990, the unmentionable 'G-word' (Genocide) again upset the indignant Khmer Rouge delegation. Khieu Samphan refused to sign any joint declaration that dared to suggest that his faction was once responsible for mass murder. Gareth Evans, Australian foreign minister, summing up the talks, claimed that they were so close to an agreement but regrettably 'it all broke down over atmospherics'.

That the issue of Khmer Rouge mass murder and genocide could be dismissed as a problem of mere 'atmospherics' was a good indication of how this massive Cambodian fear about the return of genocidal past was far down the list of the international community's priorities.

If the conscience of western governments had needed any pricking, the months to come provided salutary reminders of what the Khmer Rouge were all about. On 1 July 1990 the southbound train from Phnom Penh was ambushed by Khmer Rouge forces. At least 24 were killed and 52 wounded with more than ten reported missing. There were two more train ambushes in the same period killing another 80, nearly all civilians apart from a small number of security guards and soldiers.

7   Khmer Rouge soldiers at Khao Larn Khmer Rouge base near Saaphan Hin Trat province, Thailand, one of Pol Pot's HQs in the 1980s. Access to these zones was blocked by the Thai military engaged in enforcing martial law along the Thai–Cambodian border. (Tom Fawthrop)

France, UK, Sweden, Canada, Italy and the European Community as a whole were variously reported as preparing to withdraw support for the Khmer Rouge-dominated CGDK in the forthcoming session of the UNGA. Then on 18 July 1990 US Secretary of State James Baker announced a major shift in policy, at a time when Congress was considering cutting off assistance to the coalition, saying that the US would no longer continue to support the seating of the CGDK in the United Nations.[30]

8   The Chinese connection. Pol Pot haggles over the price of a watch in Beijing in the early 1990s, but he is far better known as the tyrant who abolished money in 1975. China has exerted great pressure on the Cambodian government to abandon the tribunal. (Nhem Eng, KR photographer)

On 10 September 1990 the Jakarta International Meeting agreed on the establishment of a twelve-person Supreme National Council, to be the 'repository of Cambodian sovereignty' to represent Cambodia at the UN and on the delegation of certain functions to the UN leading up to elections, finally agreeing to allocate a 50/50 split between the State of Cambodia and the Coalition Government of Democratic Kampuchea. The CGDK did not nominate Sihanouk among the twelve members, but he was later appointed as Chairman. The agreement called for the establishment of the United Nations Transitional Authority in Cambodia (UNTAC) to which the Supreme National Council would agree to delegate 'all powers necessary to ensure the implementation of the comprehensive agreement, including those relating to the conduct of free and fair elections and the relevant aspects of administration of Cambodia.'

The first meeting of the Supreme National Council was held on 18 September 1990 in the Cambodian Embassy in Bangkok. No agreement was reached on either a ceasefire or on the members of the Cambodian delegation to the UN General Assembly. The 45th (1990) UNGA in New York left the Cambodian seat 'temporarily unattended', but the CGDK representatives continued to use the offices and letterhead of the Permanent Mission of Cambodia to the UN.

If only India's empty-seat formula had received the same support back in 1979, perhaps Cambodia could have been spared the long debilitating eleven years of war and all the millions of landmines might never have been planted. As noted in Chapter 2, in 1979 the UK's Foreign Office had argued against leaving the Cambodia seat vacant on the grounds that it was somehow a 'bad legal precedent'. But new international realities in 1990 made the empty-seat formula suddenly attractive and all the previous doubts and legal dissension evaporated.

POL POT AND THE PEACE PROCESS COMES TO PATTAYA

The Pattaya seaside resort in Thailand in 1991 had achieved an international reputation less for its natural beauty than its unbridled nightlife. It catered to every whim of sex-hungry American sailors, regularly disgorged from visiting US warships. Many towns have red-light districts but Pattaya is different. The town is synonymous with its continuous red-light zone of bars, brothels and massage parlours, a focal point and symbol of Thailand's thriving sex-tourism trade.

Pattaya was not perhaps an obvious haunt for the infamous Khmer Rouge supremo Pol Pot who had imposed a totalitarian puritanism on everyday life with his plan for a Cambodian utopia. He visited Pattaya several times during the 1980s according to the former Tuol Sleng photographer Nhem Eng. When he strolled the streets of Pattaya, did Pol Pot ever compare the excesses of Thai freedom with the murderous excesses of his own social engineering? Did he ever stop to reflect on his Khmer Cultural Revolution, which made China's Cultural Revolution look almost tame?

He normally travelled to Pattaya in a four-wheel drive vehicle with dark-tinted windows from his headquarters, code named '87', in Trat province near the Thai village of Saaphan Hin. Any journalist from Bangkok who went looking for Pol Pot encountered the Thai military marine camp blocking any further access up the mountain to the Khmer Rouge HQ. This was the Thai military's most closely guarded secret for a whole decade. In spite of the large number of correspondents based in Bangkok and the region who made frequent trips to the Thai-Cambodian border, not one of them cracked the *cordon sanitaire* of the Thai military's secret Unit 838 and the marine camp at Saaphan Hin in Trat.

Pol Pot and all Khmer Rouge leaders when operating inside Thailand were escorted by the secret Unit 838, its soldiers usually dressed in civilian attire. Drawn from Thai Special Warfare Command stationed in Lopburi, they functioned as a border liaison force supervising Khmer Rouge bases, camps and military warehouses in Thailand (as discussed in more detail in Chapter 4). They also coordinated with the top generals in Bangkok and with military Unit 315 – the special unit for coordinating Kampuchea operations, strategy and intelligence.

9   Pol Pot with Thai special forces Unit 838. Pol Pot is waiting to meet some VIPs near Pattaya in Thailand. Unit 838 provided protection and transportation for Khmer Rouge leaders in Thailand. (Khmer Rouge photos)

In June 1991 the Thai government hosted a critical meeting of SNC at the five-star Royal Cliff Hotel in Pattaya. The Khmer Rouge delegation was headed as usual by Pol Pot's front man in the diplomatic arena since 1979, Paris-educated Khieu Samphan. The other Khmer Rouge representative was the overtly sinister Son Sen, the former interior minister, the man who had been directly responsible for the secret police and their S-21 interrogation headquarters.

10   Son Sen (left), in charge of defence and security from 1975–79, pictured here as the Khmer Rouge delegate to a meeting of the SNC (Supreme National Council) held in the Thai beach resort of Pattaya in November 1991. Son Sen was murdered on the orders of Pol Pot in 1997. The second figure is KR diplomat Im Sopheap. (Tom Fawthrop)

Most delegates agreed that the next meeting of the SNC should be held in Phnom Penh, but the KR delegates refused to provide a definite answer and the session had to be adjourned. The reason was simple: this matter had to be referred to a higher authority in the Khmer Rouge, Pol Pot.

Thai army chief General Suchinda Krapayoon had met with the Khmer Rouge 'Brother Number One'[31] shortly before the Pattaya talks started. General Suchinda told a visiting US senator back in April that

'Pol Pot was a nice guy' and repeated the positive opinions of Pol Pot that he had expressed at pre-Pattaya meetings held at the residence of the Thai prime minister Chatichai Choonhavan.

But then some may question General Suchinda's fitness as a character witness. The Thai army chief masterminded the bloodbath in Bangkok in 1992 when hundreds of soldiers opened fire on a peaceful pro-democracy demonstration. General Suchinda, like the Khmer Rouge leadership, never expressed any remorse for the acts of barbarism he so clearly countenanced.

During the conference adjournment the man the Khmer Rouge delegates were all waiting for secretly arrived in Pattaya.

Rumours about Pol Pot's presence were rife among the hundreds of foreign and local press covering the peace talks. One enterprising reporter decided to try to find out if he was actually staying at the Royal Cliff Hotel.

There was a mystery name on the list of Khmer Rouge staying at the hotel. Number two in the delegation was an unknown 'Mr. Chea Chheng' listed ahead of Son Sen, and allocated a separate room, like Khieu Samphan and Son Sen, while the others in the delegation shared rooms. Chea Chheng was surely a cover for Pol Pot. The enterprising journalist scribbled Pol Pot's real name 'Mr Saloth Sar' on a piece of paper and gave it to the hotel receptionist. Minutes later hotel guests were greeted with a loudspeaker announcement: 'This is a call for Mr. Saloth Sar – can you please come to reception.' The Cambodia watchers and better-informed media hooted with laughter.

To the disappointment of the assembled hacks Pol Pot did not come to the hotel reception desk but he did preside over an all-night session of the Khmer Rouge delegation somewhere in Pattaya, whether at the Royal Cliff Hotel or elsewhere. Only Pol Pot had the authority to authorise acceptance of the peace plan. After the conference, Khieu Samphan on the orders of Pol Pot accepted a critical proposal for the SNC to meet in Phnom Penh. After his secret intervention Pol Pot was spirited away by his Unit 838 escorts and the story was reported by Nayan Chanda in the *Asian Wall Street Journal*.[32]

Many were sceptical of Nayan Chanda's report at the time in spite of the fact that he was the author of the highly acclaimed *Brother Enemy*, a brilliant account of Indochina diplomacy during the 1980s. But US diplomatic sources knew Pol Pot was there and leaked it to Chanda. The authors were able to confirm his presence with Nhem Eng, a Khmer Rouge photographer who was present at Pattaya. 'I knew Pol Pot came to Pattaya. I never saw him but In Sopheap (also in the Khmer Rouge delegation) told me he was there.'

That a man reviled by the world and convicted of genocide could be secretly chaperoned around a world-famous seaside resort under the noses of the leading diplomats from the Permanent Five nations surely defies imagination. In all the many years of keeping Pol Pot's whereabouts in Thailand a secret (shared only with the CIA and a few other intelligence agencies) spiriting him in and out of a major international conference was little short of a diplomatic coup by Bangkok's military intelligence.

During the course of 1990 and 1991 changes on the international stage heavily favoured a peace settlement brokered largely on Chinese terms fully backed by Washington. The Cambodian government's principal allies – Vietnam and the USSR – while harbouring serious misgivings about the terms of the settlement, also pushed Phnom Penh to clinch the deal, as they were themselves in dire economic circumstances and in no way able to continue their previous role of underpinning the State of Cambodia and its military forces.

During the two years from the first round of Paris in 1989 to the final signing of the Paris Peace Agreements on 23 October 1991, no western country backed Phnom Penh's call to hold the Khmer Rouge accountable for their crimes. Japan in early 1991 proposed a special commission of inquiry into the crimes committed but US Assistant Secretary of State, Richard Solomon, tried to kill this initiative with his comment that such a commission was 'likely to introduce confusion in the international peace efforts'.[33]

Diplomats over the years had frequently tried to convey an impression that they detested the DK leadership as much as anyone, and the US government and others were quietly pushing Pol Pot and others to go into exile in China. This was a case of diplomatic disinformation obfuscating a rather different story. Another US diplomat, Kenneth Quinn, let the cat out of the bag as to where the pressure was really being applied in his address to the Global Business Forum in September 1991. While pressure on China was no more than rhetoric, Quinn told the assembled businessmen that pressure on Hanoi was intense 'to see that Vietnam holds Hun Sen's feet to the fire'.[34]

Prince Norodom Sihanouk confirmed that all parties had agreed at a second SNC meeting at Pattaya in August 1991 and that 'Pol Pot would enjoy the same rights as all other citizens.' But, as if to reassure the world, he added, 'I know that Messrs. Pol Pot, Ieng Sary and Ta

Mok will not be candidates ... But they might encourage their party and its candidates during the election campaign.'[35]

One of the key men in US intelligence operations directed against Phnom Penh, Colonel Mike Eiland, promoted to be DIA's regional chief of military intelligence in the mid-1980s, was seen lurking on the stage with the Cambodian leaders at the end of the Pattaya conference at the Royal Cliff Hotel.

11   UN police chief, Brigadier General Van Roos, wearing a blue beret, in conversation with leading genocide suspect Khieu Samphan, 1993. At that time the UN had still not recognised the crimes of the Khmer Rouge regime. (Tom Fawthrop)

On the eve of the Paris Peace Agreements, a gesture was made to put the historical record straight by an organ, however small, of the United Nations. Some twelve and a half years after the overthrow of Pol Pot, on 23 August 1991, the UN Human Rights Commission's Sub-Commission on Prevention of Discrimination and Protection of Minorities mentioned 'that it is the duty of the international community to prevent the recurrence of genocide in Cambodia.'

But such words were not to find their way into the final text of the agreement signed in Paris exactly two months later, in which all references to the genocidal past of the Khmer Rouge were expunged in favour of the vaguest of euphemisms, 'the non-return to the unacceptable practices of the recent past', allowing the Khmer Rouge to evade any responsibility. Hun Sen's demand that the international community should insist that the Khmer Rouge should renounce the genocidal policy of their past regime fell by the wayside. Key nations that might be expected to care about human rights, such as Australia, France, UK and the US, stayed silent. Their commitment to not upsetting China won the day.

The Beijing-brokered deal insisted on equal rights for the Khmer Rouge party – no sanctions, no penalties, no exclusions and no references to genocide in the final text. In other words, full and unconditional legitimation of the Khmer Rouge.

Many aspects of the Paris Peace Agreements were anathema to Hun Sen and his SOC delegates but they were forced to accept them. Cambodia was devastated by two decades of war and genocide from 1970–1991 and was no longer receiving military and economic support from Vietnam and the former Soviet Union and its allies. Bereft of other options, the State of Cambodia had to go along with a deal that would at least usher in a new era of peace, aid and development once a UN-organised election had taken place.

Above all, the war-weary population craved peace. But it was a peace imposed by external forces and without any concern for justice or guarantees of protection from attacks by the Khmer Rouge. It would soon become clear that the architects of the peace deal had failed to provide any sanctions against factions that violated the basic provisions and defied the implementation of the agreements.

6
Peace Without Justice

The Paris Peace Agreements created an extraordinary opportunity for the Khmer Rouge. It handed them legitimacy, putting them on an equal footing with the other three factions. Now they had the right to set up their delegation headquarters in Phnom Penh.

The last time Khieu Samphan and Son Sen had been in Phnom Penh was the first week of January 1979 just before fleeing towards the Thai border as Vietnamese troops advanced on the capital. At the time they were senior leaders of the Democratic Kampuchea regime – Khieu Samphan as head of state and Son Sen holding the portfolio of Defence and Internal Security with special responsibility for S-21 (Tuol Sleng).

In November 1991 they returned to the capital as the Khmer Rouge delegation to the Supreme National Council. Only a few months earlier, if the Khmer Rouge team had dared to set foot in Phnom Penh they would have surely been arrested for their crimes and membership of an illegal organisation.[1] Overnight they had been legalised and legitimised. Now they were back in town not as prisoners but as VIP diplomats under the protection of the Paris Peace Agreements. However this did not protect them from an angry protest from which they were rescued by government forces, Khieu Samphan emerging with 'his bleeding head ignominiously bandaged with a pair of Y-fronts'.[2] They were escorted straight to the airport and took the next flight to Bangkok.

The Khmer Rouge delegation agreed to return to Phnom Penh only after firm guarantees of security from both UNTAC and the State of Cambodia. They were provided accommodation behind the high walls of the compound of the Royal Palace. Lor Chandara, the former deputy director of Tuol Sleng museum, expressed incredulity that these two had been permitted to return to Phnom Penh.

From the start of the UNTAC mission key UN officials were uncomfortable with the contradictions and preferred that no one mentioned the impolite 'G-word' (genocide). The political etiquette that had been laid down in Paris and UN HQ in New York was to stress peace, national reconciliation and the protection of human rights. But even the human rights mandate was tarnished. UNTAC's human rights component, headed by Dennis McNamara, supported the creation of a number of local human rights NGOs but was gagged by the Paris Peace Agreements from delving into the biggest human rights issue of all – the crimes of the Khmer Rouge, including genocide.

UNTAC's chief, Japanese diplomat Yasushi Akashi, was on several occasions invited by the Cambodian star of *The Killing Fields* film, Dr Haing Ngor, to join him on visits to the Tuol Sleng Genocide Museum. Haing Ngor, who played the part of Dith Pran in the movie, had since the early 1980s actively campaigned for Khmer Rouge leaders to be brought to justice. According to the late Dr Ngor, Mr Akashi's reply was always, 'I am too busy', but Dr Ngor believed that was not the real reason. He felt Akashi was afraid that the Khmer Rouge and possibly others would denounce him for visiting a museum that exposed the crimes of the Khmer Rouge in stark clarity, and had been established with the help of Vietnamese advisors.[3] The Cambodian doctor who had endured the ordeals of the Pol Pot regime confided, 'I know that Mr Akashi does not want to offend the Khmer Rouge. It is a political decision but genocide is above politics.'

According to Cambodia analyst Raoul Jennar, 'Haing Ngor was never ideological and didn't like politics.' The way he saw it, Tuol Sleng did not belong to any faction, but rather it transcended all politics as a national shrine and museum for all victims.[4]

General John Sanderson, the Australian military commander in charge of UN peacekeeping forces, berated journalists on more than one informal occasion for focussing too much on Khmer Rouge crimes, thereby undermining the spirit of national reconciliation and making his job all the more difficult.

Issues of international law, and the status of the UN Convention on the Prevention and Punishment of Genocide became legally fuzzy under the terms of the Paris UN mandate. Cambodia had acceded to the Genocide Convention way back in 1950. And what of the death sentences passed on Pol Pot and Ieng Sary by the 1979 People's Revolutionary Tribunal? Had the Paris Peace Agreements provided immunity from prosecution? Tom Fawthrop put these questions to Michael Williams working for UNTAC Human Rights. If Pol Pot were arrested, would UNTAC demand his release in the name of national reconciliation and the spirit of the peace agreement? Williams, a former BBC journalist, was stumped for an answer, saying only, 'That's a good question!'

Hun Sen, addressing the same basic question at a Phnom Penh press conference, said his government did not know if the verdicts of the 1979 tribunal were still valid after signing the peace agreements, but he stressed 'the UN conventions on genocide cannot be overridden by the Paris Peace [Agreements].... Right now I wish very much to implement that UN convention.'[5]

There was nothing in the text of the Paris Peace Agreements that dared to spell out the obvious implications – that no legal action should be taken against Khmer Rouge leaders until after the UN-supervised election. UNTAC's human rights experts were handicapped by a mandate that was based not on the Universal Declaration of Human Rights and the UN Commission on Human Rights, but on the particular political compromises of the Paris Peace Agreements.

12 Thai military intelligence agent Colonel Chaiwat Maungnol, left, partying in Pailin with a Cambodian gem-dealer in 1995. (Khmer Rouge officers were also in the group.) The Thai-Khmer Rouge military officers also diversified by 1989 into a lucrative smuggling operation deaing in Pailin's gems and logging. (Tom Fawthrop)

UN Human Rights Day, 10 December 1992, was celebrated in Phnom Penh. Yasushi Akashi invoked the UN Declaration of Human Rights. The UN press release reported that UNTAC would do its utmost to ensure that human rights were respected in Cambodia. In deference to the sensitivities of the Khmer Rouge, though, he did not even use the standard euphemism that there must be no return to 'the unacceptable practices of the recent past'. Nor was there any mention of ongoing human rights violations in Khmer Rouge-controlled Pailin and Anlong Veng, where the UN peacekeepers had been barred from entering.

At an UNTAC-sponsored conference to mark the occasion, members of the Committee to Oppose the Return of the Khmer Rouge (including Ben Kiernan and Helen Jarvis) were even prevented from handing out a leaflet referring to the crimes of the Khmer Rouge[6], whose representatives were seated as dignitaries!

Despite the official rhetoric that all four factions would have to submit to equal UNTAC supervision, in reality almost all of UNTAC's scrutiny was focussed on the State of Cambodia. The two 'non-communist' factions virtually abandoned their zones along the border with Thailand to come to town and join in the political game. However, it was neither the State of Cambodia nor UNTAC that took over these zones, but rather their partner in the CGDK, the Khmer Rouge, thereby significantly increasing the areas under its control.

UNTAC was almost totally excluded from entering Khmer Rouge-controlled zones. In one famous incident UNTAC's political and police chiefs (Akashi and Brigadier General Van Roos, head of CIVPOL) declined to assert their right to pass through a roadblock consisting of a single bamboo pole! Such was UN humiliation over the incident that its own film footage was prohibited from the usual distribution for use by local and foreign TV stations.[7]

The Khmer Rouge refused to implement a single one of the pledges it had signed in Paris and in 1993 they withdrew from their Phnom Penh office with accompanying threats to disrupt the UN-supervised election.

Most importantly, they refused to disarm and instead continued to terrorise and intimidate people in many parts of the country, including perpetrating a number of atrocities against people of ethnic Vietnamese origin. Even UNTAC itself suffered high casualties – 20 of its personnel were killed by hostile action and 58 seriously wounded, and a number of personnel were taken hostage.[8]

The success of the peace plan depended on the cooperation of the three neighbouring countries – Laos, Thailand and Vietnam, all signatories of the Paris Agreements – to cut off any arms supply to the four Cambodian parties. According to UNTAC's military observers, Laos and Vietnam strictly complied, but the Thai military made no attempt to sever its long-standing links, both commercial and military, with the Khmer Rouge.

China, a member of the P5, had by 1990 accepted the need to disengage from bankrolling Pol Pot's forces, but by then the Khmer Rouge operations were well financed by the looting of Cambodia's natural resources, particularly gems and timber. Earth-moving machinery moved into ruby-rich Pailin along with numerous Thai logging companies. Khmer Rouge revenue from this trade was estimated at $100–150 million,[9] more than the annual budget of the State of Cambodia government during the period of 1990 to 1991.

That kind of money flowing from Thai logging and mining companies made it easy for the Khmer Rouge to buy everything they needed, food, gasoline, and ammunition from Thailand, and to thumb their noses at the UN. Thailand's National Security Council and the post-coup Thai regime run by General Suchinda Krapayoon obstructed attempts by UNTAC to clamp down on this illegal cross-border trade. During 1992 foreign minister Arsa Sarasin openly defended the right of Thai businessmen to trade with the Pol Pot faction. Ieng Sary, who had been the conduit for Chinese financial aid to the Khmer Rouge during the 1980s, continued to play the role of Khmer Rouge point man for gem and illegal logging trade along the Thai-Cambodian border and was widely reported to have siphoned off a percentage for himself.

The UN Security Council passed a resolution imposing petroleum sanctions on any parties not complying with the military provisions of the Paris Peace Agreements (i.e., the Khmer Rouge) in November 1992, but it was a toothless measure that could only request, but not compel, international cooperation.

Mr Akashi made several attempts to garner Thai support to stop the border collusion between the Thai military and the Khmer Rouge, including an offer to place UN military observers on the Thai side of the border. His overtures met with uniform hostility especially from the Chairman of Thai National Security Council General Charan Kulavanijaya who frequently lambasted UNTAC. But to independent observers it was clear that the Thai military–Khmer Rouge relationship from '1992–94 depicts a comprehensive military alliance – and not one of ad-hoc assistance measures'.[10]

The attack by KR soldiers on 1 August 1993 on the UN Cambodia-Thai border checkpoint CT 1, and the capture of UN military observers and peacekeepers, dramatically showed the close ties between the Thai military and Pol Pot's forces in the border region. The shelling of CT 1 forced the UN team to flee across the border into Thailand for safety where they were intercepted by a Khmer Rouge unit.

The four UN military observers from Australia, Britain, China and France together with 19 Pakistani soldiers were held by the 25-strong Khmer Rouge unit for eight hours on the Thai side of the border. The local Thai military commander, Lt Col Suchet, eventually negotiated their release with the Khmer Rouge commander. UNTAC's investigation into the border incident strongly blamed the Thai authorities for allowing the Khmer Rouge to use Thai territory to launch an offensive against the Cambodian checkpoint.[11]

Akashi was outraged and strongly recommended to New York that the UN Security Council censure the Thai government for violating Article 7 (2) of the Paris Accords. UN headquarters replied to the effect that Thailand was a 'respected member of the region' that had provided considerable logistical support and supplies to the UN peacekeeping operation, and declined to take any further action.[12]

UNTAC never called the Khmer Rouge to account for flagrant violations of the agreements their leaders had signed. Prince Norodom Sihanouk remarked:

> The Khmer Rouge sees that the gentlemen of UNTAC are very kind. If there is a fight somewhere, UNTAC does not intervene. On the contrary, it withdraws. The Khmer Rouge know that the UN will never make war against them. The Cambodian people believed that the UN blue berets were like Jupiter threatening to unleash lightning against the Khmer Rouge. What do people see? UNTAC pulls back.[13]

Instead, it was the Khmer Rouge itself that took the decision finally to withdraw even from the pretence of participating. In April 1993 they suddenly closed down their Phnom Penh headquarters, escalated their attacks on UN peacekeepers and threatened to disrupt the forthcoming election.

David Hawk, from the US-based Cambodian Documentation Commission, expressed some anxiety about another possible scenario: 'Had the Khmer Rouge not withdrawn from the peace plan, or even more likely, if they had rejoined the election at the last minute, it is probable that some of Pol Pot's closest henchmen would be ministers in the new Cambodian government.'[14]

The United Nations had descended on Cambodia with 22,000 officials and soldiers and hundreds of four-wheel drive land cruisers in an exercise that cost some US$3 billion over less than two years. Cambodia is widely hailed as one of the UN's peacekeeping success stories, glossing over the fact that peace was not achieved and that the UN did little to assuage the Khmer Rouge threat to the fragile new democracy. In September 1993 Khmer Rouge forces, aided and abetted by the Thai army, captured the ancient tenth century Khmer temple of Preah Vihear straddling the border. UNTAC was unable or unwilling to do anything to return it to government control. It was deeply symbolic of a major failure of the UNTAC mission.

On the other hand the UN mission did chalk up some successes: the smooth repatriation of over 350,000 Cambodian refugees, staging the 1993 elections and helping to open up Cambodian society to press freedom, pluralism and grassroots organisations independent of the state and governing party.

But did it really require such a vast unwieldy UNTAC to achieve these positive outcomes? If western governments had thrown their weight behind the Sihanouk-Hun Sen agreement in Jakarta May 1989, based on the concept of a tripartite coalition without the Khmer Rouge, the Cambodian people would not have been forced to swallow the legitimisation of the Pol Pot forces – inviting the tiger inside the tent.

7
Waking up to Genocide

The era of Khmer Rouge legitimation thanks to the Paris Peace Agreements was over. The UNTAC mission had left Cambodia but Cambodia was still at war. In July 1994 the National Assembly passed a law that declared the Khmer Rouge once again to be insurgents and outlaws. The path had been cleared. Khmer Rouge impunity could now be addressed. Cambodians had the right to expect that Michael Kirby, an Australian jurist appointed in November 1993 as the UN Secretary General's Special Representative for Human Rights in Cambodia, would move on the genocide issue.

Kirby reported to the Secretary General on human rights violations, the legal system, the prisons and courts. But, with his focus on the present, he paid no particular attention to the most egregious violation of human rights in Cambodia's history – the Khmer Rouge genocide – despite continuing entreaties and proposals by a number of experts and NGOs who continued to advocate the need for an international tribunal.

UNTAC's human rights component was re-vamped into the Cambodia Office of the United Nations High Commission on Human Rights but it, too, paid no attention to the Khmer Rouge. The UN's abysmal record on the Khmer Rouge was perpetuated right up to 1997, long after the Khmer Rouge themselves had declined to take advantage of the offers of political rehabilitation extended to them under the Paris Peace Agreements.

But a number of important developments forced the issue of the Khmer Rouge back into international focus.

On 1 April 1994 the US Congress passed the Cambodian Genocide Justice Act, prohibiting the US government from cooperating in any way with the Khmer Rouge and mandating the State Department to collect evidence on the Khmer Rouge's genocidal crimes. The State Department was instructed to fund two projects: a study into the legal accountability of the Khmer Rouge and also a major programme of research and documentation of the Khmer Rouge period. The US government's role in regard to the Khmer Rouge was now forced to change course dramatically.

The policy change has been derided as hypocritical and three arguments are advanced to support this view. First, the actions were belated, and came at a time when the Khmer Rouge had been finally rendered harmless. Second, it is widely believed that it was precisely actions by the US that had done most to bring that brutal regime to power – support for the coup that overthrew King Sihanouk in 1970, followed by the massive bombing in the 1970s. And third, US support had been pivotal in keeping the Khmer Rouge alive in the 1980s partly motivated by a desire for revenge over Vietnam, the only country to have inflicted defeat on the superpower.

Whether hypocritical or not, 'Better late than never' was the reaction from many people, including the well-known Cambodian actor and writer Dr Haing Ngor.

In any event, this new focus was carefully formulated to rule out consideration of any actions by the US before 1975 or after 1979, including Nixon and Kissinger's 'secret' bombing campaign.

The US policy shift in the 1990s was not a spontaneous result of government officials finally seeing the light. A sustained public campaign had been mounted through the 1980s in opposition to the to US policy that furnished material and political support to the Khmer Rouge dominated CGDK Coalition (as described in Chapter 5).

Leading a new push was the Campaign to Oppose the Return of the Khmer Rouge (CORKR), launched in the late 1980s. This NGO coalition was founded in 1989 to press for major changes in US policy towards Cambodia.

Operating under the umbrella of the Asia Resource Center in Washington, DC, CORKR managed to gain backing from over 100 NGOs, including both religious and secular groups, such as the American Friends Service Committee, Church World Service, the Union of American Hebrew Congregations, the Maryknoll Fathers, the Federation of American Scientists, Oxfam America and many other organisations. They were united in opposing a US policy that was more hostile to the Cambodian victims than to the Khmer Rouge guerrillas, still threatening to grab power for a second time. CORKR had regional offices in nine US cities and affiliated groups in the UK and Australia.

CORKR's Executive Committee included Cambodian activists Chanthou Boua and Borasmy Ung, and among its more prominent members were academic Ben Kiernan, lawyer Gregory Stanton, film-maker David Munro and journalist John Pilger. Its energetic Executive

Director was Craig Etcheson, whose PhD thesis had been on 'The rise and demise of Democratic Kampuchea'. His attention was principally focussed on lobbying the Congress and the State Department to reverse US policy on the Khmer Rouge.

Among issues addressed by CORKR were the termination of Thai military assistance to the Khmer Rouge guerrillas, the ending of the aid and trade embargo against Cambodia, expansion of humanitarian assistance and the problem of landmines.

The most successful project launched by CORKR was the Cambodian Genocide Justice Act. The bill was initiated in 1991 by CORKR's Justice Committee, chaired by Greg Stanton, and drafted by Craig Etcheson working with the legislative staff of Senator Charles Robb from Virginia, a Democrat. It was presented unsuccessfully to two sessions of Congress. At last, after a deal in which the State Department agreed to drop its opposition to the bill,[1] it was eventually passed by the US Congress on 1 April 1994 and signed by President Bill Clinton in May.

The Cambodian Genocide Justice Act made it 'the policy of the United States to support efforts to bring to justice members of the Khmer Rouge for their crimes against humanity committed in Cambodia between April 17, 1975 and January 7, 1979'. The Office of Cambodian Genocide Investigations was established. The law also directed the US State Department to arrange for researchers and independent organisations to carry out expert investigation into Khmer Rouge crimes during the 1975–79 period.

In fact many US government officials were far from enthusiastic about the new mandate, fearing that it might also turn up incriminating evidence concerning US bombings and other acts of warfare against the countries of Indochina.

Lawyers Jason Abrams and Stephen Ratner were commissioned to prepare a legal analysis of the culpability of members of the Khmer Rouge regarding war crimes, genocide and crimes against humanity. They concluded by finding *prima facie* culpability for all three, and weighed various avenues for prosecution that might be followed.[2] In 1998 Stephen Ratner was appointed to be one of the UN's Group of Experts, whose report drew on the research Ratner and Abrams had undertaken in 1994–5.

Yale University's Cambodian Genocide Program (CGP) won the public tender contract for research, documentation and training. The founding Director of the CGP was Professor Ben Kiernan, an Australian historian and specialist on the Khmer Rouge at Yale

University. Craig Etcheson was appointed Program Manager; Helen Jarvis was Consultant for Documentation; and Youk Chhang headed the CGP's office in Phnom Penh, known as the Documentation Center of Cambodia.[3]

The initial grant of nearly half a million US dollars for two years was followed by a second grant of 1 million, enabling the mounting of an unprecedented effort to collect, organise, catalogue and make available primary source materials from the Khmer Rouge regime.[4]

In late 1995 an international conference was held in Phnom Penh, hosted by the CGP and the Documentation Center of Cambodia. The then two Co-Prime Ministers (Norodom Ranariddh and Hun Sen) spoke and Abrams and Ratner presented the results of their analysis of legal options.

In 1995 and 1996 the Cambodian Genocide Program held legal training courses for Cambodian government officials, judges and others involved in issues relating to grave violations of human rights. The Schell Center of Yale University was a partner in these programs.

By early 1997, at the end of its first phase, the Cambodian Genocide Program and the Documentation Center had amassed an enormous wealth of primary source documents and had begun to make them publicly available on the internet.[5]

The nature and number of documents collected in Phnom Penh greatly exceeded all expectations. Some 40,000 documents are being catalogued and analysed. They included confessions, photographs, prison note books, and personnel records from Tuol Sleng, as well as from other parts of the Khmer Rouge security apparatus, and a complete set of the court documents presented at the 1979 People's Revolutionary Tribunal.

The image database contains scanned images of more than 5,000 photographs from Tuol Sleng prison (S-21) – from one quarter to one third of the total number of people who were held there during the period of Khmer Rouge rule, most of whom were executed at Choeung Ek on the outskirts of Phnom Penh.

The biographic database by the end of 2002 contained records on more than 20,000 people, including over 10,000 who were detained in S-21, based on interrogation notes, confessions and prison records. It contains data on Khmer Rouge cadres detained as 'traitors' and many other Cambodian prisoners as well as those who served in the security apparatus.

The mapping of genocide sites throughout the country is an important aspect of the work of the CGP and the Documentation

Center. Sites were indicated by physical evidence and documents and interviews with villagers. The precise locations of over 550 genocide sites in 20 provinces have been recorded, using Global Positioning System (GPS) technology and the task is by no means complete. Every single district, sub-district and in fact almost every village in Cambodia appears to have some physical evidence of the crimes of the Khmer Rouge.[6]

The mapping field teams have to endure some of Asia's worst roads and many sites cannot be reached by car. The range of other transportation that has to be used includes ox-cart, motorbike, speedboat, boat rowed by a single oar and walking. Especially in the early years of this work teams were frequently provided with armed escorts by the provincial or local authorities, due to fear of harassment from residual Khmer Rouge forces, or from bandits. On one occasion in Kampot (1996), a team left a site just 15 minutes before a Khmer Rouge unit crossed the only access road. Another ever-present danger comes from the estimated 6 million mines that litter Cambodia's countryside. Demining is a painfully slow operation and most of the areas visited carry some risk, making a local guide an imperative.

Despite these obstacles, by May 2003, 170 of Cambodia's districts had been visited in 24 provinces. The teams had mapped 551 sites: 348 burial sites with 19,471 mass graves; 169 prisons and 77 memorials. The Documentation Center reports that information obtained during the site visits indicates that the graves may contain the remains of between 1,386,734 and 2,038,735 people. The estimates of how many died during the Pol Pot regime can safely be concluded as more than a million. The evidence points to more than 1.7 million and still counting but the precise figure cannot be declared with certainty.[7]

The Documentation Center of Cambodia became an independent NGO in January 1997. CGP's impressive series of research and publication activities includes *Sveng Rok Kapet* (Searching for the Truth), a Khmer language magazine with a circulation of over 20,000 copies each month, distributed free to every commune and district throughout the country. The magazine covers latest research and highlights some of the key documents from DC-Cam's voluminous archives, as well as reporting on legal, historical and political issues relating to the trial. Some of the articles are translated and published in an English-language version of the magazine.

In addition to the magazine, the Documentation Center has begun to publish books in both Khmer and English reporting the results of its research and also translating other works of relevance to its mission. In 2001 it launched an Accountability Project involving 'scouring the existing archives and examining newly arriving primary documentation to bolster individual case files for top Khmer Rouge leaders'. This was later extended 'to seek to locate and interview former cadres who served in the Democratic Kampuchea regime between 1975 and 1979'. In 2002 a new forensic project to study human remains at several memorial sites was launched.[8] A much earlier research project had been carried out by Vietnamese experts in 1988–89. The exhumed skulls at Choeung Ek were measured by a team from Ho Chi Minh University led by Professor Quang Quyen.[9]

The Documentation Center is seeking funding for a permanent home suitable to house the documents and provide research facilities. A competition for an architectural design was launched and in 2000 the Cambodian government donated a piece of land adjacent to the Tuol Sleng Genocide Museum for this purpose.[10]

The work of the Cambodian Genocide Program and the Documentation Center of Cambodia rekindled interest in a tribunal and presented a mass of potential evidence, available and waiting to be tapped by a prosecutor. Their work gave substance to the recommendations proposed in Abrams' and Ratner's legal study.

HAMMARBERG LIFTS THE LID

Thomas Hammarberg, the second Special Representative of the Secretary General for Human Rights in Cambodia, arrived in Phnom Penh in June 1996 bringing with him a very different outlook from that of his predecessor, Michael Kirby.

This former Swedish ambassador had in 1980 been appointed executive director of Amnesty International in London, and before that he had been a prominent Vietnam antiwar activist in the 1970s. David Hawk's photographic exhibition of Tuol Sleng prisoners was shown in Stockholm with his assistance.

After so many years of the UN saying nothing and doing even less over the Khmer Rouge justice issue, Thomas Hammarberg was from the outset determined to address this bitter record of international neglect. He took the view that contemporary human rights violations could not be solved while these crimes against humanity were ignored.

Thomas Hammarberg later recalled how he was compelled to act:

During my first mission to Cambodia (June 1996) it immediately became clear to me that the Khmer Rouge crimes in the 1970s still cast a paralysing shadow over Cambodian society. The killings of educated professionals had left gaps that still crippled the judiciary, the government administration, including the health and education structures. The moral impact was even more profound. The fact that no one had been held accountable for the mass killings and other atrocities had clearly contributed to the culture of impunity which was still pervasive in Cambodia.

Wherever I went in Phnom Penh or in the provinces I made a point of discussing the Khmer Rouge legacy and what ought to be done. One message became clear: the crimes were not forgotten. Almost everyone I met was personally affected, had suffered badly and/or had close relatives who died. Even now, more than two decades later, the overwhelming majority wanted those responsible to be tried and punished. The only argument against arrests and trials was the risk of further unrest and civil war. However, I heard many voices saying that not even that should be accepted as a reason to avoid seeking justice.

Decision-makers, almost without exception, had emotional and painful memories of the Democratic Kampuchea period in the seventies. King Sihanouk had tried to reason with the Khmer Rouge, been humiliated and even had family members killed. Hun Sen and several of his CPP colleagues had joined the Khmer Rouge movement, and had later defected to the Vietnamese side. Several of them had also lost family members. It is important to recognise this dimension of the Cambodian drama....[11]

The timing for Thomas Hammarberg's arrival on the scene could not have been better. The mid-1990s was a time of enthusiasm for the development of international law and justice to cope with massive human rights violations. The establishment of *ad hoc* international criminal tribunals to deal with the former Yugoslavia in 1993 and Rwanda in 1994[12] was accompanied by efforts to put international tribunals on a permanent footing. The Statute of Rome, adopted in July 1998, laid out the foundation for the ongoing international court that had been envisaged 60 years before. International justice and the enforcement of the UN Genocide Convention were finally starting to happen, albeit on a highly selective basis. An initiative to settle the long-overdue case of the Khmer Rouge crimes was likely to be well received, particularly by those who felt the actions of the international community needed to be set right.

The kidnap and execution of Christopher Howes, a de-miner working for the British NGO MAG (Mines Advisory Group) in March 1996, and his Cambodian partner Houn Hourth once more alerted the world to the continuing menace posed by the Khmer Rouge.

Pressure on the UK government resulted in two Scotland Yard detectives being deployed in Siem Reap province where the kidnapping took place. The Khmer Rouge predictably denied any knowledge of Howes and his fate remained a mystery for more than two years.

It was not until May 1998 that it was finally confirmed that Howes had been taken by a Khmer Rouge unit to Ta Mok's headquarters in Anlong Veng. The internal Khmer Rouge revolt against Ta Mok's leadership in Anlong Veng led to the first real evidence in the case and a Khmer Rouge defector, interviewed in Phu Noi camp in Thailand, provided eyewitness testimony of how the British de-miner was shot from behind on the orders of Ta Mok and his deputy General Kem Nguon who supervised the killing and was the last one to speak to Howes.[13]

The Khmer Rouge abducted and killed at least ten foreign tourists during the 1994–1998 period but Howes was the only one clearing landmines who received the same treatment. A Khmer Rouge defector, Major Phuan Phy, recalled that Khmer Rouge Colonel Kong clearly explained their motive for killing the de-miner, addressing a meeting of Khmer Rouge in 1996: 'We spend a lot of money and effort to lay mines and they come along and remove our mines. The Britisher disrupted our operations and our security, so he is the enemy.'[14]

Christopher Howes's important and dangerous work in trying to make Cambodia a safer place was honoured with the naming of a Phnom Penh street after him and he was posthumously awarded the Queen's Award for Gallantry.

Solving the Howes murder case involved unprecedented cooperation between Cambodian military intelligence chief, Colonel Dom Hak, Scotland Yard detectives and the Thai military.

Derek Fatchett, British Minister of State of the Foreign and Commonwealth Office, met with Hun Sen in May 1998 and strongly urged the Cambodian government to arrest Howes's murderers. He handed over Scotland Yard's final report on the case, naming those responsible including Ta Mok, General Khem Nguon, Colonel Kong, the cadre who pulled the trigger and three members of Khem Nguon's bodyguard unit, known only as Rim, Lim and San.

However it was a trifle difficult for Phnom Penh to arrest most of the people listed in the British investigation into Howes' murder case as Ta Mok and most of his gang that fled the mutiny in Anlong Veng were now known to be part-time residents of Thailand, hanging out just inside the Chong Sa-Nam Pass and protected by elements of a Thai infantry division stationed along the border. Such reports presumably had also reached the ears of the British military attaché and the ambassador in Bangkok. General Nhek Bun Chhay in an interview with Tom Fawthrop commented that, 'The Thai military wish to hide the role of Ta Mok and Khem Nguon and blame it all on Pol Pot because he is dead. The British Embassy [in Bangkok] knows this very well.'[15]

The Scotland Yard report failed to mention that Ta Mok's deputy, Khem Nguon, who arranged the execution party and offered a durian fruit to Howes for his last supper before he was shot, had been working closely with the Thai military over many years, and was in regular communication via his Thai-registered mobile telephone. In the circumstances, if Derek Fatchett had wanted to see the speedy apprehension of the suspects, the logical course was surely to pressure the Thai military to hand them over to Cambodian authorities to stand trial. Officially the Thai government again denied – as it had denied ever since 1979 – providing any sanctuary and support to the Khmer Rouge.

However the UK government's cosy ties with Thailand and strong business apparently precluded any strong pressure on the Thai military. It was far more convenient to divert responsibility for further action to the Cambodian authorities.

In December 1998 Generals Khem Nguon, Tem and Kong all returned to Cambodia on the understanding that if they surrendered to Phnom Penh authorities they would not be arrested. In response to energetic lobbying by Stephen Bridges, the British ambassador in Phnom Penh, deputy prime minister Sar Kheng has said any prosecution must wait until the time is right. Until March 2004 – nearly ten years after his kidnap and death – nobody had been charged with the Howes murder.

The Howes case was another illustration of how western governments turned a blind eye to Thai military's extensive links with their Khmer Rouge comrades throughout the UNTAC period and beyond. Indulgence of Thailand's violations of the 1991 Paris Peace Agreement, and failure to apply real pressure on the Thai military to sever their links with the Khmer Rouge, tragically prolonged the war in Cambodia. Up till 1990 western support for the Khmer Rouge is widely known. What is less well understood is the failure of the US,

Britain and France in the post-UNTAC period of 1993–1998 to take any action against Bangkok to end the continuing Khmer Rouge insurgency, fuelled with Thai logistics and other support.

In the second half of the 1990s within Cambodia too, an unprecedented opportunity to seek judicial accountability was presented by the Khmer Rouge's virtual disintegration under pressure from the government's 'push and pull' strategy. Military campaigns and internal divisions were the pushing factors, while cadres were pulled into defecting by offers of various kinds by both Funcinpec and the Cambodian People's Party. Convincing Ieng Sary and his forces to abandon Pol Pot in September 1996 was the most dramatic manifestation of this strategy.

Thomas Hammarberg decided that something should and indeed could be done to show the UN's determination to act. The genocide issue was raised in discussion of his first Cambodia report during the UN Commission on Human Rights session in April 1997 and, on the initiative of the United States, the following paragraph was included in its Cambodia resolution 1997/49:

> [The Commission] Requests the Secretary-General, through his Special Representative for Human Rights in Cambodia, in collaboration with the Centre for Human Rights, to examine any request by Cambodia for assistance in responding to past serious violations of Cambodian and international laws as a means of bringing about national reconciliation, strengthening democracy and addressing the issue of individual accountability.

In June Thomas Hammarberg reported the positive signal from the UNCHR to Cambodia's two Co-Prime Ministers and they both agreed to sign a letter to the Secretary General making such a request.[16]

On 21 June 1997 the letter was sent to the Secretary General asking 'for the assistance of the United Nations and the international community in bringing to justice those persons responsible for the genocide and crimes against humanity during the rule of the Khmer Rouge from 1975 to 1979'. The letter further stated:

> Cambodia does not have the resources or expertise to conduct this very important procedure. Thus, we believe it is necessary to ask for the assistance of the United Nations. We are aware of similar efforts to respond to the genocide and crimes against humanity in Rwanda and the former Yugoslavia, and ask that similar assistance be given to Cambodia.

We believe that crimes of this magnitude are of concern to all persons in the world, as they greatly diminish respect for the most basic human rights, the right to life. We hope that the United Nations and the international community can assist the Cambodian people in establishing the truth about this period and bringing those responsible to justice. Only in this way can this tragedy be brought to a full and final conclusion.

This letter was later to be cited as evidence that the prime ministers had initially requested an international tribunal and that Hun Sen later backtracked in rejecting such a solution. However, while the phrase 'similar efforts to respond to the genocide in Rwanda and the former Yugoslavia' certainly suggests an approach like the two international criminal tribunals for the former Yugoslavia and Rwanda, on the other hand the letter does not specify the form of assistance, nor the nature of the legal response requested.

13   The UN sees the light. Mary Robinson, UN Human Rights Chief in January 1998 was the first high-ranking UN leader to pay respect to the victims of the Khmer Rouge at the historical site of the Tuol Sleng extermination camp, now the genocide museum. Next to her, former deputy director, Lor Chandara, a survivor of the 'Killing Fields', who was one of those who originally set up the museum in 1979. (Tom Fawthrop)

The signing of the appeal to the UN was almost the last joint act by the Co-Prime Ministers. Within days relations between them were dangerously polarised, breaking down in early July into factional fighting on the streets between units of the armed forces aligned to Hun Sen and Prince Norodom Ranariddh respectively.

For two days the streets of Phnom Penh echoed with the sound of automatic gunfire and tank battles on the outskirts of the city. More than 70 civilians were killed and several Funcinpec military officers executed. First Prime Minister Prince Norodom Ranariddh fled into exile with many of his supporters. The CPP-aligned sections of the highly factionalised army emerged triumphant, but the government was then faced with a crisis of legitimacy. The US immediately halted all assistance to Cambodia (a situation that continues today, except for certain categories of aid channelled through NGOs). Other countries suspended or downgraded their assistance. Asean postponed consideration of Cambodia's admission to full membership.

The Credentials Committee of the United Nations General Assembly voted to hold the Cambodian seat vacant following a spirited intervention by opposition forces including Prince Norodom Ranariddh, Sam Rainsy and Son Soubert (all of whom had played a role in the Coalition Government of Democratic Kampuchea during the 1980s).

To add to the confusion of the time, the Khmer Rouge was entering into its final disintegration. The ageing Pol Pot had provoked a major leadership crisis in the Khmer Rouge a month earlier in Anlong Veng. On 9 June he ordered the murder of Son Sen, the Khmer Rouge leader most directly responsible for security and mass killings in his role as Minister of Defence from 1975–79.

The brutal elimination of Son Sen was entirely in keeping with the terror tactics of Democratic Kampuchea. Following Khmer Rouge 'best practice', his entire family was also put to death. The murders provoked an internal split and an anti-Pol Pot faction under the leadership of Ta Mok challenged 'Brother Number One' who fled into the jungle, headed for the Thai border. Pol Pot, ill and being carried in a hammock, and his small group of seven were soon captured by Ta Mok's forces and brought back to Anlong Veng.

The extent of the Khmer Rouge internal rifts was revealed in a kangaroo court trial of Pol Pot held on 25 July 1997, in which he was convicted of crimes against others in the leadership: of murder (of Son Sen and others) and of detention and attempted murder (of Ta Mok and Nuon Chea). There were no lawyers present, and Pol Pot was not allowed to present any defence.[17] No mention was made of any crimes against the people of Cambodia or under international humanitarian law during his period in power. He was sentenced to life imprisonment and his final months were lived out under house arrest in Anlong Veng, a few kilometres from the Thai border.

In a sudden reversal to the many years of US support for the Khmer Rouge, President Bill Clinton embarked on a new policy: to 'Get Pol Pot'. Following months of planning in early 1998, executive orders were made to the State and Justice departments to proceed towards the capture of Pol Pot and to prepare the logistics for spiriting him away to a third country.[18] Pol Pot at last appeared to be an easy target. According to some reports Ta Mok was offering to barter the disgraced and ailing 'Brother Number One' in exchange for large quantities of rice and other supplies.

But while he may have dangled the carrot for some tactical advantage there is serious doubt that Mok would ever have trusted US spooks enough to have brokered such a bizarre deal. Ta Mok's former deputy, Ke Pauk, provided a more convincing account of Mok's intentions: 'Ta Mok will never hand over Pol Pot to other country, because he is afraid that Pol Pot will incriminate him. More likely Ta Mok will kill him.'[19]

According to the Washington script, reportedly authorised 'at the highest level' and agreed to by the Thai military and by Cambodia, US special forces would enter Cambodia from Thailand, grab Pol Pot and bring him across the border. He would then be delivered to a US air force helicopter on standby and flown off to a Pacific island to be held in US custody until such time as a tribunal was set up, or a court found that was willing to try him. The favourite candidates included US-controlled Wake Island or the independent Pacific country of Palau.[20]

If US intelligence agencies had wanted to arrest Pol Pot at any time after 1979 it would have been a fairly simple task. He was a regular visitor to Thailand – really a part-time resident who spent many years enjoying sanctuary and protection. From 1979 Pol Pot ran strategy sessions, standing committee meetings and the war from his various Thai safe houses and Khmer Rouge bases dotted along the border and strongly protected by the Thai military. Close US-Thai military ties, including shared intelligence and joint military exercises, ensured that US intelligence agents monitoring the Cambodian border knew exactly where Pol Pot could be found. In the early 1980s he was ensconced in Saphan Hin and Borai in Trat province.[21] During the

UNTAC period he was based at Phnom Tum and Phnom Chat, north of the most important land border crossing at Aranyaprathet. Pol Pot's former photographer, Nhem Eng, confirmed that he was more often in Thailand than in Cambodia.[22]

Many Cambodians were cynical about Washington's plan to 'get Pol Pot'. Kim Bophana, a former Tourism Ministry employee who counted a total of 38 relatives killed during the Pol Pot regime, was not impressed. 'The US had the power to arrest Pol Pot 20 years ago. I feel angry they left it so late. Why did they wait so long?'[23]

During the 1980s it was the Phnom Penh government, Vietnam and their allies who advocated the arrest of Pol Pot, not western governments, who are usually the most vocal over human rights. It was not until the late 1990s that President Clinton and his advisors calculated that it was the politically convenient time to plan to capture the isolated and debilitated Pol Pot, and show concern over Khmer Rouge impunity.

In contrast to its attitude during the invasion of Panama and the spiriting away of General Noriega, a former CIA asset who became a thorn in Washington's side, the US government was circumspect about its role on Thai territory. It was decided that the Thai military had to be included in the operation, but Washington seemed to ignore one crucial fact. Thai generals, Khmer Rouge leaders and China all had a good many reasons to block any tribunal at which Pol Pot might name other names, parties and governments that had backed him over the years. The Thai military, with its long history as a military ally and business partner in gems and logging, was hardly likely to turn over Pol Pot for the sake of international justice. While the Pol Pot posse in Washington made optimistic statements that they had secured full cooperation from the Thai authorities and were only a hair's breath away from pulling it off, Thai generals and Bangkok's foreign ministry denied that they ever had approved of the plot.[24]

The 'get Pol Pot policy' also apparently met with resistance from CIA and US military intelligence that had been engaged in covert support for the Khmer Rouge insurgency since 1979. Clinton was forced to issue a presidential directive in a bid to get everyone on board with this policy shift.

The US plan had several alternatives. First choice was the establishment of an *ad hoc* UN tribunal (as for the former Yugoslavia and Rwanda). A draft resolution to create one was circulated at the UN by Ambassador David Scheffer. However, it was withdrawn before ever being formally introduced. The reason given was that members of the Security Council were suffering 'tribunal fatigue', but undoubtedly the real reason was the threat of a veto from China.

The US had a fall-back option, which counted on finding a country with universal jurisdiction. Germany, Canada, Belgium, Sweden, the Netherlands and Spain, for instance, had established such laws to prosecute ageing World War II war criminals. Some countries, especially Belgium, had already used such laws against those responsible for genocide in Rwanda and Bosnia.[25] But the willingness of these countries to host a Pol Pot tribunal was not at all clear. After the news of US intentions was leaked, Canadian authorities expressed some surprise that their country was in the list and denied any prior consultation.

But, whether or not it would be an international tribunal or a trial in another country, in keeping with the US unilateralist approach to international relations, the plan involved the US acting as the world's policeman rather than assisting Cambodia to bring Pol Pot to justice. As with the plan to snatch former President Noriega of Panama, grabbing Pol Pot would be another case of Washington exercising extraterritoriality as opposed to developing institutions of international justice. Other nations that were working energetically at that time to establish the International Criminal Court saw the US plan as diversionary from that process. Certainly such unilateral law-enforcement was consistent with the then US policy of weakening, and eventually refusing to join, the International Criminal Court.

On 9 April 1998 the *New York Times* reported the leaked story of the plan to capture Pol Pot. Six days later he was dead. Did the news of an impending arrest hasten his demise? Was he suffocated or poisoned by other Khmer Rouge leaders, or perhaps by an agent of a foreign power anxious to silence him for ever? Or did he die because he was a 73-year-old man with breathing problems and other ailments?

Serious doubts linger over the cause of death as no autopsy was permitted by the Thai military forces which controlled all access across the border to the Pol Pot deathbed. A Thai military medical team took blood samples and their spokesperson hurriedly declared that, 'Pol Pot died of natural causes'. But his body was cremated with indecent haste and the Thai military's medical report was never made public.

Although Pol Pot was known to be in poor health and needed oxygen equipment, several claims have been made that Pol Pot's death resulted from foul play. As mentioned above, Ke Pauk had predicted only two weeks earlier that Ta Mok would rather kill Pol Pot than surrender him. Other sources, including Funcinpec commander General Nhek Bun Chhay and Thai army chief General Surayud Chulanond, have alluded to the real cause of death being suffocation or poisoning. General Surayud delayed his revelation by many years and it was not until 2002 that the *Bangkok Post* reported that the Thai military medical team had misled the public at the time and had kept their true findings a secret. The Thai army commander admitted that the medical findings indicated that Pol Pot had not died from natural causes[26] but he did not reveal whether Ta Mok, the Thai military, China or another party should be held responsible for allowing Pol Pot to evade answering for his crimes in a court of law.

THE UN SEES THE LIGHT

Thomas Hammarberg reports that he met both Hun Sen and Norodom Ranariddh in New York in September 1997 and that they both confirmed that they still stood by the request of 21 June. 'As a strange historic coincidence, the issue that could have become deeply divisive, turned out to be the only one on which all political forces now agreed. On that basis I urged the General Assembly to respond positively and generously to the Cambodian request for assistance.'[27]

China made it clear to Thomas Hammarberg that it would not support the matter were it to be raised in the Security Council, the organ that had provided the mandate to establish the *ad hoc* tribunals for both the former Yugoslavia and Rwanda. So it was brought onto the agenda of the 53rd Session of the General Assembly, which included the following paragraphs in its resolution on the agenda item 'The human rights situation in Cambodia':

> Recognizing that the tragic history of Cambodia requires special measures to assure the protection of the human rights of all people in Cambodia and the non-return to the policies and practices of the past, as stipulated in the Agreement signed in Paris on 23 October 1991;
>
> Desiring that the United Nations respond positively to assist efforts to investigate Cambodia's tragic history, including responsibility for past international crimes, such as acts of genocide and crimes against humanity ....
>
> *Endorses* the comments of the Special Representative that the most serious human rights violations in Cambodia in recent history

have been committed by the Khmer Rouge and that their crimes, including the taking and killing of hostages, have continued to the present; and notes with concern that no Khmer Rouge leader has been brought to account for his crimes;

Requests the Secretary General to examine the request by the Cambodian authorities for assistance in responding to past serious violations of Cambodian and international law, including the possibility of the appointment, by the Secretary General, of a group of experts to evaluate the existing evidence and propose further measures, as a means of bringing about national reconciliation, strengthening democracy and addressing the issue of individual accountability.[28]

In December 1997, then, almost 19 years after the events, for the first time one of the two major organs of the UN acknowledged that massive human rights violations had occurred in Cambodia during the Democratic Kampuchea period of 1975–1979.

The Secretary General responded in July 1998 by appointing a Group of Experts with the following mandate: to evaluate the existing evidence with a view to determining the nature of the crimes committed by Khmer Rouge leaders in the years from 1975 to 1979; to assess, after consultation with the Governments concerned, the feasibility of bringing Khmer Rouge leaders to justice and the apprehension, detention and extradition or surrender to the criminal jurisdiction established; and to explore options for bringing to justice Khmer Rouge leaders before an international or national jurisdiction.

Sir Ninian Stephen (Australia) was appointed chairman of the group, whose other members were Judge Rajsoomer Lallah (Mauritius) and Professor Steven R. Ratner (United States). David Ashley (United Kingdom), who had written his PhD thesis on the Khmer Rouge, served as the group's advisor on Cambodian affairs and the Khmer Rouge, and as Khmer language interpreter.

After two decades of delay in bringing the Khmer Rouge to justice, in early 1999 the tide was decisively turning towards the setting up of a tribunal, with the presentation of its comprehensive 64-page report[29] – the touchstone for much of the later discussion and negotiations regarding the tribunal.

The Group of Experts' principal recommendation was to establish an *ad hoc* international tribunal such as those already in operation for Rwanda and the former Yugoslavia. 'Only a United Nations tribunal can be effectively insulated from the stresses of Cambodian politics ... that we believe would ultimately prove fatal to the viability of a Cambodian court ... from our perspective, the more insulated the tribunal can be from domestic politics, the better.'

The Group of Experts reported its recommendations under the following headings:

Evidence

First, the evidence gathered to date by researchers, scholars, the Documentation Center and others makes clear the commission of serious crimes under international and Cambodian law ... Second, the Group is of the opinion that sufficient physical and witness evidence currently exists or could be located in Cambodia, Viet Nam, or elsewhere to justify legal proceedings against Khmer Rouge leaders for these crimes.

A considerable part of the report examined the problems and prospects for successful prosecution of a number of different crimes, concluding:

Criminal nature of the acts committed

'Based on our review of the law and available evidence, the Group believes that it is legally justifiable to include in the jurisdiction of a tribunal that would try Khmer Rouge leaders for acts during the period from 1975 to 1979 the following crimes: crimes against humanity, genocide, war crimes, forced labour, torture and crimes against internationally protected persons, as well as the crimes under Cambodian law' of homicide, torture, rape, physical assault, arbitrary arrest and detention, attacks on religion and other abuses of governmental authority.

The Khmer Rouge in contemporary Cambodian politics and society

The Group of Experts stated that it could not 'act as legal experts in a vacuum', but rather had to take into account 'special political factors unique to Cambodia, and, in particular, the views of the Cambodian people and the role of the Khmer Rouge in domestic politics.'

It reported hearing 'an unambiguous demand for trials' from Cambodians in and out of Government. Although voiced by some non-Cambodians, no Cambodians took the view that 'Cambodia needs to move forward and no longer look at its past ... None suggested that peace and trials were irreconcilable, or that Cambodians saw peace as a substitute for justice ... We believe, based on our consultations in Cambodia, that, after 20 years of waiting, Cambodians are ready for trials and would embrace them.'

Feasibility of bringing the Khmer Rouge to justice

Although atrocities were undoubtedly committed by thousands of individuals, the Group of Experts concluded that the targets of investigation should be limited, due not only to logistical and financial implications, but also because 'a reopening of the events through criminal trials on a massive scale would impede the national reconciliation.'

They recommended that 'any tribunal focus upon those persons most responsible for the most serious violations of human rights during the reign of Democratic Kampuchea. This would include senior leaders with responsibility over the abuses as well as those at lower levels who are directly implicated in the most serious atrocities.' While refraining from offering any numerical limit, they suggested that the number tried 'might well be in the range of 20 to 30', and that the prosecutor 'should fully take into account the twin goals of individual accountability and national reconciliation.'

Options for bringing persons to justice

In examining options for a tribunal, the Group of Experts made what turned out to be its most controversial recommendations. The Group was 'of the opinion that domestic trials organized under Cambodian law are not feasible and should not be supported financially by the United Nations' due to corruption and manipulation by political forces resulting in lack of confidence in the Cambodian legal system. These factors likewise caused the Group to reject 'a mixed Cambodian-foreign court'.[30]

On the contrary, the Group strongly recommended 'the establishment of an ad-hoc international tribunal by the United Nations'. The Group preferred that this be done under the Security Council, although it presented a fall-back recommendation for General Assembly action.

Jurisdiction

The Group is of the strong opinion that ... the temporal jurisdiction of such a tribunal should be limited to the period of the rule of Democratic Kampuchea, i.e., 17 April 1975 to 7 January 1979 ... consideration of human rights abuses by any parties before or after that period would detract from the unique and extraordinary nature of the crimes committed by the leaders of Democratic Kampuchea.

The Group believes that a United Nations tribunal must have jurisdiction over crimes against humanity and genocide. These two crimes, especially crimes against humanity, constituted the bulk of the Khmer Rouge terror....' It went on to caution against including war crimes because of the fact that if war crimes were included in the jurisdiction of a court for Cambodia, it would have to include war crimes by persons from other States during the period of Democratic Kampuchea ... we believe this would divert the attention of the court from the bulk of the atrocities, and we thus believe war crimes should not be included.

Structure

The Group believed that there should be 'at least two trial chambers of three judges and an appeals chamber of five judges'. While it felt that 'ideally' the tribunal should include at least one Cambodian judge, 'it might be difficult for the United Nations to locate' such a person, but it recommended 'that the United Nations actively seek a qualified, impartial and appropriate Cambodian.'

Ignoring the problems that sharing a prosecutor had already caused the International Criminal Tribunals for the former Yugoslavia and Rwanda, the Group recommended that the Prosecutor of the International Criminal Tribunals for the former Yugoslavia and Rwanda should also take on the duty of being the Prosecutor for the proposed Cambodian tribunal, with 'a highly-qualified deputy specifically assigned to the Cambodia prosecutions with significant authority over day-to-day decisions.'

It specifically precluded the choice of a Cambodian Prosecutor or deputy, a decision that is absolutely essential in order to insulate them from the political pressures noted above and provide them with the independence to indict and try persons as they see fit in the best interests of justice and national reconciliation although they did admit the desirability of including Cambodians 'on the staff of the Prosecutor ... provided they in no way compromised the independence of the Prosecutor.'

Location

The Group 'reluctantly concluded that trials in Cambodia are fraught with too many dangers and that a United Nations tribunal should be located elsewhere' and they went on to recommend 'a city in a State situated somewhere in the Asia-Pacific region' in order to 'preserve for Cambodians the sense that trials were taking place in their own part of the world and not, for instance, in distant Europe, and would enable Cambodians to follow them closely. At the same time, its location would be insulated from the political pressures of Cambodia.'

The main office of the Deputy Prosecutor should be located at the site of the tribunal, but it should have a 'Phnom Penh-based investigations office'. The model was clearly based on the International Criminal Tribunal for Rwanda, whose location outside Rwanda has greatly weakened its impact on the country.

It went on to recommend that the UN cooperate with the Cambodian government to 'establish effective mechanisms for the dissemination of the proceedings to Cambodia. A dedicated television channel and radio channel, free of government control, is one option.'

The Experts' Conclusions

The Group of Experts concluded its report with a more detailed reasoning and justification for an international tribunal 'based upon our rejection of the option of trials in a Cambodian court'.

More than five years down the track, it is interesting to note that one of the reasons they argued against an unprecedented hybrid court, known as a mixed tribunal, was that 'the negotiation of an agreement and the preparation of legislation for and its adoption by the Cambodian National Assembly could drag on' and 'the Cambodian Government might insist on provisions that might undermine the independence of the court'. The Group opposed this solution as 'it seems likely ... to prolong the impunity of the Khmer Rouge leaders until many of the likely defendants have died or, equally bad, make the United Nations a party to a process not meting out impartial justice.' This assessment finds many echoes in subsequent legal critiques of the Khmer Rouge Tribunal Law that was promulgated in 2001 and the agreement of cooperation with the UN (analysed in Chapters 9 and 10).

The Group also considered and rejected other options such as 'an international tribunal established by multilateral treaty ... along the model of the International Military Tribunal at Nuremberg through a treaty among interested States' as well as trials established 'by and in a State other than Cambodia ... as a matter of international law under the theory of universal jurisdiction'. The latter idea could, however, be followed in the absence of a UN court. They considered that 'other forms of individual accountability beyond criminal trial', especially an 'investigatory commission, commission of inquiry, or truth commission' could be a useful supplement, but 'could not replace prosecutions for Cambodia in terms of the goals of justice, closure and accountability.'

In addition to its recommendations on the tribunal itself, the Group proposed that: 'following the establishment of a tribunal to try Khmer Rouge leaders, Cambodia enact a statute requiring all persons convicted by the tribunal to be thereupon barred from holding public office' (lustration); and 'the wealth of Khmer Rouge leaders convicted by a tribunal should represent a form of monetary reparation for the victims of the Khmer Rouge.'

The Report went on to make brief comments on more peripheral although still controversial issues, such as: avoiding delays; incorporating some aspects of civil law procedure, especially regarding admission of evidence; the importance of protection of evidence and witnesses; cooperation from other States; and, finally, the idea of incarceration in prisons meeting international standards in a State other than Cambodia.

The last section of the Group of Experts' report concluded:

> In asking for United Nations assistance, the Government of Cambodia has responded to what we sense is the desire of the Cambodian people for justice and their knowledge that it is impossible to simply ignore the past. Rather, it is necessary to understand the past and move beyond it by seeing justice done for those responsible for it. This process has been too long delayed for Cambodia and the time for action is here. If these and our other recommendations are pursued by the United Nations now, with the support of the Government of Cambodia, we believe they will lead to a process that will truly enable Cambodia to move away from its incalculably tragic past and create a genuine form of national reconciliation for the future.

The Group of Experts commissioned by the UN Secretary General had, then, concluded that given the weak state of the Cambodian legal system, the most credible option was an international tribunal, in which the only role reserved for Cambodians was as defendants. But the Cambodian authorities had as little confidence in UN-run legal shows as the international jurists who compiled the report had in the Cambodian legal system.

In January 1999 the conclusions of the Group of Experts began to be leaked, even before the report had been formally presented to the Cambodian government in February and to the General Assembly and the Security Council in mid-March.

Prime Minister Hun Sen was extremely vocal in response, insisting that Cambodia should conduct the trials, in contrast to the international tribunal favoured by the UN Group of Experts. Citing national sovereignty and Article 6 of the Genocide Convention, under which Cambodia is the primary state obligated to act, the Prime Minister argued the case for national trials but with international assistance. Furthermore, he reiterated his government's intention of meeting international standards of justice, this being one of the main reasons for requesting expert assistance, in addition to gaining international credibility and acceptance, especially from those states that had previously supported the Khmer Rouge.

The Cambodian Prime Minister indicated to Kofi Annan that the Cambodian government would not tamely accept the recommendations for the UN to set up an international tribunal.[31] Hun Sen upped the ante by suggesting that the scope of the trials should be expanded to include crimes committed before 1975 – including the saturation B52 bombings secretly ordered by Kissinger and Nixon – and after 1979, which would involve the complicity and culpability of other parties, both within and outside Cambodia.

Such a proposal taps into ideas to widen the jurisdiction of international law, holding accountable not only the easy targets among third world despots like Pol Pot and Slobodan Milosevic, but also those accused of war crimes at the top of the global power chain like the former US Secretary of State Henry Kissinger. Hun Sen was well aware of the political pressures and realities that would make any such widening of the scope of a tribunal a non-starter. But he evidently took some delight in reminding certain 'great powers' of their complicity both before 1975 and after the Pol Pot regime was toppled.

On 3 March 1999 the Cambodian government officially responded to the Group of Experts' report in a letter from the Foreign Minister, Hor Namhong, to the Secretary General cautioning that any decision to bring the Khmer Rouge leaders to justice must take account of Cambodia's need for peace and national reconciliation. There was an understandable fear that if the trial were not handled with care and confining the prosecution to the top Khmer Rouge leaders, it could sow panic among rank and file defectors and even trigger a renewed guerrilla war.

The government was at odds with the jurists' report on two key points: the report argued that trials should be held outside Cambodia, and second they should be completely controlled by the UN and international jurists. Many western human rights advocates airily dismissed Phnom Penh's expression of concern over the social impact of trials so soon after the country had put war and insurgency behind it. Amnesty International based in the UK, Human Rights Watch in the US and human rights groups inside Cambodia sharply opposed the Cambodian government position, depicting the Prime Minister as a power-hungry 'strongman' who opposed an international tribunal because of his desire to control and direct the court. While one side of the brewing controversy would inevitably focus on prime minister Hun Sen and his reputation for interfering in the administration of Cambodian courts, there was also another critical dimension to this UN-Cambodian legal tussle.

Many observers would agree that the UN had compromised its moral authority over Cambodia by its dismal record of complicity with the Khmer Rouge in the 1980s and even beyond. It was not only Hun Sen that faulted the UN on this score but also the third Special Representative of the Secretary General for Human Rights in Cambodia, Peter Leuprecht. During a Phnom Penh visit in 2002 the law professor from Canada appointed by Kofi Annan pointed out, 'the UN should be aware of its past record on Cambodia, a record that is not all glorious.'[32] From the outset relations were handicapped by the fact that not only did the UN not trust the Cambodian government, but equally the Cambodians had plenty of historical reasons for not trusting the UN. Unfortunately too many media reports were one-sided and neglected to mention the Cambodian grounds for distrust.

On 6 March 1999, the arrest of Ta Mok[33], one of the Khmer Rouge's most feared leaders, suddenly changed the possibility of a trial from the theoretical to the immediately tangible.

During the Democratic Kampuchea period Ta Mok had been commander of the southwest zone and a member of the Standing Committee of the Communist Party of Kampuchea. From early days during the Khmer Rouge regime, Pol Pot entrusted him with implementing major purges. After 1979 he established a guerrilla stronghold in Anlong Veng, the last bastion of the Khmer Rouge to fall to government forces.

After the death of Pol Pot and a Khmer Rouge mutiny in its Anlong Veng northern command in April 1998, Ta Mok led his loyalist forces across the border into Thailand and, courtesy of the Thai military's special Unit 838 and an Infantry battalion, they settled in a secure base near Nga-Sgaam Pass in Thailand's Sisaket province.

In early March 1999 the US pressured Thailand to abandon its long support and sanctuary to the Khmer Rouge leader and Ta Mok was pushed across the border by Thai authorities. The Cambodian government was tipped off and sent forces into the area to effect his arrest. After his capture he was flown in a helicopter to Phnom Penh and placed in a military jail, charged initially with violating the 1994 Law to Outlaw the Khmer Rouge and later with crimes against humanity.

Foreign Minister Hor Namhong met with the Secretary General on 12 March and conveyed the decision of the Cambodian government to put Mok on trial before a Cambodian court and to seek foreign assistance and expertise to that end. He expressed the government view that, under Article 6 of the Genocide Convention, Cambodian courts were fully authorised to conduct any such trial. Furthermore, he again queried the credibility of a UN international tribunal in the light of the General Assembly's support for the Khmer Rouge throughout the 1980s.

In submitting the Experts' Report to the Security Council and the General Assembly, Kofi Annan also had to bear in mind that Phnom Penh had welcomed the recommendations to try the Khmer Rouge leaders, but rejected the model proposed – an international tribunal.

The Secretary General remained concerned about 'the credibility of any trial process' and, given the poor assessment by the experts of the Cambodian legal system, he held the view that 'if international standards of justice, fairness and the process of law are to be met in holding those who have committed such crimes accountable, the tribunal in question must be international in character.' He concluded: 'I stand ready to assist the General Assembly, the Security Council, the Government and people of Cambodia in bringing about a process of judicial accountability, which alone can provide the basis for peace, reconciliation and development.'

Then on 9 May a second significant arrest was made – of Kaing Khek Iev, known widely as Duch, the director of S-21 (Tuol Sleng prison, the very icon of Khmer Rouge barbarism). Like Mok, Duch was charged with violating the 1994 law banning the Khmer Rouge, and additionally was charged with murder.[34]

The arrest of Duch followed press revelations of his whereabouts. British photographer Nic Dunlop was the first one to stumble upon him in the remote western district of Samlaut. The arrest was clearly a response to this publicity, because it had long been rumoured that Duch was living in western Cambodia and it seemed probable that military authorities knew his whereabouts in spite of his assumed identity as a born-again Christian named Pin, who had acquired employment with Battambang's branch of the Education Ministry. The fact that the Cambodian government had two prime suspects in custody exerted considerable pressure on the UN Secretariat to consider options other than an exclusively international tribunal as recommended by their Group of Experts.

The Secretary General's letter of 15 March provided a way out by suggesting that the trial could be acceptable to the United Nations, if it were 'international in character'. Translating the algebraic formula 'domestic in form, but international in character' into a judicial process that would be acceptable to both sides was to take years of complex, and at times tense, negotiations.

8

The Trauma of a Nation: Searching for Truth, Justice and Reconciliation

25 December 1998 was one of the strangest days in the history of Cambodia. Two of the world's most wanted men, Nuon Chea and Khieu Samphan, prime suspects for the Cambodian genocide tribunal, were star attractions at a government-organised press conference at a luxury hotel in Phnom Penh.

Nuon Chea, known as 'Brother Number Two', and Khieu Samphan sat without handcuffs. They had just returned from a sanctuary in Thailand under a deal that guaranteed them police protection instead of police custody. The Thai government had imposed a 'no arrest 'condition on the Cambodian government in exchange for repatriating them.

1998 was the final year of the Khmer Rouge insurgency. Their last bastion, Anlong Veng in the north of the country, fell in April after a mutiny that ousted Ta Mok. Government forces chased Ta Mok, Nuon Chea and Khieu Samphan across the border, where they received the protection and hospitality from the Thai military they had become accustomed to in the years since 1979.

When they appeared in Phnom Penh they got a taste of public outrage when a retired civil servant angrily heckled them outside their Thai-owned luxury hotel, the Royal Phnom Penh. A survivor of their slave labour camps shaking with anger, 68-year-old Veng Khieng declared that 60 of his relatives had died during the Khmer Rouge reign. He shouted at and cursed the pair as they left Phnom Penh for the final leg of a Government-arranged tour of the country they had turned into a prison. The VIP tour included a trip to the seaside at Kampong Som and the temples of Angkor. 'Why put them in an air-conditioned hotel? They should sleep in a rice field like we had to when we were under their rule,' Veng Khieng told reporters after the guerrilla leaders' motorcade left. 'I feel relaxed inside after cursing them, but I would have been more satisfied if I'd had the opportunity to punch them three or four times.'[1] Other Cambodians over the years had wanted to inflict much worse on their tormentors. The VIP treatment bestowed on Khieu Samphan and Nuon Chea after they arrived in Phnom Penh outraged many.

It was 20 years since the Pol Pot regime had been ousted. The Khmer Rouge war was over. Guerrilla zones had been liberated and all territory was once again under government control. Cambodia was at peace for the first time since 1970. Two principles – the need for national reconciliation and the longstanding demand for a Khmer Rouge tribunal – came into sharp collision over the VIP welcome accorded to Nuon Chea and Khieu Samphan. While people acknowledged the need to receive them as defectors (and not prisoners) signifying the end of the war, even members of the ruling CPP were astonished by the red carpet treatment. Im Sethy, currently Secretary of State for Education, confided to the authors 'we were very shocked by Khieu Samphan and Nuon Chea being received as VIPs'.[2] Hun Sen perplexed and even infuriated many by his comment after a cabinet meeting: 'If we bring them to trial it will not benefit the nation, it will only mean a return to civil war. We should dig a hole and bury the past.'

This was a defining moment in Cambodia's culture of impunity. Most major crimes in the country were never solved. Both political and non-political crimes are seldom seriously investigated. Thomas Hammarberg, the UN's Special Human Rights representative for Cambodia, had concluded, 'The major human rights problem in Cambodia, in my assessment, is impunity ... They see these mass murderers going scot-free, and even treated as VIPs, while people with minor crimes go to jail.'

Many people could not see why they should be punished for a single murder or robbery if the Khmer Rouge leaders who had killed thousands could nonchalantly walk free. Moeun Chhea Nariddh, a Cambodian journalist, commented that even after 20 years, putting the Khmer Rouge on trial is vitally important.

> It would be a lesson: that you cannot escape justice. It would be fair to minor criminals – thieves and robbers who have been tried for stealing a bicycle or stealing some money. I share the idea of releasing all these criminals if you don't put the Khmer Rouge killers on trial.[3]

Cambodian legal rights and human rights NGOs strongly backed the tribunal not only to bring Khmer Rouge leaders to justice, but also to serve as a legal cornerstone symbolising an end to impunity.

Hun Sen received so much flak that he felt obliged to clarify his position and defend himself in a six-page declaration issued on 1 January 1999. Had he forgotten about a trial for the Khmer Rouge leaders? Hun Sen declared, 'It is not that I forgot to mention it. But ... I am having to talk about peace before anything else.'

Now for the first time he decided to go public on the secret diplomacy with Bangkok over the return of these two Khmer Rouge leaders. The Prime Minister stated that 'the neighbours' (meaning Thailand) would only hand them over 'if we accept to reintegrate them back into the fold of the nation'.[4] Given Thailand's long history of support for the Khmer Rouge, it is not very surprising that Bangkok's conditions for handing them over to Phnom Penh stipulated no arrests.

Hun Sen went on to refute any suggestion that he had promised them amnesty or pardon, 'I have provided no guarantee to any particular persons to be free from the charges of the court.' And he concluded by saying, 'The real victory of peace does not mean killing all the enemy but to do everything possible so that the enemy stop fighting in a peaceful way.'

Later Hun Sen later commented wryly on the hypocrisy of many who criticised his actions:

Compare the way I received Khieu Samphan and Nuon Chea and the way others have received them in the past. I received these people as they surrendered to the government, to live a life as normal citizens. From 1979 to 1994 others received Khieu Samphan as head of state and even provided him with escort cars when he went with Pol Pot and Ieng Sary to speak in New York at the UN. They were received as equals with other heads of state. Before the 1993 elections, when I met Khieu Samphan at the Royal palace, I carried with me the Genocide Convention of 1948. I read the articles of the Genocide Convention to Khieu Samphan and told him: you have to be arrested. Then, nobody did anything to Khieu Samphan! In fact, I was ordered by UNTAC to provide them with better security. The ones who supported the Khmer Rouge in the past should be courageous enough to state the facts.[5]

Indeed, the December 1998 reception of Khieu Samphan and Nuon Chea raises many of the same issues as were generated by the special treatment accorded to Ieng Sary. Former Pol Pot foreign minister Ieng Sary, a man that a great many Cambodians want to see arrested for crimes against humanity, today lives in a lavish twelve-room mansion in the capital Phnom Penh, eats in the best Chinese restaurants and attends wedding parties. He even travelled for several years on a diplomatic passport, courtesy of foreign minister Hor Namhong.[6]

Ieng Sary, once deputy prime minister in a regime that abolished family life and eradicated money, has metamorphosed into a member of Cambodia's wealthy elite owning houses in Bangkok, Pailin and Phnom Penh. (He has at least two houses in Phnom Penh and his daughter and grandchildren occupy the Bangkok house.)

The generosity of the government's treatment of Ieng Sary in permitting him to keep his ill-gotten wealth based on smuggling gems and logs, and to build a luxury mansion in Phnom Penh, makes many people uneasy and even outraged. Heng Sophal, a renowned Phnom Penh artist who like millions of other Cambodians will never forget the killings, the pain and the trauma of the Pol Pot period commented, 'I am very, very angry when I see Ieng Sary's face. He brought Cambodia down to zero. It is an insult to what the people suffered under his regime to see how well Ieng Sary lives today.'[7]

Ieng Sary's death-sentence from the 1979 trials was revoked under a Royal Pardon granted by the King in 1996 at the request of Prime Minister Hun Sen and his then Co-Prime Minister Prince Norodom Ranariddh. This pardon was Ieng Sary's condition for leading a mass defection of the Khmer Rouge based in Pailin and Phnom Malai which accelerated the final collapse of the Pol Pot insurgency. It was accompanied by an amnesty for prosecution under the 1994 Law to Outlaw the Khmer Rouge.

Hun Sen argued: 'For the sake of the nation we had to do it. To destroy 70% of the KR forces, we needed to pay a price too – that was the amnesty provided to Ieng Sary.'[8]

Some observers, including Hans Corell's team, saw this as an indication that Hun Sen would not respect the independence of a tribunal and would actively obstruct a prosecution of Ieng Sary. However, local diplomats and other observers are more used to the conflicting signals of the loquacious prime minister. Former US ambassador to Cambodia Kent Wiedemann confided: 'In private conversations the prime minister agreed that the tribunal would lack credibility without the prosecution of Ieng Sary.'[9]

Hun Sen's public utterances sometimes sowed confusion and dismay among those who yearned for justice. There were fears that a badly handled prosecution could panic rank and file Khmer Rouge defectors into thinking they could be arrested. In the countryside there was almost no public information about the terms of reference of the tribunal. The issue of whether the prosecutors would only charge the top leaders or go after smaller fish was not even clearly understood among the more sophisticated urban populace of the capital, never mind those in the remote districts of Pailin and Anlong Veng who seldom saw a newspaper.

Exactly these fears surfaced during the 2003 election campaign. Former Khmer Rouge who made up most of the Pailin electorate expressed strong anxiety about the forthcoming tribunal. These fears were exploited by opposition leader Sam Rainsy who suggested only a vote for his party would protect them from being prosecuted.

Both Pailin candidates came from the ranks of the Khmer Rouge. The victorious CPP candidate Y Chhien was at one time a Pol Pot bodyguard and later became a Khmer Rouge general in command of the Pailin zone. After the 1996 defections led by Ieng Sary, which split the guerrilla movement, Y Chhien was appointed as Pailin's governor. The rival candidate, from the Sam Rainsy Party, was Ta Mok's niece, Ven Dara.

The arrest of Ieng Sary would no doubt spark anger from his son, Ieng Vuth (now the Deputy Governor of Pailin) and a small coterie of his supporters and perhaps cause some more general apprehension. But after years of futile fighting most defectors are in no mood to return to the battlefield.

Whatever one may think about the tone of the reception given to Nuon Chea and Khieu Samphan, the amnesty accorded to Ieng Sary, or the death of Pol Pot, following five years of complex strategy by Hun Sen, it was the last gasp for the Khmer Rouge. What the UN with its huge budget and 12,000 strong peacekeeping forces had failed to do – disarm the Khmer Rouge – had now been accomplished by the Cambodian government. The Khmer Rouge insurgency had been eliminated and, after 30 years of war, the nation could finally savour peace. But Cambodia emerged from this long period of conflict with weak political and economic institutions based on a severely damaged culture and society.

PUBLIC REACTIONS

Among Cambodians who had waited for nearly 20 years for the opportunity to hold these Khmer Rouge leaders accountable, the government's seemingly inconsistent attitude towards a trial caused confusion and anxiety. The CPP's legitimacy was based on being the only major party that had fought the Khmer Rouge in every venue – on the battlefield, at UN forums and at the Paris Peace talks.

This sudden twist in the direction of coddling some former Khmer Rouge leaders in the eyes of many Cambodians went far beyond the legitimate need for reconciliation. It flew in the face of the distinction made in the Salvation Front platform of December 1978 between rank and file Khmer Rouge being accepted back into the community, but the leaders being called to account for their 'blood debts'. Were the lines now becoming blurred by some CPP leaders and others who had lost their appetite for a serious examination of the past? Hun Sen's ill-chosen words about digging a hole to bury the past hit a raw nerve in a Cambodia already littered with mass graves.

For many who had heard the government rail so often against the leaders of the genocide and called so many times for them all to be put on trial, this 'softly softly' treatment stuck like a fish-bone in the throat and smacked of betrayal. Some CPP supporters even tore up their party membership card in disgust at this apparent about-face by the prime minister.[10]

The genocide tribunal, a subject that had lain dormant in the Khmer psyche for some years, was re-awakened by the defections. Dr Kao Kim Hourn, who heads the Cambodian Institute for Cooperation and Peace (CICP) observed, 'This is the major topic now that people talk about,' he said. 'People from all walks of life have begun to question what happened in that period. They share a common past, a common suffering and therefore a common outrage when they see these mass killers returning to the mainstream of society.'

Educated in the US, Dr Kao Kim Hourn returned to Phnom Penh during UNTAC time and became a respected political analyst. He is president of the recently established University of Cambodia. Reflecting on Cambodians becoming more assertive he concluded,

It is becoming difficult for the government to just dictate to the people and ignore public opinion. People have reached a certain level of maturity. They have more access to information. With popular emotions stirring, internal pressure on the government has begun to build up ... National reconciliation at all costs? Bury the past? Forgive and forget? No. I don't think that is the case now.

Hun Sen's declaration spurred Cambodians to make their feelings known. The Cambodian Human Rights Action Committee circulated a petition to the Secretary General of the United Nations. Despite harassment by local authorities in six provinces and even one threatened arrest, they managed to gain 84,195 signatures for the petition, which read: 'We, the people of Cambodia whose signatures and thumbprints are attached, request the United Nations to establish an international tribunal to try the Khmer Rouge leaders for the mass killings and crimes against humanity committed during their rule from 1975 to 1979.'[11]

Chea Sophara, former governor of Phnom Penh and a member of the CPP Central Committee is a vocal supporter of a tribunal. During the Pol Pot regime his father died from lack of food and medicine, and seven out nine died from among his immediate family. Even after he was sacked from the governorship as a scapegoat for the anti-Thai riots in January 2003, Sophara retained a popular following among the citizens of Phnom Penh. 'We must not forget justice,' Chea Sophara told the authors. 'Among CPP members, ninety percent strongly want a tribunal.' 'Ieng Sary? A must. He was a leader, he must be included.'[12]

At other times when there are no defections, arrests or other focussing events to spur public reaction, most Cambodians may appear to be rather quiescent on a subject of such magnitude. Many foreigners – diplomats, aid workers and consultants – over the years have argued that the average Cambodian is more concerned about economic survival than about a tribunal. This has given rise to a common misconception that it is really the international community, and not the Cambodians themselves, who are pushing for a Khmer Rouge Tribunal and that Cambodians are far more concerned with improving their meagre living standards.

But in the view of several psychologists who have started to study the legacy of trauma in Cambodia, other factors have contributed to pushing the demand for justice on to the back burner of everyday consciousness.

During the mass killings of the late 1970s Cambodians had no choice but to become experts at remaining silent. Men, women and children learned to contain and repress the horrors they had witnessed.

One of the few studies carried out on the subject, the Truth, Justice, Reconciliation and Peace in Cambodia project directed by Laura McGrew reported:

A common view is that villagers are only thinking about their next meal and how to survive ... However, in the few discussions held with villagers, several started out by saying they didn't think about the trial (several had not even heard of the possibility of a trial), but by the end of a several-hour discussion, obviously had views on the issue of accountability for the KR regime, and some felt very strongly there should be a trial.[13]

International aid workers and journalists in Cambodia during the 1980s were constantly bombarded with personal accounts of family members savagely murdered. Economic survival has always been a pressing concern. But at that time the day-to-day battle for survival co-existed with passionate feelings about the need for revenge, justice or accountability and anger was never far beneath the surface. It is only after so many long years of being denied the opportunity for a Khmer Rouge trial that many ordinary people have gradually eliminated it as a topic of everyday conversation. In an effort to rebuild their lives and move on, they have built their own mental warehouse in which to store away their tortured memories.

THE NATIONAL TRAUMA

That Cambodians were traumatised by the horrors of the Pol Pot regime has been widely accepted as political fact, yet almost nothing has been done to repair the damage inflicted on the national psyche.

Although there is little systematic research with which to attempt to measure the trauma, it is evident that the memory of the Khmer Rouge period has resulted in many tens of thousands of Cambodians suffering from depression and other mental illness, sometimes termed as post-traumatic stress disorder.

In the years of reconstruction of Cambodian society after 1979 psychological diagnosis and treatment were not seen as priorities. While political acknowledgement was made of the national trauma, the crisis faced by individuals was not addressed and they mostly suffered in silence.[14]

A medical sociologist at the University of Cambodia in Phnom Penh, Dr Nou Leakhena, says that untreated mental health problems among Cambodians have became an epidemic, but the government is not addressing the issue. 'The country needs a national therapy session.' The US-trained sociologist argues, 'What keeps Cambodia in stagnation for so long is that the psychological past remains unresolved. Putting the Khmer Rouge leaders on trial is a start. The tribunal can be a first step in the healing process and it would show that the people's suffering has not been ignored.'[15]

Most research studies on the traumatisation of Cambodians who lived under the Pol Pot regime have been confined either to the refugee camps in Thailand or to Khmer refugees in the US. These studies have not accounted for anxiety-specific patterns seen in those who have remained inside the country. For example, adults may have heightened anxiety symptoms during *pchhum ben* (season of honouring ancestors and others who have died) because they experience the roaming spirits of deceased ancestors. If they cannot make the obligatory pilgrimage to seven pagodas during this time, their symptoms increase.[16]

The only available mental health services after 1979 were provided by monks, traditional healers, fortune tellers and physicians who lacked psychiatric assessment or counselling training. In 1992, the Ministry of Health created a Mental Health Sub-committee and began developing psychosocial health strategies.

Cambodia today has only one psychiatric hospital, Takhmau Hospital in Kandal, which was built in 1935 and in colonial times was the only psychiatric hospital for the whole of Indochina.[17] Takhmau Hospital is linked to the Khmer Rouge not only by reason of the traumas of its current patients: in 1975 the hospital was used by the Khmer Rouge as the site for the S-21 prison, before it was moved into the Tuol Sleng high school in Phnom Penh proper in mid-1976.

The Transcultural Psychosocial Organization (TPO), is one of the few NGOs to focus on mental health inside the country, and it is now under the direction of a Cambodian specialist in the field, Dr Sotheara. TPO provides specific and intense education to psychiatrists. Both Dr Sotheara and Dr Nou Leakhena advocate integrating mental health services into the community and enlisting village support.

Psychiatrists expect that the tribunal will trigger many painful memories and that some Cambodians, in coming to grips with the past, may well suffer the phenomenon of re-traumatisation.

Dr Peg LeVine, psychologist and anthropologist from Monash University in Australia, has conducted a longitudinal study on couples married by the Khmer Rouge. She contemplates 'the implications for a potential Khmer Rouge tribunal with regard to people's well being and the lingering presence of the animistic context – dynamics worth pondering for any strategic prevention and intervention.'[18]

But on balance a well run tribunal is seen as an important landmark in the mental health of the nation. Cambodia's mental health director,

Dr Ka Sunbaunat, commented, 'some patients see the Khmer Rouge trial as therapy in itself. Exposure of wrongdoing helps them put their lives back together again'. Many others argue that the tribunal can also assist in making some historical sense of the past.

The widespread demand for justice is often tempered by a concern that it should not be at the expense of peace. The newfound peace is still fragile and tens of thousands of former Khmer Rouge soldiers need to be integrated into mainstream society. The demand for justice has to be balanced with the needs of reconciliation. The same challenge faces other post-conflict societies, including South Africa, Sierra Leone and East Timor. Laura McGrew acknowledges that 'Justice must be balanced with political realities, and international human rights with national considerations.'[19] But in the case of Cambodia, the harsh judgement of many NGOs of the Khmer Rouge Law passed in 2001 lacked any sensitivity towards such 'national considerations' (see Chapters 9 and 10).

By the year 2000, UN and Cambodian legal teams were engaged in complex negotiations over setting up a tribunal but, as Chea Vannath observed, while the positions of the international community and the government on a tribunal were heard, the voice of the Cambodian people was missing. The Center for Social Development (CSD), a Cambodian NGO funded from abroad, organised a series of public forums in Battambang, Phnom Penh and Sihanoukville in which hundreds of people, including former Khmer Rouge soldiers, were given a rare opportunity to speak their mind and express their ideas on how to deal with Cambodia's tragic past. One of these debates was televised. CSD published a booklet providing a summary of views expressed.[20]

WHY A TRIBUNAL?

The myriad reasons why Cambodia needs a tribunal can be broken roughly into two categories: to address the wide-ranging concept of justice for the victims and the survivors; and to contribute to the rule of law, accountability and the foundations of the Cambodian legal system.

Justice for all

The one thing that just about all, Cambodians and foreigners alike, can agree on is that a trial of the Khmer Rouge leaders would not be the same as a routine murder or robbery case. A Khmer Rouge

CENTER FOR SOCIAL DEVELOPMENT SURVEY ON
KHMER ROUGE TRIALS COMPILED FROM 632 VOTES RECEIVED

Questionnaire One

Which solutions can bring about a true national reconciliation?
(multiple choice allowed)

There is no need to try the former Khmer Rouge leaders. The past should be forgotten
55 votes (9%)

The former Khmer Rouge leaders should publicly admit their faults and apologise
187 votes (30%)

A public religious ceremony should be held to put the bad karma of the past to an end
95 votes (15%)

More time should be spent educating people to be more aware before the Khmer Rouge trial takes place
155 votes (25%)

The former Khmer Rouge leaders must be tried
429 votes (68%)

The trial should apply to persons of all regimes, both before 1975 and after 1979, and not just to Khmer Rouge leaders
320 votes (51%)

Questionnaire Two

Will the trial of former Khmer Rouge leaders be advantageous or disadvantageous to true national reconciliation?
(multiple choice allowed)
advantageous: 517 votes (82%)
disadvantageous: 217 votes (34%)
abstentions: 10 votes (2%)

Tribunal is intended to deliver judgment on how various senior leaders participated in a series of massive and systematic crimes committed during a four-year period, 1975–79.

Above all it is expected to come to grips with the darkest chapter in Cambodian history, to record and explain the past. Time and again Cambodians have expressed a hunger for answers. 'The tribunal has to answer questions about what really happened? Why did the Khmer Rouge kill their own people?' asked Dith Munty, one of Cambodia's few surviving lawyers in 1979 and now chief judge of the Supreme Court.[21]

But the tribunal could disappoint those who expect the Khmer Rouge leaders to confess everything and tell the truth, the whole truth and nothing but the truth. Occasional interviews with Nuon Chea and Khieu Samphan have demonstrated their stubborn state of denial.[22]

Much will depend on the willingness of Kaing Khek Iev, known as Duch (the head of the S-21 prison at Tuol Sleng, who in later years converted from torturer-in-chief to an evangelical disciple of Jesus) to explain how other Khmer Rouge leaders directed his machinery of interrogation, torture and death.

Many of the victims see the tribunal in terms of the catharsis of justice. After decades of suffering they look forward to that day when all Cambodians will finally get the chance to catch a glimpse of the Khmer Rouge leaders being arraigned as prisoners of the court and forced to account for their crimes.

None can express this feeling with more poignancy than the survivors of S-21, the Tuol Sleng extermination centre. Chhum Mey, now 70 years old, is one of only three survivors from S-21 who were still alive at the time this book was written.[23] During an interview he broke down crying as his memories of the screams, the repeated electric shocks and other tortures crowded his mind once more.[24]

Youk Chhang from DC-Cam feels all Cambodians 'live under a cloud and cannot have peace of mind until this terrible chapter is resolved. Without closure the Cambodian psyche remains tormented. The past is always with us and will always haunt us.'[25]

In his editorial in the August 2003 issue of *Searching for the truth*, the monthly magazine of the Documentation Center of Cambodia, Youk Chhang wrote of the need for individual victims to achieve psychological healing by letting go of their anger and blame against all the Khmer Rouge, contrasting this with the tasks and objectives of a trial – to bring the perpetrators to account for their crimes. Youk Chhang suggests that 'forgiveness' has a place in the former setting but not in the latter – at least not until after trial and sentencing has been carried out.

For many Cambodians the revelations of a tribunal, the painful recounting of the horror, is a necessary part of the healing process. The CSD survey found that 52 per cent of survivors were willing to come forward and give evidence in a trial.

But the tribunal cannot be a complete panacea. The idea of a truth commission has been raised many times to address lower-ranking Khmer Rouge as part of the national reconciliation process. But much of the documentation function of such a truth commission has been carried out by the Cambodian Genocide Program and DC-Cam. At the same time a process of community reconciliation has been taking place in rural villages since 1979, accelerating after the 1993 elections.

Some critics of a tribunal ask why should a poor developing nation like Cambodia spend so much time, energy and resources on a tribunal? Why not concentrate on building the future rather than dwelling on the past? Supporters of a tribunal dismiss this kind of thinking as a false dichotomy – the issue is not a choice between more food or more justice. Human rights is about both. One cannot be a substitute for the other.

Likewise, one is not forced to choose either to deal with the past or to focus on the future. The Khmer Rouge Tribunal will deal with both, past and future. Thun Saray, director of Adhoc, one of the leading local human rights NGOs, argues that the tribunal must be a deterrent to future generations: 'Who will guarantee genocide does not happen again in Cambodia if we don't prosecute now?'[26] Beyond issues of law and justice it has the potential to address the conscience of future generations to understand that what happened once must never happen again.

The tribunal also has to take into account the shocking ignorance of young Cambodians (more than 60 per cent of whom are under the age of 24) who have little or no knowledge of the Khmer Rouge period. Even university-educated graduates have been known to say, 'we don't believe Cambodians killed their own people. It must have come from some foreigners behind Pol Pot.'

The schools stopped teaching about the Khmer Rouge regime after the 1991 Paris Peace talks were signed. Education ministry official Im Sethy vividly remembers that during UNTAC an international staff member of Unicef chastised him for the using the word 'genocide' on the grounds that UN-era of peacekeeping had swept the whole subject under the carpet of reconciliation between all factions. After the 1993 election, the CPP and Funcinpec were unable to reach any agreement on how to teach the history of the Khmer Rouge in the classroom.

In 2001 a fresh effort was made to introduce a chapter on Cambodian contemporary history into the school curriculum, but Funcinpec objections to the resulting text (on points unrelated to the Khmer Rouge) led to it being withdrawn and re-written and it has not yet been re-introduced into the schools. To this day only two sentences in Cambodian secondary school history texts refer to the Khmer Rouge era. With so many parents unable to discuss it with their children, it can be concluded that a whole generation has grown up in ignorance of the most tragic chapter in Cambodian history.

Law, Accountability and the Foundations of the Cambodian Legal System

The realm of justice is far broader in scope than the cold mechanics of law. Law is essentially no more than a set of rules by which a democratic society hopes peacefully to attain the objective of justice.

All too many cases in Cambodia, including political murders, have never been seriously investigated. Even a senior CPP government official stated that Funcinpec Secretary of State Ho Sok was murdered while in police custody inside the Ministry of Interior headquarters in July 1997. No one has ever been arrested, although an eyewitness implicated a high-ranking police officer.

Thomas Hammarberg put it thus:

> People in positions of power, people with money, people with weapons – they can do whatever they want against the small people. It's like a cancer in society. It makes people feel vulnerable and powerless. Part of the violence we see in Cambodia, with people settling scores with weapons on a local level, is that they do not trust the system of justice.[27]

Human rights NGOs have set their sights on utilising the Khmer Rouge Tribunal to revamp the legal system and end the climate of impunity. The failure to prosecute the most serious human rights crime of all – the Cambodian genocide – has set the worst possible precedent and undermined the credibility of the entire legal system. A fair trial of the Khmer Rouge and the punishment of the guilty after due process is widely seen as the only way to lay the foundation for human rights.

CAMBODIAN COURTS, NGOS AND THE QUALITY OF JUSTICE.

Cambodia's vocal NGO community often expresses the hope that the tribunal will provide a model to guide Cambodian courts out of their current malaise, riddled with corruption and incompetence. Of all the many reasons why Cambodians and foreigners alike see the compelling need for a tribunal, the notion that it would become the model of 'flawless justice' has generated the most dissension and confusion.

Nearly all the other objectives of a tribunal – justice for the victims, accountability of the senior Khmer Rouge leaders and bringing a closure to the Khmer Rouge trauma – find common ground between ordinary citizens, human rights activists, and the government's Task Force for setting up the tribunal. But the grey area of uncharted legal territory – the mixed tribunal and the issue of the quality of justice – has led to bitter differences among Cambodians, NGOs, international lawyers and jurists.

The whole justice system in Cambodia is currently undergoing a slow and gradual process of reform prodded by the international donor community. Most Cambodians don't trust their courts, which are largely in the hands of poorly trained judges and lawyers. Corruption is rife and independent judgments in the face of police pressure or political interference are a rarity.

In their letter to the Secretary General in 1997 Co-Prime Ministers Hun Sen and Norodom Ranariddh cited the weakness of the Cambodian legal system as the major reason for requesting UN assistance to set up a tribunal.

A major difference then emerged over the issue of how much international assistance. Amnesty International and Human Rights Watch Asia from the beginning advocated a position that the only fair tribunal would be one taken completely out of the hands of the suspect Cambodian judiciary – meaning nothing less than the hugely costly framework of a fully-fledged international tribunal.

But an international tribunal has always been an unlikely prospect, threatened by a Chinese veto in the Security Council and unattractive to other UN members because of the enormous costs of the International Criminal Tribunals for the former Yugoslavia and Rwanda. In any event, Phnom Penh wanted UN assistance but within the framework of Cambodian sovereignty.

Several Cambodian human rights NGOs took their cue from their international brethren and expressed serious doubts about the 'mixed tribunal' that was soon canvassed as the most appropriate and practical trial formula.

Thun Saray, who knew better than most the failings of local courts, predicted, 'We know our government will manipulate the tribunal.' While he supported the principle of Cambodian involvement, Saray and other human rights activists considered that upholding international legal standards was the key to ensuring a credible trial. 'We are concerned that if we can't have a fair trial it will set a bad example. It is better to have no tribunal than a bad tribunal.'

The most controversial of all the provisions was the ratio of international to Cambodian judges. In arguing that a majority of international judges was imperative, the UN legal team had the backing not only of the major international human rights organisations (most vocally Amnesty International and Human Rights Watch), but also of the Cambodian Human Rights Action Committee – a coalition of 17 Cambodian human rights groups that monitored all the developments towards the tribunal.

They considered that the Cambodian judges could well be politically pressured to block the possibly more independent deliberations of the international jurists. It was an argument favouring international legal expertise over Cambodian sovereignty.

The refusal of the Cambodian government to concede to the UN's lawyers appeared at first glance to be unreasonable given that all parties accepted the chronic weakness of the Cambodian judiciary. But this tribunal was not just an issue demanding legal expertise and command of international justice. The Cambodian government is concerned to ensure that society is not destabilised nor should the process degenerate into a witch-hunt.

This side of the argument never got much of a public airing and the international debate was dominated by the repeated claim that the government had no stomach for a fair trial. But the critical issue of whom to indict provided ample grounds for suspicion of a hidden agenda unrelated to the tribunal itself. Certainly some of those who joined the debate, including right-wing US congressmen, were not coy about their demand for regime change in Cambodia.

The most extreme case is the Cambodia Democracy and Accountability Bill introduced into the US Senate on the eve of the 2003 national elections, in which Mitch McConnell held out a carrot: 'an additional $21,500,000 shall be made available for assistance for Cambodia above the fiscal year 2004 budget request of $43,000,000' and a stick: provided that 'new leadership in Cambodia has been elected in free and fair elections, and that Prime Minister Hun Sen is no longer in power'. It also provided that 'assistance may be provided to support, directly or indirectly, a Khmer Rouge tribunal, trial, or other legal venue established by the Government of Cambodia with the assistance of the United Nations if the US President determines and reports to the appropriate congressional committees that such tribunal, trial, or other legal venue –

(1) is not subject to the control or influence of the ruling Cambodian People's Party;
(2) includes participation of judges of high moral character;

(3) is supported by democratic Cambodian political parties; and
(4) meets international standards of justice.[28]

The Washington lobby for regime change in Cambodia has made little secret of their all-out support for opposition leader Sam Rainsy, a French-trained lawyer and banker who sees himself as America's 'freedom-fighter' in Phnom Penh. Both Sam Rainsy and his rightist Republican allies in the US Congress were effective in pressuring the US government to delay financial support for the tribunal until after the July 2003 elections. It appears that their chief enthusiasm is not for a Khmer Rouge Tribunal as such, but rather the avenues it might open up to indict Hun Sen and the CPP leadership in the event of a 'Starr' Chamber prosecution.[29]

WHOM TO INDICT FOR CRIMES AGAINST HUMANITY? PROSECUTION, CONFUSION AND SUSPICION

Few people wished to see low-ranking Khmer Rouge officials and soldiers, perhaps tens of thousands of individuals, being rounded up for their involvement in each and every serious act of murderous brutality. This would disrupt progress made towards reconciliation across the country, sowing fear and panic among the ranks of Khmer Rouge defectors and endangering the fragile new order of peace and stability.

Logic and justice dictate that prosecution must be selective and must identify those with primary responsibility. But how far down the chain of command to go is not at all clear. At the CSD Public Forum in Battambang, several participants expressed apprehension at being caught up in an open-ended prosecution they described as shrimp soup. Some defectors elaborated: 'Imagine a soup, in a broth with many shrimps. Their long tentacles become entangled, so when you try to take a spoonful, a whole string of shrimps is pulled out.'

Rather, the main focus of justice has been directed at the surviving senior leaders of the Khmer Rouge at the top of the chain of the command, in an attempt to hold them accountable for the policy decisions that authorised, encouraged and often directed mass executions. Cambodia's Khmer Rouge Trial Law, welcomed by the UN General Assembly, refers to those who can be indicted as 'senior leaders of the Khmer Rouge and those most responsible for the serious crimes', but it stops short of defining who is a Khmer Rouge leader.[30]

Researcher Craig Etcheson maintains that a clear definition of a 'Khmer Rouge leader' as a member of the Pol Pot regime's Standing Committee or Politburo, would have clarified who was a serious candidate to be prosecuted and thereby avoided public misunderstanding and confusion. Thun Saray from Adhoc has stated that he would like to see the definition of leaders extend as far as the Central Committee, a position also held by Youk Chhang in 2001,[31] but few wish to go further.

Lack of clarity on this point has afforded opportunities for unchecked rumour and rampant speculation. The Truth, Reconciliation and Justice Project reported the anonymous views of some participants in the survey that 'many Khmer Rouge leaders are still in power. Now they govern the country.' The author, Laura McGrew, treated this as if it was a matter of fact, neglecting to question these extremely grave allegations about some current members of the government. Given that both government and civil society ostensibly had the same goals – to put Khmer Rouge leaders on trial – such loose allegations reported in a serious research study only exacerbated distrust between the two. McGrew's sample of civil society surprisingly lacked any declared CPP adherents, who see their party as the one party that had always supported bringing the Khmer Rouge to justice.

In the last election, opposition leader Sam Rainsy and Funcinpec scarcely mentioned the Khmer Rouge genocide at all. But the CPP constantly reminded voters of how they had successfully negotiated with the UN a tribunal that would finally deliver justice.

Laura McGrew unfortunately fails to connect a fragmented civil society today with other parts of society that still remember 1979, and those who defended Cambodia against a return of the Khmer Rouge throughout the 1980s.

Characterisation of Hun Sen as a 'former Khmer Rouge leader' has been taken as good coin and slipped into the media's vocabulary to an alarming extent. The *New York Times* has been known to use this turn of phrase to describe him.[32]

This category is periodically widened to include various others. For example, on 6 April 1999 an editorial in the *Nation* (Bangkok) noted: 'Many of the current cabinet ministers including Hun Sen, Chea Sim, Hor Namhong and Sar Kheng, among others, are former Khmer Rouge leaders.' And on 9 January 2001 the *Cambodia Daily* published an article entitled 'Prosecutors must decide who KR leaders are' opining, 'They could ... include some government officials who were part of the Khmer Rouge regime, like Finance Minister Keat Chhon and Foreign Minister Hor Namhong ... .'

As if this weren't enough, on 7 August 2001, the BBC pulled out all the stops when correspondent Clive Myrie referred, erroneously, to Foreign Minister Hor Namhong as having once been the director of 'a Khmer Rouge torture centre'. While allegations have been levelled against the foreign minister's collaboration as a detainee in the Boeung Trabek camp for returnee intellectuals and diplomats, there is absolutely no evidence to suggest that he ever directed a torture centre.[33]

This failure to define 'senior Khmer Rouge leaders' has opened the way for scurrilous character assassinations. The aim has been to discredit the government by dragging Hun Sen's name alongside notorious Khmer Rouge leaders Pol Pot and Ieng Sary. Resolution 553, introduced by Dana Rohrabacher, and passed by the US Congress in December 1998, named Hun Sen as one of the 'leaders of the Cambodian genocide' and called for his 'indictment for genocide and crimes against humanity before an international tribunal'.

Prince Norodom Ranariddh's Cabinet chief, Kong Vibol, also weighed in with the comment: 'We support [the resolution] because Hun Sen is a second Pol Pot.'[34] These wild accusations against CPP leaders, designed to saddle them with responsibility for the crimes of the Pol Pot regime, are red herrings drawn across the path towards a trial of the real KR leaders.

In reality Hun Sen joined the *maquis* as an 18-year-old, heeding the appeal of the deposed Prime Minister Norodom Sihanouk. As later a battalion commander and later deputy regimental commander in Kampong Cham province during 1975–77,[35] he would hardly have been privy to the grand designs of the top leaders. Genocide researchers have been asked hundreds of times about any evidence that linked the current prime minister to the atrocities of 1975–79 period and the answer has always been: there is no such evidence.[36]

Two Cambodian scholars, Craig Etcheson and Steve Heder, issued a joint letter to all US congressmen strongly criticising the Rohrabacher resolution. They pointed out, 'It is a disservice to the rule of law and truth to make baseless or grossly exaggerated allegations to achieve a political end.' Further, the letter explained that a *'prima facie* case may exist to implicate Hun Sen' in serious human rights violations after 1985 (when Hun Sen became Prime Minister) but 'egregious as these human rights crimes may be, they do not cross the threshold into genocide, crimes against humanity or war crimes as defined in international law.'[37]

The Khmer language service of two US radio stations – *Voice of America* and *Radio Free Asia* – have devoted much air time to Rohrabacher and McConnell's small coterie of fellow congressmen and senators. Cambodian listeners often assume that these radio stations speak for the US government. Frequent statements on air calling for the arrest of Hun Sen convinced thousands in Phnom Penh and in the provinces that Washington was about to send troops and arrest the Cambodian Prime Minister in the aftermath of post-election protests staged by the opposition in August 1998.

Kenneth Quinn, the US ambassador in Phnom Penh at the time, was reported to have engaged in heated exchanges with Sam Rainsy and his wife, Thioulong Saumura, over statements claiming Washington was ready to send missiles or marines to topple Hun Sen. The chorus of neo-conservatives trying to impose their *pax Americana* and regime change on Cambodia was noisy enough to provoke extreme nervousness in Phnom Penh and legitimate concern that a Khmer Rouge Tribunal could be exploited to undermine the Cambodian leadership. Brad Adams, Director of Human Rights Watch Asia, observed: 'attempts to bring Hun Sen to an International Tribunal will undermine [the tribunal's] credibility [and] discourage Cambodian government cooperation.' Adams added Rohrabacher's moves 'could make Hun Sen nervous about a US plot to get him'.

Reacting to those threats several internal CPP meetings debated the pros and cons of opening Cambodia's legal system to participation of foreign judges under the auspices of the UN. There is much speculation about so-called factional divisions within the CPP. Craig Etcheson gives one analysis of the wide spectrum of views on whether to go ahead with a tribunal:

There are at least three groupings in the ruling party who oppose a UN tribunal. The 'nativists' oppose any UN involvement in a tribunal, reflecting an abiding revulsion at external interference in Cambodia's internal affairs; after nearly a century of French colonialism, Japanese occupation in World War II, the US intervention in the early 70s, the Vietnamese occupation of the 80s, and the UN peacekeeping mission of the early 90s, it is easy to understand why some Cambodians are jealously protective of Cambodia's sovereignty. The 'rejectionists' oppose the idea of any tribunal at all on the grounds that it could be harmful to national reconciliation, and a threat to Cambodia's new-found security and stability. The 'protectionists' oppose any international involvement in a tribunal on the grounds that several important members of the ruling party have skeletons in their closets, and party elders are reluctant to sacrifice any core members over this issue.

There are also several groups in the ruling party who strongly support the idea of UN participation in a Khmer Rouge tribunal. These include the 'internationalists', who understand that cooperation with the UN on the tribunal can bring many side benefits, from increased bilateral and multilateral aid to greater political credibility in regional fora such as ASEAN and global fora such as the UNGA. The 'modernizers' look to the domestic political benefits of a well-conducted tribunal, including combating the Culture of Impunity, weeding out undesirable elements in the party, and providing a salutary example of an independent judiciary. Finally there are the 'triumphalists', who view a full-scale, fully internationally legitimated tribunal as the final act of revenge against those who destroyed Cambodia's revolution and wrought so much havoc, as well as the final 'proof' of the correctness of the party's perception of its own historical role.[38]

The extent to which such clear formations or factions exist within the party is open to question, but this picture of diversity of opinion within the CPP is unquestionably true, and stands at odds with many media reports claiming the CPP to be a monolithic party. Likewise, the frequently pushed notion that the CPP has no political will to establish a tribunal fails to take account of the strong tendencies inside the party committed to see justice done. At both the level of the central committee and among the rank and file they are known to be in the overwhelming majority. The Cambodian People's Party was pushing for a tribunal at least a decade before the issue became fashionable with international human rights groups and western governments.

9
Uneasy Partners

By the end of 1997 the UN had finally acknowledged in a General Assembly resolution that genocide had occurred in Cambodia two decades previously, and had come round to the idea that Cambodians also deserved some justice. One era of controversy – ignoring the genocide – was over, but a new chapter of controversy and tortured UN-Cambodia relations was about to begin over what kind of tribunal would be the most viable, given all the circumstances, including the widely discussed opposition of China.

Who would be in control of the Khmer Rouge trials was the key issue over which the Cambodian government and the United Nations constantly locked horns. This underlay all the points of controversy and compromise in the three rounds of negotiations, numerous exchanges of letters and interventions by third parties from 1999 until 2003.

In March and again in mid-May 1999 Thomas Hammarberg, then Special Representative of the Secretary General for Human Rights in Cambodia, pursued the challenging task of seeking common ground between the parties. Hammarberg, a Swedish diplomat and former executive director of Amnesty International, had been instrumental in formulating the original May 1997 letter from the Co-Prime Ministers to the Secretary General requesting United Nations assistance in the process of bringing the Khmer Rouge to account for their crimes. He launched into his last major foray as Special Representative, with typical enthusiasm and optimism that a way forward could surely be found, if the two sides genuinely wished the process to succeed.

US Senator John Kerry met Hun Sen in April and gained tacit Cambodian support for pursuing the option of a mixed tribunal. Hammarberg's meetings with the Prime Minister and other officials during May transformed this support into a formal position, with both sides agreeing that 'it would be very appropriate' that United Nations experts should assist Cambodia in drafting the legislation to ensure that it would meet international standards, and that such experts should arrive as soon as possible. Hammarberg was of the opinion that the trial that would emerge from such a process of drafting would be a 'mixed tribunal', a then unprecedented institution in international law.

Just as the path towards this rather exciting new concept in international justice was beginning to evolve out of the previous deadlock, other forces threw obstacles in the way. Hammarberg was widely respected but his commitment to work for a mixed tribunal was greeted with alarm and considerable consternation in some quarters. Hammarberg's proposal, it was argued, could lead the UN into a process over which it had no control and was received with at best apprehension. Fellow Swede Hans Corell, the chief of the UN's Office of Legal Affairs, was reportedly miffed with Hammarberg for exceeding his mandate and insisted that the matter of the Khmer Rouge tribunal was the exclusive prerogative of the Office of Legal Affairs. A UN turf-war erupted even before any serious negotiations over the tribunal had begun.

Apparently there was also a fear in the Office of Legal Affairs that the mixed tribunal formula would open the door to demands for similar structures elsewhere. In retrospect it is clear that the Office of Legal Affairs never really overcame its initial scepticism of the whole idea.

Other voices supported the compromise reached by Hammarberg and Hun Sen, feeling that in Cambodia, as indeed in other places too, the mixed tribunal approach might indeed be more appropriate than the cumbersome *ad hoc* international tribunals of the Yugoslavia and Rwanda type. Balakrishnan Rajagopal, a professor in international humanitarian law from the Massachusetts Institute of Technology, who had previously worked in the UN Centre for Human Rights in Cambodia, commented on the UN's prevailing mindset. He characterised it as 'legal fundamentalism' and a fear of venturing into uncharted legal territory.[1]

In January 1999, Rajagopal had proposed a mixed tribunal, an idea floated within the State Department 18 months previously in Gregory Stanton's 'Options to try Pol Pot' paper. In addition to arguing for his solution on legal grounds, Rajagopal made the pragmatic argument that 'the request by the Cambodian government could be directly acted upon by the Secretary General (SG) of the UN as a technical assistance request', on the basis of a Memorandum of Understanding between the Cambodian government and the UN, without requiring either Security Council or General Assembly approval.[2]

Rajagopal went on to say:

The SG has taken a first crucial step by appointing the three-member expert Commission, without getting any endorsement from the Security Council. What is needed now is principled and courageous follow-through by the UN, acting through Hammarberg, to conclude an MOU with the Cambodian government. The MOU should be preceded by a dual effort: one on the part of the western countries to encourage Hun Sen to agree to this process, without preconditions; and two, on the part of the UN to mobilize financial support for the mixed-tribunal, preferably from Scandinavia, the Netherlands and Canada. Many of those countries were recently at the forefront of the battle to conclude the Rome Charter [of the International Criminal Court]. They should show similar foresight and determination to back this long-overdue effort to bring the KR to justice.

The potential advantages of the mixed tribunal were that it would be less unwieldy, more accessible to the local people and far less costly. In answer to the argument that mixed tribunals might compromise the UN's reputation, Rajagopal and other advocates pointed out that the United Nations could withdraw at any time if it felt the process was not meeting international standards.

During the course of the debate over what kind of tribunal should be established, critics of the Cambodian model (notably Amnesty International, Human Rights Watch and Cambodian human rights groups) constantly returned to the track of a fully-fledged UN *ad hoc* international tribunal.

But these groups neglected to address the virtual certainty of a Chinese veto of any tribunal resolution that might be brought before the UN Security Council, even if Hun Sen could be persuaded to drop his objections. All *ad hoc* tribunals to date had been established by this body, but Beijing, the prime supporter of the Pol Pot regime, had on several occasions indicated that it would block any such resolution for Cambodia. Rather than emanating from a Security Council Resolution, the UN mandate on Cambodia derived from human rights resolutions passed through the General Assembly.

DRAFTING THE LAW FOR A MIXED TRIBUNAL

The UN legal assistance that Hammarberg had offered, and Hun Sen had welcomed, never arrived. Drafting a Khmer Rouge tribunal law incorporating both domestic and international law was an immense legal task. Cambodia clearly needed help and several countries were ready to fund an assistance package proposed by the UN's Office for Human Rights in Cambodia. Senior international jurist, Antonio Cassessi had apparently indicated a willingness to work with Cambodia to ensure impeccable legal standards. However, the lawyers in New York were already penning a UN draft and saw no need for consultation with, let alone assistance for, their Cambodian partners.

At the end of July 1999 the *New York Times* leaked the principal points that were contained in the draft law being prepared by the United Nations Office of Legal Affairs. It was presented to a meeting of members (consultation of the whole) of the Security Council, on 30 July, briefed by Alvaro de Soto, Assistant Secretary General for Political Affairs. On 4 August Ralph Zacklin, deputy director of the OLA, sent a 12-point memorandum to Ouch Borith, the Cambodian Permanent Representative to the United Nations.

The OLA memorandum attracted criticism from all sides. Those who held fast to the wholly international tribunal were dismayed by the UN's change of heart in accepting the mixed tribunal concept. Other critics questioned the proposed 'Nuremberg style' group trial[3] and the idea of allowing no appeals (single chamber of both first and final judgment) which were considered to violate the International Covenant on Civil and Political Rights, 1966. A number of international human rights organisations felt the proposed structure would give the Cambodians too much say, while the Cambodian side objected to the proposed international majority of judges and prosecutors, viewing this as a blueprint for an international tribunal by another name.

From the Cambodian perspective, however, perhaps even more upsetting than the content of the memorandum was the way in which the understanding with Hammarberg had been scuttled in the corridors of the OLA in New York. The fact that the contents were leaked to the press and discussed with members of the Security Council, before being given to the Cambodian government, made it all the more galling. The optimistic spirit that had prevailed after Thomas Hammarberg's May visit had all but evaporated.

The Cambodian government's disquiet with the direction being taken was strengthened by a paper passed on to it in August reporting comments by Ramsey Clark, former US Attorney General, an outspoken critic of many US and UN policies and of the legitimacy of the International Criminal Tribunals for the former Yugoslavia and Rwanda. Ramsey questioned many aspects of the trial process envisaged by the OLA and emphasised the importance of retaining Cambodian sovereignty in any trial.[4]

NEGOTIATIONS BEGIN – ROUND ONE

In early August the composition of the UN delegation was announced: it would be headed by Ralph Zacklin, Assistant Secretary General in charge of the Office of Legal Affairs, and would have representatives from the Department of Political Affairs as well as from the UK and France.[5]

The Cambodian government responded with the creation of a high-level Task Force for Cooperation with Foreign Legal Experts and Preparation of the Proceedings for the Trial of Senior Khmer Rouge Leaders on 10 August 1999. Chaired by Senior Minister Sok An, it included senior legal officials and political advisors.[6]

The two negotiating teams assumed their places along opposite sides of the highly polished tables in the imposing room generally used by the Council of Ministers (the Cambodian government's cabinet) for its weekly meetings. A generous flower arrangement was placed in the centre, signifying the places to be taken by the respective heads of delegation. Formality was the order of the day in this initial meeting and this set the tone for all subsequent rounds of negotiation, with discussion almost entirely limited to the heads of delegation, very occasionally prompted or amplified by the other members. Ralph Zacklin presented an aloof and somewhat imperious image, while Sok An's style was softer and he made the rather unusual gesture of speaking in English throughout (official international negotiations in Cambodia are normally conducted in Khmer with translation as required for the visitors).

Sok An opened the negotiations by welcoming the UN delegation and placing on the table a Cambodian Draft Law. While the UN had been developing its draft over the previous months the Cambodian government had done likewise, with assistance from French legal academic, Professor Claude Gour, advisor to the Council of Jurists, who had a long association with Cambodia, having taught law there in the 1960s, with Prince Norodom Ranariddh as one of his students.

The Cambodian draft took a diametrically opposed approach from the UN's. It was a general enabling law, designed to incorporate into Cambodian domestic law international law provisions concerning crimes against humanity and the crime of genocide, as all countries are expected to do under Article 6 of the Genocide Convention.

It assumed that the special court or tribunal would operate under the jurisdiction of the existing Cambodian court structure and under Cambodian laws of procedure. Foreign judges would be invited to participate at each level of the court, but would hold the minority of positions. Provision was made for the possibility of a foreign co-prosecutor, who would issue indictments jointly with the Cambodian co-prosecutor. All judges and prosecutors would be appointed by the Supreme Council of the Magistracy, but the foreign judges and prosecutors would be recommended by the Secretary General, or by Member States of the United Nations.

Two particularly controversial points were Article 18: 'This law is retroactive', and Article 15 which extended the definition of the crime of genocide beyond that included in the Genocide Convention to include not only 'a national, ethnical, racial or religious group' but also 'any other group determined on the basis of any criterion, such as assets, degree of education, sociological group (urban/rural), allegiance to a political regime or system (old people/new people), social class or category (business person, civil servant etc.)' – similar to the definition used in the new French Penal Code of 1992.

It was quite obvious that the United Nations' delegation had not expected to receive a Cambodian draft, which Minister Sok An requested be considered as the sole working draft in the negotiations. The UN team ignored this request and the next day went ahead to put on the table their own quite different draft, as well as some comments on the Cambodian text. By the time it was presented officially to the Cambodian side, some of the most criticised elements of the UN's initial memorandum had been dropped (including the group trials and the absence of appeals).

Many aspects of the two drafts were similar (for instance the crimes and their penalties), but the UN draft took a quite different approach regarding the nature of the court. The UN's proposed tribunal would be an independent entity separate from the existing court system and would have a majority of foreign judges at each of the two levels proposed. All judges and prosecutors and the registry staff (both Cambodian and foreign) were to be appointed by the Secretary General and specific Rules of Procedure and Evidence were proposed for this tribunal (along the lines of the International Criminal Tribunals for the former Yugoslavia and Rwanda).

Two particularly controversial points in the UN draft were Article 5: An Exception to the Principle of *non-bis-in-idem*, which allowed for the subsequent retrial of persons previously tried under a Cambodian court for crimes under this law; and Article 6: Amnesty which stated, 'There shall be no amnesty for the crime of genocide. Any amnesty granted to any person falling within the jurisdiction of the Tribunal shall not be a bar to prosecution.' Both of these articles were clearly designed principally to prevent any loopholes in the prosecution of Ieng Sary, Pol Pot's deputy prime minister and foreign minister during the DK regime.

Canadian Jurist William A. Schabas remarked at the time:

In late August, a high-level UN delegation came to Phnom Penh with draft legislation modelled on the statute of the International Tribunal for Rwanda. The mixed character was largely symbolic. International in all but name, it allowed for only a minority participation by Cambodian judges. Mr. Annan was to appoint the prosecutor. The tribunal was to sit in Phnom Penh but be run out of New York. There were unfortunate overtones of arrogance in the UN's involvement that Cambodians were quick to pick up.

Schabas was equally damning in his criticism of the Cambodian model:

The Cambodians themselves proposed a 'mixed' tribunal that, on closer inspection, amounted to nothing but their own miserable court system complemented by a minority participation of foreign experts. Under such a system, a Cambodian-directed prosecutor would be tempted to pick and choose among the guilty, sheltering those Khmer Rouge leaders who had made political deals with the current regime.[7]

With two quite different drafts on the table, and each side holding firmly to its own approach, there was little room for manoeuvre. Nevertheless, the atmosphere of the talks was cordial, with both sides adopting a positive tone, something that had seemed unlikely from the press statements made by both sides in the preceding days. It was agreed that the Cambodian side would come up with a second draft, revised in the light of the discussions and comments and of the points raised by the United Nations.

At the end of the first round of negotiations a pattern was set of revealing a minimum of information on the discussions to the pressing crowd of journalists. Both Hans Corell and Sok An declined to divulge any drafts or details of their respective positions, citing a 'gentlemen's agreement' to maintain confidentiality.

AS TIME GOES BY

An indication of the strained aftermath of the first round of negotiations is given in the letter that Hun Sen wrote to UN Secretary General Kofi Annan in September 1999 in which he offered three options for UN involvement in a Khmer Rouge tribunal: 1) provide a legal team and participate in a tribunal conducted in Cambodia's existing courts; 2) provide a legal team which would only act in an advisory capacity to the tribunal; or 3) withdraw completely from the proposed tribunal. Kofi Annan never responded to the letter, but its subtext – that Cambodia was prepared to go it alone – continued to hover in the background.

Two years were to pass before a Cambodian tribunal law was promulgated. It was crafted from these two drafts and advice given to the Cambodian Task Force by experts from several countries, including France, India, Russia, Australia and the United States.[8] Sok An's speech introducing the Draft Law to the National Assembly at the end of 2000 outlined the process of negotiation between the United Nations and the Cambodian government Task Force. Along the way a number of compromises were reached, facilitated mainly by the US Ambassador for War Crimes, David Scheffer, and by Senator John Kerry, who had long been one of the main advocates of normalising US relations with both Vietnam and Cambodia.

The key issues that required compromise included the following:

1) The UN insistence on a majority of international judges and Cambodia's refusal to submit led to deadlock. Both sides had rational grounds for holding to their respective positions. It required skilful mediation from outside to resolve this impasse with the formula of 'super-majority' decision making to ensure that no decision could be taken by a simple majority of three Cambodian judges acting in concert against the two international judges. All decisions therefore would require the agreement of at least one of the foreign judges.

2) Each side wanted to hold the positions of prosecutor and investigating judge. The solution reached was to appoint co-prosecutors and co-investigating judges.
3) The hypothetical problem of a disagreement between the two 'co's' as to whether to proceed with a prosecution or investigation needed resolution. The solution was that they would be mandated to attempt to reach agreement, with a fallback pre-trial chamber to resolve any disputes and deadlocks, and with neither side able to block the process.

Thomas Hammarberg later denigrated this process, saying 'it would have been important to build [the tribunal's] construction on principles rather than on political compromise.'[9] Such a dismissive remark rather flies in the face of the role he himself played in 1999 in achieving the initial compromise that got the discussions under way – that the UN and Cambodia should work together to formulate an unprecedented mixed tribunal that was neither purely international nor purely domestic. Without Hammarberg's willingness to seek a compromise no progress would have been made and the same applies to the later compromises brokered between the two sides.

There is more than one principle at stake here. 'Delivering justice to the Cambodian people is the first priority,' said Chea Vannath. 'Any tribunal conducted in Le Hague will have little meaning for Cambodians. It is important to have the trial here so that Cambodians can be a part of the process.'[10] The Genocide Convention itself gives primacy to the active role of the people concerned as victims and perpetrators, as does the newly established International Criminal Court.

The Cambodian government just managed to achieve its target of completing the second draft of the Khmer Rouge law before the end of 1999, sending it to the United Nations on 20 December. Hun Sen stated in his covering letter that the government would not wait beyond Friday, 24 December, for a response before proceeding to send the draft to the legislature. Giving such short notice to the UN Secretariat was not the best way to garner its support for the Cambodian draft law.

On 23 December Hans Corell, the UN Legal Counsel, responded, expressing many concerns relating to key provisions in the Draft Law: the composition of the court; the form of majority required; the notion of co-prosecutors and the role of investigating judges. He also objected to the proposal for the court to be funded entirely through the proposed United Nations Trust Fund. In conclusion, he stated his opinion that it would be premature to submit this draft to the National Assembly, and sought further meetings in order to find 'solutions that will accommodate the concerns of the Organization and would allow it to continue to get engaged in the process'.

At its final Cabinet meeting for the year, on 24 December 1999, the Cambodian government made minor amendments to the draft so that some trial expenses previously to be paid by the UN would be paid by Cambodia, and to make provision for other countries to act directly in sending judges or prosecutors to the proceedings. In so doing, it took into account the financial comments made by Hans Corell in his letter of the previous day, but no substantive changes were made to the juridical structures and procedures envisaged in the draft. This revised draft was then re-submitted to the United Nations, again requesting urgent comment.

On 5 January 2000 Hans Corell handed over the UN's comments on the second draft of the Cambodian law. These were in the form of a 'Non-Paper', a peculiar UN practice that allows an undated and unsigned memorandum to circulate without any official standing. This practice was familiar to the Cambodians as it had occasionally been employed during the protracted discussions preceding the 1991 Paris Peace Agreement.

The Non-Paper questioned the addition of a number of items of applicable law in the Cambodian second draft and implied that any prosecutions should be limited to genocide and crimes against humanity. It went on to assert that the super-majority procedure and the appointment of co-prosecutors 'will inevitably lead to paralysis', and made a number of other criticisms on the role of the investigating judges, on amnesty and pardon and on financing, before insisting that 'the international component among the judges must be more substantive' and 'the decision making process should be such as to command international credibility'.

The Non-Paper was pervaded by a negative and condescending tone, exemplified by the sentence, 'Otherwise, the United Nations could be accused of assisting what many would describe as a sham trial' and the concluding reproach '... we would like, yet again, to invite the Government of Cambodia to enter into constructive negotiations with the United Nations ...'. Given that the Cambodian government had repeatedly stated its intention of trying to meet international standards, and had just completely rewritten its first draft in accordance with points made by the UN and the US, this gratuitous comment was perceived as insulting.

> This Non-Paper – quintessential Hans Corell – was a defining moment in what was from the outset a marriage of convenience, in which neither groom nor bride understood or trusted each other.

Tensions were running high as the new millennium began. The UN Legal Counsel was obviously irate at the short amount of time that the UN was given to respond to the Second Draft and no doubt the timing at Christmas and New Year was not convenient for many of his staff, even though these Yuletide dates mean little in Cambodia.

On 27 December 1999 Ta Mok's lawyer, Benson Samay, announced that he was planning to file subpoenas for several former world leaders to appear at the tribunal. It was his intention to call three former US presidents (Jimmy Carter, Ronald Reagan and George Bush) to question them on their support of the Khmer Rouge during the 1980s, as well as former British Prime Minister Margaret Thatcher and, for an earlier period, former US Secretary of State Henry Kissinger, who was with Richard Nixon jointly responsible for the 'secret' bombing of Cambodia in the 1970s.

The possibility of widening the scope of the Khmer Rouge trial to include both the post-1979 and the pre-1975 periods continued to hover behind the negotiations. This was a wild card that the Cambodians hinted at playing whenever the going got tough. None of the big powers, the Permanent Five of the Security Council, wanted any process that stepped out of the 1975–1979 period, for fear they would find themselves in the dock. This time it was Ta Mok's lawyer playing the card, but on many other occasions this possibility, which some interpreted as a threat, came from the mouth of the Prime Minister himself.[11]

THE DRAFT LAW AND ITS RECEPTION

Despite the objections raised in the UN's Non-Paper, on 6 January 2000 the Cambodian cabinet approved the draft law in principle, while it allowed for further revision before the final draft would be sent to the National Assembly. On the suggestion of visiting Japanese Prime Minister Keizo Obuchi it was modified to include a foreign co-investigating judge.

On 18 January the draft law was handed over by Minister Sok An to National Assembly President Norodom Ranariddh. In the view of the government, the responsibility for making any further changes was now in the hands of the legislature – a view that caused some disquiet in the UN Office of Legal Affairs, as was to be seen over the following months.

The same day that the law went to the National Assembly, Chhouk Rin, a former Khmer Rouge commander who had defected to the Cambodian army in 1994, was arrested and charged in connection with the July 1994 train attack in which at least 13 Cambodians were killed and three western tourists and some Cambodians taken hostage. The three westerners had been executed in late September. Although this same train had been ambushed many times by southwestern Khmer Rouge forces in the 1990s, it was only the capture of three foreigners and the ensuing international publicity that engendered sustained pressure for a trial.

After Cambodian troops captured the Phnom Voar (Vine Mountain) base in Kampot province on the southern coast of Cambodia, with the help of more than 100 defecting Khmer Rouge led by Colonel Chhouk Rin, the two top regional Khmer Rouge leaders fled westwards and went to ground. General Sam Bith defected in 1996 and was promptly rewarded with the rank of two-star general in the Cambodian army in line with the policy of national reconciliation. The Khmer Rouge commander in charge of Phnom Voar, General Nuon Paet, had by 1996 taken refuge among the ranks of former Khmer Rouge in Pailin, a fact that did not escape the attention of Cambodian military intelligence.

While the government's paramount concern in this period was to bring an end to the war by encouraging splits among the Khmer Rouge, the three western embassies involved in the Kampot hostage saga constantly pressured Sar Kheng, the Interior Minister and Prime Minister Hun Sen to deliver justice for the families involved. Media reports that Nuon Paet was living quietly in Pailin encouraged the Australian, British and French ambassadors to press the government harder for action. Phnom Penh's line was 'Be patient, it will happen when the time is right.'

It was clear to Hun Sen that sending an arrest party to the den of the former Khmer Rouge commander who exercised autonomy in their gem-rich zone of Pailin, bordering Thailand, could be a risky move. After the 1998 election Hun Sen gave the order for his generals to lure Nuon Paet from Pailin to Phnom Penh with a bogus offer of a lucrative business deal. He was brought by helicopter to Phnom Penh and formally indicted for the train ambush, kidnapping and murder of 13 Cambodians and three foreigners.

During his pre-trial detention in T3 prison, Phnom Penh, Nuon Paet was interviewed by Tom Fawthrop. In a rare filmed interview the former Khmer Rouge commander admitted the hostages were under his care and protection, but denied any part in their execution.[12] He blamed his regional boss, General Sam Bith, and Pol Pot for ordering them to be killed. However, radio transcripts proved not only the guilt of Pol Pot and Sam Bith, but also that of Nuon Paet himself who received and transmitted messages under the code name of '75'. Pol Pot was '99' and Sam Bith '37'. The transcripts were used by the prosecution in the trials of Nuon Paet and later Sam Bith and helped to secure their convictions.

Chhouk Rin testified at the June 1999 trial of his immediate superior General Nuon Paet, in charge of the Phnom Voar (Vine Mountain) guerrilla zone, the first Khmer Rouge officer to be convicted and jailed. Nuon Paet's appeals were dismissed by the Appeals Court (October 2000) and the Supreme Court (September 2002).

Cambodian authorities announced that they were also seeking the arrest of (now General) Sam Bith, another defected former Khmer Rouge commander, for his role in the same events. Some anxiety was expressed about whether these and other Khmer Rouge commanders could be prosecuted in light of the article offering amnesty in return for defection, in the 1994 legislation to ban the Khmer Rouge. Indeed Chhouk Rin was released on 18 July 2000, the first day of his trial, because of this amnesty, but was, on appeal by the prosecution, convicted *in absentia* in September 2002.[13] General Sam Bith never showed up. The Defence Ministry informed the court that they were unable to track him down even though he was listed as a two-star general on the payroll.

Later the missing Sam Bith, fugitive from justice, was found – not by Cambodia's judicial or military police, but through investigations conducted by Tom Fawthrop, reporting for the *Age* newspaper in Melbourne, who revealed the exact location. Whereas Cambodian authorities claimed they could not locate his whereabouts, Fawthrop found him living right next door to the police station at Sdao on the road from Battambang to Pailin.

CONTROVERSY GROWS OVER THE CAMBODIAN TRIBUNAL

The trial negotiations were always two-sided high-level affairs that afforded little opportunity for popular participation. But ordinary Cambodian people who had clamoured for justice for so long had every right to have their say in what kind of tribunal was being designed by the two negotiating parties – the UN legal team and their government.

In the early months of 2000 a number of interested parties commented on the Draft Law in response to an invitation for comment from Manh Sophan, Chair of the Legislation Committee of the National Assembly. Although earlier versions had been leaked to the press, this was the first time that a concrete draft was made available for public scrutiny and comment.

The voices of international human rights organisations were the first to be heard. On 1 February the US-based international non-governmental organisation, Human Rights Watch, submitted its comments to the National Assembly and the Ministry of Justice. Human Rights Watch made sweeping criticisms of the Draft Law, concluding that it 'does not meet international standards' and 'would allow the judicial and prosecutorial processes to be subject to political pressures that could compromise both the selection of suspects for prosecution and the fairness of the trials they receive'. This response from HRW and also from the Cambodian Human Rights Action Committee (a coalition of local human rights organisations) set the tone for a polarisation of perspectives on the Cambodian model of a mixed tribunal, in which international judges did not have a majority vote. Human Rights Watch and later Amnesty International both demanded the scrapping of the mixed formula in favour of a fully-fledged UN-run *ad hoc* tribunal. Once again these organisations ignored the issue of a probable veto in the UN Security Council of such a tribunal. Neither did they consider the positive aspects and potential advantages of a mixed tribunal.

The opposition Sam Rainsy Party with 15 members seated in the National Assembly initially took the same line, indicating that it rejected the proposal for Cambodian Extraordinary Chambers with international participation, and instead called for an international tribunal along the lines of the International Criminal Tribunals for the former Yugoslavia and Rwanda.[14]

Recognising the need for real involvement of the people, the Center for Social Development embarked upon an ambitious programme of public forums discussing the whole issue of justice for crimes committed by the Khmer Rouge. CSD also furnished a detailed commentary on the Draft Law, including some constructive proposals that were eventually incorporated into the Law.

The first public forum was held in the northwestern town of Battambang in January 2000 followed by Phnom Penh (February) and Sihanoukville (March) at which hundreds of people, including former Khmer Rouge soldiers, had the opportunity to voice their opinions. The forums revealed overwhelming support for a trial (68 per cent). The opposition was primarily from former Khmer Rouge soldiers and officials. More details of the responses are given in Chapter 8.

NEGOTIATIONS – ROUND TWO

On 8 February 2000 Kofi Annan wrote to Prime Minister Hun Sen putting officially on to the negotiating table the main concerns raised in the earlier Non-Paper. The letter identified four key issues that required further discussion and change in the Draft Law before the UN would agree to participate in the process:

- guarantees for the arrest and surrender of indictees;
- exclusion of amnesty and pardon for genocide and crimes against humanity;
- a single independent international prosecutor and an investigating judge; and
- a majority of international judges, appointed solely by the Secretary General.

The Cambodian Task Force met immediately to consider the Kofi Annan letter and concluded that, whereas the first two points were in principle acceptable to the Cambodian side and required discussion only as to their formulation in the legal texts, to comply with the last two positions would be seriously at odds with Cambodian position on the tribunal and would fly in the face of compromises already mooted in discussion with the UN and with various member states. If the two latter points were to be accepted, this would mean a return to the original UN formula of international control, a scenario that had been rejected outright by the Prime Minister in March 1999.

The Prime Minister sent a short letter to the Secretary General in which he did not respond to the points made, but rather expressed surprise at 'the gap between the positions raised in your letter and ours which has already been supported by a number of distinguished Member States' (alluding to the support from United States, France, India and Russia) and suggested that further understanding might be reached in a future UN delegation visit to Cambodia.

Hun Sen's more colourful remarks to the press included his comment that the only jobs the Secretary General would give to Cambodians to do would be to 'go into the jungle to capture the tiger' and to be 'the watchdog for the UN'.[15] In other words the Cambodians would carry out the arrest and detention of the major suspects, while the trials should be left in the hands of international legal experts. Given that all those same experts and institutions in the 1980s never got round to dealing with the scandal of the UNGA seating of the Pol Pot gang, Hun Sen was entitled perhaps to think that the UN attitude was more than a little patronising.

What seemed like an almost unbridgeable chasm between the two sides appeared to be traversed when the two leaders met face to face on 12 February 2000 on the sidelines of a UN trade conference in Bangkok. Both Hun Sen and Kofi Annan said they were optimistic that a new UN mission to Cambodia could resolve differences, but tensions remained high in the following weeks. On 24 February the European Parliament passed a motion calling for an *ad hoc* international tribunal, while on 6 March Hun Sen said that three former UN Secretaries General should be held accountable for the KR's occupation of Cambodia's UN seat during the late 1970s and 1980s.

The seriousness that the Secretariat placed on this second round of talks was shown by the composition of the UN delegation. It was led by Hans Corell himself, the chief UN Legal Counsel, who had previously directed successful negotiations with Moammar Ghadafi, as well as being instrumental in the establishment of the International Criminal Tribunals for the former Yugoslavia and Rwanda. Kofi Annan made a positive gesture by including Lakhon Mehrotra, who had recently stepped down from his term as Special Representative of the Secretary General on Cambodia, during which he developed a good working relationship with the Cambodian government, including the Prime Minister.[16]

The overall atmosphere was considerably more positive and less stiffly formal than during initial round of talks. Hans Corell seemed more relaxed and convivial than Ralph Zacklin had been, with occasional jocular remarks about his leg being in plaster and coming with a (walking) stick in hand. Certainly his tone seemed light years away from that conveyed in the Non-Paper and the Secretary General's letter of 8 February.

Perhaps it is in the nature of things that civility is likely to pervade person-to-person meetings, especially when the eye of the television camera is trained on the interlocutors, and joint press conferences after each session helped to develop a positive attitude with the negotiations treated as a common enterprise. The positive spirit engendered was reinforced by the delegation's decision to lay a wreath at the Choeung Ek memorial to victims of the genocide on the outskirts of the city, where Hans Corell remarked that 'the shadow of the killing fields has been present throughout in our meeting rooms'.

Nevertheless, inside the walls of the Council of Ministers' meeting rooms, talk was pretty blunt and even heated at times, though it was muted somewhat by the decision not to focus discussion on the four points of the Secretary General's letter but rather to deal with the contentious issues as they arose, working through the draft texts for both the law and the agreement to be signed between both parties.

While there were still a number of points of incompatibility between the Draft Law and the UN text presented at this meeting, the major issue was not one of content, but rather how to proceed. The Cambodian position was that, once agreement had been reached with the UN on the legal basics and structure, the Draft Law should be debated first in the National Assembly. They felt that any agreement with the United Nations should be on how to implement that law and that it should not be signed, initialled or authorised with the UN until the National Assembly had had a chance to debate the draft and make its decisions.

Both inside the meeting and outside Corell expressed impatience to the press with what he termed this 'irregular' procedure of sending the Draft Law to the National Assembly before the international agreement had been signed, rather than ratifying it after signature, as is the normal practice with international treaties.

For the Cambodian delegation, however, the agreement to be signed was never seen as a typical international agreement or treaty to be ratified by many countries after multilateral agreement on the text. This was a matter that specifically concerned Cambodia, as the scene of the crimes, and Cambodians, as both victims and perpetrators, and they felt it was right and proper that it be enacted first at the national level, albeit on the basis of formulas agreed to in negotiations with the UN.

Whatever the relative merits of these two positions as to which document should be signed first, it is extraordinary that this could later become one of the main justifications given by the United Nations for aborting the negotiations.

During this second round of negotiations in March 2000, after lengthy debate acceptable compromises were reached on all the four issues raised in Annan's letter. Hans Corell eventually accepted the formula of co-prosecutors – one international and one Cambodian – while reserving a final decision until agreement could be reached on how to resolve deadlock situations if the two co-prosecutors could not reach agreement on whom to indict.

Much ground was covered on a large number of what might be seen as mechanical or logistical issues concerning methods of appointment, financial arrangements, privileges and immunities, administration and protection of witnesses and victims.

On Annan's fourth issue – amnesty – Sok An gave the delegation a letter clarifying the current situation, namely that only one person had been granted a pardon in 1996, relating only to a conviction for genocide. Although not spelled out in the letter, this referred to the case of Ieng Sary, who was in 1996 given a pardon for his 1979 *in absentia* conviction by the People's Revolutionary Tribunal, as discussed in detail in Chapter 3. Ironically, in granting the pardon to Ieng Sary the King conferred a degree of legal recognition of the tribunal that had been so ignored up until that time.

Prime Minister Hun Sen said at the time,

> If you study the wording of the Royal [amnesty], you will see that there is still the possibility to try the crimes committed by Ieng Sary … We paid much attention to the wording of the pardon … there are no words in it which ban the accusation of Ieng Sary in front of a court which may be formed in the coming times. Therefore we should speed up the investigation of the crimes of Pol Pot so that we can bring all those responsible to justice. And then if Ieng Sary can get rid of being accused, at least he can become a witness because he has much evidence. So we should speed up the investigation into the [crimes] of Pol Pot.[17]

Although defence lawyers at a future tribunal would be likely to plead that their client had a pardon, and could not be tried twice on the charge of genocide, such a plea would not help the defendant on other equally serious indictments including crimes against humanity. Any astute international lawyer knows that, whereas proving genocide can be very problematic because of the legal complexities relating to the definition of the crime, conviction for crimes against humanity is far more likely, based on the evidence that has been compiled so far against all the Khmer Rouge leaders including Ieng Sary. (The problems and pitfalls of seeking prosecution under each of the items of applicable law are discussed in Chapter 10.)

During this second round of negotiations, the United Nations' delegation accepted the Cambodian majority of judges at all levels, as moderated by the super-majority decision making process, but Hans Corell stipulated that this be part of a package that would give the co-prosecutors and investigating judges the right to act independently of each other.

From the vantage point of architects of the international tribunals in The Hague, the concept of an international prosecutor carried with it notions of independence and impartiality. But the Cambodians were wary and less ready to take this at face value. The recent attempt to impeach President Bill Clinton was fresh in their minds, and the spectre of a very political 'Independent Prosecutor' Ken Starr hovered in the air. There was a fear that the international prosecutor might run amok or cast too a wide a net, undoing progress towards national reconciliation. The counter argument to this would be that requiring the two prosecutors to reach agreement on whom to indict or investigate would give the Cambodian prosecutor a potential veto over the process.

After lengthy discussion the two sides agreed that the prosecutors should strive to work together, but the problem remained as to what was the way out if they had irreconcilable differences.

Sok An suggested that a mechanism be found to break any such deadlock between the prosecutors or investigating judges. Hans Corell responded positively and made several suggestions for how this might be implemented, including establishing some kind of pre-trial chamber.

The feeling after this second round of negotiations was that great distance had been travelled by both parties and a way out of the impasse over Kofi Annan's four points had been found. The only remaining major issue – deciding on the mechanism to resolve differences between the co-prosecutors – was not seen by the Cambodian side as anything that could derail the whole process. But the determination of the UN delegation to hold firm on this point, at the Secretary General's insistence, precluded a full agreement after this second round of negotiations.

With hindsight, though, the issue of the relative status of two documents – the Cambodian law and the international agreement – had not been satisfactorily resolved and would come back to haunt the negotiations.

Hans Corell's parting press conference conveyed a tension and ambiguity:

> We have not yet arrived at an overall agreement. A few issues still divide us. But we have made great progress, and I am pleased to confirm that we are much further along the road to success than we were a week ago. I must say that these were negotiations in which all issues were discussed fully and solutions sought. In some instances both sides have altered their positions in order to accommodate the legitimate concerns of the other side. I have left my Cambodian interlocutors in no doubt about the limits within which the United Nations has to act in this unprecedented endeavour. They in turn have explained that they cannot conclude a final agreement with us until their Parliament has debated the necessary legislation. Of course, it would have been easier if a draft law had not already been forwarded to the National Assembly. Naturally, however, we respect the sovereign right of Cambodia, a UN Member State, to resolve the remaining issues within its own constitutional processes.[18]

AND THEN THERE WAS LIGHT : BREAKTHROUGH ON THE CO-PROSECUTORS

After Hans Corell left Phnom Penh the US got back into the fray, with both Ambassador for War Crimes David Scheffer and Senator John Kerry (apparently after discussion with Hans Corell) coming up with an approach as to how to deal with any conflict between the two prosecutors or investigating judges.

On 17 April 2000 – the 25th anniversary of the Khmer Rouge coming to power – at Pochentong Airport on his return home from a non-aligned movement meeting in Havana, the Prime Minister announced that he accepted the new solution. The Secretary General then formally proposed the idea of a pre-trial chamber to resolve any differences of opinion between the co-prosecutors or the co-investigating judges.

While in-principle agreement had been announced, the devil was in the detail: would the agreement of this chamber be needed to block or to proceed with a prosecution advocated by only one of the co-prosecutors? The joint project went close to going off the rails yet again as this was worked through. Hun Sen sent two letters to the Secretary General in April and May. The letters conveyed his agitated mood at the time, clearly expressed in a speech highly critical of the UN role and threatening to extend the jurisdiction of the trials:

In the past, the Khmer Rouge existed and who supported the Khmer Rouge? These are the subjects that the [National] Assembly will question and answer. If they ask the government, the government will refer to the United Nations and I myself will not answer in order to implicate no one else but the three Secretary Generals, Kurt Waldheim, Xavier Perez De Cuellar and Boutros Boutros Ghali. So if a question to the government is raised: 'Why were the Khmer Rouge part of the Paris Peace Accord?', I will refer to the UN Secretary Generals. If the Secretary Generals answered further that this was because of votes in the UN General Assembly, then go and see what countries voted to support the Khmer Rouge seat in the UN, and go and see which countries provided the Khmer Rouge with weapons, territory, shelter and all the things. It was for these reasons that in the previous talks I limited the period to 1975–79. But when they refused and they treated Hun Sen so badly, the momentum for [a trial to extend beyond] the period 1975–79 has swollen up. That is why I feel regret. I do not know how much further the law will go but I want to reaffirm that I will keep up efforts on what we have agreed with the legal experts from the United Nations, France, India, Russia, and the United States to submit [the draft law] to the Assembly and to protect the position of the Royal Cambodian Government. Nonetheless, the position of the Royal Government shall not be [to] put pressure on the Assembly on how to pass the law. We will respect the Assembly, nothing beyond this. This is a separation of powers.[19]

Like many of the Prime Minister's controversial statements about the tribunal, this threat annoyed the UN Secretariat. In spite of this public and private posturing on 19 May 2000, Hun Sen and the Secretary General reached agreement on the final structure and workings of the tribunal.

An amendment would be made to the Draft Law before its consideration by the National Assembly, providing for a pre-trial chamber to settle disputes. The pre-trial chamber would comprise three Cambodian and two foreign judges (again with a super-majority requirement for decision making). A key provision was contained in the last sentence: 'If there is no majority, as required for a decision, the investigation or prosecution shall proceed.' These words made clear that the Cambodian side could not block the international co-prosecutor from pursuing a case, even if all the Cambodian parties (both co-prosecutor or co-investigating judge and three judges in the pre-trial chamber) disagreed with it.

The far-reaching implications of this provision seem to have been lost on most observers and have received very little publicity. Newspaper stories continue to claim that the legal framework is designed to handicap a serious prosecution.

In giving no 'braking power' to the Cambodian side to halt prosecution or investigation of any suspect, this formula provided a balance to the decision making arrangements for the trial chambers. At the prosecution and investigation stages, a lack of consensus cannot prevent an indictment from proceeding. However, at the stage of deciding the verdict, a lack of consensus must result in acquittal, in accordance with the international standard of presumption of innocence until proven guilty.

As the impasse reached in March had been resolved via external mediation, there was a need for another round of negotiations to bring all the new formulations reached since January into both the Draft Law and the draft Agreement to be signed between both parties.

ROUND THREE – HANS CORELL'S TEAM
RETURNS TO PHNOM PENH JULY 2000

Hans Corell once again led the third UN delegation.[20] The meetings held on 5 and 6 July 2000 in Phnom Penh re-examined article by article both the Draft Law as well the draft Articles of Cooperation, concentrating especially on amendments needed to incorporate the changes already agreed to between Kofi Annan and Hun Sen.

Despite (or perhaps because of) the progress made by outside mediation from the US, tension was palpable as the first session convened. Hans Corell opened by saying, 'I am pleased to be back – this time without a stick,' a remark that clearly carried a double meaning. In March he had come with a walking stick in hand, but his other 'stick' was an instruction from Kofi Annan to withdraw if the main issues were not resolved.

Over two days of discussions, agreement was clear on a number of points, while on others Sok An raised objections, or alternative wording, or simply did not express acceptance or dissent and merely suggested moving on to the next item on the agenda. In a clear case of cross-cultural misunderstanding, the UN apparently regarded silence as indicating consent. Hans Corell later repeatedly referred to the drafts as agreed texts while the Cambodian side considered them as just the latest working drafts.[21] Once again, lack of public disclosure of the documents allowed unfettered speculation as to their contents, with the Cambodia side later lambasted for having reneged on the July 'agreements' while in reality no accord had been reached on several contentious points. Neither side initialled or signed the drafts, which were prepared by the UN team and dated and handed over on 7 July – the day after the negotiation round had finished.

At the conclusion of the two days of discussions the prospects for an eventual trial became more tangible as the delegations donned hard hats and were taken on a tour of the Chaktomuk Theatre, the government's suggested venue for the trial, which in mid-2000 was under renovation as a prestige venue for meetings and performances. Chaktomuk, in the centre of the city on the river front and close to the National Assembly, the Palace and most ministries, would be easy to secure. It was large enough to be able to accommodate the large number of observers and media that the trial would attract. Finally, it carried symbolic significance as the site of the 1979 People's Revolutionary Tribunal.

As 2000 drew to a close, external and seasonal forces served to delay things even further. Cambodia experienced its worst floods for at least 40 years, leading to 347 deaths, displacing one-third of the rural population and washing away one-fifth of the year's main rice crop, hundreds of bridges and over 900 kilometres of main roads. All activities of the government – even Cabinet meetings – were put on hold for over a month as the Prime Minister and other senior officials went on daily food distribution trips to the worst affected districts. And the normal series of post-rainy season traditional and religious holidays was followed by the landmark visit by China's president, Jiang Zemin, the first such visit for 37 years.

Pundits had for the past few months suggested that the National Assembly would be unlikely to take any action that could in any way be interpreted as critical of China in the lead-up to this historic visit. Clearly China would not welcome any mention of its role as the major backer of the Khmer Rouge, both during its rule and for many years afterwards, and the Cambodian government was hoping for a positive and uneventful state visit during which a significant aid package would be signed.

In September Lee Kwan Yew's memoirs were published, confirming what had been known for years – that China had paid over 1 billion US dollars in cash and weapons to the Khmer Rouge during the 1980s when it mounted armed opposition to the government. This news made the visit even more delicate. The anti-government Democratic Front of Khmer Students and Intellectuals and the Student Movement for Democracy staged small demonstrations before the visit, presenting petitions demanding China apologise for its backing of the Khmer Rouge; refrain from using its influence to block a trial; and pay compensation to the survivors of the genocide (citing the statutes of the International Criminal Court on this point).

An Associated Press release on the eve of the visit, 12 November 2000, reported comments by Thomas Hammarberg, the ex-UN Special Human Rights envoy to Cambodia. Hammarberg related that during private discussions with the Prime Minister, Hun Sen 'often referred to international pressure, including ... pressure he was receiving from China'. 'The implication was that China didn't want a trial,' Hammarberg said.[22]

Small demonstrations were mounted in several parts of the city, while crowds of school children and civil servants were assembled to stage an official welcome and the large Chinese community also held several colourful processions and performances. In any event, the visit went off without unrest.

A series of bilateral agreements were signed and both sides denied that the issue of the Khmer Rouge trial came up in their talks. When asked by the press, the Chinese spokesperson repeated the official Chinese position: 'It should be up to the Cambodian people to decide without foreign interference,' Foreign Ministry spokesperson Zhu Bangzao said. 'China has not and will never apply pressure on the Cambodian government over this question.'[23] This is a quotation that could rank as among the least credible ever uttered on the complex subject of China–Cambodia relations.

It could well be true that the Khmer Rouge tribunal was never explicitly mentioned during the course of the state visit. It would simply be too vulgar to bring up a bone of contention during an exercise in toasting China–Cambodia friendship. Explicit diplomatic pressure against a tribunal would more likely be exercised by the Chinese ambassador in Phnom Penh or in New York. Kent Wiedemann, the US ambassador in Phnom Penh, noted that on several occasions after he emerged from meetings with the Prime Minister urging him to move forward with the tribunal negotiations, the next visitor was waiting to lobby Hun Sen. It was none other than the Chinese ambassador.[24]

And Thomas Hammarberg concluded in his memoir on the history of the tribunal negotiations:

> The Chinese were actively working against any further UN initiative. In a meeting I had with the Chinese Ambassador in Phnom Penh, he argued that the issue of the Khmer Rouge was an 'internal' matter and should not be dealt with by the UN – not even on a Cambodian invitation.[25]

A week before Jiang Zemin's visit it was announced that Vietnam's president, Tran Duc Luong, would also make a state visit within several weeks, presumably to balance the impact of the Chinese visit and to reassure Cambodia's former close ally of continuing amity. However, unexpected events prevented that visit. Just two days before Luong was due to arrive, on the night of 23/24 November, an armed attack was launched on several key buildings in Phnom Penh, including the Ministry of Defence and the Council of Ministers. The attack was put down before dawn, but eight people were reportedly killed in the fighting and some hundreds arrested in various parts of the country in the following days, including Richard Kiri Kim, a leader of the Cambodian Freedom Fighters, based in California. On hearing of the unrest Luong announced the postponement of his visit.

Despite the tension arising from this attack, the Draft Law's long gestation period came to an end in the final days of November, with the United States once again playing midwife. US Senator John Kerry took the opportunity, after joining President Clinton in his historic first visit to Vietnam made in the final days of his presidency, to call into Phnom Penh. Kerry pressed the Cambodian government to step up the pace and pass the Draft Law without further delay, preferably before the (as yet undeclared) new US president was inaugurated on 20 January.

LEGAL HISTORY IS MADE IN PHNOM PENH : THE NATIONAL
ASSEMBLY PASSES THE KHMER ROUGE TRIBUNAL LAW

Acting with new found enthusiasm, the National Assembly moved swiftly to fulfil Prime Minister Hun Sen's expressed wish that the law be dealt with before the end of the year and on Friday 29 December 2000 began its debate in plenary session.

National Assembly President Norodom Ranariddh opened discussion by calling on the Chairperson of the Legislation Committee, Manh Sophan, to report on the committee's deliberations. Representatives from each of the three parties represented in the National Assembly stated their agreement in principle with the law and, less than an hour after the opening of the session, the 98 members of the National Assembly present voted unanimously to endorse the overall contents of the Draft Law and to proceed with discussion chapter by chapter.

The Minister responsible for the Draft Law, Sok An, then made a major speech introducing the draft. On the first day Chapter One (Article 1) was passed by 96 votes of 96 cast following some fairly brief debate, in which all parties went on record as supporting the purpose of the law as being 'to bring to trial senior leaders of Democratic Kampuchea and those responsible for the crimes and serious violations of Cambodian penal law, international humanitarian law and custom, and international conventions recognised by Cambodia, that were committed between 17 April 1975 and 6 January 1979.'

Debate resumed on Tuesday 2 January 2001. In the absence of Prince Norodom Ranariddh who took a day off to celebrate his birthday, the session was chaired by Heng Samrin, Deputy President of the National Assembly and former President of Cambodia from 1981 to 1993. While some observers read Ranariddh's absence as a political statement against any trials, or against the Draft Law, this was not borne out by his subsequent involvement on the legislative process. And it is true to say that nobody expected the discussion to move so quickly that he would miss the entire remaining debate by a single morning's absence. While some questions and reservations were expressed in the debate, and Chapters 3, 4 and 11 received one fewer vote than the total number of members present, the Draft Law was finally adopted by a unanimous vote of 92/92. Sok An made a brief concluding speech and the session was over before noon.

Ranariddh signed the Draft Law on the following day and forwarded it to the Senate. On 9 January the Senate Legislation Committee discussed the text and debate in plenary session began on Thursday 11 January. The Senate members had had an additional week to consider the text and also to take on board criticism that the National Assembly debate had been perfunctory. Perhaps also this was an occasion on which the Senate (established only in 1999) wished to show its stature and assert its role as the house of review. In any event, the Senate debate turned out to be lengthier and definitely more emotional and searching than that of the National Assembly. Again, the members gave unanimous approval (54/54) to the Draft Law.

The vote was historic for two reasons: it made international legal history by promulgating a mixed tribunal (what has become known as 'the Cambodian model') and, domestically, it was the first time since 1993 that the National Assembly had voted unanimously in support of any piece of legislation.

A slight contretemps arose during and after the Senate debate concerning a letter sent by Hans Corell to Sok An on 9 January, expressing extensive criticism of the Draft Law as passed by the National Assembly, mentioning eleven problems and 'insisting' that a number of points be 're-introduced' into the text in accordance with his understanding of what was agreed to in the July 2000 negotiations. The letter was leaked to the press and several Senators asked for it to be read in the debate so that its contents could be known prior to a vote.

Sok An resisted this call, taking the view that nothing in the Draft Law contradicted any agreement reached with the United Nations and that the points raised in the letter could be clarified or amplified in the Articles of Cooperation to be signed between the two parties. His reluctance to take up any of the specific criticisms expressed by Corell stemmed also from the fact that any changes suggested by the Senate would require the whole legislative process to be undertaken all over again. Furthermore, he feared that introducing even amendments he would favour would open the door to any number of further amendments – friendly and hostile alike. He considered that the safest course of action was to keep the Draft Law text intact as passed by the National Assembly.

If the UN objections had been made public before the National Assembly session, it might well have stimulated a serious debate in which any differences with the UN would have received a public airing. Sad to say that did not happen and many observers felt that neither the strengths nor weaknesses in the draft law had been thoroughly debated.

Because it established a new legal structure (the Extraordinary Chambers), the Draft Law required review by the Constitutional Council. Its first meeting was postponed due to an electricity blackout, a reminder that Cambodia's infrastructure still suffered from the effects of past troubles. The Constitutional Council concluded its work on 12 February, issuing a decision and a reasoned opinion that Article 3 contained a contradiction with the Constitution's explicit ban on the death penalty in its reference to certain articles of the 1956 Penal Code that specified such a sentence.

Some degree of consternation and uncertainty resulted from the Constitutional Council's decision. At the very least it caused a delay in the Draft Law's heretofore smooth progression through the legislature, making it impossible for the King to sign it into law before his departure to Beijing on 21 February. Indeed, some suggested that this might have been by design, to save him the unpleasant task of sealing the fate of his former allies, although in the event it was his signature that promulgated the law several months later after he had returned to Cambodia.

The Constitutional Council decision did not specify what course of action was required. There were two ways to deal with this legal problem. The Prime Minister and Sok An said they understood that Article 3 would have to be amended,[26] but another reading of the decision would suggest that the Council gave approval to the Draft Law, and only noted that any reference to the death penalty would be unconstitutional – a point that could perhaps be clarified by the person who was to sign it into law, by the government, or by the Extraordinary Chambers when constituted.

UN spokesperson Fred Eckard issued a statement expressing disappointment at the Constitutional Council ruling, saying the process was 'starting at the bottom of the ladder again – it's a set-back, time-wise', and Hans Corell later spoke of the amendments as being 'completely unnecessary'. Prime Ministerial advisor Om Yentieng said, 'They always teach us to do things by the law, and we are abiding by the law,' but there was indeed a basis for questioning whether the complicated process of amendment was really necessary. Despite the fact that the Prime Minister had said it 'could be done in 15 minutes', the amendment process actually delayed the Law's promulgation for six months.

Various reasons were proffered for what many regarded as excessive delay: the Prime Minister and Minister Sok An both stated on several occasions that the government had other more pressing business to attend to, and any observer would note quickly that the Cambodian body politic was plagued by a chronic lack of delegation and consequent over-commitment by a handful of senior individuals.

But the delay was undoubtedly caused largely by renewed pressures from various quarters to derail the tribunal. While the CPP is well known for being tight lipped, it is widely understood that before the debate in the National Assembly in late 1999 consensus had been achieved within the party to go forward with the trial. The loss of momentum caused by the amendment process allowed former doubts and questions to re-surface, and Sok An was now obliged to convince, assure and win over a range of key individuals and institutions, especially within his party, the CPP, which held the majority within the ruling coalition.

It was not until after the CPP Plenum of July 2001renewed its endorsement for the Draft Law that the government was ready to re-present it to the National Assembly with an amendment regarding the death penalty. Not only had he secured a new consensus within his party, but Hun Sen also had gained assurance of support from the other two parties.

However, perhaps even more decisive than domestic considerations in delaying the Law's progress were the machinations of great powers, which have dogged this issue since 1979. With China in perennial opposition, but taking the public position of leaving it up to Cambodia to decide, the momentum for a trial has been largely dependent on counterweight pressure applied by mostly western governments and especially the United States.

The invisible pressures from China were not understood by many critics and nor apparently by the UN Secretariat. Hans Corell constantly harped on the theme of the Cambodians dragging their feet and interpreted the delay as a clear indication of their lack of political will. Whenever a high-ranking emissary from Beijing visited Phnom Penh, diplomats noted nothing moved on the tribunal. Stephen Bridges, the British ambassador in Phnom Penh, observed in early 2001 that hardly a week went by without a Chinese delegation coming into town to strengthen and consolidate the myriad fields of Sino-Khmer cooperation and aid agreements. China, which for more than a decade had been Phnom Penh's most bitter enemy and the key backer of the Khmer Rouge, had since 1997 gradually metamorphosed into Cambodia's special friend, providing substantial interest-free loans, aid and investment. Singapore's ambassador in Phnom Penh, Verghese Matthews, told Hans Corell that he [Corell] simply did not understand the Asian style of diplomacy. Matthews elaborated that any Asian government would have shown the same aversion to embarrassing their guests.[27]

At the same time, in the first half of 2001 the Cambodian government was waiting anxiously to see what would be the attitude of the incoming US administration of George W. Bush. The Clinton administration had taken a high profile in pushing for the Khmer Rouge tribunal. As discussed above, on several occasions key individuals like US Ambassador for War Crimes David Scheffer and Senator John Kerry had been instrumental in helping to break deadlocks between Cambodia and the UN's legal team. Equally importantly, though rather less obvious to the public eye, were the ongoing efforts in support of the tribunal made by Kent Wiedemann, US ambassador in Phnom Penh, and two former ambassadors to Cambodia, Kenneth Quinn and Charles Twining.

When George W. Bush came into the White House, Washington changed course on a range of foreign policy issues, showing little interest in pursuing multilateral diplomacy. On the issue of the Khmer Rouge tribunal no public statements were made, but insiders noted that the level of interest subsided markedly. Craig Etcheson remarked:

> It was obvious to the UN's Office of Legal Affairs that Washington had new priorities after the Bush Administration came into office. During the last years of the Clinton Administration, OLA was deluged with practically daily calls and meetings about the Khmer Rouge tribunal from senior US officials. In contrast, OLA staffers could remember only two calls from Washington about the tribunal during the first two years of the Bush Administration. Clearly there was a new sheriff in DC town, and he was not particularly focused on bringing the Khmer Rouge to justice.[28]

Meanwhile other Member States, notably Australia, India and the European Community, continued or even increased their open support. The United Kingdom pledged $500,000, and Japan and India offered judges to serve in the Extraordinary Chambers.

When eventually handed back to the legislature, the amended Draft Law moved speedily, being passed by the National Assembly on 11 July 2001 and approved by the Senate on 23 July. It was pronounced both legally and constitutionally valid by the Constitutional Council on 7 August 2001, and then signed into law by the King on 10 August 2001.

A number of governments issued congratulations to Phnom Penh for its achievement. To get this far towards establishing a credible legal framework for pioneering a new kind of genocide tribunal was in itself a significant achievement, but the UN Secretariat made no acknowledgement of the immense legal and political hurdles that had been overcome.

The endgame now depended on the UN's broad acceptance of the framework of the law as the basis of a working relationship with Cambodia, to be enshrined in a formal agreement between the two parties. Sok An sent the text of the Law to Hans Corell and, on 28 September, invited the UN to come to Phnom Penh to finalise the agreement (referred to by the Cambodian side as Articles of Cooperation).

It was hoped that this would be completed in the final months of 2001, but the events of 11 September and the establishment of the Sierra Leone Special Court diverted the attention of the United Nations away from Cambodia. It also soon became clear that the Cambodian assumption that the Khmer Rouge Trial Law was for the most part an acceptable and accepted legal framework in the eyes of the Office of Legal Affairs was ill-founded.

Hans Corell responded to the passage of the Law with an abrasive letter of 10 October 2001 criticising the Law and reiterating the eleven points of disagreement with the Law that he had made in January. This led to a polarisation of positions and opened a new phase of legal and political impasse.

Sok An sent a further two letters: in November he wrote clarifying the Cambodian position on the relationship between the Law and the agreement, and in January he responded to each of the eleven points.

Corell had insisted that the agreement must have the status of an international treaty and 'in case of difference between the Law and the Agreement, the latter shall prevail'. Sok An put forward a different perspective:

The Law, which was adopted by the Cambodian legislature under the Constitution of Cambodia, has determined the jurisdiction and competence of the Extraordinary Chambers as well as their composition, organisational structure and decision-making procedures, while the Articles of Cooperation are to determine the modalities of cooperation between the Royal Government of Cambodia and the United Nations in implementing those provisions of the Law concerning foreign technical and financial support.

While the Articles of Cooperation may clarify certain nuances in the Law, and elaborate certain details, it is not possible for them to modify, let alone prevail over, a law that has just been promulgated.

Sok An's January letter addressed Corell's eleven points, optimistically suggesting that none was insuperable and all were open to further negotiation:

... we believe that we will be able to find mutually acceptable resolutions to the points you have raised, as the Law passed by the Cambodian legislature does not contradict any of the fundamental principles we agreed on in our negotiations. You will see in our response that most of the points you raised can be clarified in the Articles of Cooperation, while certain points appear to reflect a misunderstanding of Cambodian circumstances.

COMMUNICATION FAILURES AND FLAWED NEGOTIATIONS

Apart from all the conflicting political pressures on both sides, the integrity and smooth flow of the negotiations were also constantly undermined by misunderstandings and the information gap between New York and Phnom Penh. The dialogue and negotiating process could be characterised as essentially erratic and lacking clear coordination. It constantly had to be rescued by third party mediators. Chea Vannath, president of the Center for Social Development, saw the urgent need for closer cooperation: 'I think the UN and Cambodian government should work more closely together. There should be a joint working group here in Phnom Penh instead of both teams working separately and pointing accusing fingers at each other.'[29] During nearly two years of legal drafting and complex negotiations there were long periods with little or no contact between the two sides.

Diplomats and NGOs suggested that the UN in New York could have fast-tracked the negotiations by assigning a Phnom Penh-based UN staffer, with special responsibility for liaison work. Two UN agencies – UNDP and the UN Centre for Human Rights, with offices in the Cambodian capital – were well-placed to act as the much needed facilitators. Appeals from concerned parties, including Phnom

Penh embassies, for the UN to improve its level of communications with the designation of a UN coordinator to the tribunal to be based in Phnom Penh, fell on deaf ears.

The challenge of setting up the world's first ever 'mixed tribunal', dubbed initially as the 'Cambodian model', was bound to require constant feedback, dialogue and sensitive facilitation between Phnom Penh and New York. Several Phnom Penh diplomats were astounded that the UN legal team in faraway New York had never understood the need for UN liaison to be based on the ground in Phnom Penh.[30]

On the Cambodian side control was also held firmly in a few hands. The country has little if any delegation of authority. All important decisions are still made by a few people at the top. The Khmer Rouge trial was certainly no exception. This means that the Khmer Rouge trial, like any other issue, never gets their undivided attention. Senior Minister Sok An, the chairman and chief negotiator from the Cambodian side, was reportedly at the same time holding down no less than 47 other portfolios, ranging from administrative reform, legal and judicial reform and demobilisation, to being Chairman of the National Commission of Unesco, and even at one stage to running the national airline. A Cambodian reporter once quipped, 'Mr Sok An can best be described as "the minister for everything".'

The progress of these intricate negotiations has been followed with great interest by the media, human rights NGOs and a wider public. But the key documents and communications were almost always regarded as secret affairs governed by the rules of diplomacy, rather than the public interest. The joint press conferences were dominated by the usual platitudes and real information was seldom disclosed. Both sides can be blamed for stifling public debate and for a lack of transparency.

The Cambodian government probably suffered the most as a result of this information black-out. Many human rights NGOs in Phnom Penh were all too ready to adopt adversarial positions to any agreement that fell short of a fully-fledged international tribunal. The absence of dialogue between Cambodian civil society and the government reinforced their worst suspicions. On many current problems affecting Cambodian society in dealing with poverty, injustice and the negative impacts of unbridled privatisation and 'capitalism sauvage' the government has done very little to inspire public trust.

Clearly the two sides had much to discuss and there was no doubt that the outstanding issues could not be resolved at arm's length.

The Cambodian side was anticipating a new round of face-to-face negotiations in early 2002. But they were to be disappointed. Hans Corell in New York had no intention of making another trip to the Kingdom, preferring to continue to communicate by phone, fax and letter. Subsequent events indicate that he had made up his mind and now had very different plans up his sleeve.

10
The Gangs of New York

Out of the blue on 8 February 2002 a bombshell exploded. The UN walked out of the Cambodia tribunal talks. Without responding either to the invitation to come to Phnom Penh, or to Sok An's replies to the issues he had raised in his letter of 10 October, Hans Corell suddenly announced that the UN was aborting negotiations. The dramatic announcement was made in New York without any warning to other parties involved. UN member states and officials of the Cambodian government were shocked by this sudden pull out.

The Spokesperson of the Secretary General summarised the UN position as follows:

> First, on a review of the entire process of the negotiation, the United Nations has concluded that as currently envisaged, the Cambodian court would not guarantee independence, impartiality and objectivity, which are required by the United Nations for it to cooperate with such a court.
>
> Second, the Government rejected the United Nations proposal that the assistance that the United Nations would provide will be governed by the agreement between the United Nations and Cambodia. Cambodia insists that only its own rules would govern such assistance.

The Cambodian Permanent Representative to the UN was given a copy of the press statement only 45 minutes before the press conference (held at midnight Friday Phnom Penh time). Also taken by surprise were the member states, especially those which had been heavily involved in the process (particularly United States, France, United Kingdom, Japan and Australia) whose UN Ambassadors were given only 15 minutes' notice.

Cambodians who had survived the 'Killing Fields' ordeal and yearned for two decades that justice would one day be done were bitterly disappointed. Their hopes for a credible internationally backed tribunal were shattered by the UN's unilateral decision. Some people blamed the UN. Others blamed the Hun Sen government. To abandon the process in mid-stream was also to abandon the UN's obligation to Cambodian people, offering nothing in return except one more round of justice denied.

Cambodian government officials expressed astonishment and dismay at the UN pull out, while emphasising that the door remained open to a resumption of talks. Sok An decided to place on public record the text of the Khmer Rouge Trials Law, as well as his letters to Hans Corell of 23 November 2001 and 22 January 2002, in order to clarify what he saw as misinterpretations, if not misrepresentations, of the Cambodian position.[1]

As if to underline the fragility of the whole exercise and the drastic implications of further delay in organising the trials, Ke Pauk, one of the Khmer Rouge senior military leaders likely to be indicted, died of liver failure on 15 February. His death was a timely reminder that all the surviving Khmer Rouge leaders were getting old – mostly in their 70s – and several were suffering health problems. Many feared that if the UN and the Cambodian authorities did not get their act together soon the potential defendants would all be dead before any tribunal could be convened. The UN walkout was to set back negotiations by more than a year.

Several ambassadors in Phnom Penh rushed to assure Hun Sen that member states would not accept this 'scuttle' diplomacy by the UN Secretariat against the consensus of UN member states. Australia, France, Japan and the UK went into overdrive to lobby New York for a reversal. On 13 March the Secretary General said that about a dozen ambassadors had come to see him to lobby for a resumption of talks. Kofi Annan reported, 'I advised them that I thought it would be more effective if they made a démarche in Phnom Penh,' reflecting the UN Secretariat's belief that all the blame for the collapse of negotiations lay on the Cambodian side.

Not all in the UN system felt the same way. On a visit to Phnom Penh in March, Special Representative of the Secretary General for Human Rights in Cambodia, Peter Leuprecht, said, 'I personally regret the situation with which we are now confronted, and I very much hope the last word has not been spoken.'[2] He added that he had written to Hans Corell expressing his views. On another occasion he was quoted as saying, 'the UN should be aware of its past record on Cambodia, a record that is not all glorious.'[3]

The two sides hardened their positions. While not a single government supported the unilateral decision of the UN to withdraw, the major human rights organisations applauded the move. The tenor of the two views can be gleaned from an exchange in the pages of the *Washington Post*. Balakrishnan Rajagopal, director of the Program on Human Rights and Justice of the Massachusetts Institute of Technology, argued: 'Given its history of disregard for justice in Cambodia, the United Nations sounds altogether too sanctimonious in insisting on international standards of justice as the reason for pulling out of the negotiations.'[4] Mike Jendrzejczyk, Human Rights Watch's Washington Director for Asia hit back:

> ... it is the Cambodian government that is to blame for the impasse. UN negotiators bent over backward to meet its demands, but it went ahead and adopted a tribunal law that didn't meet basic international standards. The most glaring defect of the law is that it could prevent prosecution of Khmer Rouge leaders who have received pardons or amnesties.[5]

Jendrzejczyk's analysis was challenged by the US ambassador in Phnom Penh, Kent Wiedemann,

> As much as I respect Human Rights Watch, and Mike in particular, he is simply misinformed, and his comment to the Washington Post is therefore wrong. The Khmer Rouge Law and all agreements with the UN clearly ruled out amnesty and pardon for Ieng Sary or any other defendant. Hans Corell at the UN has obfuscated and misrepresented this fact to his dishonour ... the world looks to the UN for truth, not calumny. He served us, and more importantly, the Cambodians, poorly.[6]

It is worth noting that the UN's legal experts chose to sever negotiations after no face-to-face talks for 18 months (since July 2000). It seems unimaginable that the UN would rely on remote communication via fax and occasional phone calls for the final stages of negotiations for such an unprecedented and complex process. In Asia face-to-face contact is considered the essential element in establishing trust, a commodity that was sorely lacking between the two legal panels.

Chea Vannath, president of the Center for Social Development (CSD) stressed the need for closer cooperation: 'I think the UN and Cambodian government should work more closely together. There should be a joint working group here in Phnom Penh, instead of both teams working separately, and pointing accusing fingers at each other.'[7]

Sok An had an opportunity to present the Cambodian position at the Stockholm International Forum on Truth, Justice and Reconciliation in April 2002.[8] This forum was attended by delegates from many countries grappling with these problems, including South Africa, East Timor, the former Yugoslavia and Rwanda.

Also in April the United Nations Human Rights Commission passed a strong resolution, in which it recognised 'the need for the Government of Cambodia and the United Nations to cooperate, appeals to the parties to resume discussions on the establishment of a tribunal for such a purpose and also appeals to the international community to provide assistance in this regard'.[9]

During this political standoff the Cambodian side undertook intensive work to prepare a 'state of the art' draft agreement designed to meet internationally accepted standards. Assistance to the Cambodian side in this task was given by a number of international lawyers and experts and several governments indicated that they were ready and willing to provide funding. Such were the politics of the situation, however, that these governmental expressions of intent – in one case a formal decision at ministerial level – failed to materialise into concrete assistance. Reliable diplomatic sources have reported that the governments backed off following 'pressure from New York'.

Given that Australian assistance to the Cambodian Task Force had ceased in late 2001, the Cambodians were left to work on their own meagre resources or with voluntary assistance, except for two small grants from the Open Society Institute to the Cambodian Genocide Project to enable Dr Payam Akhavan, a former Legal Advisor to the Prosecutor of the International Criminal Tribunal for the former Yugoslavia, to visit Cambodia in August 2002, and Dr Gregory Stanton, Director of the Cambodian Genocide Project, to assist the Cambodian delegation during negotiations at the United Nations in January 2003 and to travel to Cambodia in September 2003 to assist the Task Force, especially relating to procedure and evidence.[10]

Prime Minister Hun Sen, who is well known for his acerbic tongue and colourful language, was unusually muted as the various diplomatic overtures were played out. Initially he said that the United Nations had three months in which to return to the negotiations before Cambodia would move to Plan B – the explicit fallback provisions in the Law if the United Nations refused to participate.

If there were to be no UN-backed trial then the law allowed for a series of options: firstly bilateral arrangements with foreign judges being recommended by member states and not through the UN

Secretariat. The next possibility would be for direct recruitment from among the ranks of well-known international jurists. If neither of these options worked, the last resort would be to establish a wholly Cambodian domestic court.

As the United Nations showed no interest in a resumption of talks, on 14 May 2002 Hun Sen stated, 'I now suspect that political tricks are being played by the United Nations to protect the Khmer Rouge,' again recalling the record of UN support for the Khmer Rouge during the 1980s. He went on to say, in an allusion to Plan B, 'The ball is in the UN's court, but they should not forget there is another ball.' India had already made public its willingness to supply a judge even without the United Nations.

For four months both Hans Corell and Kofi Annan maintained stubborn resistance even to discussing the issue, despite ongoing intense lobbying for renewed talks. It appeared to many that it was the end of the road, best summed up by Craig Etcheson's comments at the Foreign Correspondents Club of Cambodia: 'The UN is out of the picture, period. They aren't coming back. That chapter is history. The second coming is more likely than Hans Corell coming back to Phnom Penh.'[11]

The Secretary General's resistance to dialogue was softened only by the efforts of Ambassador Hisashi Owada, a very senior Japanese foreign affairs official, who had served as Japan's Permanent Representative to the United Nations from 1994–98. Owada, a member of the select United Nations Foundation, was able to kick-start a resumption of talks by persuading Kofi Annan to talk to Hun Sen on the phone.

Once again, though, things were not as they seemed on the surface. Kofi Annan introduced a new hoop for Cambodia to jump through – he insisted on receiving a 'clear mandate' from either the Security Council or the General Assembly. This requirement, disarmingly innocuous and easy to achieve (at least as far as the General Assembly was concerned), was therefore all the more puzzling. The General Assembly had voted every year since 1997 for the United Nations to be involved in the trial, most recently with a specific welcome of the 2001 Cambodian Khmer Rouge Law, urging 'the Government and the United Nations to conclude an agreement without delay so that the Extraordinary Chambers can start to function promptly, and appeals to the international community to provide assistance in this regard, including financial and personnel support to the Chambers'.[12]

Why did Kofi Annan not accept as a mandate the six General Assembly resolutions from 1997 to 2001, which were also backed up by the April 2002 United Nations Human Rights Commission resolution? If there were any doubts about the views of member states on the issue, then the persistent lobbying he received from countries that expressed an opinion on the issue should have convinced him that a mandate was staring him in the face.

And if a fresh mandate were now required, what would the Secretary General require it to say? When the news of the mandate became public, announced by the Secretary General's spokesperson, Fred Eckhard, on 20 August, some optimism was expressed, but also a considerable degree of caution. 'I think this is a door opening after the deadlock,' said Prince Norodom Ranariddh, president of Cambodia's National Assembly.

Meanwhile the Cambodian legal system was coming to grips with more recent crimes committed by the Khmer Rouge. In 1994 Khmer Rouge forces had ambushed the Phnom Penh–Kampot train; 13 Cambodians were killed and three western backpackers taken hostage and later executed. On 4 September 2002 the Supreme Court upheld the conviction of General Nuon Paet, who had held the three foreign hostages in custody. Two days later the Appeals Court convicted Colonel Chhouk Rin, the leader of the military unit that had attacked the train.[13]

Both decisions appeared to indicate a willingness by the authorities to get serious about Khmer Rouge prosecutions, albeit belatedly and following sustained pressure from the foreign embassies and families of the victims. The December 2002 conviction of General Sam Bith, the third Khmer Rouge officer implicated in the crimes, who was Pol Pot's Kampot regional chief with command responsibility, was another sign of resolve.

Cambodian judges have often been dismissed as hopelessly corrupt, ill-trained and lacking independence. But in the case of the Sam Bith trial, US lawyer George Cooper from Legal Aid of Cambodia, who represented the family of Mark Slater, one of those executed, noted that, 'this is one of the better trials I have attended. The judge was competent in handling the proceedings, the rights of the accused were respected, and justice was seen to be done.'[14]

DELIVERING THE MANDATE

The 57th session of the UN General Assembly presented the opportunity to deliver the Secretary General his required mandate.

It was a difficult exercise despite the concerted efforts of a number of member states and the express opposition of none.

Japan took the lead role in coordinating interested member states to draft a new mandate. On 26 September a meeting of 27 countries calling themselves the Group of Interested States discussed their strategy. The Cambodian Permanent Representative to the UN, Ambassador Ouch Borith, explained that Cambodia supported their efforts to do what was required to re-engage the United Nations. The Group of Interested States debated several alternative strategies and decided to go ahead with a special resolution in the Third Committee (which covers social, cultural and humanitarian affairs). At Japan's request, Australia took on the task of drafting the resolution.

During October and early November a resolution to mandate the UN secretariat to resume negotiations with the Cambodian government was drafted and circulated among the Group of Interested States. It went through several drafts incorporating amendments proposed by Cambodia and other countries. Considerable energy was expended on arguing semantic points, none of which should have been allowed to stand in the way of moving towards the trial with all possible speed.

Tensions were riding high in early November as the deadline approached for filing resolutions for the 57th UNGA. The Group of Interested States was still trying to finalise the text and gradually, almost imperceptibly, a new condition was imposed on Cambodia – to co-sponsor the resolution.

Rumours began to fly that Australia would not proceed with its sponsorship of the resolution if Cambodia did not join as a co-sponsor. On the last day (13 November) the rumour was confirmed when Australia withdrew. At the eleventh hour France and Japan came to the rescue by sponsoring a draft resolution with some slight amendments.

On 16 November Prime Minister Hun Sen affirmed to the sponsors that Cambodia supported the final text of the draft resolution despite not wishing to be a co-sponsor, and it was debated and put to the vote in the Third Committee on 20 November.[15] The Chairman reported that some delegations had asked for a 24-hour postponement, partly in order to hear the views of the Secretary General and Legal Counsel (Hans Corell) and partly to eliminate supposed uncertainties or ambiguities in the text, though details of these were not given. The proposal to defer the matter was debated and defeated by a vote of 14 in favour to 90 against, with 59 abstentions.[16] The substantive resolution was then debated and adopted by a recorded vote of 123 in favour including China to zero against, with 37 abstentions. 'We found the changes to weaken the text, but we were not prepared to vote against it,' said Ambassador John Dauth of Australia.[17]

While the margin of the vote in the Third Committee was overwhelming, a bad taste was left by the debate and particularly by the conspicuous abstention of some states that had been strong supporters of the process (notably Sweden and the United Kingdom). Evidently some of the 37 countries abstained because they were convinced by the arguments of Hans Corell that international legal standards could not be guaranteed by the existing legislation.

The passage of the resolution was a clear slap in the face to the UN Secretariat for pulling out of the negotiations in 2002. In addition to calling on the Secretariat to re-open talks, it stipulated that negotiations be resumed from where they left off in 2002 and it affirmed that the 2001 Khmer Rouge tribunal law should be accepted as the legal framework.

A last-minute campaign swung into action to stop the General Assembly from endorsing this strong mandate from the Third Committee for the United Nations Secretariat to return to Cambodia and carry on negotiations from the point where they had been scuttled in 2002.

Amnesty International issued a strong press release on 19 November calling 'upon the UN General Assembly to ensure that any new resolution for the establishment of the tribunal be based upon new negotiations starting afresh with the Cambodian authorities'. In Amnesty's view the new mandate did not address the 'totally-flawed Khmer Rouge Law' and all that had been achieved so far should be scrapped.

> Cambodians deserve the same high standards of justice as provided in the statute of the newly established International Criminal Court, which Cambodia itself has ratified ... We believe that the so-called 'mixed tribunal' agreed upon in 2000 comprising a majority of Cambodian judges over international judges, without an international prosecutor, fell short of required internationally recognized standards and did not provide full guarantees of independence, impartiality and credibility required to ensure that justice be done, and be seen to be done ... Moreover the Extraordinary Chambers which would be created would only be

required to act on international human rights standards that are severely limited in the draft resolution.

The Amnesty International position was backed by Human Rights Watch and a number of Cambodian Human Rights NGOs. It should be noted that the Amnesty statement was factually wrong in stating that the Law provided for no international prosecutor and it ignored the fact that the resolution (on Cambodia's specific suggestion) included reference to the need to comply with Articles 14 and 15 of the International Covenant on Civil and Political Rights in the conduct of the trial. On 21 November veteran writer on Cambodia, Elizabeth Becker, gave a highly negative assessment in the *New York Times*:

> But the resolution that ultimately passed in a key committee had been watered down to meet Cambodia's approval ... 'This resolution does not even ask the Cambodian government to live up to the very minimum international standard for a fair trial, much less build in guarantees that those standards will be adhered to', said Stephen R. Heder, a Cambodia scholar at the University of London.[18]

These critics were answered, also in the *New York Times*, by David Scheffer, then senior vice president of the United Nations Association of the United States, who had played a key role in the Cambodian negotiations as US ambassador at large for war crimes issues.

> Every judicial action would require the approval of at least one international judge ... The few issues that caused the talks to collapse must not be allowed to derail the process again. Lingering concerns about legal representation, amnesties and the influence of the United Nations have long been resolvable. Human rights activists call for a United Nations-dominated international criminal tribunal for Cambodia – an approach sought long ago and blocked – and insistence on near perfect justice risk losing the good for the sake of the unattainable....
>
> After more than 20 years, senior Khmer Rouge leaders are finally on the verge of standing trial in an open and credible courtroom. How tragic it would be if advocates for international justice helped them get off the hook.[19]

Despite all the furore, on 18 December 2002 the General Assembly adopted Resolution 57/228 by a margin of seven votes higher than

14   Hans Corell, UN legal chief, and Sok An, chairman of the Cambodian Task Force for setting up the tribunal, clink glasses at the 6 June 2003 signing ceremony. This landmark agreement for a mixed tribunal has been dubbed the Cambodia model. (Sokunthea)

when it was passed in the Third Committee – 150 in favour, zero against, with 30 abstentions. Again China voted with Cambodia. The following day Kofi Annan invited Hun Sen to send representatives 'to an exploratory meeting at United Nations headquarters in New York in order to prepare for the resumptions of negotiations', and the Prime Minister instructed Sok An to accept.[20]

BACK TO THE TABLE – OR TO THE DRAWING BOARD?

As the talks began on 6 January 2003 the UN headquarters were shrouded in snow and the atmosphere inside was no less frosty. Even though the Cambodian delegation had been warned that Hans Corell would be tough, nobody expected that he would go so far as to seek to annul the structure, composition and decision making methods of the Extraordinary Chambers as previously negotiated more than two years between Cambodia and the UN and now incorporated in the Khmer Rouge Law promulgated in August 2001.

In the opening session of the talks Corell gave an hour-long monologue with no translation, before which he put on the table another of his 'Non-Papers'. In a breathtaking move Corell proposed returning to the model presented by the UN back in August 1999 – an international majority in both chambers, a single international prosecutor and investigating judge – and scrapping the pre-trial chamber.

Ignoring the General Assembly resolution's explicit welcome of the 2001 Khmer Rouge Law and the clear mandate for the Secretary General to resume talks on the basis of previous negotiations, Corell based his wholesale revision of the proposed structure on the General Assembly resolution's call for credibility, which he said presented a 'new situation'. Further, he advanced the argument that the UN's experience in Sierra Leone had convinced him that the formerly negotiated structure needed 'simplification'.

The Cambodian delegation was exasperated by this U-turn. They could not see how the spirit of the new UN mandate, which instructed negotiations to be resumed not started all over again, was not being implemented. There is no way that anyone could have expected Cambodia to agree to throw out everything that had been carefully crafted over years and was now enshrined in Cambodian law. The delegation certainly felt like walking out in disgust, but knew that there was too much at stake. Sok An was adamant that they must continue talking and attempt to reach agreement. The Cambodian Task Force had previously resolved that they would never be the ones to 'break the bridge'.

The Cambodians went back to their hotel, and spent 7 January, the 24th anniversary of the overthrow of the Khmer Rouge, preparing their own Non-Paper in response to Corell's. The only way to prevent a rift was to concentrate on items on which progress could be made, putting to one side what were referred to as 'core elements' defining the structure, composition and decision making of the Extraordinary Chambers. Sok An said he had no mandate from the Cambodian government to re-negotiate these core elements.

One evening the Cambodian delegation went to the movies. They chose the most popular show in town, *The Gangs of New York*. How appropriate for the atmosphere they found themselves in – a knock-down, drag-out war between 'native' New Yorkers (the Secretariat) and interloping 'foreigners' (Cambodia and the other member states).

Hans Corell repeatedly stressed that the position he was presenting was fully supported by the Secretary General and, indeed, Kofi Annan did present the same hardline stance in his 15-minute meeting with Sok An. The delegation was surprised by his cool demeanour, which contrasted to his public persona exuding warmth and enthusiasm. A timer was prominently placed on the table in front of him – hardly conducive to a free and cooperative discussion.[21]

On 29 January 2003, within two weeks of the New York meetings, anti-Thai riots erupted in Phnom Penh. Cambodia's rising international stature after its competent hosting of the seventh Asean Summit hosted in November 2002 was dramatically undermined as mobs torched the Thai Embassy and a number of Thai businesses and hotels, following a build-up of racist resentment and unfounded press rumours of insults by a Thai actress and killings of Cambodian embassy staff in Bangkok. The immediate property damage was calculated at $50 million – money Cambodia could ill afford. But far greater damage was wreaked on Cambodia's international reputation and to its people's hard-won sense that peace had come at last to their country. Gone in a single night was the confident and calm image presented in November as Cambodia hosted the Asean summit, and the Asean Tourism Ministerial Meeting that ushered in 'Visit Cambodia Year 2003'. And as far as the Khmer Rouge Trials were concerned, the riots were manna from heaven for those who doubted the government's ability to stage trials in an atmosphere upholding the rule of law and guaranteeing the security of witnesses, defendants and judges alike.

Meanwhile, member states began to hear of the U-turn proposed by the Secretariat in New York and they were horrified. Six members of the Group of Interested States met with the Secretary General on 13 February 2003 to insist that he carry out the will of the member states by resuming negotiations where they left off, without any new conditions. They made it clear that they considered the position put to the Cambodian delegation in January was not in accordance with the spirit of the December UNGA resolution. They were extremely concerned that Kofi Annan had said he was not yet ready to send a delegation to Phnom Penh to resume negotiations (as stipulated in the UN mandate) but had introduced a pre-condition, that Prime Minister Hun Sen should confirm in writing acceptance of all the articles in the UN's latest version of the draft agreement except those articles relating to the core elements.

In the meeting with the Group of Interested States Kofi Annan complained about interference and 'micro-management' by the member states but he agreed to send the delegation to Phnom Pen with no new conditions. This was a clear victory for the member states over the UN Secretariat's diversionary manoeuvres that had threatened to stall negotiations all over again.

The scope for autonomous policy making by the UN Secretary General without the consensus of member states is not clearly defined in the UN charter. In this case the only fig leaf of justification for not complying with the will of member states was to point to the fact that the resolution had not gained unanimous approval in the General Assembly. However, 30 abstentions when pitted against 150 votes in favour and none against, was a rather threadbare justification for going against a General Assembly resolution.

The Secretary General's eventual decision to send the delegation without any prior conditions was welcome news in Cambodia, but there was not much basis on which to build the mutual confidence that was sorely needed to clinch the final agreement.

FINAL TEXT INITIALLED

The Cambodian team was confident that their insistence on retaining the previously negotiated structure had the explicit support of the UNGA mandate and was also backed by the member states. They were ready to negotiate on all other points and proposed revised wording that quickly led to agreement on most of the articles, with several set aside for more lengthy discussion.

In withdrawing from the negotiations a year earlier Hans Corell had cited international standards of justice and the relationship between the Law and the Agreement as the most contentious issues. With regard to international standards, even before the UN withdrawal Cambodia had (in Sok An's letter of 22 January 2002) expressed a willingness to add more explicit guarantees regarding the defendants' right to free choice of counsel (the only standard Corell had explicitly mentioned in his criticism of the Law). During the negotiations in New York Sok An agreed to make direct reference in the Agreement to the key international treaty regarding the conduct of trials and the rights of defendants (Articles 14 and 15 of the International Covenant on Civil and Political Rights), which had, at Cambodia's request, been inserted into the UNGA Resolution of December 2002.

Perhaps the key remaining point of contention was, then, the relationship between the two documents, which was resolved in March. The Cambodians objected to the UN wording that the Law 'shall at all times conform to the present Agreement' and 'in case of inconsistency between the text ... the Agreement shall prevail', finding it crass and one-sided. Instead, Sok An proposed that the Agreement should state that it would be subject to the application of the Vienna Convention on the Law of Treaties. In discussion, particular reference was added to Articles 26 and 27. Article 26 is the famous *pacta sunt servanda* dictum that 'every treaty in force is binding upon the parties to it and must be performed by them in good faith', while Article 27 states that 'A party may not invoke the provisions of its internal law as justification for its failure to perform a treaty.' The UN side agreed, adding that they also had thought of taking that way out of the impasse on this point.

Late on Sunday evening both delegations gave their approval to the latest text. Hans Corell said it could only be initialled at this stage and that signature would have to await endorsement by the General Assembly. Diplomats and other close observers of the process expressed surprise that the two sides had arrived at this positive outcome, particularly since Hans Corell had been quite pessimistic in discussions with them as the negotiations proceeded. What, they wondered, was the magic potion that had suddenly brought about such a breakthrough?

The real explanation for the turnaround was somewhat more mundane. The final text was a vindication for those who had argued that the differences between the two camps were not that great when the UN abandoned the process with its walk-out in 2002. Where there is a political will, there is a way to find agreement. Historians may conclude that whereas the UN Secretariat backed out a year earlier because it lacked the will and conviction to see the process through, the member states took a more positive view. The fresh mandate delivered in December by the UNGA left little room for manoeuvre and Hans Corell confided to local NGOs that 'this time my hands are tied.'

A final text of the Draft Agreement was initialled by Sok An and Hans Corell in the presence of Prime Minister Hun Sen on Monday 17 March – one day before Kofi Annan was to present his report to the General Assembly requested within 90 days from the UNGA Resolution 57/228.

At a luncheon he gave in honour of Hans Corell and the UN delegation, Sok An was beaming with delight as he announced that the final text had been initialled hours before. He called for a toast to the visitors and to the agreement, praising the Cambodian model as a contribution to international justice.

Hans Corell responded in more sombre mode. He referred to his visit to the killing fields of Choeung Ek three years before, stating 'the world community owes a debt to Cambodia, and if this Agreement works, we can do something to pay this back.' As to the content of the Agreement, he remained guarded: 'it is not for me to express an opinion on the result. I am merely a civil servant carrying out my duty.' At his departure press conference he made more public his reservations on the Cambodian model, saying it was cumbersome and complex: 'as a professional judge, I would say a more simple structure would be an advantage.'

Both sides clarified that the initialling of the text was only the conclusion of the 'technical phase' of the negotiations, and that it now needed the political approval of the General Assembly and then ratification by Cambodia.

ENDORSEMENT BY THE GENERAL ASSEMBLY

After the celebration lunch in March at Hotel Le Royal in Phnom Penh where the entire diplomatic corps toasted the hard-won agreement, it remained only for both sides to endorse the text. Approval by the UNGA appeared to many to be a straightforward formality, but it was made more complicated by a last-ditch effort from the UN Secretariat to query some provisions and foster doubt about the viability of the agreement.

On 6 April 2003 the UN Secretary General released his Report to the General Assembly on the Khmer Rouge Tribunal. It was rather amazing that Kofi Annan could not find even one positive thing to endorse in the draft agreement and did not recommend its adoption by the General Assembly. The sole recommendation in his 20-page report related to the need to assure appropriate salaries and status of the international judges, co-prosecutor and co-investigating judge.

The highly negative report clearly reflected the stand of the Office of Legal Affairs, which was far closer to the attitude of Amnesty International than to that of key member states.

Annan's report expressed doubts three times, concerns about credibility seven times and twice emphasised that the draft agreement allowed for UN withdrawal if it were to be violated by the Cambodian Government.

The Secretary General chose to devote most of his report to revisiting every step of the negotiations, apportioning blame to the Cambodian side for any delays and seeking to criticise the general situation of human rights in Cambodia and the weakness of the judiciary. He defended the Secretariat decision to withdraw from negotiations in February 2002 and implicitly criticised those member states who opposed the scuttling of the talks.

One good thing that can be said about the report was that it publicly confirmed that at the January 2003 talks in New York the Secretariat had made a U-turn in their negotiations with Cambodia and attempted to create a Sierra Leone-type court with an international majority in all aspects. Up until the Secretary General's report was released this was not widely known.

The Secretary General for the first time made an estimate of the budget for the Extraordinary Chambers – $19 million over three years. While not made clear in the report, it would seem that this figure referred only to the international costs, overwhelmingly for personnel ($18.2 million). The estimate did not include renovations of premises, travel for witnesses, UN share of utilities and services or remuneration of defence counsel, nor any expenses by the Cambodian side. Annan reiterated the Secretariat's preference for funding the Extraordinary Chambers through the regular budget of the United Nations, citing the problems experienced in gaining sufficient funding for the Sierra Leone Special Court.

Amnesty International (and also Human Rights Watch) went even further than the Secretary General's report, explicitly urging the General Assembly not to accept the Draft Agreement as it stood:

> Amnesty International urges all members of the General Assembly to study carefully the UN Secretary-General's report which expresses explicit reservations about the proposed Extraordinary Chambers given the precarious state of Cambodia's judiciary as well as the observations made by Amnesty International below before voting on the present draft. The organization urges the General Assembly to make the improvements necessary to bring this agreement into line with international laws and standards.[22]

A point by point rebuttal of Amnesty International's objections was made by Gregory Stanton in an article entitled, 'Perfection is the enemy of justice', published in the *Bangkok Post* and widely circulated on the Internet.[23]

The strongly-worded public denouncements of the Draft Agreement were accompanied by feverish behind-the-scenes activity by right-wing forces in the US Congress with support from the Cambodian opposition. Pressure was exerted on the State Department to refrain from supporting the Draft Agreement at the United Nations, as part of a policy of withholding anything that could be seen as support of the Cambodian People's Party during the 2003 national election campaign. Congress threatened to block any US funding for the Extraordinary Chambers if the State were seen to support the government in any way. A last-minute deal exchanged silence by the US delegates at the Third Committee for agreement by Congress to allow funding for the Extraordinary Chambers, provided it would not be requested until after the Cambodian elections.

Despite these manoeuvres, the Third Committee on 2 May and the plenary session of the General Assembly on 13 May approved the Draft Agreement, specifying that the Extraordinary Chambers should be funded by voluntary contributions.

For the convenience of the US delegation, the vote was taken by consensus on both occasions. Nevertheless, the US delegation dissented from the consensus. The UN official press release on the meeting reported:

> In explanation of vote, the representative of the United States said his country supported the substance of the current resolution, but dissociated itself from the consensus due to concerns about the timing. It would have been better to delay consideration of the text until after the elections for the Cambodian National Assembly in July.

THE SIGNING CEREMONY

Finally, then, almost six years after being requested to assist, on 13 May 2003, the United Nations had given its assent to the Agreement with Cambodia to establish the Khmer Rouge trials. To become official the document now had to be signed and then ratified by Cambodia.

Hans Corell quickly proposed that he come to Phnom Penh for the signing ceremony and Sok An suggested that it be held on 20 May, the memorial day for victims of the Khmer Rouge crimes. Unfortunately, it proved impossible for Hans Corell to make that date, due to pressing legal concerns in New York in connection with the Security Council discussions on the UN's status in Iraq, so the ceremony was postponed for a few weeks.

The signing ceremony was held on 6 June 2003 in the historic Chaktomuk Theatre. The auditorium where the 1979 People's Revolutionary Tribunal had taken place was once again packed –

this time with representatives of the diplomatic corps, government, parliament, UN agencies, NGO workers and the press.

Hans Corell headed back to New York with one copy of the blue bound and ribboned signed Agreement under his arm and the other copy was retained in Phnom Penh, to be deposited in the Legal and Consular Department of the Ministry of Foreign Affairs and International Cooperation.

RATIFICATION BY CAMBODIA

Now the ball was firmly back in Cambodia's court to undertake the ratification of the Agreement. Certainly, the Prime Minister seemed keen to move fast and the Council of Ministers endorsed the Agreement at its meeting of 13 June, forwarding it to the National Assembly with a request that it be dealt with as a matter of urgency.

Yet, as had so often been the case, a seemingly simple step proved to be hard to take. Gaining approval by the UN had taken so long that when the signing ceremony was held, Cambodia was already in campaign mode for the 2003 national elections. During late May and early June the National Assembly failed repeatedly to gather a quorum of members to deal with a number of items that had been on its agenda for some time, as members were already out on the hustings and priming the pump in their constituencies.

Besides electoral distraction, another factor may well have played a part in the National Assembly's lack of action on ratification. This was the perennial factor of outside intervention. The writing was already on the wall at the UNGA meeting in May with the United States dissociating itself from the consensus (a rather strange concept indeed), expressing a desire to delay approval until after the elections in July, in deference to those who were campaigning against Hun Sen and the CPP.

As the elections drew closer the pressure increased. As discussed in Chapter 8, on 26 June 2003 Senator Mitch McConnell introduced into the Senate the Cambodia Democracy and Accountability Bill offering increased funding to Cambodia, including its allocation specifically for the Khmer Rouge trial, but conditional on free and fair elections – but only if they resulted in regime change. Their concern was not so much about free and fair and elections as getting rid of Hun Sen, presumably replacing him with 'our man in Phnom Penh' – Sam Rainsy.

While those unfamiliar with Cambodia's political history of foreign intervention berated the government for 'dragging its feet' over ratifying the Agreement, the Cambodian government was extremely wary of giving the US government any pretext for intervention in the pre-election period. The National Assembly's failure to make a special effort to gain a quorum and ratify the treaty with the UN before the elections sadly became of matter of political convenience to all the parties.

The delay over ratification was one of several manifestations of Cambodia's acquiescence to US pressures during this sensitive period. On the eve of US Secretary of State Colin Powell's visit to Cambodia in early June to attend the Asean Regional Forum, the authorities closed several Islamic schools and arrested four people as suspected terrorists at the behest of US intelligence reports. Considerable pressure was also exerted by Washington to get Cambodia to sign an 'Article 98' exemption agreement, whereby Cambodia and the US pledged not to send each other's nationals to the International Criminal Court. It was a testimony to Cambodia's weakness that it felt obliged to make such an undertaking when less than a year earlier, in its capacity as the first southeast Asian signatory of the International Criminal Court and one of its founding members, Cambodia had proudly hosted a conference promoting the International Criminal Court.[24]

So the ratification was put on hold until the formation of a new government. And that turned out to be a long time coming. In the July ballot the CPP won 73 seats, Funcinpec 26 and the Sam Rainsy Party 21 seats. The CPP won a clear majority and was the only party to campaign on the genocide issue. Indeed, much of the loyalty of Cambodian voters to the ruling party is attributed to their historic role in 1979 in delivering the country from the Khmer Rouge in alliance with the Vietnamese army.

But the CPP majority was still nine seats short of the two-thirds majority required under the Cambodian constitution to vote in a new government. Unlike 1993 and 1998, Funcinpec this time declined to take part in open talks on a coalition government and instead joined forces with the opposition Sam Rainsy Party to create a new Alliance of Democrats. The Alliance used the two-thirds majority rule to block any progress on forming a new coalition government unless the CPP accepted their terms, including the choice of prime minister. This led to a stalemate.

In October the new National Assembly members were sworn in and the King convened several meetings in November in an attempt to break the stalemate, but the year ended with the new government still out of reach four months after the declaration of the poll.

The old government continued to function, albeit without the participation of most former Funcinpec members. As far as ordinary Cambodians were concerned, the impasse seemed to have little effect on their day-to-day lives and only served to increase their already high level of cynicism with politics and politicians. But the failure to elect the officials and committees of the National Assembly meant it was not formally in session.

Ratification of the Agreement with the United Nations was one of the casualties of this situation. What a pity that this simple vote was not held before the elections when it might have been anticipated it would have been supported unanimously, as the Khmer Rouge Law had been in 2001. In the increasingly polarised political situation at the end of 2003, Sam Rainsy Party parliamentarian, Son Chhay, said that his party would not vote to ratify the Agreement and wanted to set up a purely international tribunal.[25] While a vote against, even by all 21 Sam Rainsy Party members, would not prevent ratification, which requires only a simple majority, it would signal the end of the consensus that the government had managed to nurture on this issue of national importance.

Despite the pending status of the Agreement's ratification, the government and the United Nations continued to work on preparations for the tribunal, in the expectation that the political crisis would be resolved sooner or later. The Task Force continued its work throughout the election and post-election period, concentrating its efforts on collecting and translating documents that would be needed by the court. Developing the web site and examining staffing and space requirements with a view to refining budget estimates also moved the process forward.

On 1 October 2003, the Secretary General appointed Mr Karsten Herrel as Coordinator for United Nations Assistance to the Khmer Rouge Tribunal (UNAKRT), a new unit established in the Office of Programme Planning, Budget and Accounts within the UN Secretariat. Herrel is a long-term senior United Nations administrator, most recently heading the operations in Bosnia. He expressed pleasure to be able to return to Cambodia, recalling memories from over a year spent as UNTAC's Chief of Administration.

Herrel's Technical Assessment Mission to Cambodia made a productive week-long visit in December 2003, working with the Cambodian government Task Force on inspections, details of staffing, budget, legal matters, documentation and security.

The Joint Press Statement was very positive. 'We have achieved a common concept of operations on which to base our planning,' said Mr Herrel. The two sides would continue to work together from afar translating the data gathered during the mission into a detailed staffing profile, budget and time-line, to be included in the Secretary General's final report which would be accompanied by an appeal for funds from member states.

The two sides agreed to develop a coordinated budget with two sources of funding – the proposed United Nations Trust Fund and the Royal Government of Cambodia. The RGC indicated it would be seeking bilateral funds to contribute to its side of the budget.

Senior Minister Sok An assured the UN team and stated publicly that, 'Ratification of the Agreement will be the highest priority for the new government and National Assembly, to be addressed immediately on resolution of the current political deadlock.'

Perhaps more important than the concrete achievements of the mission, was the good working relationship that the two teams developed. It was the first time since the Cambodians had requested United Nations assistance over six years earlier that a real sense of common purpose had been achieved, with both sides finally rowing in the same direction.

11
Clinching Convictions – the Challenge for the Prosecution

The world believes that the key lieutenants of Pol Pot are guilty of some of the worst crimes ever committed in the twentieth century. The senior leaders of the Khmer Rouge rank as world class murderers in the premier league with Hitler and Stalin. There is overwhelming documentary proof and testimony that terrible crimes took place. In the eyes of many Cambodians justice means only one thing – that all the leaders will surely be found guilty and then perhaps Cambodia can be at peace. But there is one problem. In a free and fair trial the accused are entitled to the presumption of innocence until the case is proven beyond a reasonable doubt, referred to as 'intime conviction' in the French civil law system.

Most of the surviving Khmer Rouge leadership have so far denied either knowledge or responsibility for crimes committed by the Pol Pot regime. Nuon Chea denied just about everything in a rare interview with the BBC in 2002. BBC's Phil Rees commented after the interview at Nuon Chea's house in Pailin,

It did not matter that the questions were about mass murder. Torture. The annihilation of nearly a quarter of the Cambodian nation. They still brought a smile to his lips and a chortle or two. 'Good humour is in my nature,' he told me, 'I have no worries.' Nuon Chea was clearly not troubled by any trifling matters of conscience in stating categorically 'I have never stayed awake at night or shed any tears. Referring to his role in the power structure he said 'Pol Pot was the party secretary. I was just the deputy secretary and sometimes I had no influence.'[1]

Those indicted will probably argue that they were not privy to leadership decisions about internal security, purges and campaigns to eliminate enemies of the state. One can predict that the defendants will seek to place the full blame on others – especially 'Brother Number One' Pol Pot, who is conveniently dead.

Most Cambodians have little or no notion of the delicate balancing act known as the scales of justice and such complicated notions as the burden of proof and the rights of the defence. If the unthinkable were to happen and a Khmer Rouge leader were acquitted on the basis of insufficient evidence, this could provoke popular anger against the tribunal judges and particularly the international jurists. Supporters of a tribunal have to place faith in the ability of the prosecutors to prove their case. At the same time they have to recognise that strong as the evidence is, conviction is by no means a forgone conclusion.

This chapter moves our focus from the political and historical plane to the legal in examining the challenges for the prosecution in building cases against individual defendants for their role in the commission of specific crimes enumerated in the Khmer Rouge trial law. We remain at the level of painting the general picture and have deliberately refrained from making allegations as to individual culpability, or anticipating lines of defence to be pursued by likely defendants.

We consider three aspects of the task faced by the prosecutors and the investigating judges: evidence, jurisdiction and legal proof of the elements of the crimes.

Their main task is to find evidence that directly incriminates individual Khmer Rouge leaders. They will be searching for evidence that would prove some of the following key points:

1) that a defendant was a high-ranking leader of the Khmer Rouge regime who was involved in policy-making decisions *or* was personally responsible for serious crimes;

2) that the instructions and policies of the Khmer Rouge leadership from 1975–79 were instrumental in promoting a culture of mass killings, purges and the elimination of enemies in pursuit of the purification of society;

3) that the central command structure of the regime was such that the leadership could exert control over the regions and that the mass killings were not local phenomena but were widespread and systematic – the logical result of policies, instructions and orders carried out according to a clear chain of command or responsibility.

Observers used to the Anglo-American adversary or common law systems will be unfamiliar with the significant role of the investigating judge in the inquisitory or civil law system followed in Cambodia. In this system the largest part of the process takes place in the investigating phase, outside the court room, and the trial phase is relatively brief. The case is passed from the prosecutor to the investigating judge for substantiation and in-depth evaluation. Only if and when the investigating judge confirms that there is enough evidence to support the charges issued against the defendant will the case go forward to trial.

Another characteristic of a trial under Cambodian law is the potential role of victims as parties to a criminal case. They may elect to join the process and to seek compensation for loss resulting from the offences. In this way, victims take a civil action within the framework of a criminal process and forego their right to launch a case in the civil courts. In such cases, following its sentencing of the convicted criminal, the criminal court decides on an award for compensation to be made by the convicted criminal to individual victims. This was the route taken in the backpacker trials against Chhouk Rin and Sam Bith (discussed in Chapters 9 and 10), where the families of those murdered and the railway officials joined the cases and were awarded compensation. It is, however, difficult to imagine how the millions upon millions of survivors from the KR regime could be represented in the coming trials or adequately compensated for their losses. The court will need to plan a careful approach to this issue.

THE RANGE OF EVIDENCE AVAILABLE TO THE COURT

Stored away in the vaults of the Cambodian genocide research project known as the Documentation Center of Cambodia is a veritable treasure-trove of Khmer Rouge documents and photographs which have been meticulously arranged, catalogued, analysed and translated.

Thousands of incriminating documents, many from the archives of S-21 (Tuol Sleng) and other parts of the prison system, will undoubtedly form much of the legal foundation of the prosecution case. These include over 200,000 pages of internal files from the security apparatus (the Santebal) and nearly 20,000 biographies, mainly compiled from S-21 prisoners' confessions.

Annotations on some documents indicating they were passed up for the approval of party leaders may be critical in helping to determine the role played by individual defendants. Other documents can lead the prosecutors to mass graves throughout the country which may provide physical forensic evidence, or may identify perpetrators and witnesses, both victims and lower-level Khmer Rouge cadres, who could be called to testify in person at the trial.

The Law provides that the Khmer Rouge trials will be organised in accordance with Cambodian legal procedures, although these may be supplemented from international practice when Cambodian procedure is seen to be imprecise or lacking. The Rules of Procedure developed for the two existing International Criminal Tribunals (for the former Yugoslavia and Rwanda), the International Criminal Court and the Sierra Leone Special Court all combine aspects of common and civil law, and they will provide the main points of outside reference for the Khmer Rouge trials.

Some commentators from common law countries following the Anglo-Saxon legal tradition, such as the US and most of the former British colonies, are so steeped in their own legal tradition that their criticisms have failed to take heed of major differences that will apply to admissibility of evidence in the tribunal as a court in the Cambodian system, modelled on the civil law system of France, the former colonial power.

Under the 'common law' legal system severe restrictions are placed on what types of evidence are admissible in court for presentation to the jury.

By contrast, 'civil law' systems have no jury, and the prosecutors and investigating judges have the right to decide according to the law what types of evidence to take into account, and to pass on to the trial judges to consider.

In both common and civil legal systems, however, the weight accorded to any item of evidence varies according to a number of factors.

DOCUMENTARY EVIDENCE

Two factors are of primary importance in advancing documentary evidence: the authenticity of the document; and its provenance – where it comes from, including its chain of custody (all the people who have ever had possession of the document).

Authenticity

This should ideally be established by the author of the document appearing in person at the trial, but in many cases such testimony is

214 Getting Away With Genocide?

impossible. Many documents that will almost certainly be presented as evidence were written by prisoners who were subsequently executed. Others were compiled by prison guards who may have died, or whose current whereabouts are unknown.

Some authors, however, may be traceable and brought to the court to give testimony. One of the prison photographers, Nhem Eng, has been interviewed several times in recent years, as have several guards, such as Kok Sros and Him Huy.[2] These people could assist in establishing the authenticity of at least some of the documents. Other individuals, including several who are likely to be defendants – most notably, of course, Duch, the S-21 prison director – annotated, signed and dated many of the documents that passed through their hands. To supplement the testimony of individuals involved in the creation of the documents, handwriting and paper experts could be called to testify.

The court will presumably require submission of the original documents and, in many cases, this should not be a problem, as the originals are in archival storage under the custody of the Documentation Center of Cambodia. After the original has been sighted and authenticated, for the convenience of the court, copies (photocopy, print, microfilm or scanned images) will probably be used. In cases where the original has disappeared or deteriorated, individuals who have held custody may be found, and could testify as to the authenticity of the copy.

Provenance and chain of custody

Most of the documents did not come into the custody of the Cambodian Genocide Program or the Documentation Center of Cambodia until 1995 at the earliest, although some were given to researchers as early as 1981. Most of the documents have passed through the hands of various Cambodian governments since 1979 (the People's Republic of Kampuchea, the State of Cambodia and the Kingdom of Cambodia) and therefore may well be subject to challenge from the defence. The court would need to be convinced that the documents were neither fabricated nor altered during the last two decades. Many of the documents have been sorted and listed by archival teams working in the Ministry of the Interior and it may be possible to call individuals who carried out this work to testify as to when and where the documents were found.

WITNESSES

Because of the difficulties of proving the authenticity and provenance of documents, courts generally place a great deal of importance on the oral testimony of witnesses who appear in court and are subject to cross-examination by lawyers for both the defence and the prosecution.

As in all cases of crimes against humanity, most of the victims of the Khmer Rouge's atrocities cannot be called to testify, as they did not survive the crimes. There were, however, small numbers of people who did survive, against all odds – people who climbed out of graves over the bodies of the others, people who were left for dead but who revived and managed to escape and a few people who were tortured or persecuted but not taken away for execution. Others witnessed the crimes, either accidentally, from a hiding place, or as participants – guards and drivers who transported prisoners to their place of execution and of course those who actually carried out the killing. Many of these people may have died during the period since the crimes were committed. The prosecutors will certainly be anxious to find and interview any of these potential witnesses who survive today.

It would clearly be impossible to call all witnesses to the stand to testify in court. In similar cases with such an overwhelmingly large crime base, prosecutors at the Nuremberg Trials and at the International Criminal Tribunals for the former Yugoslavia and Rwanda have followed the practice of calling witnesses on the basis of establishing a 'representative sampling' of these crimes.[3] In some cases the defence may not even challenge the crime base, as the real focus of the trials would rather be on linking the crimes to individual defendants.

But here, too, there are a number of challenges to be faced, even after witnesses are identified and found. Above all, the court will need to be convinced that their memories are still sound after an elapsed time of a quarter of a century since the crimes took place. It can be expected that they will be challenged as to their recollection of contemporary events, as well as their unquestionable identification of the defendants as the persons who committed the purported crimes. Vigorous interrogation along these lines has knocked out many witnesses presented at trials for suspected Nazi war criminals.

A second challenge will be for the witnesses to prove that their testimony is pure and uncontaminated by other people's accounts of what happened. The length of time that has elapsed since the crimes took place is a problem here too, for during this quarter century many books and films have been made and circulated inside Cambodia, and many people have spoken on the television and radio or given interviews to journalists or researchers. If it can be shown that the witnesses themselves have been previously interviewed, were their first statements recorded, and did the interviewer/s ask neutral questions? If they have previously been asked leading questions that suggested the line of response, then not only is such response problematic in and of itself, but it may be used to challenge the witnesses as unreliable, reducing the value of their testimony as the basis for a conviction.

The prosecutors may decide to introduce testimony presented at the People's Revolutionary Tribunal in 1979, testimony given within months of the overthrow of the Pol Pot regime. The existence of complete sets of the court documents in Khmer, French and English, and the publication of an English language version of an almost complete set of the PRT documents in 2001, will provide a valuable and accessible starting point for consideration of this possibility.

There are a variety of ways in which testimony from a former trial may be admitted into evidence which can lead to increased efficiency, while at the same time fully according with the accused's rights to a fair trial. For instance, certain of the witnesses at the 1979 trial could be made available for cross-examination (a right of the defence that was not utilised in 1979).[4]

PHYSICAL/FORENSIC EVIDENCE

The S-21 prison (Tuol Sleng) was found only a day after it had been abandoned by fleeing Pol Pot forces. Cheung Ek, the principal execution site for Tuol Sleng, was found soon afterwards. Other prisons and burial sites in Siem Reap, Kampong Cham, Kampong Speu and Kandal were identified over the following months and their existence reported to the August 1979 People's Revolutionary Tribunal. The PRT judges were taken to see several sites outside Phnom Penh.

Although the local authorities in every province had rudimentary maps of genocide sites in their area, no overall map had been compiled until 1995 when the Cambodian Genocide Program and the Documentation Center of Cambodia launched a programme to map such sites throughout the country.[5] By May 2003 some 551 sites had been mapped: 348 burial sites with 19,471 mass graves; 169 prisons and 77 memorials. The Documentation Center reports that information obtained during the site visits indicates that the graves may contain the remains of between 1,386,734 and 2,038,735 people.[6] In 1988 Vietnamese forensic scientists and doctors from Ho Chi Minh University conducted the first examinations of the skulls at Cheung Ek to establish age, sex and cause of death. The team led by the late Professor Quang Quyen, and Dr Tran Hung, was invited by the Phnom Penh Municipality. They examined 8,000 skulls during three field trips to Cambodia.[7]

In 2002 a new project of forensic studies of human remains began, led by Dr Michael S. Pollanen of the Coroner's Office in Ontario, Canada, in conjunction with the Documentation Center of Cambodia and Dr Craig Etcheson.

The prosecution will possibly wish to carry out its own forensic studies or may wish to examine previous reports. Besides determining date and probable cause of death, it is sometimes possible for a forensic study to yield ancillary data (such as spent bullet cases, ropes, blindfolds) on the methods of killing, (clothes or papers) on the identity of the victims or even of the perpetrators. The size and shape of graves, types of shackles and the pattern of cell construction in prisons can also help to establish a nationwide pattern of atrocities, belying attempts by the defence to claim that any killings were random excesses committed by local authorities.

But, again, the length of time that has elapsed since the period under examination by the court presents a range of challenges. Almost all sites (burial sites, prisons and memorials) visited during preliminary research have been found to be in an alarming state of decay. Every rainy season washes away crucial evidence (as at an ethnic Cham village in Kampong Cham province, where the graves are being cut right through as the Mekong River bank erodes) and most sites are completely unmarked and unsupervised. In many instances (as at the well-known Cheung Ek site, near Phnom Penh) graves were excavated by the Cambodian government in the early 1980s. Remains were often removed from the graves and placed in a memorial structure nearby, or at times taken from the site itself to be placed in a temple for security and as a mark of respect. At some sites memorial sheds or stands have since fallen down, and skulls have been trampled and even eaten by cows or pigs or removed by visitors. Over the years most of the graves have been sacked by robbers.

Secondary sources as guides for the prosecution

In the International Criminal Tribunals for the former Yugoslavia and Rwanda, and in the national trials in Rwanda and the Sierra Leone Special Court, the prosecutors have had to seek data on which to build their cases. By contrast, in Cambodia there is almost a surfeit of existing documentation, personal accounts, surviving victims and witnesses ready to testify, and identified sites. The initial task will be for the prosecution to find a way to sift through the data, focussing on selecting material that helps develop individual cases.

The prosecutors and investigating judges are likely to need pathways into the huge mass of data described above. This is not the place to give an overview of the already extensive secondary literature that has been produced on the Khmer Rouge period in Cambodian history – autobiographical, biographical, historical, demographic, legal and literary.[8]

Suffice it here to refer to Annexe B which refers to several recent publications that are of particular importance for building an understanding of the crimes of the Khmer Rouge and the legal problems in their prosecution.

WHO WILL STAND IN THE DOCK?

Article One of the Khmer Rouge Law on the Establishment of the Extraordinary Chambers states clearly:

> The purpose of this law is to bring to trial *senior leaders of Democratic Kampuchea and those who were most responsible for the serious crimes and violations* of Cambodian penal law, international humanitarian law and custom, and international conventions recognised by Cambodia, that were committed during the period from 17 April 1975 to 6 January 1979. [Italics added by authors.]

But the Law gives no further guidance as to who might fit this definition. Although it was often suggested that the negotiators should be more specific, both sides agreed that it would be contrary to legal procedure to name names in the wording of the law. The task of defining more precisely who will be liable for prosecution has been left for the tribunal to determine.

The Law specifies two possible criteria for liability for prosecution: '*senior leaders of Democratic Kampuchea, and those who were most responsible for the most serious crimes and serious violations ...*'.

It must be emphasised at the outset that people are to be indicted and tried for specific crimes committed as outlined later in the Law and not for their rank as 'senior leaders of Democratic Kampuchea'.

The Law is clear that a person indicted may fall into either or both of these two groups. The words 'and those who were' introduces a second category that may or may not overlap with the first. This establishment of two categories is clear, too, in the official Khmer version of the law (*ning chun teang laay dael totuel koh trew kpus bomphot*) and in the French (*et ceux qui sont les plus hautement responsables*). All three texts lead to the conclusion that a person would not need to satisfy the first criterion before being considered for the second.[9]

Senior leaders of Democratic Kampuchea

The formulation 'senior leaders of Democratic Kampuchea' would seem to include leaders of both the state and the ruling party. The temporal jurisdiction of the court is defined as 'from 17 April 1975 to 6 January 1979', but the state of Democratic Kampuchea did not officially come into being until 5 January 1976, with the adoption of a new constitution for Cambodia. Ben Kiernan reports that during 1975 party records used the term *Prates Kampuchea* (country of Kampuchea).[10]

The government announcement on 17 April 1975 set in place as the government of Cambodia the existing government-in-exile in Beijing, the Royal Government of the National Union of Kampuchea (generally known by its French acronym GRUNK). Some token posts were initially awarded to Sihanoukists (e.g., the Prime Minister was the Sihanouk loyalist Penn Nouth), but the majority of significant positions were held by members of the Communist Party of Kampuchea, with Khieu Samphan as Deputy Prime Minister, Minister of Defence and Commander-in-Chief of the armed forces. In August 1975 Ieng Sary was named Deputy Prime Minister in charge of Foreign Affairs and Son Sen Deputy Prime Minister in charge of defence.

Although this was on paper the new regime, the Sihanoukists, did not actually return to Phnom Penh until September 1975, and played only a cosmetic role until they were formally relieved of their positions after just six months.

From 17 April 1975 the Head of State was Prince Norodom Sihanouk, who was replaced on 2 April 1976 by Khieu Samphan.

Some of Sihanouk's critics have suggested that he too should stand trial for alleged complicity with the Khmer Rouge regime. Sihanouk, now deemed 'inviolable' by virtue of his role as constitutional king of Cambodia, has angrily retorted that he was 'prisoner of the Khmer Rouge' under conditions of palace arrest.[11] Although he was nominally a 'senior leader of Democratic Kampuchea for some months', he was clearly powerless and resigned his position at an early stage of the regime.

Elections (of a sort) were held on 20 March and the one and only session of the People's Representative Assembly was held on 10 April 1976 at the old National Stadium and at Chaktomuk Theatre in Phnom Penh on the following day. The People's Representative Assembly selected Nuon Chea as its President, Ta Mok as first Vice-President and Khek Penn as second Vice-President.

The new government, approved by the People's Representative Assembly, was partially revealed on 14 April 1976 – the new Prime Minister was an unknown Pol Pot. (Not until 1978 was his identity confirmed as the veteran Communist Party of Kampuchea leader, Saloth Sar.) Three Deputy Prime Ministers were appointed – Ieng Sary (Foreign Affairs), Vorn Vet (Economics) and Son Sen (Defence). The Cabinet also included Hu Nim (Information); Thiounn Thioen (Health); Ieng Thirith (Social Action); Toch Phoen (Public Works); and Yun Yat (Culture). A State Presidium was appointed, consisting of Khieu Samphan as Chairman, and So Phim and Nhim Ros as first and second Vice-Chairman, respectively.

It will be up to the prosecutors to decide if they wish to consider the survivors among such state, governmental and legislative office-holders as falling within the definition of 'senior leaders of Democratic Kampuchea' for consideration of any crimes they may have committed, or whether they will concentrate their efforts on the party structure that always held and wielded the real power. It seems to be the case that the ministries and other organs of state hardly existed, and certainly neither government nor military had independence from the party. In particular, the non-CPK state and governmental office-holders in the GRUNK would appear to have had no power either to make or implement policy.

The Khmer Rouge, as with most rebel movements, operated as a clandestine organisation prior to taking power on 17 April 1975. Unlike most others, though, after becoming the effective government of the country it carried on this clandestine mode of operation. Ben Kiernan refers to 'the mysteries of a new government run by unknown names and composed of unnamed ministers. The new, formal face of Democratic Kampuchea was no more open than the old one.'[12] Not until 27 September 1977 did Pol Pot reveal that the unnamed *Angkar* (organisation) that had been ruling the country for over two years was in fact the Communist Party of Kampuchea of which he was the head. Elizabeth Becker maintains that it was Chinese pressure that forced him into this revelation of the existence of the party, if not his own identity.[13]

It seems that no complete list of the structures and membership of what was called 'the Centre' (*machhim*) of the Communist Party of Kampuchea has yet been found. Various researchers have combed vital documents and come up with lists of people mentioned as being the members of key committees at various times. One of the most complete lists was compiled by Timothy Carney, a US diplomat, and published in 1989.[14]

For a detailed summary of key Khmer Rouge personnel, see Annexe A.

WHAT CRIMES CAN BE PROSECUTED? (SUBJECT MATTER JURISDICTION)

The Khmer Rouge Tribunal Law embodied many compromises between the Cambodian government and the UN, particularly as regards the structure and composition of the courts, methods of decision making and procedure to be followed in the trials, as has been discussed in Chapters 9 and 10.

By contrast, there was almost total agreement between both sides as regards the crimes to be prosecuted (what is known as substantive law or subject matter jurisdiction) and the Law as passed in 2001 reflected almost exactly what was suggested by the Group of Experts in 1999. The only significant exception was war crimes (Article 6 of the Law), discussed below.

Agreement on substantive law does not preclude the possibility of serious challenges to successful prosecution under each of the six articles defining the substantive law for the Extraordinary Chambers (Articles 3–8).

Reflecting the mixed nature of the tribunal, the six articles include both Cambodian domestic law (covering murder, torture and religious persecution) as well as relevant international law on genocide and crimes against humanity and other international crimes.

During the drafting of the tribunal Law, questions were asked as to whether so many items of substantive law should be included. After considering the range of crimes that were committed and also the challenges that might be mounted to each charge, it was concluded that it would be wise to keep a number of options in order to have the greatest chance of securing conviction.

Article 3 – Cambodian domestic law

The following articles of the 1956 Penal Code of Cambodia have been included in the Law:

a)   Homicide (Articles 501, 503, 504, 505, 506, 507 and 508)
b)   Torture (Article 500)
c)   Religious Persecution (Articles 209 and 210)

All accounts indicate that during the Khmer Rouge regime there was no functioning legal system, nor any respect for the rule of law. However, in the absence of any formal repudiation or replacement of the previously existing penal code, the pre-existing Cambodian domestic law is legally held to have been still in force throughout the period of Democratic Kampuchea. Hence its inclusion as part of the 2001 Law. The decision to make this the first article outlining the crimes to be punished was a conscious one, to emphasise the fact that the trials will mix both Cambodian domestic law and international law.

One area of potential dispute relates to the issue of the length of time that has expired since the crimes were committed. The 1956 Penal Code established a ten-year statute of limitations, but the Law extended this for an additional 20 years for the crimes enumerated above, to a total of 30 years. This retroactive extension was itself enacted over 20 years after the crimes were committed and over ten years after the original statute of limitations had expired.[15]

Article 4 – Genocide

In Cambodia the crimes of the Khmer Rouge have been referred to consistently since 1979 by the government and in common parlance as genocide. Genocide was the only charge prosecuted by the 1979 People's Revolutionary Tribunal.

Decree Law No. 1 on 15 July 1979 to establish the People's Revolutionary Tribunal 'to try the Pol Pot – Ieng Sary Clique for the Crime of Genocide' did not quote directly from the 1948 Genocide

Convention, although the acts prescribed in its Article II certainly resonated in the Decree Law's list of crimes:

> planned massacres of groups of innocent people; expulsion of inhabitants of cities and villages in order to concentrate them and force them to do hard labour in conditions leading to their physical and mental destruction; wiping out religion; destroying political, cultural and social structures and family and social relations.

However, a number of legal commentators and scholars have asserted that most of these crimes might not be prosecutable under the Genocide Convention, in light of its narrow legal definitions of the crime. The defence lawyers could argue that the acts of the Khmer Rouge, horrendous though they were, did not constitute genocide.

An extensive body of literature has been penned on the interpretation of the definition of genocide in general,[16] and on the Cambodian case in particular.[17]

Article II of the Genocide Convention (substantially reproduced in Article 4 of the Khmer Rouge Law) reads:

> In the present Convention, genocide means any of the following acts committed with the intent to destroy, in whole or in part, a national, ethnical, racial or religious group as such:
> a) killing members of the group;
> b) causing serious bodily or mental harm to members of the group;
> c) deliberately inflicting on the group conditions of life calculated to bring about its physical destruction in whole or in part;
> d) imposing measures intended to prevent births within the group;
> e) forcibly transferring children from one group to another group.

The clause 'with the intent to destroy, in whole or in part, a national, ethnical, racial or religious group as such' presents two problems: first, whether the Khmer Rouge intended to destroy all or part of any groups whose members it persecuted; and second, whether the groups persecuted by the Khmer Rouge fall into the defined categories, which do not include economic or political groups.

Most commentators argue that, while there is a strong chance of successful prosecution in relation to the persecution of certain non-Khmer groups (such as Vietnamese, Chinese and Cham) and the Buddhist clergy, all of which can meet the definition of national, ethnic or religious groups, the vast majority of the atrocities were carried out by Khmers against Khmers, and therefore may be deemed to fall outside the definition of genocide.

Some commentators disagree. Some of the strongest claims for the appropriateness of the term genocide for the Khmer Rouge crimes were made by the US Congress, which in the Cambodian Genocide Justice Act 1994 stated, 'The persecution of the Cambodian people under the Khmer Rouge rule, [when] the bulk of the Khmer people were subjected to life in an Asian Auschwitz, constituted one of the clearest acts of genocide in recent history.'[18]

This US law instructed the US State Department to set up an Office of Cambodian Genocide Investigation to 'develop the United States proposal for the establishment of an international criminal tribunal for the prosecution of those accused of genocide in Cambodia.'[19] Using monies granted by the Office of Cambodian Genocide Investigations, the most serious sustained investigation into the crimes of the Khmer Rouge was carried out from 1995 to 2001 as part of what is called the Cambodian Genocide Program (see Chapter 7).

However, even the narrow legal definition of genocide in the Genocide Convention has been challenged in other countries in recent years. The French Penal Code of 1994 defines genocide as the destruction of any group whose identification is based on any arbitrary criteria. Spanish judge Baltasar Garzon made three rulings in 1998 (including the well-known Augusto Pinochet case) that genocide had been committed in Argentina in the 1970s and 1980s.

International lawyer William Schabas disagrees with these attempts to push open the definition of genocide, maintaining that 'confusing mass killing of the members of the perpetrators' own group with genocide is inconsistent with the purpose of the Convention, which was to protect national minorities from crimes based on racial hatred.'[20]

On the Cambodian case in particular Schabas argues, 'A strict construction of the scope of the term ... suggests the conclusion that the Khmer Rouge atrocities were not genocide.' This position has been criticised by Gregory Stanton as 'definitionalist denial', and he points to the destruction of Cham Muslims, Buddhist monks, Christians and Vietnamese as clear cases of genocide.[21]

The Group of Experts appointed by the United Nations Secretary General agreed that the Khmer people of Cambodia did indeed constitute a national group within the meaning of the Convention, but declined to take a position on 'whether the Khmer Rouge committed genocide with respect to part of the Khmer national group [as it] turns on complex interpretive issues, especially concerning the Khmer Rouge's intent with respect to its non-minority-group victims.'[22] Argument on this point will undoubtedly be one of the preliminary issues in the forthcoming Khmer Rouge trials, and the prosecution may even attempt to gain a re-interpretation and expanded definition of the Genocide Convention.

Article 5 – Crimes Against Humanity

It is widely asserted that although many of the crimes of the Khmer Rouge may not fall within the definition of genocide, they can most certainly be classed as crimes against humanity. However, successful prosecution here, too, will need to resist restrictive interpretations.

Unlike genocide, crimes against humanity were until 1993 not codified in a precise way in a single Convention, but were considered to be a part of customary international law. Crimes against humanity were first enunciated in the Charter of the International Military Tribunal at Nuremberg in 1945. They were defined in the Statutes of the International Criminal Tribunal for the Former Yugoslavia in 1993 and the International Criminal Tribunal for Rwanda in 1994 and were spelled out more clearly in the 1998 Statute of Rome establishing the basis for the International Criminal Court.

Article 5 of the Khmer Rouge Law mentions the crimes against humanity as encompassing murder, extermination, enslavement, deportation, imprisonment, torture, rape, persecutions on political, racial and religious grounds, and other inhuman acts. As can be seen, the scope for prosecution is much wider than in the Genocide Convention and the inclusion of political grounds would cover many more of the Khmer Rouge crimes.

However, a challenge to the prosecution may be mounted as to whether the Khmer Rouge acts can be considered as crimes against humanity if they were committed during peace time. The Nuremberg Tribunal originally restricted crimes against humanity to offences committed 'before and during the war'. This is referred to as 'the nexus to armed conflict'. It is no longer deemed necessary under current international humanitarian law, as shown in the Statutes of the International Criminal Tribunal for Rwanda[23] and in the International Criminal Court.

If it is ruled that the nexus to armed conflict was still a necessary element in crimes against humanity during the period 1975–1979, then the prosecution will have to prove that such armed conflict did exist in Cambodia during that period. In fact the Khmer Rouge attacked all its neighbours continually beginning from the very first days of its rule. Raymund Johansen has made the case that not only the persecution of non-Khmers, but also much of the killing of Khmer people could also be shown to be in connection with this international conflict, in that the Khmer Rouge justified much of the internal killing on the basis of wiping out 'enemies' and specifically calling people agents of Vietnam and even 'Khmer bodies with Vietnamese minds'.[24]

Some argument can also be anticipated around the fact that there is some difference in wording between the Law and the Agreement with reference to crimes against humanity. Article 9 of the Draft Agreement mentions 'crimes against humanity as defined in the 1998 Rome Statute of the International Criminal Court', which has a wider scope than the wording in Article 5 of the Law.[25] In any event, the Law's scope offers sufficient opportunity for prosecution of crimes committed by the Khmer Rouge without the need for the prosecution to resort to the wider scope of the Statute of Rome.

Article 6 – Geneva Conventions of 1949

The Group of Experts explicitly suggested that war crimes should be excluded from the substantive law for the Khmer Rouge trials. As noted in Chapter 7, they feared that inclusion of war crimes would open the door to prosecution of non-Cambodians:

> As for war crimes, while the historical record clearly suggests their commission, the Group notes that, in establishing the International Criminal Tribunal for the former Yugoslavia, the United Nations has set the important precedent that war crimes prosecutions should not be limited to one side in a conflict. This principle would mean that, if war crimes were included in the jurisdiction of a court for Cambodia, it would have to include war crimes by persons from other States during the period of Democratic Kampuchea ... and we thus believe war crimes should not be included.

However, this argument was not followed in the drafting of the Law and the grave breaches provisions of the Geneva Conventions were included. It will be interesting indeed to see if the court deems that any non-Cambodians should be indicted for war crimes committed during the period of Democratic Kampuchea.

The issue of the presence or absence of a state of armed conflict mentioned above would again be pivotal here. The grave breaches provisions of the Geneva Conventions have normally been considered to be limited to international armed conflict.[26]

If the tribunal decides to investigate war crimes committed against neighbouring countries, then the atrocities committed by Pol Pot forces against Vietnamese villages in the Mekong Delta would be the most likely focus. Khmer Rouge forces made many cross-border raids and incursions wiping out several villages near the town of Chau Doc. A genocide museum nearby commemorates the victims. They also violated the international borders of their other two neighbours – Thailand and Laos.[27]

Article 7 – The Hague Convention of 1954 for the Protection of Cultural Property during Armed Conflict

While crimes against cultural property may pale into insignificance before genocide, crimes against humanity and war crimes, they nevertheless form part of international humanitarian law and the Khmer Rouge leaders deserve to be prosecuted for their barbaric acts in the cultural sphere as well as against life itself.

By signing The Hague Convention, Cambodia pledged not only 'to prepare in time of peace for the safeguarding of cultural property situated within their own territory against the foreseeable effects of an armed conflict' but also

> to respect cultural property situated within their own territory … by refraining from any use of the property and its immediate surroundings or of the appliances in use for its protection for purposes which are likely to expose it to destruction or damage in the event of armed conflict; and by refraining from any act of hostility directed against such property … [and] to prohibit, prevent and, if necessary, put a stop to any form of theft, pillage or misappropriation of, and any acts of vandalism [or reprisals] directed against, cultural property.

This Convention clearly states the limitation in its title, and so the issue of the existence of armed conflict during 1975–79 will be crucial to successful prosecution under this Article.

The Hague Convention has seldom been utilised in this way. Only in very recent years at the International Criminal Tribunal for the former Yugoslavia, have some such charges have been advanced, notably in the case against Strugar for the destruction of the historic town of Dubrovnik.[28] Crimes against cultural property are more usually treated as crimes of war under the Geneva Conventions.

Article 8 – The Vienna Convention of 1961 on Diplomatic Relations

In the early days of Khmer Rouge rule almost all foreigners were corralled in the French Embassy. Among the 1,046[29] were several diplomats, spouses and family of diplomats and other personnel who may be considered to have been in the category of 'internationally protected persons'. The treatment meted out to them, while by no means comparable to that experienced by the Cambodian population as a whole, may well be judged to have been a violation of the 1961 Vienna Convention on Diplomatic Relations.[30]

PROVING THE CASE IN COURT

The task of the prosecution will be to connect the personal jurisdiction and the subject-matter jurisdiction of the Extraordinary Chambers on the basis of evidence presented to the court. All defendants must have the presumption of innocence and this right is clearly inscribed into both the Law and the Agreement.

The authors are mindful of the fact that although the crimes are demonstrably a part of Cambodia's tragic history, the prosecution will not have an easy task in proving individual culpability to the satisfaction of the court. The legal conundrums and challenges outlined above under each item of substantive law foreshadow the task ahead. But linking evidence of acts performed by individual leaders to the overall conspiracy to commit genocide, crimes against humanity and war crimes will prove even more difficult.

The Extraordinary Chambers can expect challenges to every element of its jurisdiction: personal, temporal and subject matter. The defendants can rightly be expected to have the best legal support and to explore and exploit every avenue under the law to secure a dismissal of the charges against them.

A lingering legal controversy: Amnesty/Pardon

Throughout the process towards establishing the Extraordinary Chambers perhaps no issue has been more contentious than amnesty, both within the negotiating room and, debated with considerably more vitriol, in the press.

Would certain people be exempted from prosecution in any trial? Had Hun Sen made deals with various leaders at the time of their defection to the government? Certainly these allegations were made repeatedly and became items of received wisdom slipped into many media reports on the tribunal. Few journalists ever bothered to check the sources of these allegations or to notice that by recycling commonly-held suspicions and rumours about secret deals with Khmer Rouge leaders, they may have misrepresented the facts.

This issue has been discussed at several points above, most especially in Chapter 8, as part of the unfolding of the negotiations, but it seems appropriate to revisit it here, viewed in the context of the legal proceedings themselves. It is useful to clarify the main terms, since confusion over what is meant has been a hallmark of this discussion.

Black's Law Dictionary 1990 defines the terms as follows:

> Amnesty: A sovereign act of forgiveness for past acts, granted by a government to all persons (or to certain classes of persons) who have been guilty of crime or delict, generally political offences – treason sedition, rebellion, draft evasion and often conditional upon their return to obedience and duty within a prescribed time. [p. 82–3]

> Pardon: An executive action that mitigates or sets aside punishment for a crime. An act of grace from governing power, which mitigates the punishment the law demands for the offence and restores the rights and privileges forfeited on account of the offence. [p. 1113]

The distinction between the terms is not maintained in English common parlance and certainly not in the Khmer language, where the expression *kar leuk laeng touh* is almost always used for both, even in the *English-Khmer Law Dictionary*, published by The Asia Foundation in 1997.

The case of Ieng Sary was relatively clear, although this did not stop even the wildest speculation. When he defected in September 1996 a Royal Decree was issued, proclaiming:

... a pardon to Mr Ieng Sary, former Deputy Prime Minister in charge of Foreign Affairs in the Government of Democratic Kampuchea, for the sentence of death and confiscation of all his property imposed by order of the People's Revolutionary Tribunal of Phnom Penh, dated 19 August 1979; and

an amnesty for prosecution under the Law to Outlaw the Democratic Kampuchea Group, promulgated by Reach Kram No. 1, NS 94, dated 14 July 1994.

The Decree was signed by the King and, at his request, was also counter-signed by the two Co-Prime Ministers (Norodom Ranariddh and Hun Sen) and a note was added spelling out that it had arisen from a proposal by them. In addition, the King insisted that the Decree receive the support of two-thirds of the National Assembly before being publicly released. No vote or debate was held in the National Assembly; instead members were consulted privately and asked to sign indicating agreement.

The 1994 Law to Outlaw the Democratic Kampuchea Group proclaimed membership in the Democratic Kampuchea political or military wings to be illegal, and stated also that such members would be prosecuted for crimes such as murder, rape, robbery or acts of destruction of public property according to the criminal laws in effect. In debate in the National Assembly several amendments were made, including affirmation of the King's right to grant amnesty/pardon, and the law was placed on hold to offer a six-month's grace period to encourage immediate surrenders. In fact, the grace period was unofficially extended to allow the law to serve its principal intention of encouraging the self-destruction of the Khmer Rouge organisation, rather than as a means of prosecution.

The defections of Nuon Chea and Khieu Samphan in December 1998, while causing quite some furore because of the public welcome given by Prime Minister Hun Sen, were not accompanied by any public statements providing either amnesty or pardon. In fact, as described above, the Prime Minister explicitly denied giving any such commitments.

The United Nations' Office of Legal Affairs inserted in its first drafts of the Khmer Rouge Law and the Agreement between Cambodia and the United Nations the following: 'There shall be no amnesty for the crime of genocide. Any amnesty granted to any person falling within the jurisdiction of the Tribunal shall not be a bar to prosecution.'

The Cambodian delegation took the view that this wording conflicts with Article 27 of the Constitution, which states, 'The King shall have the right to grant partial or complete amnesty.' To include such a provision would be to invite the Constitutional Council to find fault with the Law.

Amnesty was one of the principal difficulties between the two sides. Kofi Annan included it as one of the four issues in his February 2000 letter to Hun Sen and it was perhaps the most heated element in the March 2000 second round of negotiations. On request from Hans Corell, Sok An gave the delegation a letter containing the clarification he had made in discussion – namely that only one person had been granted a pardon, in 1996, relating to conviction for genocide only. Although not spelled out in the letter, this referred to the case of Ieng Sary who was given a pardon for his 1979 *in absentia* conviction by the People's Revolutionary Tribunal. The wording from this letter was incorporated in Article 11 of the Agreement.

12
One More River to Cross

The pessimists said it would never happen. The UN-Cambodia Agreement was finally signed on 6 June 2003 during a ceremony held at the Chaktomuk Theatre in Phnom Penh. After marathon negotiations lasting nearly four years, UN chief negotiator Hans Corell returned for this historic moment to conclude an international treaty with the Cambodian government in front of a packed auditorium of ambassadors, government ministers, NGOs and the media.

It had taken 25 years since the overthrow of the Pol Pot regime to reach this stage of UN support for a Cambodian tribunal. There was more than a dash of irony about Corell clinking his champagne glass while only a year before he had been instrumental in pulling the UN out of the talks.

The tortuous process from 1979 to the signing ceremony in 2003 can be viewed as a history of hurdles jumped and obstacles overcome. The appeal of Cambodians and NGOs for an internationally backed Khmer Rouge tribunal in the 1980s represented the first credible attempt to invoke the UN Genocide Convention since it was passed in 1948. However, as we have seen in earlier chapters, most governments exhibited a scandalous disregard for the human rights of the Cambodian people, offering more encouragement to the Khmer Rouge than to those striving to put them on trial.

The sufferings of Bosnia, part of the former Yugoslavia in the early 1990s and the outcry of public opinion finally stirred Western governments to move towards the enforcement of international humanitarian law, a sharp contrast to their abject failure to deal with the Cambodian legacy. In 1993 when the *ad hoc* tribunal on the former Yugoslavia was set up in The Hague, the Khmer Rouge were still terrorising rural parts of Cambodia.

It was not surprising that, over the years, many pundits dismissed the Cambodian Khmer Rouge Tribunal as a pipe dream. In contrast to the Yugoslavia and Rwanda conflicts, the Cambodian case was complicated by the past support to the Khmer Rouge by so many governments, with China, Singapore, Thailand, the US, the UK and others, all having something to hide.

The end of the cold war and the increasing interest in new approaches to international humanitarian and human rights law by 1997 had influenced several western governments to change their position and include Cambodia on the agenda of international justice. The period between the release of the Group of Experts' report at the beginning of 1998 and the signing of the Agreement between Cambodia and the United Nations in June 2003 was a seesaw of alternating impasse and breakthrough. Many of those observing the process grew ever more cynical, with press reports routinely referring to Hun Sen's 'delaying tactics' and 'reluctance to hold a trial'. Such an attitude was to be expected from the anti-CPP opposition led by Sam Rainsy. But local human rights organisations also expressed scepticism, concerned that a government with such a poor record in investigating current human rights violations could not be trusted to hold a fair Khmer Rouge trial even with an international component.

Trust would be the keyword in the process – but this precious commodity was in short supply. On the international side, there was fear that Cambodian politics led by 'strongman' Hun Sen and its undoubtedly weak judicial system would necessarily compromise the process. On the Cambodian side, there was fear of surrendering national sovereignty, and suspicion of the motives of the United Nations and other outside powers. Both sets of fears were quite understandable in view of Cambodia's history and current situation. But without taking the risk of trusting each other and building something for the future, how could the process ever move beyond mutual suspicion?

Weariness from the slow pace and constant let-downs of the negotiations also prompted an increasingly negative media coverage that reflected and itself helped engender a general loss of confidence in the process. As early as mid-October 2000 the *Phnom Penh Post* led with a story entitled 'UN accepts flawed tribunal for KR'.

Day after day the press churned out stories casting the Cambodia side as having no serious interest in a tribunal:

Analysts say the Cambodian government has dragged its feet consistently and appears determined none of the top communists involved will ever be put on trial, partly for fear of upsetting the fragile political stability the country has only recently achieved. Too many people have past links with the Khmer Rouge communist regime, and many others find it too difficult to face up to the reality of the butchery, and the complicity of some of the rest of the population in the killing. Many Cambodians, from senators to government officials downwards just think it would be better to forget the past. 'Deep down inside the government doesn't want to have a trial,' said Lao Mong Hay, former executive director of the Khmer Institute of Democracy. 'My understanding is that the government is buying time until [the top leaders] die.'[1]

Others would disagree with much of this analysis, but this painfully slow progress led to serious doubts and questions about what the Cambodian government really wanted. The government failed to respond to most of the criticisms. Without explanations of the delays, critics concluded that Hun Sen's government lacked the political will to push ahead with the tribunal. Though certain figures in the government occasionally denied the allegation, and there was certainly an enormous amount of work being carried out behind the scenes by the Task Force led by Sok An, the government's public information and public relations were woefully inadequate in explaining what was going on to a sceptical public and a hostile media.

One of the biggest brakes on the negotiations was undoubtedly the behind-the-scenes pressure exerted by the Middle Kingdom (China) and its increasing role in the affairs of the Kingdom of Cambodia. Pressure from Beijing to derail the tribunal was accompanied by offers of increased bilateral aid and Chinese development assistance. Beijing's ever-closer diplomatic and economic ties to this small and desperately poor nation placed Cambodian premier Hun Sen in an awkward and delicate position. Dare he risk upsetting the communist giant to the north, the dominant power in the region?

The UN's torpedoing of the negotiations was partly due to weak communications and a clash of cultures between New York and Phnom Penh that only aggravated the deep-seated suspicions of each side. The Secretariat's assertion that the proposed tribunal did not meet international legal standards was rejected by the UN member states as a reason for withdrawing. Interested governments saw no credible basis for giving up on the Cambodian tribunal. After the dramatic UN walk out in 2002, Australia, Canada, France, Germany, Japan, UK and the US, as well as Asean, all pushed for an immediate resumption of negotiations on the basis of the Khmer Rouge Law precisely to achieve an agreement that would embody these elusive 'international legal standards'.

When the UN Secretariat washed its hands of the tribunal in February 2002 many people were shocked and disappointed. After all the negotiations and debate, the decades-long struggle to get the Khmer Rouge into court appeared to have arrived at a dead end.

But it was very welcome to at least one group in Cambodia. The news that the tribunal was apparently dead in the water was a cause for celebration and rejoicing in the Khmer Rouge hinterlands of Pailin. Once again the UN appeared to be helping the Khmer Rouge to escape justice. Peter Leuprecht, the UN's human-rights rapporteur for Cambodia commented, 'It would be a terrible irony if the UN contributed to the impunity of the Khmer Rouge leaders.' He elaborated, 'the UN should be aware of its past record on Cambodia, a record that is not all glorious'.[2]

This not so glorious record applies to the performance of the UN's permanent staff, not just the UN member states. The UN Secretariat in the 1980s failed to exercise any initiative in questioning the legal and moral contradictions of seating the Khmer Rouge, whereas in the current period the UN's Office of Legal Affairs rather perversely did the exact opposite – going out on a limb to push their own line on the tribunal contrary to the expressed will of member states. War crimes specialist David Scheffer noted, 'In the history of the UN there have been few occasions when the Secretariat had to be reminded so many times that that it is obliged to carry out the will of the member states.'[3]

The common perception, that it was always the Cambodians doing the foot dragging and that the UN legal team were being held back by politics in Phnom Penh, is not the whole story of this complex process. UN stubbornness in 2002 and their refusal to negotiate paralysed the negotiations and set back the process by a whole year. It can be argued that from the very beginning the Cambodian tribunal was based on a fragile foundation, and that both sides – the UN and the Cambodian government – contributed to an erratic game of diplomatic and legal ping-pong subjected to long periods of suspended play and stalemate.

A FLAWED TRIBUNAL?

After the final agreement between the UN and Cambodia, Sok An spoke in glowing terms of Cambodia's achievement: 'we achieved a model that we believe can contribute to the development of international humanitarian law and contribute to legal and judicial reform in Cambodia.' But that was not everyone's verdict. The moment of triumph was marred by the chorus of complaints, notably from Amnesty International in the UK and the US-based Human Rights Watch.

They criticised the Cambodian 'mixed tribunal' as nothing more than a shoddy second, or even third, class compromise by comparison with the model of an international tribunal. It was an opinion that received widespread publicity and acceptance by the media. These two organisations have earned international respect for their work on human rights in drawing attention to state repression around the globe. However their hardline position, urging the abandonment of a mixed tribunal in favour of an international tribunal, suggests that neither has yet grasped the main issues thrown up by current developments in international justice.

Is it really a case of first class justice just because it comes under the supervision of the UN Security Council? Not all jurists are so convinced of the absolute integrity and competence of *ad hoc* international tribunals.

The tribunal set up in Arusha, Tanzania to judge the perpetrators of the Rwanda Genocide is far from the pristine model being counterposed to Cambodia's mixed tribunal. US lawyer Michael Karnavas, who participated in the Arusha proceedings, complained that the Rwanda Tribunal was 'mismanaged and plagued with fraud and nepotism' and that 'the accused were denied adequate time, resources and legal assistance to mount a proper defence'. It has so far lasted almost ten years with only ten completed trials held and arguably limited impact on Rwandan society as whole given its remoteness.[4]

Accusations of political bias have also been levelled at the current *ad hoc* tribunal in The Hague, which has thrown the book at the former Yugoslav prime minister, Slobodan Milosevic.

International justice is still in its infancy and those who reflect on the likely imperfections of the Cambodian tribunal also need to accept the reality that, whatever the composition of the judges and wherever the venue of the court, all such tribunals have encountered political problems and legal flaws. It is a peculiar illusion of some human rights organisations that by transferring the Khmer Rouge case from Phnom Penh to The Hague a perfect paradigm of justice would be achieved.

On the other hand, the positive advantages of a mixed tribunal have received much less attention. The phenomenal cost of international tribunals has been a major factor in the current trend away from

The Hague, and towards alternative models of international justice. Cambodia it should be noted stands as the very first mixed tribunal model to be formulated, if not implemented. The Sierra Leone tribunal was subsequently established with inspiration from the Cambodian model.[5]

Few elements of justice are more important to the community than the principle that justice must not only be done, but must be seen to be done. For Cambodians really to see justice being done, the trials need to be held in the country where the crimes were committed and with the active participation of the local legal and judicial institutions.

The tribunal venue, the domestic legal system and the participation of the people are critical factors in making international justice less remote and more relevant to the people. Cambodian NGO leader Chea Vannath is firmly opposed to the notion that a Khmer Rouge tribunal should be staged outside Cambodia. 'A Khmer Rouge tribunal staged in The Hague would just be a remote exercise in international law but it would have no meaning for Cambodian people. We need a trial inside the country that people can feel a part of and follow the proceedings both in the court and on radio and TV.'[6]

Not only will a trial in Cambodia cost the world only a fraction of the money spent at The Hague or Arusha, but the direct impact of the trial on the affected society will carry vastly more immediacy and relevance. The director of the Documentation Center of Cambodia, Youk Chhang, similarly argues that 'it is important for the tribunal to be done here in Cambodia to involve our people. We can learn lessons and affirm our trust that Cambodians are capable, people must participate in the process.'[7] The mixed tribunal involving the local judiciary, as in the East Timor and Sierra Leone tribunals, is also part of an evolving system of justice.

US lawyer Gregory Stanton, whose commitment to a tribunal stretches back to the early 1980s, delivered a stinging rebuttal to these two renowned international organisations. Noting that, 'Amnesty International (AI) and Human Rights Watch (HRW) are superb human rights organizations', Stanton continued,

> But for Cambodia, they have insisted on another international tribunal, not a court that Cambodians will accept as their own. One of the shortcomings of the Yugoslav and Rwandan tribunals has been their lack of relationship with national legal systems ... AI expects the tribunal to help rebuild the entire Cambodian system

of justice. By setting an example of fair trials in a well-managed court, it will do so. It is also a reason for making the tribunal a special part of the Cambodian court system and locating it in Phnom Penh.[8]

The mixed tribunal formula empowers Cambodians to be participants in the trial and not be reduced to passive spectators on the occasion of the most important trial in their history. The US-trained lawyers of Human Rights Watch see the participation of Cambodian lawyers and judges only in terms of the negatives – the weaknesses of the Cambodian judiciary – but fail to acknowledge the dynamics of a participatory process. Nor do they see the wider picture: Cambodians have a legal and moral right to be directly involved in shaping the final judgment on the Pol Pot regime.

Critics, mainly from international human rights organisations, have continued to argue that Cambodia's judicial system is not capable of staging an acceptable trial and that the task should be placed in purer hands. To advocate that Cambodians should just leave everything in the hands of the foreign legal experts reeks of paternalism.

Another critical advantage of a locally-based tribunal relates to logistics. It is complicated, costly and time-consuming to be transporting witnesses from one country to another. It would also be a major deterrent to older witnesses who may be afraid to travel abroad, and many other potential witnesses would be afraid of losing their livelihood while testifying in a faraway tribunal. At the same time holding the tribunal in-country helps the international judges to understand the context for the evidence. Inside Cambodia the judges can easily visit genocide sites and come to grips with the geographical data.

The plus factors of a mixed tribunal held in-country need to be balanced with adherence to international legal standards. The two landmark legal agreements: the Khmer Rouge Tribunal Law 2001, and the Agreement between the Cambodian government and the United Nations 2003, reflect this delicate balance.

International and local media generally gave the impression that all the human rights lawyers were lined up on one side of the debate, as if there was no other view than the 'this tribunal is fatally flawed'. This notion was part of the mythology and popular misconceptions that have gathered around the tribunal.

International jurists who took the opposite view, that the Khmer Rouge Law provided a credible framework for a fair trial, received scant media attention.

The battle cry of the legal purists has been 'better no trial at all than a flawed trial', ironically a line that is more than welcome to surviving Khmer Rouge leaders who have been fervently hoping that no tribunal will ever take place. As we have noted earlier, this line also suited some conservative members of Hun Sen's ruling party with little enthusiasm for a tribunal – if for rather different reasons. A tribunal has always been viewed by a few CPP members as likely to sow panic among the ranks of ordinary Khmer Rouge defectors and to destabilise the hard-won peace.

The logic of no compromise in framing a tribunal could only have one outcome, as Craig Etcheson observed.

This would have the result that the Khmer Rouge leadership would die quiet, peaceful deaths in their beds, having successfully defended their impunity for their entire lives. It is strange to see this tacit alliance between international human rights activists and the most retrograde elements of Cambodia's ruling party, but then as they say, politics makes for strange bedfellows.[9]

Peter Leuprecht, the UN's human rights rapporteur for Cambodia, knew better than most the weaknesses of the country's legal system. But this former law professor from Vienna had no hesitation in viewing the Khmer Rouge law as clearly Cambodia's last chance for justice. 'I am a lawyer and I am sure, rather this tribunal than no tribunal,' he declared during one of his regular visits to Phnom Penh in 2002.[10]

The opponents of the Khmer Rouge Law increasingly painted themselves into a corner in their pursuit of flawless justice. US lawyer Stanton has pointed to a fundamental fallacy:

But to reject the Agreement because the court cannot do everything is equivalent to saying that because all law-breakers cannot be captured and tried, none should be. This all-or-none approach to justice for Cambodia has been characteristic of some human rights groups from the beginning. In 1981, when I asked the International Commission of Jurists to undertake investigations of the atrocities of the Khmer Rouge, the Chairman of the Board refused with the reason that if they could not investigate violations by the

Vietnamese-backed government that drove the Khmer Rouge from power, they would not investigate the Khmer Rouge mass murders. All-or-none standards are self-defeating. Perfection is the enemy of justice.[11]

In a country where authoritarian traditions and tendencies still hold sway and democratic institutions are often bypassed by those controlling the levers of power, concerns were frequently raised that Hun Sen might seek to manipulate a special tribunal. He has a known penchant for intervening in most sectors, including the courts. Distrust is frequently expressed of a prime minister who displays irritation over investigations into human rights violations by Cambodia's police and military.

But we are not dealing with a domestic court that could be easily pressured by the Cambodian executive. The Cambodian tribunal is a carefully crafted structure designed to provide sufficient checks and balances. International jurists, lawyers and judges will occupy key roles as the co-prosecutor, co-investigating judge and two out of five trial court judges, and must be a party to conviction or exoneration of any accused.

Too many critics have jumped to hasty conclusions writing off the tribunal as a script for a potential 'sham trial', without digesting all the protective provisions designed to guarantee the integrity of the process. But, in a worst-case scenario, if all these protective provisions unravel in the face of covert political manipulation that undermines the credibility of the tribunal, the agreement provides a fail-safe clause which guarantees the right of the UN and international judges to opt out of further participation in a trial.

There is no going back. The authors believe that for all its complexities and its defects, the Khmer Rouge Law 2001 and the UN-Cambodia Agreement of 2003 should be hailed as serious legal accomplishments that provide the basic foundations for the achievement of justice. Now is the time for all human rights lawyers and activists of good will to work together for its effective implementation.

INTERNATIONAL JUSTICE AND THE
MOVEMENT TO END THE CULTURE OF IMPUNITY

The Cambodia tribunal will mark one of the longest struggles to bring the perpetrators to justice, lasting more than 25 years since the day the Pol Pot regime was overthrown. By contrast the tribunals for the former Yugoslavia and Rwanda took place while the events were still fresh and well before the UN got around to addressing the Khmer Rouge legacy. For Cambodia it is a case of belated but better late than never justice.

The setting up of the International Criminal Court in 2003 is a welcome development with its mandate to deal with future egregious crimes wherever the local legal system is unable or unwilling to carry out the prosecution. Cambodia was the first Asean nation to adhere to the ICC.

But the US government's decision to withdraw from the ICC, and put itself beyond the jurisdiction of the world community, is a classic reminder that for all the progress that has been made, international justice is still hostage to power politics and the superpower agenda. In its single-minded campaign to establish immunity from prosecution for US citizens, Washington has pressured friendly and aid-dependent states to sign under Article 98, which undermines the universality and integrity of the ICC. Sadly Cambodia is on that list of compliant and vulnerable governments who have sacrificed principles for political expediency.

THE CASE OF EAST TIMOR

The tiny but heroic nation of East Timor shared a common fate with Cambodia in 1975 as victims of crimes against humanity. In that year as the Khmer Rouge drove the people out of Phnom Penh and all the urban areas, in another part of Asia the Indonesia military launched an invasion leading to mass killings and policies of deliberate starvation designed to coerce the indigenous people into submission and acceptance of Jakarta's annexation.

These crimes have never been subjected to any judicial accountability. But East Timor was to suffer barbarism at the hands of Jakarta's generals all over again in 1999 after the East Timorese voters resoundingly voted against Indonesian rule in a UN-supervised referendum. Dili was engulfed in flames. Homes, schools and clinics were systematically looted and destroyed.

A UN inquiry team recommended the setting up of an International Tribunal but there was little enthusiasm from western governments with their considerable commercial interests in the great archipelago of Indonesia. The US, UK and the Australian governments all had a long history of military aid and lucrative arms sales to Suharto's

Indonesia. They were reluctant to see indictments issued against generals who had been trained at West Point and Sandhurst.

The UN Human Rights (later Serious Crimes) Unit in East Timor set up in November 1999 as part of the UN Transitional Authority (UNTAET) requested access to Australian intelligence information on the ransacking of East Timor. But Canberra declined to cooperate. Hamish McDonald, foreign correspondent of the *Sydney Morning Herald* reported:

> The Australian Government sat on explosive intelligence material which showed the direct involvement of senior Indonesian army generals in the violence which swept East Timor in 1999. Defence sources in Canberra have given details of how Australian electronic eavesdroppers intercepted secret messages between the Indonesian officers who ran a campaign of fear to deter the East Timorese from voting for independence. But virtually none of the collected evidence, which could be vital to finding the masterminds responsible for crimes against humanity, has been shared with United Nations investigators.
>
> This is because of concerns that Indonesia would adopt countermeasures to foil future interception operations by the Defence Signals Directorate. Transcripts of the DSD intercepts revealed to the Herald show a covert chain of command down from the then President B.J. Habibie's co-ordinating minister for politics and security, General Feisal Tanjung, to army generals and colonels on the ground in East Timor.[12]

UN investigators from Dili's Serious Crimes and Human Rights unit officially requested that these 'smoking guns' from Australian intelligence should be made available to the prosecution cases being mounted in East Timor. Canberra declined without any discussion or debate.

The political enthusiasm of western intelligence agencies to supply classified intelligence data to service the prosecution of Serbian generals in The Hague, provides a dramatic contrast with their non-cooperation in the case of East Timor and it will be interesting to see if they are more forthcoming in providing such information to the Khmer Rouge trials.

The UN accepted the Indonesian government's offer to set up its own special human rights court in lieu of an international tribunal. During 2002–2003 a number of Indonesian military officers were put on trial for crimes against humanity in East Timor. The prosecution was half-hearted and most were predictably acquitted.[13]

A separate series of mixed tribunals have taken place under the court system of the newly independent government of East Timor. But with Jakarta refusing all requests for extradition of their military officers, the East Timor tribunals have only been able to prosecute the local Timorese militia leaders acting on the orders of the Indonesian military.

Indonesian generals such as Adam Damiri and Mahidin Simbolan, who were responsible for atrocities in East Timor, have since been recycled to carry out similar counter-insurgency operations against the dissidents and independence-seeking rebels in the disaffected regions of Aceh and West Papua. These are only two of the 'Masters of Terror' named in a recent study of the Indonesian military's crimes against humanity perpetrated in 1999.[14]

Many of the current shortcomings of international justice stem from the capacity of the powerful western nations to set the agenda, dictating which people accused of war crimes to target and which others should be indulged or protected. Henry Kissinger, and such despots as Generals Pinochet in Chile and Suharto in Indonesia, have managed to evade prosecution by any tribunal largely because of their most-favoured war criminal status conferred by Washington – unlike Slobodan Milosevic who has never been a friend of the western powers.

A case filed at the ICTY by the American Association of Jurists and a group of western and Russian law experts to bring war crimes charges against the NATO victors for the bombing of civilian targets, including the government television station in Belgrade, was peremptorily dismissed by the prosecutor's office despite the fact that the Geneva Convention clearly outlaws such attacks.[15]

President Nixon's Secretary of State Henry Kissinger stands accused of providing US protection, support and complicity for bloodbaths unleashed in Chile on 9/11, and East Timor in 1975. Yes, there is another 9/11 that is not on Washington's compass. On 11 September 1973 General Pinochet launched his military coup against one of the few democracies in Latin America at the time. President Salvador Allende was killed. Tens of thousands were rounded up and detained in the national football stadium, tortured and executed. We should remember 9/11. But not only Washington's 9/11. We should give at least equal attention to the victims of Santiago's 9/11 where the ultimate victim was the death of democracy resulting in rule by a military junta.[16]

15   Vann Nath, painter and one of the few S-21 prison survivors, seen here re-enacting the painting of Pol Pot inside Tuol Sleng. These pictures of Pol Pot had saved his life while he was an inmate of S-21 (see p. 251). (John Vink/Gamma photos)

The stamp of Kissinger on the aerial bombardment that shook Cambodia in the late 1960s was even clearer than that on his well-documented role in Chile and East Timor. Henry Kissinger was not only President Nixon's right-hand man and Secretary of State, but he also ranked as the chief strategist of the intensive bombing campaign directed against the neutrality of Prince Sihanouk's Cambodia. The

16   Chhum Mey another S-21 inmate who miraculously survived. Of 14,000 inmates fewer than ten lives to tell the world about the dark secrets of S-21. Tuol Sleng was a death camp rather than a prison (see p. 251). (Tom Fawthrop)

US invoked a policy of 'hot pursuit' directed against Vietcong supply lines along the Ho Chi Minh trail, passing through parts of Laos and Cambodia. Between 18 March 1969 and May 1970, 3,630 B-52 bombing raids were flown across the Cambodian frontier.

Kissinger's hands-on supervision of the bombing targets was corroborated by the White House diaries of Bob Haldemann. He recorded the first bombing operation launched over Cambodia, obscenely code-named 'Operation Breakfast', as follows: 'Historic day. K[issinger]'s "Operation Breakfast" finally came off at 2.00 PM our time. K[issinger] really excited, as was P[resident].' A year later, on 22 April 1970, Haldemann reported that Nixon, as he followed Kissinger into the National Security Council meeting, 'turned back to me with a big smile and said "K is really having fun today, he's playing Bismarck."'[17]

Kissinger 'having fun' resulted in perhaps 500,000 Cambodian lives lost. US B-52s pounded Cambodia for 160 consecutive days in 1973, dropping more than 240,000 tons of bombs on rice fields, water buffalo and villages. No surprise then that Ta Mok has instructed his lawyer Benson Samay to call Henry Kissinger as a witness at the trial. Benson Samay claims that Ta Mok has a few cards up his sleeve and some fresh revelations to tell the court about the involvement of western agencies, CIA and the British SAS with the Khmer Rouge in the 1980s.

Kissinger, it would seem, cannot be indicted in the Khmer Rouge Tribunal because the jurisdiction is limited to the period of the Khmer Rouge in power 1975–79. Cambodians knew at the outset that the only way to get international support for a tribunal was to accept that only Cambodians would be on trial, not Henry Kissinger, and not the Chinese leadership that had propped up the Khmer Rouge regime with 15,000 advisors and massive military and economic aid, nor those countries that gave diplomatic and material support throughout the 1980s.

But if Ta Mok's lawyers seek to subpoena Kissinger as a witness, his name and his role in the Cambodian tragedy will not go entirely unnoticed. Kissinger's involvement does not exculpate or lessen the responsibility of Ta Mok for the murderous purges he so ruthlessly conducted. And Henry Kissinger will certainly not answer to a court subpoena anyway. But a tribunal that managed to avoid any reference to the hundreds of thousands of Cambodians bombed into oblivion long before Pol Pot took power, would be sadly lacking in historical perspective.

International justice is still evolving. Rwanda, Sierra Leone and South Africa represent three different models of justice and reconciliation on the African continent. In Asia we have a clear failure in East Timor owing to the lack of political will from western countries to support the overwhelming case for the indictment of Jakarta's top generals. The Cambodian tribunal, despite the decades of delay, may have better prospects of success than East Timor in bringing mass murderers to account and a well-run trial could contribute a very positive addition to the practice of international justice.

GREAT EXPECTATIONS, SOBER REALITIES

At the time of concluding the final chapter of this book, in January 2004, the elusive quest for Cambodian justice is on the verge of reaching its goal. Serious preparations are under way to organise the Phnom Penh tribunal with buildings, budgets and a secretariat to run the three-year trial now being worked out. The great expectation is that after all the frustrating delays the tribunal will finally be set up in 2004.

The UN Secretary General was preparing to launch an appeal to member states to provide the financial means for a tribunal that may cost around $50 million over three years, according to figures being bandied around based on a total staff of 300 (100 international and 200 Cambodians).

This is a fairly modest sum compared to the ICTY in The Hague, which is now costing over $200 million annually, and the Rwanda International Tribunal, costing over a billion dollars so far. Still there is apprehension that it maybe be difficult to raise even that sum and the $50 million estimate may eventually have to be pruned in the face of donor reluctance. Most of the costs will be borne by the caucus of friendly member states that have pushed the project and eventually triumphed over all the objections of the UN Secretariat – Australia, Canada, France, Japan, UK and the US, as well as Asean.

The UN member states most actively involved in pushing for a tribunal are now considering putting forward the names of distinguished jurists who could serve as international judges and prosecutors. The international judges are to be appointed by the Supreme Council of the Magistracy upon nomination by the Secretary General of the United Nations. The UN Secretary General's Special Representative for Human Rights in Cambodia, Peter Leuprecht, commented,

> The Secretary-General will have to propose first class international jurists and it will be in the interests of Cambodia to appoint the best possible Cambodian judges to the tribunal. If those two conditions are met, the tribunal can have an educational role not only for the judges on the court, but also for the judiciary and the public in general.[18]

In a similar vein Suzannah Linton argued,

> I believe that Cambodians want much more than the mere spectacle of a legal process – they want a quality process that is worthy of the losses they have suffered. Here civil society has an enormous role to play in lobbying to ensure that only the finest, most ethical and principled Cambodian jurists are selected to take part. The same must be said for the candidates put forward by the UN. Cambodians have every right to demand that the UN designates only top class international personnel with the necessary experience and unquestionable integrity to the Extraordinary Chambers.[19]

A special training programme in international law to increase the competence of Cambodian jurists was in the planning stage at the end of 2003. This is one of many preparations that could and should have started much earlier. There is no question that the Cambodian judges and other legal personnel will need considerable upgrading to be able to handle the complexities of such trials in an exemplary manner under the spotlight of international media and legal scrutiny.

On the other side of the equation, credentials for selecting international jurists should not only include their mastery of international law, but also experience in developing countries and an ability to work together with their Cambodian counterparts. A mixed tribunal is a partnership both in legal deliberations and cultural interaction. Lessons can be drawn from the frosty relations that blighted the negotiations between the UN legal team and the Cambodian side, showing the need for cultural empathy and a degree of humility on both sides.

The highest calibre judges are needed to ensure the tribunal does not get bogged down over technical points, arguments over the admissibility of evidence and procedure. The President of Cambodia's Supreme Court, Dith Munty, shared this perspective, adding, 'in my opinion if Cambodian lawyers and judges don't have enough legal skills then they leave it open for international lawyers to dominate the proceedings. The tribunal is very important as a day of closure on a dark period. I think it will help people to understand the causes of why it happened – the judges will be very serious about this. Not just showy froth and bubble, but we must carry our duties from the bottom of our hearts.'[20] The workability of the tribunal depends to a great extent on the wisdom of the two international and three Cambodian judges to overcome in the court room any ambiguities or defects in the law.

Many parties now feel that the trial in 2004 has suddenly become an imminent prospect. This mood of preparation has now hit home with the suspects. Two Khmer Rouge leaders, Nuon Chea and Khieu Samphan, made public statements in December 2003, that they would plead not guilty. In early December Sok Sam Oeun, Executive Director of the Cambodian Defenders Project, disclosed that Khieu Samphan had turned up on the doorstep and requested a defence lawyer.[21]

However, Khieu Samphan's search for a lawyer was soon over. Controversial French lawyer Jacques Vergès, his classmate in Paris during the 1950s whose previous clients include Nazi war criminal Klaus Barbie and international guerrilla Carlos the Jackal, visited Pailin and offered his services. The participation of experienced international defence counsel is indeed welcome as it will ensure that the rights of the accused are fully respected, and provide an opportunity for the prosecution case to be challenged and contested.

Pol Pot's right-hand man Nuon Chea, whose house is only a stone's throw from Khieu Samphan's Pailin residence, commented that he would defend himself if charged, adding that, 'the lawyer is just for rich people, not for the poor'.[22]

The two Khmer Rouge leaders in custody, Duch, the former director of the Tuol Sleng torture and death camp and Ta Mok, the military supremo, both have Cambodian lawyers representing them at this stage. The rules of the tribunal entitle all the accused to lawyers of their choice, including foreign lawyers, and the UN is obliged to foot the bill if the defendants are unable to afford their services.[23]

Ieng Sary, another major suspect, who lives in a lavish mansion in Phnom Penh, has not made any comment about how he is planning to handle his defence.

LAW, TRUTH AND THE TRIBUNAL – WHAT CAN BE ACHIEVED?

One of the great expectations of the Cambodian people is that the tribunal will be much more than a simple court of law. People are seeking answers to questions that have long weighed them down. How could a regime commit such bestial atrocities? Who were the masterminds who unleashed such suffering on the Cambodian people? Why did they turn the Cambodian countryside into a hell on earth? These questions are far deeper than mere legal problems of proving the guilt of the accused beyond a shadow of a doubt.

Cambodian Supreme Court judge Dith Munty also expressed the understanding that the mandate of a tribunal clearly transcends an ordinary court: 'the people are expecting some answers.'[24]

Some of the key people who could have shed some light on how the leadership functioned, and their control over the mass killings, are regrettably no longer available for cross-examination. Pol Pot is dead. So too is Son Sen, the regime's defence minister whose security responsibilities included jurisdiction over S-21. One more leading suspect would surely have been indicted if still alive – Ke Pauk, a deputy military commander to Ta Mok and key player in conducting mass purges and killings. He died in the course of 2002.

But the name of Pol Pot will still echo throughout the proceedings. In their public utterances to date Nuon Chea, Khieu Samphan and

Ieng Sary have all attempted to shift the blame for the killings on to this one man – advancing the notion that only Pol Pot knew what was going on and they were all somehow kept in the dark. Since 1979 the Khmer Rouge leaders have maintained a consistently strong state of denial to any questions relating to their own responsibility.

However, with the tribunal looming Khieu Samphan broke ranks for the first time in an open letter dated 29 December 2003, admitting that he now concedes that the regime had indeed carried out 'systematic killings'. Khieu Samphan, Head of State for most of the period of Democratic Kampuchea and then Pol Pot's prime minister in the exiled regime after 1979, declared his sudden awakening:

> I must confess that I only became fully aware of the systematic character of the phenomenon of the repression only very recently, to be frank, when I saw the work of Rithy Panh (*S-21, the Khmer Rouge killing machine*). The fact that I knew nothing at the time does not change the heart of the problem: I understand we are dealing here with a State institution, situated in Phnom Penh, which cannot be passed off as an 'exception', but must be understood as part and parcel of the regime.[25]

So had Khieu Samphan not heard of the Oscar-award winning movie *The Killing Fields* released way back in 1985? Had he never encountered the mountain of personal testimony published in newspapers, journals and books? It appears that his sudden consciousness-raising has been prompted by media reports that he may find himself standing in the dock in a few months' time.

His four-page letter, written in French, concedes, 'our country must face a painful past of hatred and terror inherited from a revolution which turned out as the most radical and most violent of all revolutions that have been known so far...' which represented the first-ever admission from a Khmer Rouge leader. It is a different tune from the one he sang in 1987 when he claimed that the Khmer Rouge's only mistake was not to go fast enough and far enough in forging ahead with their brave new 'agrarian utopia'.[26]

In his December 2003 letter he goes on to ask, 'What is my share of responsibility in all this?' Although he was attending meetings of the Khmer Rouge policy making elite known as the Standing Committee in Phnom Penh yet he adds 'from 1975–78 I had never known or learned about S21 at all' and he continues to deny any responsibility for the killings.

We have little doubt that any good prosecutor equipped with Khieu Samphan's biodata will enjoy probing the credibility of a ranking leader knowing so little about the regime's internal security policies. How could he not notice that Pol Pot's Information Minister and a host of other government cadres and Khmer Rouge functionaries had suddenly disappeared, never to be seen or heard of again?

One of the heroic survivors of S-21, Vann Nath, who interrogated his former prison guards on camera in Rithy Panh's movie, also refuses to accept Khieu Samphan's attempts to squirm away from responsibility – Vann Nath commented that 'All of them must be brought to justice or the people who suffered under them will never have peace.'

In March 2004 Khieu Samphan went even further, launching his defence case even before he had been formally indicted. Five thousand copies of a 193-page book about his life hit the bookstalls of the capital Phnom Penh.[27]

While conceding that he was aware of some suffering during the Khmer Rouge, he claims that he there was nothing he could do. 'Powerless, I could only nurture my regrets and despair in silence,' he wrote. 'The accusations levelled against me – that I was "one of the architects of the genocide of Democratic Kampuchea", or that I "helped to cover up the construction of such a regime" – are totally wrong,' he wrote.[28]

But his book does not answer one of the most important questions about his loyalty to the Khmer Rouge. Why, if he entertained so many doubts about Pol Pot and the Khmer Rouge as he now claims, did he faithfully remain wedded to its top leader Pol Pot until he died in 1997, and only threw in the towel in December 1998 when all other options were eliminated?

Nuon Chea is even less apologetic than Khieu Samphan, defiantly telling a BBC reporter in 2002 that his conscience is not bothered about the past. 'I have never stayed awake at night or shed any tears.'[29]

Chhum Mey, now 70 years old, who is one of the few survivors from Tuol Sleng, is disgusted by their claims of not knowing about the tortures of Tuol Sleng. 'How can they say they don't know what happened? They are the leaders. They must know.'[30]

If the truth is really to come out in the tribunal about the extent of the leadership's knowledge about the gruesome interrogation techniques deployed at S-21, it is mostly likely to come from the lips of Duch, its former director. Duch, the born-again Christian, initially readily confessed to investigators. His witness statements are voluminous. Duch, the defendant, is potentially the star witness for the prosecution. However, his defence lawyer has advised him to deny his earlier confessions and he has stopped talking, according to Ney Thol, chairman of the military court.[31]

Given the anomaly that only two of the major suspects are in custody awaiting trial and that the other probable indictees are still at liberty, the Cambodian government is fully responsible for ensuring that they are kept under some kind of surveillance to prevent their last-minute escape. Two of the leading candidates for prosecution, Nuon Chea and Khieu Samphan, live within a few kilometres of Thailand. The UN also has an obligation to ensure the compliance of Thai authorities in blocking any attempt by Khmer Rouge leaders to seek sanctuary abroad – as they did so often in the past.

But by far the greatest fear is that with all the main suspects in their seventies, any one of them may fall sick or suffer senility unless the final stage of setting up the tribunal takes place with all possible speed. Nuon Chea complains of high blood pressure and Ieng Sary often receives medical treatment in Bangkok for various ailments. There are also concerns about the health of Ta Mok, who has been held in a military prison in Phnom Penh since March 1999.

The success of the tribunal may well depend upon the urgency with which the United Nations and the Cambodian Task Force move to expedite the establishment of the tribunal – a process that went forward on the ground in terms of technical preparation, but was unquestionably bruised politically by the inordinate delay in forming a new government and National Assembly, thus holding up ratification of the Agreement and the pledging of the significant international funds that will be needed to put it into place.

This book has catalogued the frustrations, the delays and the dashed hopes that have derailed the tribunal for a quarter of a century. Cambodians are entitled to expect an all-out effort to accelerate the final stage – the appointment of jurists, the marshalling of evidence and the preparation of indictments. The government of Prime Minister Hun Sen, the UN Secretariat and the potential donors to the tribunal all now share the responsibility of working together to make sure that this terrible chapter of Cambodia's history is finally brought to an end.

It has been a very long journey since 1979. Cambodians deserves admiration and respect for their survival after the genocide and for the way they rebuilt their society from scratch in spite of western boycotts and the Khmer Rouge-led guerrilla war.

But today Cambodian society is plagued with a myriad of problems. Land-grabbing by the rich and powerful, the rape of the forests, the constant use of bullets to settle disputes demonstrate a cult of violence that makes nonsense of the nation's Buddhist heritage and the rule of law. So many major murder cases remain unsolved.

Many relatives of the victims as well as ordinary Cambodian people say they have almost zero faith in the ability of the police to conduct serious investigations, make arrests and ensure justice is done. The cult of gun law and the impunity that goes with it are among the many legacies of the Pol Pot regime. The urgent need for a Khmer Rouge Tribunal is not only to make a judgment in history, but it is also to lay a foundation stone for justice that can start to tackle the issue of impunity.

Youk Chhang sums up his feelings,

> ... we still suffer from the legacy of Pol Pot, we have so many terrible experiences bottled inside us. I am not free. The only way to free us is to have a complete accounting, a real justice until that happens our psychological wounds cannot be healed. Without justice we will never have peace of mind.[32]

The trial of the Pol Pot regime cannot be a panacea for all the ills of contemporary Cambodian society. But at the very least it will accord some respect to nearly 2 million dead and will demonstrate that the world cares what happened and why.

The day the tribunal indicts all the surviving Khmer Rouge leaders is the day that impunity ends for a group of mass murderers that have been succoured and protected by the international community for far too long. And if, after all the evidence has been assessed and evaluated, guilty verdicts are rained down on the heads of the accused, a great lesson in accountability will have been established. Cambodia will be the provider of a fresh landmark in the international annals of justice.

No-one feels the anguish of this unresolved legacy hanging like a dark cloud over Cambodia today more than S-21 survivor Chhum Mey. During an interview he broke down in tears when recalling the horrible torture inflicted on him. 'If there is no tribunal I will keep crying until there is a trial. Only then will I stop crying.'[33]

Annexe A

Pol Pot

The person that everyone points to as the personification of the regime and bearing the greatest responsibility is Saloth Sar (widely known by his last *nom de guerre* Pol Pot). So closely is he identified with the regime and its policies that Cambodians often say 'during Pol Pot' or 'my family was killed by Pol Pot'. Undoubtedly, defendants at the trial will try to evade criminal responsibility by insisting that Pol Pot alone was in charge of everything.

The unknown figure of Pol Pot was appointed to the position of Prime Minister in the government of Democratic Kampuchea on 14 April 1976. In a visit to China in 1977 observers identified Pol Pot as Saloth Sar, who had been Secretary of the Central Committee of the Communist Party of Kampuchea since 1963, but he himself admitted this only after his regime was overthrown. Apart from a brief period in September 1976 he held the post of Prime Minister of Democratic Kampuchea throughout the regime, and indeed after its overthrow.[1]

In August 1979 Pol Pot was convicted for the crime of genocide at the People's Revolutionary Tribunal and he was sentenced to death along with Ieng Sary *in absentia* (see Chapter 3).

After his regime was toppled by the Vietnamese invasion, Pol Pot set about rebuilding his battered army and plotted a Khmer Rouge revival and return to power with strong military backing from China and critical logistical aid from the Thai military. In spite of a public relations campaign to improve the Khmer Rouge image, and claims that Pol Pot had retired, in reality he remained the supreme political leader of the Khmer Rouge party until he was arrested by Ta Mok in 1997.

Rumours about Pol Pot's whereabouts, bouts of malaria, visits to hospitals in Bangkok and Beijing and even his death, were rife once he disappeared from public view around 1980. However a steady trickle of Khmer Rouge defectors were able to confirm that far from being retired, Pol Pot remained fully in charge of the party and military apparatus until the mid-1990s.

17   Ta Mok, Pol Pot's military chief, linked to many bloody purges. In the 1980s he became a close ally of the Thai military and businessmen. He and Duch were both arrested in 1999 and are in jail waiting for the tribunal to be set up (see p. 264). (Courtesy of Chey Sopheara, director of the Tuol Sleng Genocide Museum.)

The clearest proof of his supremacy emerged in 1989 via leaks from Khmer Rouge defecting commanders during strategy sessions held in a Khmer Rouge base along the Thai-Cambodian border.[2] Our archive photos of Pol Pot in China and Thailand indicated that his direction of the Khmer Rouge insurgency was often carried on from outside Cambodia from the safety of Khmer Rouge sanctuaries on the Thai side of the border and that it was done in close collaboration with his Chinese and Thai allies who frequently hosted him.

The fact that Pol Pot was 'killed' on more than one occasion by foreign media based in Bangkok is indicative of the poor quality of

18   Ke Pauk, Ta Mok's deputy and also accused of implementing mass purges. He defected in 1998 but has since died from an illness, thus escaping justice. Siem Reap 1998 (Tom Fawthrop)

much media coverage of Cambodia over the years. For example, Pol Pot was reported dead at 11.29 am on 6 June 1996 by AFP wire-service in Bangkok. Within a few days it became obvious that the report of his death had been greatly exaggerated as the AFP 'scoop' unravelled.

Pol Pot lost the support of his loyal military commander Ta Mok over the murder of their long-time comrade-in-arms and fellow killer Son Sen, the former Khmer Rouge defence chief in charge also of internal security. A Khmer Rouge kangaroo court on 25 July 1997

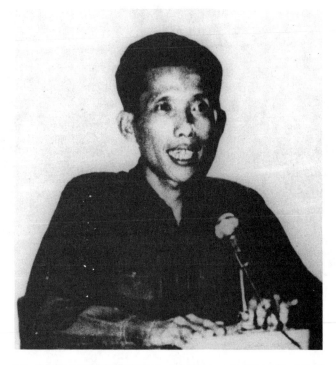

19   Duch, trusted by Pol Pot to run the secret police HQ at Tuol
Sleng. Like Ta Mok he is held in Phnom Penh pending the tribunal.
(Courtesy of Chey Sopheara director of Toul Sleng Genocide
Museum)

convicted Pol Pot of Son Sen's murder and the attempted murder
of Ta Mok and Nuon Chea. The Pol Pot revolution had reached the
ultimate stage of devouring its own. Pol Pot died on 15 April 1998,
thus depriving Cambodians of the opportunity to witness him being
finally held accountable for the misery and suffering that he had
inflicted on millions.

Pol Pot's Lieutenants

Pol Pot was known as Brother Number One among the members of
the Standing Committee (Politburo). All surviving members of this,
the highest ranking policy-making body, are potentially culpable, as
they may have been inside the loop of knowledge or responsibility
for crimes committed. All the evidence points to an inner core of
decision makers within the CPK.

20   Nuon Chea, aka 'Brother Number Two', ranked as the most powerful man after Pol Pot. He surrendered to the government in December 1998, and now lives quietly in the former Khmer Rouge stronghold of Pailin close to Khieu Samphan. Pailin 2002 (Tom Fawthrop)

Various sources give the following information on membership of the key leading bodies. (The names of those people who have died are marked with an asterisk.)[3]

The Central Committee of the Communist Party of Kampuchea

In theory, the Central Committee was the party's highest leading body responsible for 'implementation of the Party's line ... throughout the country'[4] but in reality, it appears it never met. There is no record that it was ever convened during the DK period.

Pol Pot* was secretary of the Central Committee from 1963; Nuon Chea deputy secretary from 1960; and Doeun* was administrative officer, replaced in 1975 by Khieu Samphan.[5]

The Standing Committee of the Central Committee of the Communist Party of Kampuchea

In most organisations built on the communist model, most of the work of the Central Committee is delegated to its executive body, which is always in session, known as the Standing Committee,

Permanent Committee or Politburo. In Democratic Kampuchea the Standing Committee appears indeed to have played this role.

Nine individuals were full members of the Standing Committee at various times between 1975 and 1979: Pol Pot*, Nuon Chea, Ieng Sary, So Phim*, Vorn Vet*, Ros Nhim*, Ta Mok, Son Sen* and Khieu Samphan.[6]

On 9 October 1975 the following responsibilities were assigned among members of the Standing Committee: Pol Pot* 'in overall charge of the military and the economy', Nuon Chea in charge of 'Party work, social welfare, culture, propaganda and formal education', Van (Ieng Sary) in charge of both Party and State foreign affairs, and Khieu (Son Sen)* in charge of the armed forces 'General Staff and security'[7] (which included the prison system and S-21).

A further eleven individuals were candidate members of the Standing Committee: Keu*, Khieu Thirith, Yun Yat*, Ke Pauk*, Doeun*, Nang*, Ney Sarann*, Phuong*, Chan*, Sae* and Thang Sy.*

Party Centre Military Committee (or Military Committee of the Central Committee)

This body appears to have been responsible for 'security policies and practices, which in turn circumvented the structures and processes that were formally responsible for dealing with alleged activities of ordinary people and Party members deemed to be "criminal" or "treasonous".'[8]

In November 1978 its membership was listed as Pol (Pot)*, Nuon (Chea), (Ta) Mok, Van (Ieng Sary) and Khieu (Son Sen)*.[9]

There appear to have been other sub-committees within the Military committee, including

Military (External Security) Commission

Pol Pot*, Nuon Chea, Son Sen*, Ta Mok, Sao Phim*, also Yun Yat (informal role) and Koy Thuon* (minor role).[10]

Party Centre (Internal Security) Committee

Nuon Chea, Son Sen* and Yun Yat*.[11]

The position of Nuon Chea (Brother Number Two) on this committee would appear to conflict with his denials that he knew anything about security matters.

Armed Forces

Headed by Son Sen*, Chairman of the General Staff.

Duch, as head of S-21 and Secretary of its CPK Branch, was directly responsible to Son Sen. S-21 was treated as equivalent to one of the armed forces' divisions.

Each 'Zone, Sector or Division had armed units answering to the CPK Committee at the relevant level, and agriculture cooperative chairmen had ... armed "guerrillas" or "militia" (*chhlop*) at their disposal.'[12]

A summary recapitulation of people named above as members of these top-level bodies:

The following have already died and are therefore automatically ruled out of consideration for trial:

Pol Pot*
Son Sen*
Yun Yat*
Von Vet*
Ke Pauk*
Hu Nim*
Toch Phoen*
So Phim*
Nhim Ros*
Still surviving (4 people)

Nuon Chea

Nuon Chea was born in Battambang in 1927 (an area of Cambodia occupied by Thailand during the Second World War). In the 1940s he studied at Thammasat University and was even a part-time employee at the Thai Foreign Ministry. He joined the Communist Party of Thailand and transferred to the Indochina Communist Party when he returned to Cambodia[13] in 1950, being assigned to party work in the north west as part of the Issarak insurgency.[14] He was a founding member of the Kampuchean People's Revolutionary Party in 1951 and then went to Hanoi for three years' training. In 1962 he became Deputy Secretary General of the party (at that time named the Workers Party of Kampuchea) and a member of the Standing Committee, positions he continued to hold. From 1970 to 1975 he held the position of political commissar for the revolutionary armed forces.

During the period of Democratic Kampuchea he briefly served as Prime Minister, was appointed President of the People's Assembly of Democratic Kampuchea (1976–1979), was Deputy Chairman of Standing committee of the Central Committee, Chairman of the Standing Committee of the Revolutionary Army of Kampuchea and Chairman of the Internal Security Committee.[15]

Nuon Chea surrendered (together with Khieu Samphan) to the Royal Government of Cambodia on 24 December 1998. According to statements by the prime minister at the time and subsequently, no assurances of amnesty were given as part of any deal beyond an agreement with the Thai authorities that upon their return they would not be arrested. Nuon Chea now lives quietly in Pailin assuming the role of a simple farmer, tending ducks and granting rare press interviews in which he denies culpability for genocide and other crimes against humanity. In December 2002 he came to Phnom Penh as a surprise defence witness for Khmer Rouge General Sam Bith on trial for the 1994 train ambush, hostage-taking and murder case.

Ieng Sary (Kim Trang)

Born in 1929 in Vinh Binh, now part of Vietnam, at the age of 14 he went to Phnom Penh to study at Sisowath High School. He then went on to the Institute of Political Studies in Paris, where he joined the French Communist Party and was one of the founders of the Marxist Circle of Khmer Students. He married Khieu Thirith, whose sister Ponnary married Pol Pot.

Ieng Sary returned to Cambodia in 1957 and took up a teaching position at his former high school. In 1960 he was elected to the Central Committee of the Workers Party of Kampuchea (later to become the Communist Party of Kampuchea) and in 1963 to its Standing Committee. He went underground the same year, as Sihanouk's repression of leftists increased. In 1971 he went to Beijing to join the Royal Government of Khmer National Unity (GRUNK), led by Sihanouk, and became special advisor to Khieu Samphan in 1973. He was responsible for the Communist Party of Kampuchea's international relations.

During the Democratic Kampuchea period Ieng Sary was Deputy Prime Minister and Minister of Foreign Affairs, in which capacity he was responsible for the re-education of returnees (concentration camps). Cambodians who been studying abroad, Sihanoukist diplomats and others invited to return home were held at Boeung Trabek in Phnom Penh and also in Kampong Cham. Numerous reports describe how many of these returnees were taken off and executed. Ieng Sary was a member of the Standing Committee.[16]

Convicted and sentenced to death *in absentia* for genocide by the People's Revolutionary Tribunal in 1979, he continued in senior positions within the Khmer Rouge and enjoyed close links with the Chinese government. Ieng Sary held the position of Minister for Economics and Finance in the Coalition Government of Democratic Kampuchea (1982–1991).

From 1979–1990 all financial aid from Beijing was channelled through the Chinese embassy in Bangkok and disbursed to Ieng Sary. That gave him a position of pivotal importance in coordinating logistical support from the Thai authorities and commuting between Pol Pot's bases on the border, Bangkok and Beijing.

In May 1992 he was supposedly relieved of many of his responsibilities as part of the Khmer Rouge decision to put him and Pol Pot in the background as political liabilities.

In September 1996 Ieng Sary split with Pol Pot and defected. He brought with him several thousand guerrillas from the Pailin and Phnom Malai districts, amounting to one-third of the remaining Khmer Rouge troops. He was granted a pardon for his 1979 conviction for the crime of genocide, and amnesty from prosecution under the 1994 Law to Outlaw the Democratic Kampuchea Group. The legal ramifications of the pardon are a continuing controversy and are discussed at more length elsewhere in the book, especially in Chapter 8. However, the pardon was for genocide only, and would presumably be no bar to prosecution for other charges in the Law. The Agreement signed between the United Nations and the Royal Government of Cambodia states (in Article 11) that 'the scope of this pardon is a matter to be decided by the Extraordinary Chambers'.

Ieng Sary is the only one of all the former Khmer Rouge senior leaders who continued to play any open political role after his defection. He founded the Democratic National Unity Movement (DNUM), and was behind the publication of DNUM's magazine *Phka Rik* (Flower in Bloom). Ieng Sary and his wife Ieng Thirith reside in a spacious villa in Phnom Penh. He has accumulated substantial wealth in recent years, owning at least two houses in Phnom Penh and one in Bangkok.

Khieu Samphan

Born in 1929 in the province of Svay Rieng, he was the son of a judge and was highly educated, studying at Sisowath High School, the University of Montpellier and holding a doctorate in economics from the University of Paris (1959). His thesis, entitled 'The economy of Cambodia and its problems of industrialisation' outlined autarchic policies that had considerable resonance with those adopted when the Khmer Rouge came to power 16 years later. In France he was a member of the Marxist Circle of Khmer Students and was Secretary General of the Union of Khmer Students.

Khieu Samphan returned to Cambodia in 1959 and joined Sihanouk's Sangkum Reastr Niyum. He was a professor at the Chamroeun Vichea Institute before becoming editor in chief of the newspaper *L'Observateur*. He became branded as an oppositionist by then Prince Norodom Sihanouk, and in July 1960 was beaten and humiliated in the streets of Phnom Penh, then imprisoned without trial for one month. He was later elected to the National Assembly as a representative of Sihanouk's Sangkum party in the 1962 and 1966 elections, serving as Secretary of Commerce 1962–63.

In April 1967 he went underground and was active in Kampong Speu province. He was named Deputy Prime Minister and Minister for Defence of GRUNK from 1970–76 but, unlike most of his fellow ministers, he did not go into exile with Sihanouk in Beijing, instead remaining with Pol Pot in the jungle. He was elected a candidate member of the Central Committee in 1971 and a full member in 1976.

During the period of Democratic Kampuchea, Khieu Samphan held the highest formal position, in April 1976 replacing Norodom Sihanouk as Head of State, as well other more powerful positions within the party and government, including head of the parliament.[17] After 1979 he held the positions of Prime Minister in the Democratic Kampuchea government-in-exile and President of the party, renamed the Party of Democratic Kampuchea. Throughout the 1980s Khieu Samphan was assiduously promoted by Asean and other countries as the acceptable face of the moderate Khmer Rouge, while Pol Pot and Ieng Sary were held behind the scenes.

Khieu Samphan led the Khmer Rouge delegation to the Supreme National Council from 1990 to 1993. He continued to be the Khmer Rouge's spokesperson after UNTAC left Cambodia, and was in charge of the Khmer Rouge clandestine radio station. After the 1998 mutiny in Anlong Veng, Khieu Samphan and Nuon Chea both fled with Ta Mok to Thailand.

Khieu Samphan defected (together with Nuon Chea) to the Royal Government of Cambodia on 24 December 1998. According to statements at the time and subsequently, the Prime Minister has stated that no assurances of amnesty were given as part of any deal. Khieu Samphan now lives in a modest house right next door to Nuon Chea in Pailin, close to a number of casinos and less than a kilometre from the Thai border.

Ta Mok (Chhit Choeun)

The only one of the senior leaders to have been apprehended, Ta Mok has been in military custody in Phnom Penh since March 1999.

Ta Mok was born in Takeo province, which remained his base for militant rebellion from the 1940s right up until the end of the Democratic Kampuchea period. His education was a traditional Buddhist one, including attending the Pali High School in Phnom Penh. Ta Mok was elected to the Central Committee in 1963, was appointed Deputy Secretary for the southwest zone in 1966 and Secretary and military chief of the zone in the late 1960s.

During Democratic Kampuchea he held various positions in both the party and the armed forces, notably Member of the Standing Committee of the Central Committee,[18] Secretary of the southwest zone and later Secretary of the northern/central zone, Chief of the General Staff and Member of the Military (External Security) Committee, as well as First Deputy President of the parliament.

He continued to command the Khmer Rouge forces after 1979 and set up a series of logistical bases and arms caches in Sisaket province in Thailand in close coordination with the Thai military. For many years he occupied a spacious mansion in the Thai town of Khukan and operated a lucrative trade in smuggling logs from Cambodia. Later he became a business entrepreneur and partner in at least three Thai petrol stations. His business transactions in Thailand were handled by Nou Noeu.

In 1997, in a Khmer Rouge leadership split, Ta Mok wrested control from Pol Pot whom he put on trial in Anlong Veng. A year later Ta Mok's leadership was challenged by a mutiny in Anlong Veng and he was forced to flee across the Thai border.

Unlike the other Khmer Rouge leaders, Ta Mok never surrendered or defected to the Royal Government of Cambodia, but was captured in March 1999. Initially charged with violating the 1994 law banning the Khmer Rouge and with crimes against domestic security, in September 1999 he was charged with genocide under Decree Law No. 2 of 1979. Since February 2002 he has been detained for crimes against humanity under the 2001 Khmer Rouge Law.[19]

Beyond the Standing Committee

Besides the above-mentioned members of the most significant bodies of the Communist Party of Kampuchea, especially the Standing Committee, other individuals may also be considered to be 'senior leaders of Democratic Kampuchea' by virtue of their function or position.

The degree to which the various zones were independent of each other and of the Centre is a matter of some contention. Kiernan says that the evidence indicates a highly centralised structure, albeit with some regional variation. Heder says that the zones, and even districts, enjoyed a large measure of autonomy.

Zone Secretaries

The Secretaries of the seven zones that the country was divided into would be foremost among those whose roles should be examined. It would appear, though, that as the regime turned ever inward in waves of purges and 'purification', regional bosses who had the potential to develop individual power, were eliminated one by one. The only Zone Secretary to survive was Ta Mok, who was already named above due to his membership of the Standing Committee and the Military Committee. So the expansion of the focus to the zone level does not add any further names to the list of prime suspects.

The Zone Secretaries were:

East – So Phim*
Southwest – Ta Mok
Northwest – Ros Nhim*
West – Thang Si*
North (later renamed **Central** in December 1977) – Ke Pauk *[20]
Northeast – Ya*
New North (from December 1977) – Kang Chap*

Women

All the above people mentioned are male. Few women seem to have made it to the top of the Khmer Rouge hierarchy, although there are many reports of cruelty being inflicted by female guards and particularly by young women in positions of local authority.

Three who did rise high were the Khieu sisters, Thirith and Ponnary (who were married to Ieng Sary and Pol Pot respectively) and Yun Yat*, married to Son Sen.

Khieu Thirith (also known as Ieng Thirith)

Candidate Member of Standing Committee of the Central Committee; Minister of Social Affairs. As Minister for Social Affairs in Democratic Kampuchea, she could be held to be at least partially accountable for the social policies of the Khmer Rouge that caused extreme suffering. She went on to be a vociferous defender of the Democratic Kampuchea regime long after its demise, and will presumably at least be called as a material witness, or as an accused.

Khieu Ponnary*

Chair of the Democratic Kampuchea Women's Association. Khieu Ponnary evidently was already seriously deranged by 1975 and seems scarcely to have played any role in the regime. Given the fact that she had for so many years been no longer in control of her faculties, she was never considered as a potential witness or defendant. She died in Pailin in mid-2003.

Yun Yat*

Candidate Member of Standing Committee of the Central Committee; Minister of Culture, Education and Instruction; parliamentary representative of Phnom Penh factory workers. Yun Yat was murdered by Pol Pot together with her husband Son Sen in 1997.

KEY KHMER ROUGE PERSONNEL –
THOSE MOST RESPONSIBLE FOR SERIOUS CRIMES

As mentioned above, under the Khmer Rouge Law the Co-prosecutors can also bring indictments against other individuals who were not senior leaders but who bear criminal responsibility for the most serious crimes. One category is clearly directors of prisons such as S-21, including regional prisons like Kraing Ta Chan in Takeo[21] or people who can on the face of it be held responsible for particularly egregious tortures or massacres that took place under their command responsibility.

Duch (Kaing Khek Iev)

Kaing Khek Iev, better known as Duch, the director of the S-21 interrogation and extermination centre and held in custody since 1999, while perhaps not a 'senior leader of Democratic Kampuchea' certainly would appear to fall into the category of 'those most responsible for the most serious crimes'.

Duch was born in 1942 in Kampong Thom province, graduated top of mathematics class at university and became a teacher and then vice-principal of a school in Kampong Thom in the 1960s. He spent several years in prison (1968–1970) for subversion. Insight into his demeanour as well as his status and power at that time is provided in the memoirs of François Bizot, a researcher with the École Française d'Extrême-Orient, who was captured by Khmer Rouge forces and held near Oudong for three months in 1971 under Duch's control and interrogation.

From 1973 Duch was appointed head of security for the Communist Party of Kampuchea and was active in the liberated zones to the north and west of Phnom Penh. During Democratic Kampuchea he was Director of S-21, Chairman of S-21 Party Committee and functionally Chief of *Santebal,* the 'Special Branch' secret police.

Duch abandoned S-21 just hours before Vietnamese forces liberated Phnom Penh, fleeing to Sa Kae refugee camp in Thailand. During the 1980s he was sent by the party leaders to Beijing and was assigned to broadcast Khmer Rouge propaganda.

After his return from China little is known of his activities until, in the aftermath of the 1997 conflict in Phnom Penh, Duch was recruited by the American Refugee Committee to work inside a refugee camp in Thailand. His family had settled in the neighbouring Cambodian border district of Samlaut.

Assuming the new name of Hong Pin he became a born-again Christian. His friends described Hong Pin as a 'nice man who cares for refugees', a God-fearing Christian who wanted to bring Jesus into every home and a dedicated educator, who wanted to build schools for the poor children of Khmer Rouge defectors in this very deprived district. Kong Rian, the Cambodian administrative manager for World Vision, a Christian-based charity, met Duch several times. 'He showed me his baptism certificate. He was a very polite and very nice man.'[22]

Initially charged with violating the 1994 law banning the Khmer Rouge and with crimes against domestic security, in September 1999 he was charged with genocide under Decree Law No.2 of 1979, and since February 2002 has been detained for crimes against humanity under the 2001 Khmer Rouge Law.[23]

All the members of the Standing Committee have denied their responsibility for crimes committed. Duch so far stands alone among key suspects in cooperating with journalists and investigators. His detailed confessions include a full description of his role in the bureaucracy of death and his close links to Khmer Rouge leaders especially Son Sen. In addition to facing punishment for his own crimes, Duch's evidence could prove crucial in connecting KR senior leadership to the killings of S-21 and elsewhere in the country.

District secretaries

Heder's 2003 paper argues that district party secretaries were 'key figures in responsibility for killings nation-wide'.

The implications of Heder's latest approach would broaden the scope of prosecution or investigation to include those who held the position of Communist Party of Kampuchea Secretary in all 112 districts at any time during the Democratic Kampuchea period.[24]

One obvious effect of this extended scope would be to include at least one current CPP leader, Chea Sim, in the suspects list, given that he held the position of Khmer Rouge district secretary in the eastern zone. Chea Sim was among a group of Khmer Rouge middle ranking and minor cadres who fled to Vietnam in May 1978 in rebellion against the Pol Pot regime.

Expanding the scope to this extent would stretch the notion of 'senior leaders' beyond what was understood by both sides during the negotiations. Nevertheless, this echelon may include individuals who would fall into the second category of suspects, those who bear individual responsibility for the most serious violations of Cambodian domestic or international humanitarian law.

As we have argued in Chapter 8, justice should achieve a balance with national reconciliation, and a tribunal that engages in a sweeping inquisition of all possible suspects could do more harm than good. We do not rule out the possibility that dramatic new evidence might emerge that could incriminate someone in a leadership position. But in the absence of such evidence we are wary of attempts to widen the net, which could trigger unnecessary alarm among many rank and file defectors who are clearly outside the terms of reference of the court.

Military Officers

Among his *Seven candidates* Stephen Heder included two military officers outside the highest bodies of the Centre. These are Sou Met and Meas Muth, both of whom had risen from Ta Mok's southwest zone with powerful family connections.

Sou Met

Secretary of Central Committee Division 502, which incorporated the Democratic Kampuchea air force. Currently serving as deputy regional military commander in the Royal Cambodian Armed Forces (RCAF) based in Battambang.

Meas Muth (Khe Muth, Meah Mut)

Secretary of Central Committee Division 164, which incorporated the Democratic Kampuchea navy. He was Ta Mok's son-in-law and led the attacks on a Vietnamese island off the coast of Kampot in the days immediately after the Khmer Rouge came to power.[25] In the 1990s he was the Khmer Rouge commander in charge of Samlaut district. After joining the 1996 defections he retained his rank of general in the Cambodian army and was again assigned to Samlaut, Battambang region.

Heder claims that evidence shows that these two 'CPK Military Division Chairmen … were directly involved in the arrest and transfer to S-21' of soldiers from their divisions, and that the evidence similarly suggests that both officials may be responsible for arrests and executions perpetrated by subordinates in their respective Divisions.

Of the seven candidates cited by Heder, the other five were key members of the Democratic Kampuchea regime, but these two senior military officers are less obvious suspects. One problem with including these two as prime suspects is that it extends the scope considerably beyond the highest bodies of the Centre, raising the question of how many others held equal rank and would therefore logically be included as prime suspects. It is not clear from their exposition that the crimes committed by these two were exceptional and, indeed, such expansion is the thrust of Heder's latest work.

Annexe B

Report of the group of experts for Cambodia established pursuant to General Assembly resolution 52/135, 16 March 1999 (United Nations document A/53/850 and S/1999/231)

The main points of the Group of Experts' report were summarised in Chapter 7. For the purposes of this discussion the principal sections are 'Evidence of the criminal nature of the acts committed' and the 'Feasibility of bringing the Khmer Rouge to justice'.

The Group of Experts concluded:

> Based on our review of the law and available evidence, the Group believes that it is legally justifiable to include in the jurisdiction of a tribunal that would try Khmer Rouge leaders for acts during the period from 1975 to 1979 for the following crimes: crimes against humanity, genocide, war crimes, forced labour, torture and crimes against internationally protected persons, as well as the crimes under Cambodian law 'of homicide, torture, rape, physical assault, arbitrary arrest and detention, attacks on religion and other abuses of governmental authority.'

The Pol Pot regime: race, power and genocide in Cambodia under the Khmer Rouge, 1975–79 by Ben Kiernan (1996)

Kiernan's book was based principally on his own extensive interviews with Cambodian survivors as well as on the documentary record, particularly from the Khmer Rouge security apparatus. He argues the crucial importance of race in the evolution of Khmer Rouge policy and practice by examining in intricate detail the series of events and episodes that took place during the period of Democratic Kampuchea. Kiernan estimates the death toll at 1,671,000, and he breaks this number down into racial/ethnic groups under the two main categories used during the Democratic Kampuchea period, namely, 'new people' and 'base people'.

In addition to identifying its 'racialist preoccupations and discourse' Kiernan points to its paranoia and 'totalitarian ambitions and achievements', and he concludes, 'The DK regime was on a genocidal track. There is no reason to believe the killing would have slowed, had it not been stopped by the Vietnamese army.'

One of the most significant contributions made by Kiernan in this book is to report on rebellions and resistance both within and without the ranks of the Khmer Rouge. The enemies of the regime, both real and imagined, were hunted down in ever-narrowing circles of purges and paranoia. The details of names, places and events Kiernan provides will provide an invaluable tool for the prosecution in building its cases.[9]

Voices from S-21: terror and history in Pol Pot's secret prison by David Chandler (2000)

David Chandler describes what he refers to as the 'total institution' of S-21 (Tuol Sleng) and theorises as to its psychological and ideological roots.

This is a detailed account of the workings of S-21 as a key institution of the regime. The book is based largely on the archives of S-21, including confessions and administrative documents – manuals, lists and instructions. Most of the documents are signed or thumb-printed and dated, and many have hand-written marginal notes by the superior officers to whom they were sent for disposition. Critical to the prosecution case will be the evidence that S-21 director Duch answered directly to Son Sen in charge of defence and security, and that confessions extracted from prisoners were routinely passed on to top personnel including Nuon Chea and Ieng Sary. Chandler clearly links policy makers to the actual implementation and atrocities committed.

Seven candidates for prosecution: accountability for the crimes of the Khmer Rouge by Stephen Heder and Brian D. Tittemore (2001)[10]

Heder and Tittemore set out to demonstrate individual criminal responsibility for crimes and have selected seven 'candidates for prosecution':

> Our examination of the archival evidence suggests that there is a *prima facie* case that the seven individuals examined in this report are criminally responsible for planning or implementing these

policies under principles of individual responsibility and, in most instances, pursuant to the doctrine of superior responsibility.

The seven so named are: Nuon Chea, Ieng Sary, Khieu Samphan, Ta Mok, Ke Pauk, Sou Met and Meas Muth.

The report, written mainly by Stephen Heder,[11] is based principally on an analysis of the documents gathered by the Cambodian Genocide Program and Documentation Center of Cambodia, particularly those emanating from S-21 and the whole *Santesok* (security) apparatus. Brian Tittemore[12] prepared the legal evaluation of the evidentiary material analysed by Heder and is the principal co-editor of this report, together with Diane F. Orentlicher.[13]

However, early in 2003 Steve Heder recanted his *Seven Candidates* in a paper entitled 'Cambodia, Nazi Germany and the Stalinized Soviet Union', presented at a meeting at the German Historical Institute in Washington, DC on 29 March.[14] He threw his earlier assessment overboard, deeming it to be 'Heder's top-down temptation: seven big fish.' Acknowledging the influence of recent studies of Nazi Germany and the Soviet Union under Stalin, Heder warns that 'the greater extent to which responsibility is mistakenly laid to a restricted leadership circle at the top, the more the lower echelons are wrongly exonerated.'

His new paper divides Khmer Rouge killings into obligatory and discretionary categories. Obligatory killings, he describes as

> centrally pre-meditated and planned murders ordered by Pol [Pot] and Nuon [Chea] and carried out via what was clearly a chain of command ... But other killings – probably most – were committed by regional and local authorities acting not as part of such a tight chain of command; but of a looser and more diffuse hierarchical structure of delegated and discretionary authority...

Heder maintains that the tribunal law based on the fact that '[t]he senior-leaders formula is historically, legally and morally untenable' now argues in favour of putting thousands of Khmer Rouge defectors, including current leaders of the CPP-led government, under legal scrutiny.

This Cambodian scholar is apparently so wrapped up in his latest thesis that he neglects to take into account the need for balance in any post-conflict society between justice, truth and reconciliation (discussed in Chapter 8). What would be the impact of hauling thousands before a tribunal that might have to continue for years to finish such a massive caseload? And above all is there any evidence that the majority of Cambodians would actually wish for such a grand inquisition into the past?

While it is clear that many lower echelons of the Khmer Rouge carried out killings, and that not many people who lived under such a regime could emerge four years later with totally clean hands, it is not clear that the cause of social justice would be best served by open-ended rolling prosecutions until society is fully purged of the genocidal past. On the contrary the latest Heder formula would threaten to plunge the country into a new legal and social turmoil.

NOTES

INTRODUCTION

1. The temporal jurisdiction of the court was very limited: 17 April 1975 to 6 January 1979. This was a political deal to avoid the possibility of the court deciding to look at crimes before (especially the US bombing) and after (Khmer Rouge crimes in which support given by other countries might have been scrutinised).

2. 740,000 asserted by Michael Vickery, *Cambodia 1975–1992*, Boston: South End, 1984, p. 18; the Research Committee of the Salvation Front, 1983, claimed 3.314 million and this figure is still used by the Cambodian government; Ben Kiernan, *The Pol Pot regime: race, power and genocide in Cambodia under the Khmer Rouge, 1975–79*, New Haven: Yale University Press, 1996, p. 458. Marek Sliwinski, *Le genocide Khmer Rouge: une analyse démographique*, Paris: L'Harmattan, 1995, p. 57. Patrick Heuveline, 'Between one and three million': towards the demographic reconstruction of a decade of Cambodian history (1970–79)', *Population studies*, vol. 52, no. 1, March 1998, p. 56. See a recent summary in Ben Kiernan 'The demography of genocide in Southeast Asia', *Critical Asian Studies*, vol. 35, no. 4, 2003, pp. 585–97.

3. Heuveline, 'Between one and three million', p. 59.

4. The extent of this literature in English is shown in *Genocide: an anthropological reader*, edited by Alexander Laban Hinton, Malden, Massachusetts and Oxford: Blackwell, 2002; and William A. Schabas, *Genocide in international law*, Cambridge: Cambridge University Press, 2000. For a review of the literature on Cambodia, see especially *Genocide and democracy in Cambodia*, edited by Ben Kiernan, and Alexander Laban Hinton, 'A head for an eye: revenge in the Cambodian genocide' in *Genocide: an anthropological reader*.

5. *New York Times* editorial 24 June 1997 cited by Edward S. Herman, 'Pol Pot and Kissinger: on war criminality and impunity', *Z magazine*, September 1997.

6. Official US figures on the bombing have been released in recent years, but they do not attempt to estimate the number of resulting casualties (especially civilian). Ben Kiernan gives an estimate of 150,000 (*Pol Pot regime*, p. 25), while Christopher Hitchens reports 600,000 and adds 'these were not the highest estimates', (*The trial of Henry Kissinger*, London: Verso, 2001, p. 35). For a detailed exposition of the US bombing campaigns and their political context, see William Shawcross, *Sideshow: Kissinger, Nixon and the destruction of Cambodia*, New revised edition, London: Hogarth, 1986, *passim*.

CHAPTER 1

1. At the Nuremberg trials the crime of genocide was mentioned in the case for the prosecution, but the defendants were not actually tried for

this crime. See Chapter 3 for a detailed discussion of the 1979 People's Revolutionary Tribunal.

2. David Chandler, *Voices from S-21: terror and history in Pol Pot's secret prison*, Chiang Mai: Silkworm Books, 2000, p. 2.
3. A definite total is hard to arrive at, but more than 5,000 photos and 10,000 biographies have been catalogued. David Chandler (*Voices*, p. 35) cites concrete evidence that 13,206 people passed through the prison between 1976 and 1979, but notes that some were not recorded before they were taken off for execution.
4. Raoul Jennar, *Les clés du Cambodge*. [Paris]: Maisonneuve & Larose, 1995, p. 83.
5. See Chapter 7 for more details of the genocide sites throughout Cambodia. Henri Locard, who has focussed his research on the Khmer Rouge period on the prison system, describes it thus: 'From 17th April the entire country was to become one big prison.' He discusses factories, hospitals and re-education camps in addition to his central concern – the prison system itself, which operated on three levels, village, district and zone. *The Khmer Rouge gulag: Democratic Kampuchea 17 April 1975–7 January 1979*. Paris, Phnom Penh, Canberra, June-July 1995, prepared for the conference on 'Concentration camps: a XXth century phenomenon', Paris, 15–17 June 1995, p. 3.
6. Im Sethy interview with the authors, March 2001.
7. Tey Sambo interview by Tom Fawthrop, February 2001.
8. Chea Vannath interview by Tom Fawthrop, February 2001.
9. Described in many accounts such as that told in February 1979 to journalist Nuon Sarit by one Khmer Rouge executioner, a boy of 16 years of age. The boy recounted having killed 600 prisoners on one day in early January 1979 as all prisoners in his Kampong Thom camp were put to death. (Antonin Kubes, *Kampuchea*, Prague: Orbis, 1982, pp. 134–5). The evidence of last minute executions was recorded by those who first entered the compound.
10. Despite her initial enthusiasm, Chea Vannath and her husband fled to Thai refugee camps in 1980 because they no longer trusted the Vietnamese role in their country. In the 1990s returned to found the Center for Social Development.
11. Bui Tin, then deputy editor of *Nhan Dan* the communist daily newspaper, settled in Paris in 1990 as author and dissident. This quotation comes from his *From cadre to exile: memoirs of a Vietnamese journalist*, translated from the Vietnamese and adapted by Judy Stowe and Do Van. Chiang Mai: Silkworm Books, 1995, p. 119.
12. The full name of the Salvation Front was Kampuchean United Front for National Salvation, also referred to by the Cambodian word for front, Renakse. It was formed on 2 December 1978 in Kratie province and declared its objective to overthrow the genocidal Pol Pot regime. Eastern region dissidents Heng Samrin, Chea Sim and Hun Sen were among the leaders.
13. Dr Thong Khon interview by Tom Fawthrop, January 2002.

14. This term of description for Phnom Penh in January 1979 was coined well before Matt Dillon's movie set in Cambodia changed its title from *Under the banyan tree* to *City of ghosts*.

15. Kiernan, *The Pol Pot regime*, p. 48 cites reports of the city population being estimated at 1.8 million on the eve of the evacuation, while Ieng Sary later gave a figure of 3 million.

16. On industrial activity in Phnom Penh under the Khmer Rouge see Charles H. Twining, 'The economy' in *Cambodia 1975–1978: rendezvous with death*, edited by Karl D. Jackson, Princeton: Princeton University Press, 1989, pp. 132–4. On the city's population see Pen Khon, *Phnom Penh before and after 1997*. [Phnom Penh: s.n., 2000] p. 14 and Antonin Kubes, *Kampuchea*.

17. Frequently mentioned, as recently in an interview by Yoichi Funbashi, 'Hun Sen on the subject of nation-building', *International Herald Tribune/ Asahi*, 7 October 2003.

18. 'The Peoples Republic of Kampuchea at the Threshold of its Sixth Year', *Vietnam Courier* 1983, pp. 12–16, quoted in Irwin Silber, *Kampuchea: the revolution rescued*, Oakland: Line of March Publications, 1986 pp. 83–4.

19. As discussed more fully above in the Introduction the number of Cambodians who perished under Khmer Rouge rule (above that normally expected during the period) is estimated at around 1.7 million.

20. Kiernan, *Pol Pot regime*, p. 458.

21. *Crimes of the clique of the Beijing Chinese expansionists and the lackeys Pol Pot, Ieng Sary, Khieu Samphan in the period 1975–1979*, [in Khmer] Phnom Penh: Renakse, 1983, p. 69.

22. David Hawk, 'Cambodia: a report from Phnom Penh', the *New Republic*, 15 November 1982, p. 20.

23. Sum Mean interview by Helen Jarvis, March 2001.

24. Thong Khon, interview by Tom Fawthrop, January 2002

25. Chan Ven interview with the authors, March 2001.

26. A more nuanced view is presented in two recent studies both based on primary source Cambodian documents: Evan Gottesman *Cambodia after the Khmer Rouge: inside the politics of nation building*, New Haven, Yale University Press, 2003 and Margaret Slocomb, *The People's Republic of Kampuchea 1979–1989: the revolution after Pol Pot*, Chiang Mai: Silkworm Books, 2003.

27. Gottesman, *Cambodia*, pp. 15–146.

28. Prum Sokha interview by Tom Fawthrop, July 1997.

29. For two conflicting perspectives see William Shawcross, *The quality of mercy: Cambodia, holocaust and modern conscience*, New York: Simon and Schuster, 1984 and Eva Mysliwiec, *Punishing the poor: the international isolation of Kampuchea*, Oxford: Oxfam, 1988.

30. The story of Oxfam's early days in Cambodia is told by David Bull, *The poverty of diplomacy: Kampuchea and the outside world*, Oxford: Oxfam, 1983, p. 30–31.

31. Although the intellectuals, government officials and business people undoubtedly saw the 1960s as a halcyon age, most of the overwhelming proportion of the Cambodian population who lived in the countryside would not have seen such a great difference in their standard of living

– it has always been hard, and peasant impoverishment was on the increase throughout the twentieth century. See Jean Delvert, *Le paysan cambodgien*, Paris: École Pratique des Hauts Études-Sorbonne & Mouton, 1961, Vickery, *Cambodia*, pp. 15–17.

32. Prum Sokha interview by Tom Fawthrop, July 1997.
33. Dr My Samedy interview by Tom Fawthrop, April 2001.

CHAPTER 2

1. Paul Redicliffe, former British ambassador to Cambodia, private communication with Tom Fawthrop, 2001.
2. According to the UN High Commission for Refugees, which organised food relief for them. (Nayan Chanda, *Brother enemy: the war after the war*, San Diego: Harcourt Brace Jovanovich, 1986, pp. 214–15). This number included ethnic Vietnamese, Chinese and Khmers. On the legal issues relating to Vietnam's invasion, see Gary Klintworth, *Vietnam's intervention in Cambodia in international law*, AGPS Press, 1989 and, for a very different perspective, Stephen J. Morris, *Why Vietnam invaded Cambodia: political culture and the causes of war*, Stanford: Stanford University Press, 1999. See also Kiernan, *Pol Pot regime*, p. 389, n. 15, and Nayan Chanda, *Brother enemy*, pp. 214–15. For the Vietnamese exposition of their case at the time see *War crimes of the Pol Pot and Chinese troops in Vietnam*, Hanoi: Commission of Inquiry into the Chinese Expansionists' and Hegemonists' Crime of War of Aggression, 1979.
3. See for example the film *The last God-King: the lives and times of Cambodia's Sihanouk* by James Gerrand, Sydney: Film Australia, 1996.
4. Norodom Sihanouk, *Prisonnier des Khmers Rouges*. – [s.l.]: Hachette, 1986, pp. 337–47. Thiounn Prasith remained in New York (serving as Permanent Representative of the Khmer Rouge UN delegation until 1982, and then until 1991 of the Coalition Government of Democratic Kampuchea delegation). He is today still a resident of the US. Despite several testimonies as to his unsavoury past, the US immigration service has allowed him to stay on. Keat Chhon went from New York to the Khmer Rouge political base located in the Thai-Cambodian border zone. He underwent a remarkable metamorphosis – from Khmer Rouge intellectual to supporter of the State of Cambodia – and in 1994 he was appointed Minister of Economy and Finance, a position he still holds.
5. As recounted by Norodom Sihanouk in his *War and hope: the case for Cambodia*, translated by Mary Feeney, New York: Pantheon, 1980, p. 66.
6. Norodom Sihanouk, 'Open Letter to the Member States of the UN' in Peter Schier and Manola Oum-Schier, *Prince Sihanouk on Cambodia: interviews and talks with Prince Norodom Sihanouk*, 2nd ed., Hamburg: Institüt für Asienkunde, 1985, pp. 75–80.
7. UN Document A/34/500. *First report of the Credentials Committee of the General Assembly*, New York: 34th session: September 1979. The letter from Heng Samrin is contained in UN document A/34/472 (UN documents on Cambodia relevant to the issue of the Khmer Rouge tribunal).

8. Samantha Powers, '*A problem from hell*': *America and the age of genocide*, New York: Basic Books, 2002, p. 150.
9. *Ibid.*
10. UN Document A/34/L.3 and Add 1.
11. Details of voting patterns on the Credentials Committee reports at the UN, and on the Asean resolutions on withdrawal of all foreign forces are given in Ramses Amer, 'The United Nations and Kampuchea: the issue of representation and its implications', in *Bulletin of Concerned Asian Scholars*, v. 22 no. 3, 1990 and, by the same author, *The General Assembly and the Kampuchean issue: intervention, regime recognition and the world community 1979–1987*, Uppsala: Department of Peace and Conflict Research, Uppsala University, 1989.
12. Robert Rosenstock's position above all represented the victory of hardliners in the Carter administration led by the national security chief, Zbigniew Brzezinski.
13. Jacques Danois, 'Ted, the Man of God' in *The will to live*, Bangkok: Unicef, 1979, pp. 93–4. Hesburgh was also then President of the Rockefeller Foundation and the Emergency Committee for Cambodia.
14. Private correspondence with Derek Tonkin, former British ambassador to Thailand and Vietnam, confirmed that many small states were offered inducements to encourage a vote for Pol Pot's credentials.
15. Amer, 'The United Nations', pp. 53–4.
16. Robert Jackson, 'Preface' to Mysliwiec, *Punishing the poor*, p. iii.
17. 'Analysis prepared on behalf of the Sub-Commission by its Chairman of materials submitted to it and the Commission on Human Rights under decision 9 (XXXIV) of the Commission on Human Rights', UN Document E/CN.4/1335 (1979).
18. David Hawk, *New Republic*, p. 18.
19. Sir Robert Jackson, deputy Secretary General, United Nations January 1983, used as the frontispiece in Sydney Schanberg, *The Killing Fields: the facts behind the film*, London: Weidenfeld & Nicolson, 1984.
20. A British TV satirical comedy series that spawned several cult movies.
21. Ramses Amer, 'The United Nations', pp. 56–7.

CHAPTER 3

1. John Quigley, 'Introduction', *Genocide in Cambodia*, edited by Howard J. De Nike, John Quigley and Kenneth J. Robinson with the assistance of Helen Jarvis and Nereida Cross, Philadelphia: University of Pennsylvania Press, 2000, p. 1.
2. Point 8 of the Declaration establishing the Salvation Front on 2 December 1978. Despite such attempts to control the integration or punishment of KR cadres, many were subjected to spontaneous attack and execution by local people wanting to exact revenge for their suffering (see Gottesman, *Cambodia*, pp. 37–8).
3. Gottesman, *Cambodia*, p. 62, citing 'Work papers, Pol Pot Court, May 10, 1979 (Document 14–18)'.
4. *Ibid.*

5. De Nike et al, *Genocide in Cambodia*, p. 45. Unless otherwise indicated, all quotations in this chapter from documents of the People's Revolutionary Tribunal are drawn from this source.

6. Soviet archival sources report Vietnamese leaders describing Nuon Chea to the Soviet ambassador to Vietnam in November 1976 as 'our man and my personal friend' (Le Duan) and someone with whom 'we are able to work better, we know him better than other leaders of Kampuchea' (Pham Van Dong). Le Duan apparently held this view of Nuon Chea as late as mid-1978, cited in Morris, *Why Vietnam invaded Cambodia*, pp. 96–7, 101, 109. It is ironic that Khieu Samphan and Nuon Chea were in fact almost the last of the Khmer Rouge leaders to defect, in December 1998.

7. Chhuor Leang Huot (former judge and member of the legal unit mentioned above); Pen Navuth (former head of the Adult Education Section of the Ministry of Education and Training); Ms Chea Samy (former teacher of classical dance); Meas Savatha (Acting Battalion Chief, First Brigade); Nouth Savoeun (doctor of pediatrics); Nouth Thon (Secretary, Central Committee of the Kampuchean Youth Organisation); Ms Chhouk Chhim (Vice-President of the Kampuchean Women's Association); Kim Kun and Kim Kaneth (workers at the power plant of Phnom Penh); and Ms Lek Sarat (official in the Department of Propaganda and Education of the Central Committee of the Kampuchean People's Revolutionary Party). A further four alternate people's assessors were also appointed together with Lim Nay as Deputy Prosecutor.

8. The representation was as follows: Algeria; Omar Bentoumi (attorney in the Supreme Court, representing the International Association of Democratic Lawyers); Cuba; Francisco Varona Duque de Estrada (Deputy Presiding Judge of the Supreme Court, representing the Lawyers Association of Cuba); India: Vitendra Sharma (attorney in the Supreme Court, Secretary of the Association of Indian Lawyers); Japan: Susumi Ozaki (attorney); Laos: Oulom Souvannavong and Heuang Chantho (government officials) as observers; Syria: Mohammed Hikmet Turkmanee (attorney for the civil plaintiffs); USSR: Valentin Vasilievich Choubine (Deputy Presiding Judge of the Supreme Court of RSFSR) and Vladimir Kouznetsov (Secretary-General, Association of Soviet Jurists) as observers; USA: Hope R. Stevens (member of the Bar of the Supreme Court, Co-President of the National Conference of Black Lawyers of the United States and Canada) defending the accused, and John Quigley (Professor of International Law at Ohio State University) giving oral testimony on the question of genocide; Vietnam: Phan Anh (President of the Vietnam Lawyers Association); Madame Ngo Ba Thanh (Doctor in Law, Member of the Vietnam Lawyers Association) and Hoang Nguyen (Bachelor in Law, Member of the Vietnam Lawyers Association) as observers.

9. It was via the Permanent Mission of the Socialist Republic of Vietnam to the United Nations in New York that John Quigley was approached to seek his involvement in the PRT. Phone interview by Helen Jarvis, July 2002.

10. Sok An interview by Helen Jarvis, 14 January 2003, and mentioned in his speech in the Chaktomuk Theatre on 6 June 2003 at the signing ceremony of the Agreement between the United Nations and the Royal Government

of Cambodia Concerning the Prosecution under Cambodian Law of
Crimes Committed during the Period of Democratic Kampuchea.

11. PRT Document 1.01 bis.
12. PRT Document 3.01. As noted above, though, Decree Law No. 1 itself
    referred to the Genocide Convention.
13. *Angkar* (the Organisation) was the enigmatic name generally used to refer
    to the authorities who ruled Cambodia 1975–1979.
14. PRT Document 3.04. The controversy surrounding estimates of those
    who perished under the Khmer Rouge is discussed in the Introduction.
15. Quigley, 'Editor's note' and 'Introduction', De Nike et al, *Genocide in
    Cambodia*, pp. viii–ix and pp. 10–11.
16. *Mbenge v. Zaire,* communication no.16 /1977, Report of the Human Rights
    Committee, p. 134, U.N. Document A/38/40, cited in De Nike et al,
    Genocide in Cambodia, p. 11.
17. PRT Document 3.03 a and b.
18. UN Document A/34/491.
19. See Helen Jarvis, 'A personal view of the documents of the People's
    Revolutionary Tribunal', in *Genocide in Cambodia*, pp. xiii–xviii.
20. Quigley, 'Introduction', *Genocide in Cambodia*, pp. 17–18.
21. Private communication from Gregory H. Stanton, 11 September 2003.

CHAPTER 4

1. In early 1980 Prince Sihanouk from his residence in Pyongyang deplored
   ASEAN's continued recognition of Democratic Kampuchea, criticised
   China's military aid to the Khmer Rouge and expressed fear of the
   consequences of an immediate Vietnamese withdrawal.
2. Sir Robert Jackson, who had been Director of the UNRRA in Europe after
   the Second World War and later became UN Under Secretary responsible
   for dealing with humanitarian emergencies, speaking in 1980 to the
   Foreign Correspondents' Club of Thailand and reacting to the UN General
   Assembly resolution calling for 'immediate and unconditional withdrawal
   of Vietnamese troops from Cambodia'.
3. Correspondence with David Hawk, November 1982.
4. Jennar, *Clés,* p. 83.
5. All quotations in this paragraph from T.D. Allman, 'Sihanouk's Sideshow',
   Vanity Fair, April 1990 pp. 158–9.
6. Khmer Rouge captured documents released by the Cambodian Foreign
   Ministry, cited in Shawcross, *The quality of mercy*, p. 77.
7. China spent 'some US$100 million on the non-communist forces of
   Son Sann and Sihanouk, and over ten times that amount on the Khmer
   Rouge', Lee Kuan Yew, 'From Third World to First: the Singapore story,
   1965–2000', Singapore: *Times*, 2000, p. 379.
8. Filmmaker David Feingold witnessed five out of the consignment of 20
   tanks being delivered on 21 June 1990. The delivery was reported by
   Robert Karniol in *Jane's Defence Weekly* in 1990. The Chinese ambassador
   to the United Kingdom was cited in the House of Commons to the effect
   that they had started sending tanks from the beginning of January 1990

(*UK parliamentary debates*, 26 October 1990: 674, cited by Ben Kiernan, 'The inclusion of the Khmer Rouge in the Cambodian peace process: causes and consequences,' in *Genocide and Democracy*, n.82, p. 255). Some of these T59 tanks were destroyed in the battle of Chamkar Stung April 1991 as government forces advanced towards Pailin and Tom Fawthrop saw two of them on exhibition in Battambang in May 1991.

9. *Thai Policy vis a vis Kampuchea*, Phnom Penh: Ministry of Foreign Affairs, 1983, pp. 12–17, citing Geng Biao's Report of 16 January 1979, from *Studies of Communist China*, No.10/80, (Taiwanese periodical). See also Puangthong Rungswasdisab, 'Thailand's response to the Cambodian genocide' on the Cambodian Genocide Program web site, www.yale.edu/cgp.

10. The arms supply line started in February but most of the weapons were stockpiled along the border. The Khmer Rouge's lowest ebb was in May 1979, but after recuperation in Thai refugee camps, the Khmer Rouge was ready to take advantage of China's arms flow.

11. Tom Fawthrop interview with a Khmer Rouge defector who wishes to remain anonymous, Phnom Penh, 2002.

12. Jimmy Carter statement reported in *New York Times* 22 April 1978.

13. Memo from Steve Hochmann, dated 5 January 2000 with the subject 'President Carter and the Khmer Rouge', forwarded by him to the authors in 2001.

14. Elizabeth Becker, *When the war was over*, New York: Touchstone, Simon & Schuster, 1986, p. 440.

15. Hochmann's memo also very helpfully cited Christopher Brady's monograph *United States Foreign Policy towards Cambodia, 1977–92: A question of realities*, New York: St Martin's Press, 1999).

16. Daniel Boone was operated by the Military Assistance Command, Vietnam Studies and Operations Group, 'without the knowledge of Congress. The teams were allowed to delve up to 30 kilometres inside Cambodia and were authorised to place 'sanitised self-destruct antipersonnel' land mines as they went. Their primary purpose was supposed to be intelligence gathering; in 1,835 missions over four years they captured 24 prisoners (Shawcross, *Sideshow*, p. 65). Details of these and other clandestine operations mounted by the US in violation of the neutrality of Cambodia and Laos are now available from official documents declassified in 2003.

17. Given this role as First Secretary (Political Section) at the US Embassy in Bangkok during the 1980s,Tim Carney was a controversial choice when appointed in 1991 to head UNTAC's Public Information Department.

18. *Los Angeles Times*, 5 December 1980, I-B, p. 1 quoted in William Blum, *Rogue State: a guide to the world's only superpower*, New updated edition, London: Zed, 2002, p. 88.

19. Shawcross, *The quality of mercy*, p. 356.

20. It took direct intervention with Richard Holbrooke, Assistant Secretary of State for Asian Affairs, to break the US Treasury Department block for permits to Church World Service to donate over 1 million dollars of supplies for primary education, veterinary medicine and other relief aid

282   Getting Away With Genocide?

(private communication to the authors from Gregory Stanton, September 2003).

21. Linda Mason and Roger Brown, *Rice, rivalry and politics: managing Cambodia's relief*, South Bend, Indiana: University of Notre Dame Press, 1983, pp. 135–6, quoted in William Blum, *Rogue state*, p. 284.
22. Mysliwiec, *Punishing the poor*, p. 73.
23. *Ibid*, p. iii.
24. Bull, *Poverty*, p. 30.
25. Ok Serei Sopheak, interview by Tom Fawthrop, March 2001. After the 1993 election he became an advisor to Deputy Prime Minister Sar Kheng before moving to direct a peace and conflict studies programme with the Cambodian Development Resource Institute.
26. Rae McGrath, cited by Paul Jefferson, 'Landmines, damn lies and statistics', the *Guardian*, 9 September 1997.
27. *Washington Post*, 8 July 1985, p. 18, cited by Blum, *Rogue state*, p. 89.
28. For more on the complexities of the Cambodian–Vietnam relationship, see Gottesman, 'The Vietnamese: soldiers, advisors, and "bad elements"', Chapter 6 of *Cambodia after the Khmer Rouge*, pp. 137–69.
29. Thatcher's view of Khieu Samphan was indicated by a Foreign Office official when being filmed for John Pilger and David Munro's film, *Cambodia year ten*, ITV, 1989.

CHAPTER 5

1. These included Ben Kiernan, David Chandler, Michael Vickery and Serge Thion.
2. These and other quotations by Gregory H. Stanton in this chapter are from, 'The call', in *Pioneers of Genocide Studies*, edited by Samuel Totten and Steven Leonard Jacobs, New Brunswick and London: Transaction Press, 2002, pp. 401–25.
3. For a discussion of differing estimates see Introduction.
4. Conference of Intellectuals and Religious People, Phnom Penh, organised by the Salvation Front, 12 September 1983, 'Open Letter'.
5. For an overview of the origin and development of this anniversary, see Rachel Hughes, 'Remembering May 20 – Day of Anger', *Searching for the Truth*, no.12, December 2000, pp. 39–42.
6. Bull, *Poverty*, p. 1.
7. Jennar followed events in Cambodia very closely and issued 29 reports referred to as Cambodian Chronicles for the NGO Forum. The French edition *Chroniques Cambodgiennes 1990–1994* was published by L'Harmattan in Paris in 1995. The English edition of part of the collection appeared several years later as *Bungling a peace plan 1989–1991*, vol.1 of *Cambodian chronicles 1989–1996*, Bangkok: White Lotus, 1998.
8. Ester, Helen, *Vietnam, Thailand, Kampuchea: a firsthand account*, Canberra: The Australian Council for Overseas Aid, 1980.
9. The key publications of these scholars on the Khmer Rouge are: David Chandler, *Brother Number One: a political biography of Pol Pot*, Boulder: Westview Press, 1992 and *Voices from S-21*; Michael Vickery, *Cambodia*

1975–1982; Serge Thion, *Watching Cambodia* Bangkok: White Lotus, 1993; and Ben Kiernan, *The Pol Pot regime*. Kiernan was also the Founding Director of the Cambodian Genocide Program (see Chapter 7).

10. Hun Sen was also Prime Minister at that time, but presumably Hayden met him in his capacity as foreign minister.

11. The following quotations are excerpts from letters in the Cambodian Documentation Commission archives, donated by David Hawk to the Documentation Center of Cambodia in 2001.

12. Powers, *A problem from hell*, p. 163.

13. *Chronology of Cambodian history, 1985–1989*, www.geocities.com/khmerchronology/1985.htm.

14. Conference acclaiming the 40th Anniversary of the Convention on the Prevention and Punishment of the Crime of Genocide, 9–12–48 to 9–12–88, Phnom Penh, organised by the Salvation Front, 'Overall report of the activities of intellectuals' [in Khmer].

15. *Bangkok Post*, 13 July 1985.

16. Norodom Sihanouk, *War and hope*, p. 56.

17. T.D. Allman, 'Sihanouk's sideshow', *Vanity Fair*, April 1990.

18. Dr Kek Galabru's personal account, in an interview by Tom Fawthrop 2003. Her husband, a former French diplomat, first visited Phnom Penh in 1988 and returned to Paris convinced that a Hun Sen-Sihanouk summit was the essential first step to end the war.

19. Opposed by China and several African and Asian allies of Democratic Kampuchea, the new resolution lost the support of eleven countries because of the insertion of the anti-KR provision. However, twelve countries that had previously abstained joined because of this change, and the resolution went from 117 votes in 1987 to 122 in 1988.

20. Private communication to Tom Fawthrop from a participant at the meeting held at Prime Minister Chatichai's residence in Bangkok.

21. Mary Kay Magistad, 'Khmer Rouge are closer to new chance at power', *Boston Globe*, 17 April 1989.

22. See Tom Fawthrop, 'Thai senator urges apology', *Phnom Penh Post*, 16–29 March, 2001.

23. *Ibid.*

24. International Seminar on the Genocide Phenomena and Prevention of Their Return, Phnom Penh, 22 July 1989, Appeal.

25. 'Communication circulated to the participants at the request of the delegation of Mr. Hun Sen. Genocide in Cambodia from 1975 to 1978' (CPC/89/COM/8, issued 21 August 1989), reproduced in *Cambodia – the 1989 Paris Peace Conference: background analysis and documents*, compiled and edited by Amitav Acharya, Pierre Lizéé and Sorpong Peou, Millwood, New York: Kraus International Publications, 1991, pp. 474–77.

26. Tom Fawthrop, 'Cause for optimism: Hun Sen speaks on the Cambodian solution', *Far Eastern Economic Review*, 3 March 1988, pp. 18–19.

27. BBC, Summary of World Broadcasts, 10 August 1989, Phnom Penh home service 13:00 GMT, 5 August 1989 quoted in David Roberts, *Political transition in Cambodia 1991–99: power elitism and democracy*, Richmond, Surrey: Curzon, 2001, p. 23.

28. Edmund Muskie, *Exploring Cambodia Findings & Recommendations from Muskie's visit to Thailand, Cambodia and Vietnam*, Washington DC: Center for National Policy, October 1990, p. 21.
29. Hun Sen, press conference August 1989, as noted by Tom Fawthrop.
30. On the significance of this political decision taken by the White House and not the State Department, see Jennar, *Bungling a peace plan*, pp. 60–73.
31. The authors have found no primary source for this appellation, but David Chandler writes, 'With the Communist victory, "Brother Pol" had become prime minister. For all the talk of collectivism in Cambodia, this made him "Brother Number One"'. *Brother Number One*, p. 119.
32. *Asian Wall Street Journal*, 5 and 12 August 1991.
33. Richard Solomon, 18 March 1991 in Kiernan, *Genocide and Democracy in Cambodia*, p. 207.
34. Kenneth Quinn address to the Global Business Forum, Georgetown Club, Washington DC on 16 September cited by John Pilger, 'Organised forgetting', *New Statesman*, 1 November 1991, pp. 10–11 and then in *Genocide and democracy*, pp. 231, n. 203.
35. Reported by *Agence France Presse* and quoted in Jennar, *Bungling*, p. 259.

CHAPTER 6

1. See Hun Sen press conference 16 December 1988 listing the eight Khmer Rouge leaders whom the State of Cambodia considered unacceptable for involvement in the peace process and membership in any future national government.
2. The return of Son Sen and Khieu Samphan provoked a major protest. An angry demonstration laid siege to their villa. They were rescued by the army and fled back to Bangkok the same day. The colourful description is taken from David Roberts, *Political transition*, p. 63. It was widely believed that the student-led demonstration was organised by a faction within the CPP.
3. Dr Haing Ngor, interview in Phnom Penh by Tom Fawthrop, 1993.
4. Not all Cambodians agree and disagreement continues over the places and anniversaries marking the suffering and overthrow of the Khmer Rouge. Some see Tuol Sleng and Choeung Ek, 7 January and 20 May as too closely linked to the CPP and the Vietnamese role. Sam Rainsy has begun an annual ritual of holding a separate commemoration at Tuol Sleng on 17 April.
5. Hun Sen press conference in Chamkar Mon State Palace, Phnom Penh, 17 November 1991, as noted by Tom Fawthrop.
6. *Wanted for mass murder, genocide, war crimes*, Washington DC: CORKR, 1991.
7. A Japanese cameraman working for UNTAC TV filmed the Pailin debacle. UNTAC Information ruled that local and foreign TV should not get access to the tape. Tom Fawthrop acquired a copy of the banned tape and broadcast it as part of his special production for Dutch TV, broadcast in 1992.

8. *The United Nations in Cambodia: a vote for peace*, New York: United Nations, 1994, p. 104, quoted in Trevor Findlay, *Cambodia: the lessons and legacy of UNTAC*, Oxford: Oxford University Press, 1995, p. 156.
9. See Tom Fawthrop's exposé 'Other Side of a Khmer Rouge "Butcher"', the *Age* Melbourne, 15 May 1999, which documented for the first time details of Ta Mok's assets in Thailand, including three petrol stations.
10. Bedford, Michael and Kathy Knight, *Cambodia: still waiting for peace: a report on Thai-Khmer collaboration since the signing of the Paris Peace Accords*, Boston: Oxfam America, March 1995, p. 8.
11. The details of the Khmer Rouge attack on CT 1 are derived from 'Attack on CT1' confidential report of UNTAC's Strategic Investigations Team, dated 3 August 1993.
12. This account was confirmed by UNTAC spokesperson Eric Falt in conversation with Tom Fawthrop, September 1993.
13. *Far Eastern Economic Review*, 30 July 1992, cited by Roberts, *Political transition*, pp. 68–9.
14. Cambodian Documentation Commission, 'The UN in Cambodia: a brief evaluation of UNTAC in the field of human rights', Part II of a 3-part report, undated, p. 34, held in 'the Hawk Papers' at Documentation Center of Cambodia.

CHAPTER 7

1. Officially the State Department opposed the bill because it earmarked funds from their budget for the research. Confidential sources have informed the authors that the State Department's consent was given on the proviso that it was not required to carry out the research, but could contract it out.
2. Jason Abrams and Stephen Ratner, 'Striving for justice: accountability and the crimes of the Khmer Rouge', typescript, presented to the US State Department 1995. A revised version appeared later as part of their *Accounting for human rights atrocities in international law: beyond the Nuremberg legacy*, London: Oxford University Press, 1997.
3. Sue Cook replaced Ben Kiernan as CGP Director from 1999–2001. Craig Etcheson was Acting Director in 1997, after which he left the Cambodian Genocide Program. Following the conclusion of the State Department funding in September 2001, the CGP has continued as a program at Yale University's Center for International and Area Studies, as part of its Genocide Studies Program, under the direction of Ben Kiernan.
4. This second grant came from the Bureau of Democracy, Human Rights and Labor at the instigation of Catherine Dalpino (Deputy Assistant Secretary of State of Democracy, Human Rights and Labor in 1997) and Gregory Stanton, who had joined the State Department in 1992, and was then a member of the steering committee of the Office of Cambodian Genocide Investigations.
5. The resources were made available as the Cambodian Genocide Databases on the Cambodian Genocide Program website and published in CD-ROM format. See www.yale.edu/cgp and www.dccam.org.

6. The mapping component was initiated by a small grant of A$24,300 awarded by the Australian Department of Foreign Affairs and Trade for 1995–6; and then supported by the Netherlands government with US$130,000 for 1997, which was renewed for 1998, 1999, and by the US State Department in 2000. The Documentation Center's mapping work was directed by Phat Kosal and later by Pheng Pong Racy, with many field trips led by Sin Khin, former Director of the National Archives of Cambodia.

7. *Mapping the Killing Fields of Cambodia 1995, 1996, 1997, 1998, 1999, 2000, 2001, 2002, 2003*, prepared by Pheng Pong Racy, Phat Kosal, Chhang Youk, Sin Khin and Ouch Sam-Oeun. Phnom Penh: Documentation Center of Cambodia, 26 May 2003. For a discussion of the issue of the number of deaths during Democratic Kampuchea, see the Introduction.

8. The Forensic Study Project involves collaboration with Dr Craig Etcheson, Dr Michael Pollanen and Dr Katherine Gruspier.

9. Professor Quang Quyen's forensic study was commissioned by the Phnom Penh Municipality Department of Culture. Interview by Tom Fawthrop at Choeung Ek Genocide Memorial Site, December 1988.

10. As of October 2003 the Documentation Center had yet to gain possession of the land, which is currently occupied by a number of families.

11. Thomas Hammarberg, *Phnom Penh Post*, 14–27 September 2001, Supplement, p. A8 'Efforts to establish a tribunal against KR leaders: discussions between the Cambodian government and the UN'.

12. The UN resolutions creating the International Criminal Tribunal for Rwanda were drafted by Gregory Stanton, then in the US State Department.

13. Tom Fawthrop broke the story in 'I saw Briton shot by Khmer Rouge', the *Sunday Times* (London), 24 May 1998.

14. As revealed in an interview with Tom Fawthrop, published in the *Sunday Times* (London), 11 January 1998.

15. Nhek Bun Chhay interview by Tom Fawthrop, Surin, Thailand, May 1998.

16. Thomas Hammarberg reveals in his Phnom Penh Post article, 'Efforts to establish a tribunal', that he drafted the text of the letter.

17. US journalist Nate Thayer was invited to attend and film the proceedings, and he published reports and still photographs in the *Far Eastern Economic Review*.

18. In July 1997 a working group dubbed 'the Pol Pot Posse' was set up within the State Department. Chaired by US Ambassador for War Crimes, David Scheffer, it included Deputy Legal Advisor Michael Matheson, Deputy Assistant Secretary for Asian Affairs, Charles Kartman and Gregory Stanton of the Human Rights Bureau. It pushed policy through to decision, sometimes despite heated objections from old hands from the Vietnam War era and from conservatives in the Legal Advisor's Office. Despite the declared new policy of the US as expressed in the Cambodian Genocide Justice Act as explicitly seeking judicial accountability for the Khmer Rouge, it took considerable inside pressure to turn around the ship of State.

19. Ke Pauk interview by Tom Fawthrop in Siem Reap early April 1998. Ke Pauk, himself a leading candidate to be indicted before the tribunal, cheated his rendezvous with justice by his untimely death in February 2002, after an illness.
20. David Scheffer, personal communication to Helen Jarvis, March 2004.
21. The Thai marines' own camp at Sua Phin, above the road between Trat and Haadlek the Thai immigration border post, prevented strangers from gaining access to the secret Pol Pot headquarters on Thai soil.
22. Nhem Eng, interview by Tom Fawthrop, Feb 2001. Nhem Eng, the former Khmer Rouge photographer at S-21, joined Funcinpec as party organiser in Anlong Veng.
23. Tom Fawthrop, 'Why didn't they arrest him 20 years ago?', *Phnom Penh Post*, 24 April–7 May 1998.
24. Deputy Foreign Minister Sukhamband Paribatra interviewed by Tom Fawthrop, September 1998.
25. See the paper 'Options to try Pol Pot', written by Gregory Stanton for the US State Department in 1997.
26. Wassana Nanuam, 'Brutal KR chief poisoned', *Bangkok Post*, 19 March 2002.
27. Thomas Hammarberg, 'Efforts to establish a tribunal'.
28. UN Document A/RES/53/145.
29. 'Report of the group of experts for Cambodia established pursuant to General Assembly Resolution 52/135' (UN Document A/53/850 and S/1999/231, 16 March 1999, pp. 52–3).
30. An option advocated by Gregory Stanton in 1997, 'Options to try Pol Pot' and by Balakrishnan Rajgopal in 1998, 'The pragmatics of prosecuting the KR', *International Humanitarian Law Yearbook*, The Hague: Asser Institute, 1998.
31. Hun Sen, 'Aide Memoire and Analysis' and accompanying letter to Kofi Annan, dated 21 January 1999, to be considered as a supplement to the 21 June 1997 request for UN involvement in the process.
32. Tom Fawthrop, 'UN Aids Khmer Rouge Impunity', *Asia Times*, 12 June 2002.
33. Indictment from the Military Court No 019/99, dated 9 March 1999, of Ung Choeun, also known as Chhit Choeun, but generally referred to as Ta Mok.
34. Indictment from the Military Court N. 029/99, dated 10 May 1999. The additional charge is based on Decree Law No.2, 1979.

CHAPTER 8

1. *Associated Press* Report, 25 December 1998.
2. Im Sethy interview by Tom Fawthrop, February, 2001.
3. Moeun Chhean Nariddh, letter to *Phnom Penh Post*, 1999.
4. Hun Sen, press statement, 1 January 1999. Quoted from a press release issued by the Prime Minister's office. For a published version, with slightly different translation, see 'Hun Sen draws his line in the shifting sands', *Phnom Penh Post*, 8–21 January 1999.

5. Hun Sen interview by Helen Jarvis, 'Who helped the Khmer Rouge to survive?', *Green Left Weekly*, no. 349, 17 February 1999.
6. Tom Fawthrop, 'Pol Pot minister lives it up in Phnom Penh', *Straits Times* (Singapore), 7 January 2002.
7. *Ibid.*
8. Jarvis, 'Who helped the Khmer Rouge?'.
9. Kent Wiedemann, interview by Tom Fawthrop, March 2001.
10. This act was reported to the authors on different occasions by several CPP members who asked not to be named.
11. Cambodian Human Rights Action Committee petition, 20 January 1999.
12. Chea Sophara interview by Tom Fawthrop, March 2001.
13. Laura McGrew, *Truth, Justice, Reconciliation and Peace in Cambodia: 20 years after the Khmer Rouge*, Phnom Penh: project funded by the Canadian Embassy, 2000, p. 13.
14. Peg LeVine, 'Politics of suffering', a chapter in her forthcoming book, *Living taboo in Angkar's pageant: couples married in the Khmer Rouge* (unpublished).
15. Dr Nou Leakena interview by Tom Fawthrop, July 2003.
16. Data from paper presented by Dr Bhoomi Kumar at the Indigenous forum at the Third World Congress on Traumatic Stress Studies, Melbourne March, 2000. In 1995, Dr Marcel Roy founded the Centre for Child Mental Health, led since 1997 by Dr Bhoomi Kumar, with supportive funding from Caritas.
17. Dr Ka Sunbaunat, 'Cambodian mental health training program and organization of mental health services in Cambodia', 1998.
18. LeVine, 'Politics of suffering'.
19. McGrew, *Truth, Justice, Reconciliation and Peace*, p. 4.
20. *The Khmer Rouge and national reconciliation: opinions from the Cambodians*, Phnom Penh: Center for Social Development, April 2002, p. 23.
21. Dith Munty interview by Tom Fawthrop, 18 April 2001.
22. See, for example, BBC TV Correspondent programme, 15 March 2002.
23. According to a list sent by Youk Chhang, January 2004, which gives the names of ten survivors, four of whom are known to have died since 1979 but the exact number of prisoners who managed to emerge alive from S-21 is unknown.
24. Chhum Mey interview by Tom Fawthrop for TV programme 'Responses to Death of Pol Pot', August 1998.
25. Youk Chhang interview by Tom Fawthrop, April 1998.
26. Thun Saray interviewed by Tom Fawthrop, March 2002.
27. Thomas Hammarberg, 'Efforts to establish a tribunal'.
28. Cambodia Democracy and Accountability Act of 2003 (S 1365 IS, introduced in the US Senate on 26 June 2003 by Senator Mitch. McConnell (for himself and Senators Kyl and Leahy).
29. The Star Chamber set up by Oliver Cromwell in 17th century England was renowned for its malicious style of persecution and prosecution. Our metaphor relates also to the zealous activities of US Independent Prosecutor Kenneth Starr launched in 1998, pursuing President Bill Clinton's sexual affairs with Monica Lewinsky.

30. See Chapter 10 for a more detailed discussion of the issue of personal jurisdiction of the Extraordinary Chambers.

31. Youk Chhang wrote to Sok An on 19 April 2000 with his specific proposed wording. Note that there are no records of the Central Committee (with around 45 members) ever having met during the period of Democratic Kampuchea. In 2003 Steve Heder advocated a major expansion of those who should be considered for prosecution, as discussed in Annexe B, p. 272.

32. For example on 30 December 1998.

33. Hor Namhong at different times has successfully sued various parties for defamation of character and libel. In January 1993 he sued then-Prince Norodom Sihanouk in France for allegations that he was 'in charge of a Khmer Rouge camp, and responsible for the deaths of Sihanouk's wife's brother-in-law, among others' (*Phnom Penh Post*, 16–19 October 1998). In January 2001 he took a similar action against three journalists and the *Cambodia Daily* in the Cambodian courts for alleging that he was an official in the Khmer Rouge regime ('Reporters Without Borders', *Cambodia Annual Report 2002*). It is a matter of record that Hor Namhong, a former Sihanoukist diplomat, was during the Khmer Rouge regime a detainee at Boeung Trabek, involved in the camp administration, and not a Khmer Rouge cadre.

34. Tom Fawthrop, '"Irresponsible" and "baseless" anti-Hun Sen campaign hits US Congress', *Phnom Penh Post*, 2–15 October 1998.

35. Harish C. Mehta and Julie B. Mehta, *Hun Sen: strongman of Cambodia*, Singapore, Graham Brash, 1999, p. 45. Raoul Jennar states that he was 'number 7 in the military hierarchy of Region 21, one of the five regions of the Eastern Zone' (*Les clés du Cambodge*, p. 206).

36. To the authors' knowledge, the only specific allegation is that by Saren Thach 'when overrunning two hospitals, Heng Samrin's and Hun Sen's troops threw hand grenades and later slit the throats of critically ill patients' (in the *Washington Post*, 30 October 1989, citing the *Washington Post* of 10 September 1973, which reported the incidents without specifying the units involved, their Zone of origin, or the names of their commanders. Veteran journalist Elizabeth Becker refuted the allegations in the *International Herald Tribune*, 6 November 1989 (Cambodian Genocide Biographical Database CBIO, record Y00376).

37. Fawthrop, '"Irresponsible" and "baseless"'.

38. 'A Criminal Trial for the Khmer Rouge', by Craig Etcheson, Newsletter No. 27 Institute for the Study of Genocide, International Association of Genocide Scholars.

CHAPTER 9

1. Balakrishnan Rajagopal, 'Looking for justice in Cambodia', *National Post*, 23 September 1999.

2. Rajagopal, 'The pragmatics of prosecuting the KR', *Phnom Penh Post*.

3. The issue of group trials is a complex one, which may involve either trial of a group for conspiracy or joint criminal enterprise, or holding a single

trial to deal with a group of individuals who are charged with different, though related, offences.

4. Confidential communication dated 24 August 1999.

5. Led by Ralph Zacklin (Office of Legal Affairs), the UN delegation included Daphna Shraga (also from OLA), Jonathan Prentice (Department of Political Affairs), David Ashley (provided by the Government of the United Kingdom) and a French judge and judicial official (provided by the Government of France).

6. Chaired by Sok An (Senior Minister and Minister in Charge of the Council of Ministers) the Task Force included the Minister of Justice (Ouk Vithun); Supreme Adviser to the Government (Heng Vong Bunchhat); Secretaries of State for Justice (Suy Nou and Ly Vouch Leang – shortly afterwards promoted to be president of the Appeals Court); President of the Cambodian Government Human Rights Commission (Om Yentieng); Adviser to the Prime Minister (Chan Tany); Adviser to Deputy Prime Minister Sar Kheng (Ang Vong Wattana); and President of the Expert Group of the Council of Jurists (Leng Peng Long) – positions as at the time of appointment to the Task Force. A team of advisors to Sok An supported the Task Force, preparing commentary on all the various drafts, versions and comments on the legislation over the following year. This team consisted of Sean Visoth, Tony Kranh and Australian academic Helen Jarvis, supported from 1999 to 2001 from the Australian Government's Human Rights Fund.

7. William A. Schabas, 'Looking for justice in Cambodia', *National Post*, 23 September 1999.

8. At the same time as solutions to impasses were being submitted from the US, experts from Russia and India also came to Cambodia to give advice, in addition to that given by the resident French legal advisor and Australian member of the Task Force support team. Russia sent Professor Stanislav Chernichenko, long-time member of the Soviet delegation to the United Nations Commission on Human Rights, and Director of the Centre for International Law and Humanitarian Issues at the Diplomatic Academy of the Ministry of Foreign Affairs. Chernichenko stressed the importance of retaining Cambodian sovereignty, in particular that all judges must be appointed in accordance with Cambodian law, and not by the Secretary General of the United Nations. He also suggested that it might be appropriate to add Russian as an additional language of the court (a suggestion that was rejected by the UN as unnecessary and expensive, but which did survive into the Law as eventually promulgated).

9. Thomas Hammarberg, 'Efforts to establish a tribunal'.

10. Chea Vannath interview by Tom Fawthrop, February 2001.

11. 'Hun Sen had spoken at length [in April 1998] about a "package" into which other crimes ought to be included, such as the American bombings in the early 1970s and the Chinese support for the Khmer Rouge. This was a theme to which he was to return several times during our forthcoming discussions – and sometimes also publicly.' Thomas Hammarberg, 'Efforts to establish a tribunal', p. A2.

12. Tom Fawthrop, interview with Nuon Paet, shown on 'Dateline', Australian SBS TV, October 1998.

13. Chhouk Rin appealed that conviction and was awarded a retrial in the Appeals Court in November 2003, in which he was again convicted. He lodged a final appeal to the Supreme Court, but was never under detention in all this time.

14. It should be noted that all Sam Rainsy members of parliament voted for the proposed structure when it came before them in 2001, although in late 2003, during the impasse over the formation of the new government, Sam Rainsy Party parliamentarian Son Chhay announced that his party would oppose it, preferring instead an international tribunal (Daniel Ten Kate, 'Annan urges Assembly to OK tribunal', the *Cambodia Daily*, 11 December 2003.)

15. Annette Marcher, 'PM-UNSG agree: more talks', *Phnom Penh Post*, 18 February – 2 March 2000, quotes Hun Sen as saying 'the world body only wanted Cambodia to be a "dog guarding a house that belongs to somebody else"'.

16. In addition to Corell, the delegation included: Ralph Zacklin, assistant Secretary General and the deputy of the team; Lakhan Mehrotra, head of the Jakarta office of the United Nations Transitional Administration in East Timor; Shashi Tharoor, a director in Annan's office; John Renninger, head of the Asia and Pacific division of the UN Department of Political Affairs; Daphna Shraga, a senior officer in the UN Office of Legal Affairs; and Mark Quarterman, an officer in the Department of Political Affairs and personal assistant to Kofi Annan.

17. 'Hun Sen: Cambodia united at any price', *Phnom Penh Post*, 4–16 October 1996.

18. Hans Corell, cited in 'Deadlock on Khmer trial talks', BBC 22 March 2000.

19. Hun Sen, 'Statement at the Ceremony of the Construction Work Site for a Tuberculosis Hospital funded by the Japanese Government', 3 May 2000, translation by the Documentation Center of Cambodia.

20. This time without Zacklin or Mehrotra, but with Quarterman and Shraga giving some continuity to the team.

21. 'Statement by the Cambodian Royal Government Task Force on the Khmer Rouge Tribunal', 21 November 2000, *Phnom Penh Post*, 24 November – 7 December, 2000 and as also stated by Kofi Annan's spokesperson in July 2000.

22. 'Ex-UN official: China tried to stymie Khmer Rouge trial', Associated Press, Bangkok, 12 November 2000.

23. 'China Won't Pressure Cambodia On Khmer Rouge Tribunal', AP (Beijing) 7 November 2000

24. Interview with US ambassador in Phnom Penh, Kent Wiedemann, March 2001.

25. Hammarberg, 'Efforts to establish a tribunal'.

26. Hun Sen in a comment made on 23 February, and Sok An on 27 February 2001.

27. Verghese Matthews, interview with Tom Fawthrop, March 2003.

28. Craig Etcheson, private email communication to the authors, 15 April 2003.

29. Chea Vannath, interview by Tom Fawthrop in February 2001.

30. Ted Allegra, interview by Tom Fawthrop in February 2001.

CHAPTER 10

1. The documents were released at a press conference held on 12 February 2003 and then published on the Khmer Rouge Trials Task Force web site, www.cambodia.gov.kh/krt/.
2. Peter Leuprecht, press conference in Phnom Penh, 8 March 2002.
3. Fawthrop, 'UN Aids Khmer Rouge Impunity'.
4. Rajagopal, 'A Blind Eye to Justice in Cambodia', the *Washington Post*, 27 March 2002.
5. Mike Jendrzejczyk, the *Washington Post*, 8 April 2003.
6. Kent Wiedemann, unclassified email communication, 9 April 2002.
7. Chea Vannath, cited by Tom Fawthrop, 'No reason for standoff on Khmer Rouge law', *Phnom Penh Post*, 2–15 March 2001.
8. Sok An, *Proceedings*, Presentation to Stockholm International Forum on Truth, Justice and Reconciliation, 23–24 April, pp. 139–43.
9. UN Document, E-CN.4 2002/89, adopted 26 April 2002.
10. After the cessation of Australian government support in October 2001 Helen Jarvis continued to work with the Task Force as a volunteer until funding was provided to the Secretariat of the Task Force by United Kingdom and Sweden from June 2003 to March 2004, after which the Secretariat has remained without ongoing funding.
11. The meeting was held on 22 March 2002. Besides Etcheson, the other speakers were Khieu Kanharith, Secretary of State of the Ministry of Information, and Royal Government Spokesperson; Helen Jarvis, Advisor to the Royal Government's Task Force on Khmer Rouge Trials; and Lao Mong Hay, then Executive Director of the Khmer Institute of Democracy. It was organised by the former Foreign Correspondents' Club of Cambodia, now renamed the Overseas Press Club of Cambodia.
12. UN Document A/RES/56/169 adopted 19 December 2001.
13. As discussed in Chapter 9.
14. Tom Fawthrop, *Sunday Times* (London) report on the trial, 15 December 2002.
15. A/C.3/57/L.70 adopted 20 November 2002.
16. In favour of deferral were Belgium, Canada, Finland, Germany, Ireland, Jordan, Liechtenstein, Luxembourg, Netherlands, New Zealand, Norway, Sweden, Switzerland and the United Kingdom.
17. Elizabeth Becker, 'After 9-Month Break, U.N. Revives Plan for Khmer Rouge Trial', the *New York Times*, 21 November 2002.
18. Elizabeth Becker has substantial credentials for her past writing on the Khmer Rouge, including the highly-acclaimed book *When the war was over*. This quotation from Elizabeth Becker, 'After 9-Month Break'.
19. David J. Scheffer, 'Justice for Cambodia', the *New York Times*, 21 December 2002.
20. Sok An led a delegation of five (also including Heng Vong Bunchhat, Sean Visoth, Tony Kranh and Helen Jarvis). Besides its leader Hans Corell, the UN delegation also included Ralph Zacklin and David Hutchinson from the Office of Legal Affairs, Mr Lamin Sise (Director of Legal Affairs, Human Rights and Special Assignments, Executive Office of the Secretary

General), and two representatives from the Department of Political Affairs (Mss Beng Yong Chew and Ellen Alradi).

21. In Cambodian traditional culture it is considered inhospitable to display a clock in a room where one receives guests.

22. Amnesty International Document, ASA 23/005/2003, issued in April 2003. See also Human Rights Watch 'Serious flaws: why the UN General Assembly should require changes to the Draft Khmer Rouge Tribunal Agreement', 30 April 2003, which concluded: 'United Nations Secretary-General Kofi Annan expressed many of the same concerns in an extraordinarily candid March 31, 2003 report to the General Assembly on the draft agreement ... The Cambodians dismissed the UN team's proposals for a more robust international component, secure in the knowledge that the party demanding adherence to principles would have to capitulate to the side demanding partisan political control over the process. In the end, politics and pragmatism won out over principles.'

23. Gregory Stanton, 'Perfection is the enemy of justice', *Searching for the truth*, Special English Issue No. 2, July 2003, pp. 40–42 also published in the *Bangkok Post*.

24. Tom Fawthrop, 'Intelligence', *Far Eastern Economic Review*, June 2003.

25. Daniel Ten Kate, 'Annan urges Assembly to OK tribunal', *The Cambodian Daily*, 11 December 2003. This would be a complete turn-around in policy, as all Sam Rainsy Party members of the National Assembly and the Senate voted for the Law in 2001.

CHAPTER 11

1. 'Brother Number Two enjoys retirement', Phil Rees (reporter), 15 March 2002 on BBC 2.

2. Many of these reports have been published in the Documentation Center's publications and interaction between former guards and prisoners was the focus of Rithy Panh, *S21, the Khmer Rouge killing machine*, Film, 2003.

3. See for example the Belsen case at Nuremberg, and the Galic, Stakic and Simic cases at The Hague.

4. See for example the approach used in the ICTY (International Criminal Tribunal for the former Yugoslavia) in Galic Decision on Rule 92 bis and Milosevic Decision on 89F.

5. The mapping component was initiated by a small grant of A$24,300 awarded by the Australian Department of Foreign Affairs and Trade for 1995–6; and then supported by the Netherlands government with US$130,000 for 1997, which was renewed for 1998, 1999 and from the US State Department in 2000. The Documentation Center's mapping work was directed by Phat Kosal and later by Pheng Pong Racy, with many field trips led by Sin Khin, former Director of the National Archives of Cambodia.

6. *Mapping the Killing Fields*.

7. According to interviews of Professor Quang Quyen and Dr Trun Hung by Tom Fawthrop in Ho Chi Minh City on several occasions. The authors have not seen a copy of the final report.

8. For an indication of the wealth of such material, see Helen Jarvis, *Cambodia*, (World Bibliographical Series, vol.200), Oxford: Clio Press, 1997, especially pp. 96–107 and pp. 185–201, as well as the Cambodian Genocide Databases produced by the Cambodian Genocide Program.

9. This is notwithstanding the fact that the word *and* is in some legal systems considered to be a 'term of art' and is deemed to introduce an additional rather than an alternate criterion. It would have been clearer if the word *or* had been used in place of *and* here. The intention of two possible criteria for prosecution can be deduced also from the fact that the second would be redundant if it were simply identifying the crimes enumerated later in the law.

10. Kiernan, *Pol Pot regime*, p. 101, n.135.

11. For his account of his role during this period see especially Norodom Sihanouk, *Prisonnier des Khmers Rouges*.

12. Kiernan, *Pol Pot regime*, p. 328.

13. Becker, *When the war was over*, p. 313.

14. Timothy Carney, 'The organization of power', tables 1–4, in Jackson, Karl D. (ed.), *Cambodia 1975–1978: rendezvous with death*, Princeton, New Jersey: Princeton University Press, 1989, pp. 99–107.

15. Some commentators have criticised this retroactive element in the Law, but others maintain that retroactivity in procedure is acceptable, unlike substantive law, which is subject to the principle of *nullem crimen sine lege* (no crimes without laws).

   In any event, this issue will not be actionable during the trials because on 12 February 2001 the Constitutional Council ruled that the extension of the statute of limitations was constitutional. Under the Cambodian Constitution any ruling of the Constitutional Council is not subject to appeal.

   In the same decision, though, the Constitutional Council ruled that Article 3 needed amendment to make absolutely clear that the penalty under Articles 209, 500, 506 and 507 of the 1956 Penal Code is limited to a maximum of life imprisonment, in accordance with Article 32 of the Constitution of the Kingdom of Cambodia. These articles of the 1956 Penal Code prescribed the death penalty. The Law establishing the Extraordinary Chambers was amended to clarify this point before it was promulgated, and was declared wholly constitutional by the Constitutional Council on 7 August 2001.

16. Some argument may be expected to arise from the fact that the Khmer language official version of the Law used the term 'such as' instead of 'as such'. Unfortunately this was the term used in the Khmer translation of the Genocide Convention made in the early 1990s by the UN, and its inconsistency with the official texts of the Genocide Convention was not noticed when it was inserted in the KR trials Law promulgated in 2001.

17. The extent of this literature in English is shown in Hinton et al (eds), *Genocide: an anthropological reader*, and Schabas, *Genocide*. See especially *Genocide and democracy in Cambodia*, and Alexander Laban Hinton, 'A head for an eye: revenge in the Cambodian genocide'.

18. US Foreign Relations Authorization Act, Fiscal Years 1988 and 1989, Public Law No. 100–204, par. 906
19. US Genocide Justice Act, 1994, Public Law No. 103–236, par. 573 (b) 4.
20. Schabas, *Genocide*, p. 119
21. William A. Schabas, 'Should Khmer Rouge Leaders be prosecuted for genocide or crimes against humanity', in *Searching for the truth*, no. 22. October 2001 [Khmer version]; and Gregory H. Stanton, 'The Khmer Rouge Did Commit Genocide', in *Searching for the truth*, no. 23. November 2001 [Khmer version].
22. United Nations, Report of the Group of Experts for Cambodia established pursuant to General Assembly Resolution 52/135, UN Document. A/53/850 and S/1999/ 231, annex, para. 65.
23. Dr Gregory Stanton was responsible for drafting the Statutes for the International Criminal Tribunal for Rwanda, the first to exclude the nexus requirement.
24. Raymund Johansen, 'The Khmer Rouge communications documents and the "nexus to armed conflict" requirement for crimes against humanity', Phnom Penh, DC-Cam, September 1999. The attitude of the Khmer Rouge that those they persecuted were Vietnamese agents is clearly shown by Chhorn Hay in an statement he made to William Shawcross on the Thai-Cambodian border in the early 1980s: 'Almost every regional party secretary was a Vietnamese agent,' (Shawcross, *Quality of mercy*, p. 342).
25. The problem here is that the Statute of Rome became law long after the crimes were committed. However, the Law may be interpreted as referring to customary international law in effect when the Khmer Rouge were in power.
26. However, during the Tadic case at the International Criminal Tribunal for the former Yugoslavia, arguments were made that the grave breaches provisions may indeed apply in cases of internal armed conflict, a situation that may be easier to demonstrate, as shown by Ben Kiernan's extensive documentation of acts of resistance against the Khmer Rouge throughout the period of Democratic Kampuchea, but especially from mid-1977 (Kiernan, *Pol Pot regime, passim*). It should be noted that the 1977 Additional Protocols of the Geneva Conventions, which clarify applicability to internal armed conflict, are unlikely to be invoked, as none of the States were signatories during the Democratic Kampuchea period (although an argument could be made that the grave breaches provisions were part of customary international law before being codified in 1977). Another area of likely argument here is whether violations need to be committed 'in connection with' armed conflict, or whether it is sufficient to show that the two acts occurred contemporaneously.
27. Other provisions in the Geneva Conventions (especially Common Article 3) would appear to have been violated by the Khmer Rouge. These 'common articles' most definitely do not require international conflict and apply equally to internal armed conflict. They may therefore have provided an easier area to prosecute successfully, but Article 6 of the Law mentions only 'grave breaches', so it is unlikely that other provisions will be actionable. It is unfortunate that the common articles were not

also included in the Law, as they were, for example, in the Statute of the International Criminal Tribunal for Rwanda.

28. This case was still in trial at the time of writing this chapter, so the outcome is not yet known. Other cases at the ICTY where The Hague Convention has been invoked include Simic, and Kordic and Cerkez.

29. Francois Bizot, *The gate*, London: Harvill, 2003, p. 226. Bizot was among those held in the Embassy and he had been a prisoner of the Khmer Rouge, under the direct control of Duch, in 1971. This book is his account of the two experiences.

30. The UN draft of the law did not include the Vienna Convention of 1961 on Diplomatic Relations but rather the 1973 Convention on the Prevention and Punishment of Crimes Against Internationally Protected Persons (Article 8). However, as Cambodia has never ratified nor acceded to the 1973 Convention, and furthermore it came into force only on 20 February 1977, which was after most of the Khmer Rouge crimes against internationally protected persons are likely to have been committed (mainly in April 1975), the Cambodian side decided it would be unwise to include this as an item of substantive law, as it is unlikely that conviction would succeed. Instead, the Law includes the Vienna Convention of 1961 on Diplomatic Relations. However, a serious limitation here stems from the fact that the 1961 convention does not include penal provisions, which were introduced only in the 1973 convention.

CHAPTER 12

1. Hillary Jackson, 'Justice for Khmer Rouge victims still distant', *Reuters*, 21 October 2000.

2. Tom Fawthrop, 'UN Aids Khmer Rouge Impunity'.

3. David Scheffer private communication with Tom Fawthrop.

4. Robert Carmichael, 'Avoiding Arusha: Lessons for Cambodia Tribunal', *Phnom Penh Post*, 14 November 2003.

5. On the Cambodian model as the inspiration for the tribunals in East Timor and Sierra Leone, see Suzannah Linton, 'Cambodia, East Timor and Sierra Leone: experiments in international justice', *Criminal Law Forum*, 12, 2001, pp. 185–246, and Sok An, presentation to conference on the rule of law and the legacy of conflict, Gaborone, Botswana, 16–19 January 2003. The major difference from Cambodia is that in the Special Court for Sierra Leone international judges are in the majority over local judges, in accordance with the UN's own preference in Cambodia also, but opposed by the Cambodian government, as described in Chapters 9 and 10.

6. Chea Vannath, interview by Tom Fawthrop, 17 March 2001.

7. Youk Chhang, interview by the authors, 11 June 2003.

8. Gregory Stanton, 'Perfection is the enemy of justice'.

9. Craig Etcheson, 'Prospects for Justice for the Khmer Rouge', a public forum sponsored by Johns Hopkins University School of Advanced International Studies and the Fund for Reconciliation and Development March 22, 2002.

10. Peter Leuprecht, cited in Fawthrop, Tom, 'UN Aids Khmer Rouge Impunity'.
11. Gregory Stanton, 'Perfection is the enemy of justice'.
12. Hamish McDonald, 'Australia's bloody East Timor secret', *Sydney Morning Herald*, 14 March 2002.
13. John Aglionby, 'East Timor trial farce lets real killers stay free', the *Guardian*, 15 March 2002.
14. *Masters of terror: Indonesia's military violence in East Timor*, Canberra: Strategic and Defence Studies Centre, Australian National University, 2002 (Canberra Paper #145).
15. Samantha Powers, *A problem from hell*, p. 462. This is not the only instance of destruction of targeting media stations in time of war. Since that bombing of Yugoslav TV, US raids have twice hit offices of Al Jazeera TV – the first Arab satellite TV station. The first time was during the war in Afghanistan, and in 2003 Al Jazeera's offices in Baghdad were hit during the relentless aerial bombing against Iraq. International media organisations have strongly condemned these US military actions.
16. For a catalogue of these crimes see Hitchens, *The trial of Henry Kissinger*.
17. *Ibid*, p. 37.
18. Peter Leuprecht, press conference 8 July 2003.
19. Suzannah Linton, 'Comments on the Draft Agreement between the United Nations and the Royal Government of Cambodia Concerning the Prosecution under Cambodian Law of Crimes Committed during the Period of Democratic Kampuchea', *Searching for the Truth*, Special English edition, April 2003, p. 37.
20. Dith Munty, interviewed by Tom Fawthrop, 18 April 2001.
21. Daniel Ten Kate, 'Former Khmer Rouge president asks for legal aid', the *Cambodia Daily*, 18 December 2003.
22. Thet Sambath, 'Nuon Chea says he will not hire a lawyer', the *Cambodia Daily*, 22 December 2003.
23. The precise scope of the UN's obligations regarding payment of defence costs, particularly whether this would be limited to court-appointed lawyers, was not yet clear at the time of writing this chapter, but it was assumed to be so limited.
24. Dith Munty, interview by Tom Fawthrop, 18 April 2001.
25. Khieu Samphan, 'Second open letter to my compatriots', Pailin, 29 December 2003, translated from the French by Henri Locard, excerpted in Michael Hayes, 'The Khieu Samphan letter: smoke and mirrors', *Phnom Penh Post*, 2–15 January 2004.
26. Comments in a press conference at the conclusion of the 1987 International Conference on Kampuchea held in Bangkok and attended by Helen Jarvis.
27. *L'histoire récente du Cambodge et mes prises de position* [in Khmer], Phnom Penh: Ponleu Khmer, 2004.
28. Translation from Reuters report on Khieu Samphan's book, interview with Chhum Mey, April 2002.
29. 'Brother Number Two Enjoys Retirement', BBC Correspondent series 15 March 2002.
30. Chhum Mey interview by Tom Fawthrop, 5 April 2002.

31. Chairman of the Military Court, General Ney Thol interview by Tom Fawthrop, 6 January 2004. For Duch's earlier confessions, see Nate Thayer, *Far Eastern Economic Review*, 29 April, 6 and 13 May 1999.
32. Youk Chhang, interview by Tom Fawthrop, 22 October 1997.
33. Chhum Mey, interview by Tom Fawthrop, 5 April 2002.

ANNEXE A

1. Chandler, *Brother Number One*, p. 2 and p. 171.
2. Roger Normand, fieldwork editor of the *Harvard Human Rights Review*, published this information in several newspapers, as cited by Kiernan 'Inclusion', in *Genocide and democracy*, p. 203 and p. 254, n. 64.
3. This list was compiled from the following works Kiernan, *The Pol Pot Regime*, Heder and Tittemore, *Seven Candidates*, Carney 'Organization of Power' in Jackson, *Cambodia 1975–1978*, pp. 99–107 and Chandler *Brother Number One*.
4. CPK Statutes adopted at its January 1976 Congress.
5. Chandler, *S-21*, pp. 63–4. Khieu Samphan has denied ever being promoted to this position, *L'histoire récente du Cambodge et mes prises de position*, Paris: L'Harmattan, 2004, especially pp. 141–3.
6. Ben Kiernan, Table 1, in 'Introduction' to Kiernan (ed.), *Genocide and democracy in Cambodia*. Kiernan's spelling of names is followed throughout for consistency. Heder reports all of these except Khieu Samphan (*op cit*, p. 43) and he also mentions an unidentified 'Ke'.
7. Heder and Tittemore, *Seven candidates*, p. 43.
8. *Ibid*, p. 46.
9. *Ibid*, p. 46.
10. *Ibid*, p. 47.
11. Heder also maintains that Sao Phim was once a member of it, though that is not so clear.
12. Heder and Tittemore, *Seven candidates*, p. 48.
13. Steve Heder, *Cambodian communism and the Vietnamese model*, vol. 1: Imitation and independence, 1930–1975, Bangkok: White Lotus, 2004, p. 29, citing Nuon Chea's own accounts.
14. Khmer Issarak (free Khmers) was the collective name for a movement encompassing a wide variety of groups, individuals and even bandits operating in the north west of Cambodia in the period following the end of the Second World War. The one thing they had in common was a desire to resist re-colonisation by France.
15. Heder and Tittemore, *Seven candidates*, pp. 51–62.
16. Ibid, pp. 63–77.
17. Ibid, pp. 77–82.
18. Some sources suggest he may have only been a member of the Central Committee, not the Standing Committee.
19. Cambodian Military Court Indictments No. 019/99 and No. 044/99 and Detention Orders No. 15/DK/2002 and No. 09/03/DK.
20. Ke Pauk died in 2002 of natural causes, according to all reports.
21. The commandant of Kraing Ta Chan was reported as being 'Phen'. Apart from S-21 the records of other prisons seem to have disappeared, with

the exception of Kraing Ta Chan, whose surviving archives were copied by Ben Kiernan in July 1980. They now form a subset of the archives held at the Documentation Center of Cambodia.

22. Tom Fawthrop, 'Mass killer's double life', *The Age*, 10 May 1999.
23. Cambodian Military Court Indictments No. 029/99 and No. 044/99 and Detention Orders No. 16DK/2002 and No. 10/03/DK.
24. *DK Provinces, Zones, Regions and Districts* (a Khmer Rouge text describing the DK administrative and political geography, first published by the DK Ministry of Education for Elementary Class 2, 1977, pp. 9–10), translated by Sour Bunsou and Youk Chhang of the Documentation Center of Cambodia.
25. Kiernan, *Pol Pot regime*, p. 104.

ANNEXE B

1. Our own research shows the extent to which such opposition went. In 1998 Kampong Chhnang's military commander General Thioun Thoun (interviewed by Tom Fawthrop in September 1998) reported that in 1976 his commanding officer, Khmer Rouge General Chan Chakrey, then army deputy chief of staff, planned to assassinate Pol Pot and Son Sen and wanted to hand over power to Prince Norodom Sihanouk who was then the figurehead president. This plot is discussed by Kiernan (*Pol Pot regime*, pp. 320–23) although he cites one source as saying that Sihanouk was also a target for assassination. Such reports indicate that the regime's enemies were real as well as imagined. The proliferation of purges from 1977 on also produced its own paranoia, constantly fuelled and fed by the confessions extracted from S-21 prisoners.
2. Stephen Heder with Brian D. Tittemore and Coalition for International Justice, *Seven candidates for prosecution: accountability for the crimes of the Khmer Rouge*, Washington, DC: War Crimes Research Office, American University, 2001.
3. Dr Stephen Heder, a political scientist with the University of London's School of Oriental and African Studies, has since the late 1970s focussed his research on Cambodia. He worked on the Thai-Cambodia border 1979–1981 mainly under contract to the US State Department, served in the Information and Education section of UNTAC and has written numerous papers on the Khmer Rouge.
4. Brian Tittemore, a Staff Attorney with the Inter-American Commission on Human Rights, has previously served as Senior Research Associate and Acting Executive Director of the War Crimes Research Office (WCRO) of the Washington College of Law, American University, in Washington, DC.
5. Diane F. Orentlicher is Professor of Law and Faculty Director of the WCRO.
6. Heder, Steve, 'Cambodia, Nazi Germany and the Stalinist Soviet Union: intentionality, totalitarianism, functionalism and the politics of accountability', draft for presentation at the German Historical Institute, Washington, DC, 29 March 2003.

Bibliography

PUBLICLY AVAILABLE SOURCES

Abrams, Jason, and Stephen Ratner, 'Striving for justice: accountability and the crimes of the Khmer Rouge', typescript, presented to the US State Department, 1995.

—— *Accounting for human rights atrocities in international law: beyond the Nuremberg legacy*, London: Oxford University Press, 1997.

Acharya Amitav, Pierre Lizéé and Sorpong Peou (eds), *Cambodia – the 1989 Paris Peace Conference: background analysis and documents*, Millwood, New York: Kraus International Publications, 1991.

Aglionby, John, 'East Timor trial farce lets real killers stay free', the *Guardian*, 15 March 2002.

Agreement between the United Nations and the Royal Government of Cambodia Concerning the Prosecution under Cambodian Law of Crimes Committed during the Period of Democratic Kampuchea (UN document A/57/806).

Allman, T.D. 'Sihanouk's sideshow', *Vanity Fair*, April 1990.

Amer, Ramses, 'The United Nations and Kampuchea: the issue of representation and its implications', in *Bulletin of Concerned Asian Scholars*, vol.22, no.3, 1990.

—— *The General Assembly and the Kampuchean issue: intervention, regime recognition and the world community 1979–1987*, Uppsala: Department of Peace and Conflict Research, Uppsala University, 1989.

Amnesty International, ASA 23/005/2003, issued in April 2003.

—— various reports and statements on the Khmer Rouge trials.

Annan, Kofi, various statements as United Nations Secretary General.

Associated Press (Bangkok), 'Ex-UN official: China tried to stymie Khmer Rouge trial', 12 November 2000.

Associated Press (Beijing), 'China won't pressure Cambodia on Khmer Rouge Tribunal', 7 November 2000.

Associated Press report, 25 December 1998 and various other reports.

Asian Wall Street Journal, 5 and 12 August 1991.

Bangkok Post.

BBC TV Correspondent programme, 15 March 2002.

BBC World Service, 'Deadlock on Khmer trial talks', 22 March 2000.

Becker, Elizabeth, *When the war was over: Cambodia's revolution and the voices of its people*, New York: Touchstone, Simon & Schuster, 1986.

—— 'After 9-Month Break, U.N. Revives Plan for Khmer Rouge Trial', the *New York Times*, 21 November 2002.

Bedford, Michael and Kathy Knight, *Cambodia still waiting for peace: a report on the Thai-Khmer collaboration since the signing of the Paris Peace Accords*, Boston: Oxfam America, 1995.

Bekaert, Jacques, *Cambodian diary*, Bangkok: White Lotus, 1997–8, 2 vols.

Bizot, Francois, *The gate*, London: Harvill, 2003.

Black's Law Dictionary, 6th edn, Minneapolis: West Publishing Co., 1990.

Blum, William, *Rogue state: a guide to the world's only superpower* (New updated edition), London: Zed, 2002.

Bou Saroeun, 'Open letter to the surviving leadership of the Khmer Rouge', *Phnom Penh Post* 14–27 April, 2000.

Brady, Christopher, *United States Foreign Policy towards Cambodia, 1977–92: A question of realities*, New York: St Martin's Press, 1999.

Bui Tin, *From cadre to exile: memoirs of a Vietnamese journalist*, translated from the Vietnamese and adapted by Judy Stowe and Do Van, Chiang Mai: Silkworm Books, 1995.

Bull, David, *The poverty of diplomacy: Kampuchea and the outside world*, Oxford: Oxfam, 1983.

Burchett, Wilfred, *The China-Cambodia-Vietnam triangle*, Chicago:Vanguard, 1981.

Cambodia, Delegation to the Paris Peace Conference, 1989, 'Communication' regarding genocide, CPC/89/com/8, issued 8 August 1989, published in Acharya et al, *Cambodia – the 1989 peace conference.*

Cambodia, 'Statement by the Cambodian Royal Government Task Force on the Khmer Rouge Tribunal', 21 November 2000, *Phnom Penh Post*, 24 November – 7 December, 2000.

Cambodia, Constitutional Council, decisions dated 12 February 2001 and August 2001.

Cambodia, Law on the Establishment of the Extraordinary Chambers in the Courts of Cambodia for the Prosecution of Crimes Committed during the Period of Democratic Kampuchea, promulgated 10 August 2001.

Cambodia, Military Court Indictments No 019/99, 029/99 and 044/99 and Detention Orders No 15/DK/2002, No 16DK/2002, No 09/ 03/DK and No 10/03/DK.

Cambodia Genocide Program, Cambodia Genocide Databases, www.yale. edu/cgp.

Cambodia Daily.

Cambodian Documentation Commission archives (Hawk Papers) at the Documentation Center of Cambodia.

Cambodian Human Rights Action Committee, petition to the Secretary General of the United Nations, 20 January 1999.

Camus, Albert, *The Outsider*, translated by Stuart Gilbert, Harmondsworth: Penguin, 1961.

Carmichael, Robert, 'Avoiding Arusha: lessons for Cambodia Tribunal', *Phnom Penh Post*, 14 November 2003.

Carney, Timothy, 'The organization of power', tables 1–4, in Jackson, Karl D. (ed.), *Cambodia 1975–1978: rendezvous with death*, Princeton, New Jersey: Princeton University Press, 1989, pp. 99–107.

Center for Social Development, *The Khmer Rouge and national reconciliation: opinions from the Cambodians*, Phnom Penh, April 2002.

Chanda, Nayan, *Brother enemy: the war after the war*, San Diego: Harcourt Brace Jovanovich, 1986.

Chandler, David, *Brother Number One: a political biography of Pol Pot*, Boulder: Westview Press, 1992.

—— *Voices from S-21: terror and history in Pol Pot's secret prison*, Chiang Mai: Silkworm Books, 2000.

Chhang Youk, Editorial in each issue of *Searching for the truth*.

—— various statements and letters as Director of the Documentation Center of Cambodia.

Chronology of Cambodian history, 1985–1989, at web site, www.geocities.com/khmerchronology/1985.htm.

Communist Party of Kampuchea, Statutes, January 1976 Congress.

Conference of Intellectuals and Religious People, Phnom Penh, organised by the Salvation Front, 12 September 1983, Open Letter [in Khmer].

Conference acclaiming the 40th Anniversary of the Convention on the Prevention and Punishment of the Crime of Genocide, 9–12–48 to 9–12–88, Phnom Penh, organised by the Salvation Front, 'Overall report of the activities of intellectuals' [in Khmer].

Corell, Hans, Speech in the Chaktomuk Theatre on 6 June 2003 at the signing ceremony of the Agreement between the United Nations and the Royal Government of Cambodia.

—— various statements as Under Secretary General and Legal Counsel of the United Nations.

CORKR, Wanted for mass murder, genocide, war crimes, Washington DC: CORKR, 1991.

Crimes of the clique of the Beijing Chinese expansionists and the lackeys Pol Pot, Ieng Sary, Khieu Samphan in the period 1975–1979, Phnom Penh: Salvation Front, 1983 [in Khmer].

Danois, Jacques, 'Ted, the Man of God', in *The will to live*, Bangkok: Unicef, 1979.

Delvert, Jean, *Le paysan cambodgien*, Paris: École Pratique des Hauts Études-Sorbonne & Mouton, 1961.

De Nike, Howard J., John Quigley and Kenneth J. Robinson (eds), with the assistance of Helen Jarvis and Nereida Cross. *Genocide in Cambodia: documents from the trial of Pol Pot and Ieng Sary*, Philadelphia: University of Pennsylvania Press, 2000.

DK Provinces, Zones, Regions and Districts (a Khmer Rouge text describing the DK administrative and political geography, first published by the DK Ministry of Education for Elementary Class 2, 1977, pp. 9–10), translated by Sour Bunsou and Youk Chhang of the Documentation Center of Cambodia.

English-Khmer Law Dictionary, Phnom Penh: The Asia Foundation, 1997.

Ester, Helen, *Vietnam, Thailand, Kampuchea: a firsthand account*, Canberra: The Australian Council for Overseas Aid, 1980.

Etcheson, Craig, 'A criminal trial for the Khmer Rouge', Newsletter No. 27 Institute for the Study of Genocide, International Association of Genocide Scholars.

—— 'Prospects for justice for the Khmer Rouge', Public Forum sponsored by Johns Hopkins University School of Advanced International Studies and the Fund for Reconciliation and Development, 22 March 2002.

Tom Fawthrop, 'Cause for optimism: Hun Sen speaks on the Cambodian solution', *Far Eastern Economic Review*, 3 March 1988.

—— *Sunday Times* (London), 11 January 1998.

—— 'Why didn't they arrest him 20 years ago?', *Phnom Penh Post*, 24 April–7 May 1998.

—— '"Irresponsible" and "baseless" anti-Hun Sen campaign hits US Congress', *Phnom Penh Post*, 2–15 October 1998.

—— interview with Nuon Paet, shown on 'Dateline', Australian SBS TV, October 1998.

—— 'Mass killer's double life', *Age* (Melbourne), 10 May 1999.

—— 'Other Side of a Khmer Rouge "Butcher"', *Age* (Melbourne), 15 May 1999.

—— 'No reason for standoff on Khmer Rouge law', *Phnom Penh Post*, 2–15 March 2001.

—— 'Thai senator urges apology', *Phnom Penh Post*, 16–29 March 2001.

—— 'Pol Pot minister lives it up in Phnom Penh', *Straits Times* (Singapore), 7 January 2002.

—— 'UN Aids Khmer Rouge Impunity', *Asia Times*, 12 June 2002.

—— *Sunday Times* (London), 15 December 2002.

—— 'Intelligence' *Far Eastern Economic Review*, June 2003.

Findlay, Trevor *Cambodia: the lessons and legacy of UNTAC*, Oxford: Oxford University Press, 1995.

Gerrand, James, *The last God-King: the lives and times of Cambodia's Sihanouk*, Sydney: Film Australia, 1996.

Gottesman, Evan, *Cambodia after the Khmer Rouge: inside the politics of nation building*, New Haven: Yale University Press, 2003.

Haas, Michael, *Genocide by proxy: Cambodian pawn on a superpower chessboard*, New York: Praeger, 1991.

Hammarberg, Thomas, 'Efforts to establish a tribunal against KR leaders: discussions between the Cambodian government and the UN', *Phnom Penh Post*, 14–27 September 2001, Supplement.

Hawk, David, 'Cambodia: a report from Phnom Penh', *The New Republic*, 15 November 1982, pp. 17–21.

Hayes, Michael, 'The Khieu Samphan letter: smoke and mirrors', *Phnom Penh Post*, 2–15 January 2004.

Heder, Steve, 'Khieu Samphan and Pol Pot: Moloch's Poodle', paper presented at Australian National University, September 1990.

—— 'Cambodia, Nazi Germany and the Stalinist Soviet Union: intentionality, totalitarianism, functionalism and the politics of accountability', draft for presentation at the German Historical Institute, Washington, DC, 29 March 2003.

—— *Cambodian communism and the Vietnamese model*, vol. I: Imitation and independence, 1930–1975, Bangkok: White Lotus, 2004.

—— with Brian D. Tittemore and Coalition for International Justice, *Seven candidates for prosecution: accountability for the crimes of the Khmer Rouge*, Washington, DC: War Crimes Research Office, American University, 2001.

Herman, Edward S. 'Pol Pot and Kissinger: on war criminality and impunity', *Z magazine,* September 1997.

Heuveline, Patrick, 'Between one and three million': towards the demographic reconstruction of a decade of Cambodian history (1970–79)', *Population studies*, vol. 52, no. 1, March 1998.

Hinton, Alexander Laban (ed.), *Genocide: an anthropological reader*, Malden, Massachusetts and Oxford: Blackwell, 2002.
—— 'A head for an eye: revenge in the Cambodian genocide', in Hinton (ed.), *Genocide: an anthropological reader*.
Hitchens, Christopher, *The trial of Henry Kissinger*, London: Verso, 2001.
Hughes, Rachel, 'Remembering May 20 – Day of Anger', *Searching for the Truth*, no. 12, December 2000.
Human Rights Watch, 'Serious flaws: why the U.N. General Assembly should require changes to the Draft Khmer Rouge Tribunal Agreement', 30 April 2003.
—— various reports and statements on the Khmer Rouge trials.
Hun Sen, press conferences, letters and statements as Foreign Minister from 1979 and then Prime Minister from August 1989.
'Hun Sen draws his line in the shifting sands', *Phnom Penh Post*, 8–21 January 1999.
'Hun Sen: Cambodia united at any price', *Phnom Penh Post*, 4–16 October 1996.
International Seminar on Kampuchea, Bangkok, July 1987.
International Seminar on the Genocide Phenomena and Prevention of their Return', Phnom Penh, 22 July 1989, Appeal.
Jackson, Hillary, 'Justice for Khmer Rouge victims still distant', *Reuters*, 21 October 2000.
Jackson, Karl D. (ed.) *Cambodia 1975–1978: rendezvous with death*, Princeton: Princeton University Press, 1989.
Jackson, Robert, frontispiece in Sydney Schanberg, *The Killing Fields: the facts behind the film*, London: Weidenfeld & Nicolson, 1984.
—— preface to Mysliwiec, *Punishing the poor*.
Jarvis, Helen, *Cambodia*, (World Bibliographical Series, vol.200), Oxford: Clio Press, 1997.
—— 'Who helped the Khmer Rouge to survive?', *Green Left Weekly*, no. 349, 17 February 1999.
—— 'A personal view of the documents of the People's Revolutionary Tribunal', in De Nike, *Genocide in Cambodia*, pp. xiii–xviii.
—— 'Trials and tribulations: the latest twists in the long quest for justice for the Cambodian genocide', *Critical Asian Studies*, vol. 34, no. 4, 2002, pp. 607–24.
Jefferson, Paul, 'Landmines, damn lies and statistics', *Guardian*, 9 September 1997.
Jendrzejczyk, Mike, *Washington Post*, 8 April 2003.
Jennar, Raoul, *Les clés du Cambodge*, [s.l.]: Maisonneuve & Larose, 1995.
—— *Chroniques Cambodgiennes 1990–1994* . – Paris: L'Harmattan,1995.
—— *Bungling a peace plan 1989–1991*, vol.1 of *Cambodian chronicles 1989–1996*, Bangkok: White Lotus, 1998.
Johansen, Raymund, 'The Khmer Rouge communications documents and the "nexus to armed conflict" requirement for crimes against humanity,' Phnom Penh, DC-Cam, September 1999.
Ka Sunbaunat, 'Cambodian mental health training program and organization of mental health services in Cambodia', 1998.

Kampuchean United Front for National Salvation, Declaration establishing the Salvation Front on 2 December 1978.

Khmer Rouge Trials Task Force web site, http://www.cambodia.gov.kh/krt/krt_main.htm.

Khieu Samphan, comments at concluding press conference, International Seminar on Kampuchea, Bangkok, July 1987.

—— *L'histoire récente du Cambodge et mes prises de position*, Paris: L'Harmattan, 2004, (also published in Khmer Phnom Penh: Ponleu Khmer, 2004).

—— 'Second open letter to my compatriots', Pailin, 29 December 2003, translated from the French by Henri Locard, excerpted in *Phnom Penh Post*, January 2004.

Kiernan, Ben (ed.), *Genocide and democracy in Cambodia: the Khmer Rouge, the United Nations and the international community*, New Haven: Yale University Southeast Asian Studies, 1993.

—— *The Pol Pot regime: race, power and genocide in Cambodia under the Khmer Rouge, 1975–79*, New Haven: Yale University Press, 1996.

—— 'Bringing the Khmer Rouge to justice', *Human Rights Review*, vol. 1, no. 3, April–June 2000, pp. 92–108.

—— 'Cambodia: justice delayed', *Bangkok Post*, 17 April 2000.

—— (ed.) 'Introduction', in Kiernan, *Genocide and democracy in Cambodia*.

—— 'The inclusion of the Khmer Rouge in the Cambodian peace process: causes and consequences', in Kiernan, *Genocide and democracy in Cambodia*.

—— 'The demography of genocide in Southeast Asia', *Critical Asian Studies*, vol. 35, no. 4, 2003, pp. 585–97.

—— 'Cambodia's twisted path to justice', *The history place: points of view*, www.historyplace.com/pointsofview/kiernan.htm.

Kimmo Kiljunen (ed.), *Kampuchea: decade of the genocide* (report of a Finnish Inquiry Commission), London: Zed Press, 1984.

Klintworth, Gary, *Vietnam's intervention in Cambodia in international law*, AGPS Press, 1989.

Kubes, Antonin, *Kampuchea*, Prague: Orbis, 1982.

Kumar, Bhoomi, Paper presented at the Indigenous forum at the Third World Congress on Traumatic Stress Studies, Melbourne, March, 2000.

Lee Kuan Yew, 'From Third World to First: the Singapore story, 1965–2000', Singapore: *Times*, 2000.

Leuprecht, Peter, Press conference, 8 March 2002 and 8 July 2003.

LeVine, Peg, 'Politics of suffering' a chapter in her forthcoming book, Living taboo in Angkar's pageant: couples married in the Khmer Rouge (unpublished).

Linton, Suzannah, 'Cambodia, East Timor and Sierra Leone: experiments in international justice', *Criminal Law Forum*, no. 12, , 2001, pp. 185–246.

—— 'Comments on the Draft Agreement between the United Nations and the Royal Government of Cambodia Concerning the Prosecution under Cambodian Law of Crimes Committed during the Period of Democratic Kampuchea', *Searching for the Truth*, Special English edition, April 2003.

Locard, Henri, *The Khmer Rouge gulag: Democratic Kampuchea 17 April 1975–7 January 1979*, Paris, Phnom Penh, Canberra, June-July 1995; prepared for the conference on 'Concentration camps: a XXth century phenomenon,' Paris, 15–17 June 1995.

Magistad, Mary Kay, 'Khmer Rouge are closer to new chance at power', *Boston Globe*, 17 April 1989.

Maguire, Peter, *Law and war: an American story*, New York: Columbia University Press, 2000.

Mapping the Killing Fields of Cambodia 1995, 1996, 1997, 1998, 1999, 2000, 2001, 2002, 2003, prepared by Pheng Pong Racy, Phat Kosal, Chhang Youk, Sin Khin and Ouch Sam-Oeun, Phnom Penh: Documentation Center of Cambodia, 26 May 2003.

Marcher, Annette, 'PM-UNSG agree: more talks', *Phnom Penh Post*, 18 February – 2 March 2000.

Mason, Linda and Roger Brown, *Rice, rivalry and politics: managing Cambodia's relief*, South Bend, Indiana: University of Notre Dame Press, 1983.

Masters of terror: Indonesia's military violence in East Timor 1999, Canberra: Strategic and Defence Studies Centre, Australian National University, 2002.

McDonald, Hamish, 'Australia's bloody East Timor secret', *Sydney Morning Herald*, 14 March 2002.

McGrew, Laura, *Truth, Justice, Reconciliation and Peace in Cambodia*, Phnom Penh: project funded by the Canadian Embassy, 2000.

Mehta, Harish C. and Julie B. Mehta, *Hun Sen: strongman of Cambodia*, Singapore, Graham Brash, 1999.

Morris, Stephen J., *Why Vietnam invaded Cambodia: political culture and the causes of war*, Stanford: Stanford University Press, 1999.

Muskie, Edmund, *Exploring Cambodia Findings & Recommendations from Muskie's visit to Thailand, Cambodia and Vietnam*, Washington DC: Center for National Policy, October 1990.

Mysliwiec, Eva, *Punishing the poor: the international isolation of Kampuchea*, Oxford: Oxfam, 1988.

New York Times, editorial, 24 June 1997.

New York Times, 22 April 1979.

Norodom Sihanouk, *War and hope: the case for Cambodia*, translated by Mary Feeney, New York: Pantheon, 1980.

—— 'Open Letter to the Member States of the UN', in Peter Schier and Manola Oum-Schier, *Prince Sihanouk on Cambodia: interviews and talks with Prince Norodom Sihanouk*, 2nd ed.,Hamburg: Institüt für Asienkunde, 1985.

—— *Prisonnier des Khmers Rouges*. [s.l.]: Hachette, 1986.

Panh, Rithy, *S21, the Khmer Rouge killing machine*, Film, 2003.

Pen Khon, *Phnom Penh before and after 1997*, [Phnom Penh: s.n., 2000].

People's Revolutionary Tribunal (PRT) Documents, especially 1.01 bis, 3.01, 3.03 a and b, and 3.04, in *Genocide in Cambodia: documents from the trial of Pol Pot and Ieng Sary* and 'Work papers, May 10 1979', in Gottesman, *Cambodia*, p. 62.

Phnom Penh Post.

Pilger, John, 'Organised forgetting', *New Statesman*, 1 November 1991.

—— and David Munro, *Year zero: the silent death of Cambodia*, ITV film, 1979.

—— and David Munro, *Cambodia year ten*, ITV film, 1989.

—— and David Munro, *Cambodia – the betrayal*, ITV film, 1990.

—— and David Munro, *Return to year zero*, ITV film, 1993.

Powers, Samantha, 'A problem from hell': America and the age of genocide, New York: Basic Books, 2002.

Qiang Zhai, 'China and the Cambodian conflict, 1970–1975', on the Cambodian Genocide Program web site, www.yale.edu/cgp.

Quigley, John, 'Editor's note' and 'Introduction', in De Nike et al. (eds), Genocide in Cambodia.

Rajagopal, Balakrishnan, 'The pragmatics of prosecuting the KR', International Humanitarian Law Yearbook, The Hague: Asser Institute, 1998.

—— 'The pragmatics of prosecuting the KR', Phnom Penh Post, Issue 8/1, 8–21 January 1999.

—— 'Looking for justice in Cambodia', National Post, 23 September 1999.

—— 'A Blind Eye to Justice in Cambodia,' Washington Post, 27 March 2002.

Raszelenberg, Patrick and Peter Schier, (eds), The Cambodia conflict: search for a settlement, 1979–1991: an analytical chronology, Hamburg: Institüt für Asienkunde, 1995.

Rees, Phil, 'Brother Number Two enjoys retirement', BBC 2, 15 March 2002.

Reporters Without Borders, Cambodia Annual Report 2002.

Research Committee of the Salvation Front, 1983, Report.

Roberts, David, Political transition in Cambodia 1991–99: power elitism and democracy, Richmond, Surrey: Curzon, 2001.

Robertson, Geoffrey, Crimes against humanity: the struggle for global justice, London: Allen Lane, Penguin, 1999.

Rungswasdisab, Puangthong, 'Thailand's response to the Cambodian genocide', on the Cambodian Genocide Program web site, www.yale.edu/cgp.

Schabas, William A., 'Looking for justice in Cambodia', National Post, 23 September 1999.

—— Genocide in international law, Cambridge: Cambridge University Press, 2000.

—— 'Should Khmer Rouge Leaders be prosecuted for genocide or crimes against humanity? in Searching for the truth, no. 22. October 2001 [Khmer version].

Schanberg, Sydney, The Killing Fields: the facts behind the film, London: Weidenfeld & Nicolson, 1984.

Scheffer, David J., 'Justice for Cambodia', New York Times, 21 December 2002.

Searching for the truth, a magazine of the Documentation Center of Cambodia published monthly in Khmer (Sveng Rok Kapet) and irregularly in English.

Seminar on the Genocide Phenomena and Prevention of their Return to remind the world of the crimes of the Khmer Rouge and of their continued recognition, Phnom Penh, organised by the Salvation Front and the Ministry of Information, July 1989.

Shawcross, William, The quality of mercy: Cambodia, holocaust and modern conscience, New York: Simon & Schuster, 1984.

—— Sideshow: Kissinger, Nixon and the destruction of Cambodia, new revised edition, London: Hogarth, 1986.

Silber, Irwin, Kampuchea: the revolution rescued, Oakland: Line of March Publications, 1986.

Sliwinski, Marek, *Le genocide Khmer Rouge: une analyse démographique*, Paris: L'Harmattan, 1995, p. 57.

Slocomb, Margaret, *The People's Republic of Kampuchea 1979–1989: the revolution after Pol Pot*, Chiang Mai: Silkworm Books, 2003.

Sok An, Presentation and comments to the National Assembly on the Draft Law on the Establishment of the Extraordinary Chambers in the Courts of Cambodia for the Prosecution of Crimes Committed during the period of Democratic Kampuchea. Phnom Penh: Office of the Council of Ministers, 2001, see also www.cambodia.com.kh/krt/

—— Presentation to Stockholm International Forum on Truth, Justice and Reconciliation, 23–24 April 2002, *Proceedings*, pp. 139–43. See also www.cambodia.com.kh/krt/

—— Presentation to Conference on the Rule of Law and the Legacy of Conflict, Gaborone, Botswana, 16–19 January 2003.

—— Speech in the Chaktomuk Theatre at the signing ceremony of the Agreement between the United Nations and the Royal Government of Cambodia, 6 June 2003. See also www.cambodia.com.kh/krt/

Stanton, Gregory H., 'Options to try Pol Pot', drafted for the US State Department in 1997.

—— 'The Khmer Rouge Did Commit Genocide', in *Searching for the truth*, Number 23, November 2001 [Khmer version].

—— 'The call' in Totten, Samuel, and Steven Leonard Jacobs (eds), *Pioneers of genocide studies*, New Brunswick and London: Transaction Press, 2002, pp. 401–25.

—— 'Perfection is the enemy of justice', in *Searching for the truth*, Special English Issue No. 2, July 2003, pp. 40–42, also published in the *Bangkok Post*.

Ten Kate, Daniel, 'Annan urges Assembly to OK tribunal', *Cambodia Daily*, 11 December 2003.

Thailand, Ministry of Foreign Affairs, *Thai Policy vis a vis Kampuchea*, Phnom Penh 1983.

Thayer, Nate, *Far Eastern Economic Review*, 29 April, 6 and 13 May 1999.

Thet Sambath, 'Nuon Chea says he will not hire a lawyer', *Cambodia Daily*, 18 December 2003.

Thion, Serge, *Watching Cambodia*, Bangkok: White Lotus, 1993.

Twining, Charles H. 'The economy' in Jackson, Karl D. (ed.), *Cambodia 1975–1978: rendezvous with death*, Princeton: Princeton University Press, 1989.

United Nations, 'Analysis prepared on behalf of the Sub-Commission by its Chairman of materials submitted to it and the Commission on Human Rights under decision 9 (XXXIV) of the Commission on Human Rights' E/CN.4/1335 (1979).

—— Report of the Group of Experts for Cambodia established pursuant to General Assembly Resolution 52/135 (UN Document. A/53/850, and S/1999/ 231).

—— various other documents on Cambodia relevant to the issue of the Khmer Rouge tribunal especially UNGA Resolution 57/228 (A and B), and Report of the Secretary-General (A/57/769).

'The UN in Cambodia: a brief evaluation of UNTAC in the field of human rights', Part II of a 3-part report by the Cambodian Documentation

Commission, undated, p. 34, held in 'the Hawk Papers' at Documentation Center of Cambodia.

United States, Foreign Relations Authorization Act, Fiscal Years 1988 and 1989.

—— Cambodia Genocide Justice Act of 1994.

—— Cambodia Democracy and Accountability Act of 2003.

Vickery, Michael, *Cambodia 1975–1992*, Boston: South End, 1984.

Vietnam Courier, 'The Peoples Republic of Kampuchea at the Threshold of its Sixth Year', 1983, pp. 12–16, in Silber, *Kampuchea: the revolution rescued*.

Vietnam: *War crimes of the Pol Pot and Chinese troops in Vietnam*, Hanoi: Commission of Inquiry into the Chinese Expansionists' and Hegemonists' Crime of War of Aggression, 1979.

Wassana Nanuam, 'Brutal KR chief poisoned', *Bangkok Post*, 19 March 2002.

Yoichi Funbashi, 'Hun Sen on the subject of nation-building', *International Herald Tribune/Asahi*, 7 October 2003.

Unpublished interviews and private communications

Allegra, Ted, interview by Tom Fawthrop, February 2001.

Chan Ven, interview by the authors, March 2001.

Chea Sophara, interview by Tom Fawthrop, March 2001.

Chea Vannath, interview by Tom Fawthrop, February 2001 and March 2001.

Chey Sopheara, interview by Tom Fawthrop, March 2001.

Chhang Youk, interview by Tom Fawthrop October 1997 and April 1998.

—— interview by the authors, June 2003.

Chhum Mey, interview by Tom Fawthrop, August 1998 and June 2002.

Chhuor Leang Huot, interview by Helen Jarvis, March 2001.

Dith Munty interview by Tom Fawthrop, April 2001.

Etcheson, Craig, private communication, April 2003.

Haing Ngor, interview by Tom Fawthrop, 1993.

Hawk, David, interview by Helen Jarvis, February 2002.

Hochmann, Steve, memo 5 January 2000, forwarded by him to Tom Fawthrop.

Holloway, John, interview by Helen Jarvis, May 2000 and May 2001.

Hun Sen, interview by Helen Jarvis, 27 January 1999.

Im Sethy, interview by Tom Fawthrop, February and March 2001.

Ke Pauk, interview by Tom Fawthrop in Siem Reap, April 1998.

Matthews, Verghese, interview by Tom Fawthrop, March 2003.

Men Sam An, interview by Helen Jarvis, September 2000.

Min Khin, interview by the authors, March 2001.

My Samedy, interview by Tom Fawthrop, April 2001.

Ney Penna, interview by the authors, March 2001.

Ney Thol, interview by Tom Fawthrop, January 2004.

Nhek Bun Chhay, interview by Tom Fawthrop, May 1998.

Nhem Eng, interview by Tom Fawthrop, date???.

Nou Leakena interview by Tom Fawthrop, July 2003.

Prum Sokha, interview by Tom Fawthrop, July 1997 and 2003.

Ok Serei Sopheak, interview by Tom Fawthrop, March 2001.

Quang Quyen, interview by Tom Fawthrop, December 1988.

Quigley, John, phone interview by Helen Jarvis, July 2002.

Redicliffe, Paul, private communication with Tom Fawthrop, 2001.

Scheffer, David, private communications with the authors.

Sok An, interview by Helen Jarvis, January 2003.

Stanton, Gregory H., private communication with Helen Jarvis, 11 September 2003.

Sukhamband Paribatr, interviewed by Tom Fawthrop, September 1998.

Sum Mean, interview by Helen Jarvis, July 1999 and in March 2001.

Tey Sambo, interview by Tom Fawthrop, February 2001.

Thioun Thoun, interview by Tom Fawthrop, September 1998.

Thong Khon, interview by Tom Fawthrop, January 2002.

Thun Saray, interview by Helen Jarvis, June 2001 and by Tom Fawthrop, March 2002.

Tonkin, Derek, private correspondence with Tom Fawthrop.

Trun Hung, interview by Tom Fawthrop in Ho Chi Minh City, 1995.

Uch Kiman, interview by the authors, June 2002.

Wiedemann, Kent, interview by Tom Fawthrop, March 2001 and unclassified email communication, 9 April 2002.

Index

Note Cambodian names are listed under first name, eg. Hun Sen not Sen, Hun

pre-trial chamber, 163, 176
Prum Sokha, 21, 22, 276, 277
Pung Peng Cheng, 83

Quang Quyen, Vietnamese forensic
    specialist, 113, 217
Quigley, John, 40, 45, 47, 50
Quinn, Kenneth, US ambassador to
    Cambodia, 98, 153, 184

Radio Free Asia, 153
Rajagopal, Balakrishnan
    proposal for a mixed tribunal,
    156, 191
Rajsoomer Lallah, Judge, 124
Ranariddh, Norodom, see Norodom
    Ranariddh
Ratner, Steven R., 110, 124
Reagan, Ronald, US president, 62,
    70, 63, 80, 82, 86
    as possible defence witness in EC,
    165
Rees, Phil, 210
refugee camps, 59
    and KR control of, 33, 35, 38, 67
repatriation, 107
relationship between Law and
    Agreement, 171
religious persecution, 4, 15, 50,
    221–4
Research Committee into the
    Crimes of the Pol Pot Regime,
    72, 73
retroactivity, 160
Ridge, Tom, US congressperson
    supporting KRT, 86
riots, anti-Thai, Jan 2003, 200
Rithy Panh, 250
Robb, Charles, US senator
    supporting KRT, 110
Robert Rosenstock, US delegate to
    UN, 29–30
Robinson, Mary, UN High
    Commissioner for Human
    Rights, 118
Rohrabacher, Dana, US
    Congressman, 152
Roos, General Klaas Van, head of
    UNTAC's police, 104

Ros Nhim, 265
Rosenblatt, Lionel, 62
Royal Government of the National
    Union of Kampuchea
    (GRUNK), 219
Rules of Procedure and Evidence,
    see Extraordinary Chambers,
    procedure
Russia
    assistance to Task Force, 162

S-21, 9, 41, 78, 95, 101, 132, 142,
    145, 216, 249, 250, 251, 259,
    260, 266–9, 271–2
    photographs, 111
    prison records, 70, 111, 212, 214
    survivors, 145, 251, 253, 244, 245
    see also Tuol Sleng Genocide
    Museum
Sa Kaeo, Thailand, 35
Saaphan Hin, Thailand, 92, 94, 95
Salvation Front
    and formation of PRK, 13
    composition of, 16
    documentation of DK crimes, 72,
    173
    on post-DK population
    movement, 12
    founding document of, 40
    petitions to UN, 73, 88
    policy on judicial accountability
    of KR, 42, 139
Sam Bith, 166, 167, 194, 261
Sam Rainsy, 119, 138, 150, 151,
    153, 168, 206, 208, 284, 290,
    293
    on EC, 233
Sanderson, John, General,
    commander of UNTAC peace-
    keeping forces, 102
Schabas, William A., 161, 224, 274,
    290, 294
Scheffer, David,
    and negotiations, 162, 174, 184,
    286, 292, 296
    article in New York Times, 197
    draft resolution to Security
    Council, 121
    on UN withdrawal, 235